Advances in Information Systems
and Management Science

Band 22

Advances in Information Systems and Management Science

Band 22

Herausgegeben von

Prof. Dr. Jörg Becker
Prof. Dr. Heinz Lothar Grob
Prof. Dr. Stefan Klein
Prof. Dr. Herbert Kuchen
Prof. Dr. Ulrich Müller-Funk
Prof. Dr. Gottfried Vossen

Christian S. Brelage

Web Information System Development

Conceptual Modelling of Navigation for Satisfying Information Needs

Logos Verlag Berlin

 λογος

Advances in Information Systems and Management Science

Herausgegeben von

Prof. Dr. Jörg Becker, Prof. Dr. Heinz Lothar Grob,
Prof. Dr. Stefan Klein, Prof. Dr. Herbert Kuchen,
Prof. Dr. Ulrich Müller-Funk, Prof. Dr. Gottfried Vossen.

Westfälische Wilhelms-Universität Münster
Institut für Wirtschaftsinformatik
Leonardo-Campus 3
D-48149 Münster

Tel.: +49 (0)251 / 83 - 3 81 00
Fax: +49 (0)251 / 83 - 3 81 09
http://www.wi.uni-muenster.de

Bibliografische Information Der Deutschen Bibliothek

Die Deutsche Bibliothek verzeichnet diese Publikation in der
Deutschen Nationalbibliografie; detaillierte bibliografische Daten
sind im Internet über http://dnb.ddb.de abrufbar.

ISBN 3-8325-1189-X
ISSN 1611-3101

D 6 2005

Logos Verlag Berlin
Comeniushof, Gubener Str. 47
10243 Berlin

Tel.: +49 (0)30 / 42 85 10 90
Fax: +49 (0)30 / 42 85 10 92
http://www.logos-verlag.de

Foreword of the Editor

Web information systems are a cornerstone of current IT architectures and are used for a wide variety of applications ranging from knowledge management portals and intranets to web-based e-commerce applications. However, recent studies have shown that the development of web information system is still erratic, prone to errors and, therefore, often fails to achieve the intended objectives. Organizations respectively employees and managers ultimately depend on the provision of relevant and accurate pieces of information. Seeking information is time-consuming and costly.

The conceptual design of information systems is one of the cores of the information systems discipline which is positioned at the intersection of business administration and computer science. It is widely accepted that conceptual modelling can potentially help to improve the development process. By using semi-formal languages, conceptual modelling intends to create abstract artifacts of the information systems and its components in order to facilitate the communication within the development team. Christian Stephan Brelage contributes to the body of knowledge in the information system discipline in a twofold manner: firstly, a conceptualization of web information systems is created that serves as a reference model for the analysis and description of web information systems. Secondly, a conceptual modelling approach is constructed on the basis of this conceptualization. The modelling approach is constructed with special regard to the navigational design of web information systems. A sound specification of navigation is crucial for web information systems since navigation structures mainly determine a user's ability to retrieve the desired information.

This thesis is an important and original work. Brelage's approach of creating a conceptual modelling approach for web information systems is well-founded and excellently illustrated in this thesis. His conceptual modelling approach is a valuable contribution to our discipline and can have substantial impact for information technology.

Münster, February 2006

Jörg Becker

Preface

During my time at the European Research Center for Information Systems I worked on several practical projects as well as on rather scientific and theoretic topics. Despite the variety of application domains and topics, two particular problems seemed paramount. How can information system developers describe an information system and how can the communication process between potentially very diverse team members be facilitated? In other words: how to *speak* about information systems? This is neither a mere technical nor a purely conceptual problem. It is both and, thus, the core of the IS discipline. I investigated this problem for a particular subtype of information systems within this thesis, that is web information systems. I was particularly interested in navigational means that support information seeking tasks, hence, providing the "extension of the human brain" hypertext pioneers envisioned decades before "the Web" actually emerged. I am utterly convinced that new ideas for information structuring and access have to be developed in order to keep information technology usable.

Research is collaborative by nature and so is this work (albeit a monograph). I am extremely grateful to my friends at the European Research Center for Information Systems for their helpful comments, encouragement and critical discussions. In particular, I am greatly indebted to Michael Ribbert and Michael Thygs, who helped me to get started with my research and contributed to my work with several ideas. Alexander Dreiling provided "unconventional" and new ideas to approach research work. Karsten Klose and Thorsten Falk always had the right view and pragmatism that helped me to keep going when my work lost focus. Additionally, I like to thank Roland Holten and Ralf Knackstedt who laid the (conceptual) foundations for my research with their work and triggered my interest in the topic.

I am thankful to Prof. Dr. Jörg Becker, who gave me the opportunity to do research and write my thesis in a rather open-minded, creative and free atmosphere at his chair. Likewise, I would like to thank Prof. Dr. Gottfried Vossen for his willingness to co-supervise my thesis and his helpful comments on earlier drafts.

The greatest thanks go to Daniela Groba for providing me not only with inspiring linguistic support but also with abundant love. Most of all, I would like to thank my parents, Werner and Elisabeth Brelage. I would never have been able to finish this work without their infinite support, encouragement and help. This book is dedicated to them.

Münster, February 2006

Christian Stephan Brelage

Contents

List of Figures

List of Tables

List of Abbreviations

APD	Abstract Presentation Diagram (modelling concept of OO-H)
Ass.	Assignment
CASE	Computer Aided Software Engineering
cf.	compare (Latin: confere)
CGI	Common Gateway Interface
CSS	Cascading Style Sheet
e. g.	for example (Latin: exempla gratia)
ERM	Entity Relationship Modelling
ERP	Enterprise Resource Planning
HDM	Hypertext Design Model
HTML	Hypertext Markup Language
i. e.	that is (Latin: id est)
ibid.	in the same place (Latin: ibidem)
IEC	International Electrotechnical Commission
IETF	Internet Engineering Task Force
IR	Information Retrieval
ISO	International Organization for Standardization (Greek: isos for equal)
IS	Information Systems (Discipline)
JSP	Java Server Pages
NAD	Navigational Access Diagram (modelling concept of OO-H)
OLAP	On-Line Analytical Processing
OOHDM	Object Oriented Hypertext Design Model
PDA	Personal Digital Assistent
PERL	Practical Extraction and Reporting Language
PHP	Personal Hypertext Preprocessor
RFC	Request For Comments
SGML	Standard Generalized Markup Language

URI	Uniform Resource Identifier
URL	Uniform Resource Locator
W3C	World Wide Web Consortium
WebML	Web Modelling Language
WIS	Web Information System
XML	eXtensible Markup Language

Chapter 1

Exposition

1.1 Motivation, Problem Statement & Relevance

Web information systems have become a cornerstone of information technology architectures in organizations in the course of the last years.[1] They have found widespread use in a broad variety of application types including traditional internet information systems, intranets and knowledge portals in organizations as well as in e-commerce applications.[2] Virtually all organizations use some kind of web information system and migrate 'traditional' applications to web environments.[3] The ongoing diffusion of web information systems has changed their characteristics fundamentally. Having started as a vision of an extension of the human mind and having evolved to simple applications for information exchange between scientists, web information systems became fully fledged applications that are virtually identical to traditional applications concerning application scope and complexity.[4]

The undamped growth of data available in organizations as well as private environments enhances information technology at the present time. More and more business processes are carried out or supported electronically in order to decrease costs and processing time.[5] As a result, electronic documents (for instance, invoices, delivery notes and orders) replace their respective paper-variants. Additionally, emerging technologies like wireless sensor networks[6] and radio frequency identification[7] will result in

---

[1]   Cf. Isakowitz, Bieber & Vitali (1998), p. 78 and Ginige & Murugesan (2001), p. 14.
[2]   Cf. Ginige & Murugesan (2001), p. 14.
[3]   Cf. Ginige & Murugesan (2001), p. 14.
[4]   Cf. Ginige & Murugesan (2001), p. 14 and Section 2.2.3 for an overview of the historical development of web information systems respectively hypertext.
[5]   Cf., for instance, Mullock, Birch & Breems (2004).
[6]   Cf. Akyildiz, Sankarasubramaniam & Cayirci (2002); Estrin et al. (2002); Mattern & Römer (2003); Hill et al. (2004) and Culler & Hong (2005).
[7]   Cf. Borriello (2005) and Angeles (2005).

a drastically increasing amounts of data stored in information systems. A considerable amount of data processed in organizations is semi-structured, for instance, documents, e-mail, pictures as well as videos and resources on the Web. More and more heterogeneous and distributed information sources are available for individuals as well as organizations. Companies build 'knowledge portals'[8] in order to provide employees with a unified access to all pieces of data they potentially need and researchers have full-text access to thousands of journals. This vast 'data-pool' is *potentially* useful for individuals and organizations. However, due to the dramatic growth of available data it becomes more and more difficult to find and assess those pieces that are relevant for a particular information need. The phenomenon of being unable to find *relevant* information in an abundance of information is well-known from daily life and metaphorically circumscribed as *infoglut*[9] or *information overload*[10].

This phenomenon causes costs and results in a decreased employee productivity since a considerable amount of time is spent on seeking and assessing relevant information in large data pools (for instance, files on a hard drive, e-mail or an intranet). In general, two concepts of information access can be differentiated. Firstly, considerable research has been made on *searching* technologies like those known from web search engines.[11] Relevant pieces of information are supposed to be identified by using key words and search terms. However, it is well documented that users are *usually unable* to express their information need by means of a search query.[12] In particular, users with vague information needs usually do not 'know' what kind of information they actually seek. Their information need is actively shaped, reformulated and refuted during the information retrieval process.[13] Thus, it is unlikely that users will be able to identify relevant pieces of information by searching *efficiently*. The second area of research is concerned with *browsing* technologies which is a promising approach for web information systems in particular. Browsing intends to provide means that allow users to navigate the data-pool

---

[8]   Cf. MACK, RAVIN & BYRD (2001).

[9]   Cf. KUROPKA (2003), p. 2.

[10]   Cf., for instance, BERGHEL (1997), pp. 19 f.; MACDONALD & OETTINGER (2002), pp. 44 f. and FARHOOMAND & DRURY (2002), pp. 127 f. LEVY aligns the problem of information overload with BUSH's seminal article 'As We May Think' and discusses its social implications on work-life (cf. LEVY (2005), pp. 281 f).

[11]   Cf., for instance, ARASU et al. (2001) and JANSEN & SPINK (2006) as representatives for this research direction.

[12]   Cf. PAPAZOGLOU, PROPER & YANG (2001), pp. 3 f. and HOFSTEDE, PROPER & WEIDE (1996), pp. 1 f. The page information refers to a reprint. BERGHEL notes that internet search engines are inherently ill-equipped to 'judge' the quality and credibility of resources from the Web (cf. BERGHEL (1997), p. 21).

[13]   Refer to Section 2.3 for a conceptualization of information needs.

respectively the information space efficiently. 'Queries' or 'search terms' are explicated in an information structure that is supposed to guide users into the right direction. Each element of the information structure represents a (potentially large) amount of information. The research on browsing and related subjects like classification has a long tradition in the information systems discipline as well as in related areas.[14]

Despite considerable research efforts, the development of information systems in general and web information systems in particular is still a considerable challenge for developers, users and stakeholders. A recent study reports that the majority of web application development projects *fail* to achieve the intended goals with regard to time, budget and quality: 84 % of the projects do not achieve the intended goals, 79 % are not completed on time, 63 % have budget overruns, 53 % lack functionality and 52 % do not meet the necessary level of quality.[15] In analogy to the term 'software crisis', GINIGE & MURUGESAN refer to this situation as the 'web crisis'.

1.2 Goal Statement

This thesis proposes an information systems view on the phenomenon 'web information systems' and its development that explicitly acknowledges a social dimension and focuses on the conceptual specification of navigational means allowing users to satisfy their information needs. Thus, the thesis focuses on browsing rather than searching in information spaces. It is argued that a solely technical view on the phenomenon is insufficient to explain and describe web information systems, their development as well as their usage holistically and adequately. Conceptual modelling of navigation is proposed as a tool to foster communication among developers and users in order to overcome inefficient web information system development practices.

In particular, the goal of this thesis and its contribution to the body of knowledge in the IS discipline is twofold. Firstly, this thesis develops a comprehensive *conceptualization* of web information systems. This conceptualization describes *what* web information systems are. It identifies and specifies elements of the system, their 'meaning' as well as the relations of elements. The conceptualization serves as a *reference model* for web information systems and provides a sound, holistic and comprehensive terminology of the phenomenon. Research on web information systems, whether positivistic or interpretative, ultimately depends on the existence of a sound terminology and the conceptualiza-

---

[14] Compare, for instance, the review of related work on navigation in Section 2.2.3.

[15] Cf. CUTTER CONSORTIUM; GINIGE & MURUGESAN (2001), p. 15; GINIGE (2002), p. 721 and KAPPEL et al. (2004), p. 3. Similar results have been reported for information system development in general (cf. STANDISH GROUP).

tion of the phenomenon to be investigated. If such a conceptualization is not used, the comparison and evaluation of research becomes impossible since the question whether two research approaches actually investigate the same subcomponent of the phenomenon cannot be accessed. The conceptualization reflects a particular understanding of the perception of reality. Additionally, it is developed with a specific understanding of human information processing and, particularly, the role of navigation for satisfying human information needs. The conceptualization is 'encoded' by metamodels that depict the elements of web information systems and their relations.

Secondly, the conceptualization provides a sound basis for the development of a *conceptual modelling approach*. The development of this approach is the second goal of this thesis. The modelling approach intends to provide suitable means for the conceptual specification of web information system which can be used by information system developers and by users of the system as well as by other project stakeholder. Information system developers and users are enabled to achieve a *mutual understanding* of the development project, its goals as well as the means to achieve them by using the modelling approach. Special regard is given to issues of navigation which are considered to be crucial for the successful development of web information systems. Metamodels serve as the starting point for the development of a conceptual modelling approach. The elements identified in the metamodels are mapped to suitable representation forms that allow depicting 'knowledge' about web information systems in a comprehensive and consistent way by using an easy-to-use notation.

The modelling approach constructed in this thesis claims to be a general approach for modelling information systems intending to satisfy the information needs of the users. Particularly, it is neither restricted to a specific group of users (for instance, top-management) nor specifically designed for a certain domain. Although, application domains (for instance retailing, industry or services) pose specific challenges for information system developers, this thesis aims at providing a general approach for modelling efficient and effective information systems. However, given the nature of the research approach used in this thesis, it is possible to extend the modelling approach by integrating new aspects.

Having outlined goals, it is necessary to outline aspects that are *not* covered by this thesis. This thesis does not cover methods or approaches dealing with information requirements specification or the modelling process as such. The process of model creation is heavily influenced by social issues like imbalances with regard to power and the empathy between among members. However, the question *how* models are created is beyond the scope of this thesis. Instead, the thesis provides means to enable the documentation of issues on which a group of people has achieved an agreement. It is concerned with languages enabling the agreement upon models and the concepts they depict. However, *processes-in-the-small* that describe partially how a specific model can be created (for instance, naming conventions and usage of icons) are covered by the modelling method.

Moreover, this thesis is *not* concerned with technical issues. It is assumed that the technical means for the development and deployment of web information systems are available and can be used efficiently. Thus, advantages, disadvantages of different techniques (e. g. PHP versus any other scripting language) or in-depth-descriptions of programming languages are not covered by this thesis. The reader may refer to the numerous publications covering these topics.

Finally, this thesis concentrates on web information systems that can be characterized as *data collections*. Interactive systems that provide a high degree of user interactions and are used in order to support business process like order management or procurement are not discussed. Typical web information systems covered by this thesis are intra-organizational knowledge portals like intranets.

1.3 Structure of the Thesis

The structure of this thesis is as follows: Firstly, the scientific background adopted for the purpose at hand is outlined in Section 2.1. The scientific background describes the 'setting' in which the development and application of web information systems takes place. It reflects a particular understanding of how researchers, developers and users are able to perceive, describe and use the subject of research. The research approach used to develop the conceptualization and the modelling approach is discussed in Section 2.1.3.

The terminology needed to describe web information systems is introduced in Sections 2.2.1 and 2.2.2. After a brief overview of the system theory, the terms 'data', 'information' and 'knowledge' are discussed in order to provide a sound understanding for the purpose at hand. Subsequently, the term 'information system' is discussed. Information systems are defined as socio-technical systems. Web information systems are defined as a subtype of information systems that are characterized by a particular technical background, an aspect of individuality as well as a distinct concept of information access. Additionally, some characteristics of web information systems are discussed. A classification framework for web information systems is developed in order to describe and classify the subject of research more precisely. Section 2.2.3 elaborates extensively on the hypertext origin of web information systems. The concept of navigation is described in detail in this chapter. Additionally, the related works on navigational issues are discussed. Section 2.2.4 gives an overview of the technology used in web information systems. Information system development and conceptual modelling are discussed in Sections 2.2.5 and 2.2.6. Conceptual modelling is defined as a tool used by information system developers in order to achieve a mutual understanding with users about problems, goals and procedures of the development project. Section 2.2.7 discusses related conceptual modelling approaches for web information systems and outlines commonalities as well as differences of the approach presented in this thesis in relation to existing approaches. In order to align navigation with human information processing, an information retrieval model is developed in section 2.3. The model is based on the prior works on human information processing and is designed with regard to the scientific background of this thesis.

The modelling approach is developed in Chapter 3. After some preliminary remarks on the metalanguage used as well as an overview of naming conventions, the linguistic means needed to specify web information systems are constructed systematically. The discussion is subdivided into five parts respectively model types depicting different aspects of web information systems and conceptualize the linguistic means needed to model web information systems. Firstly, *information space models* are discussed. They are used to specify the structural composition of the web information systems. Information space models explicate the information structures used to organize all pieces of information in the system. Secondly, *property models* are discussed. Property are used to subclassify pieces of information stored in the system. Thirdly, *content models* represent a sound conceptualization of content. A content represents any piece of information stored in the systems and is annotated with metadata. Fourthly, the concept of *navigation* 'encoded' in the conceptualization is outlined. Additionally, it is shown that navigation-paths in the system can be used to enrich the 'semantics' of a link. Therefore, users are enabled to construct statements about the objects they investigate. Finally, a *personalization* concept is presented.

Although the research approach used in this thesis is speculative by nature, a validation and illustration of the approach is developed in Chapter 4 by means of an informed argument. A fictitious case is developed illustrating the usage of the modelling approach for the conceptual specification of a web information system. Additionally, the modelling approach has been applied during a case study in order to analyze and describe an existing web information system. A summary and an outlook to further research prospects concludes the discussion. The structure of the thesis and major interdependencies of some Sections are illustrated in Figure 1.1

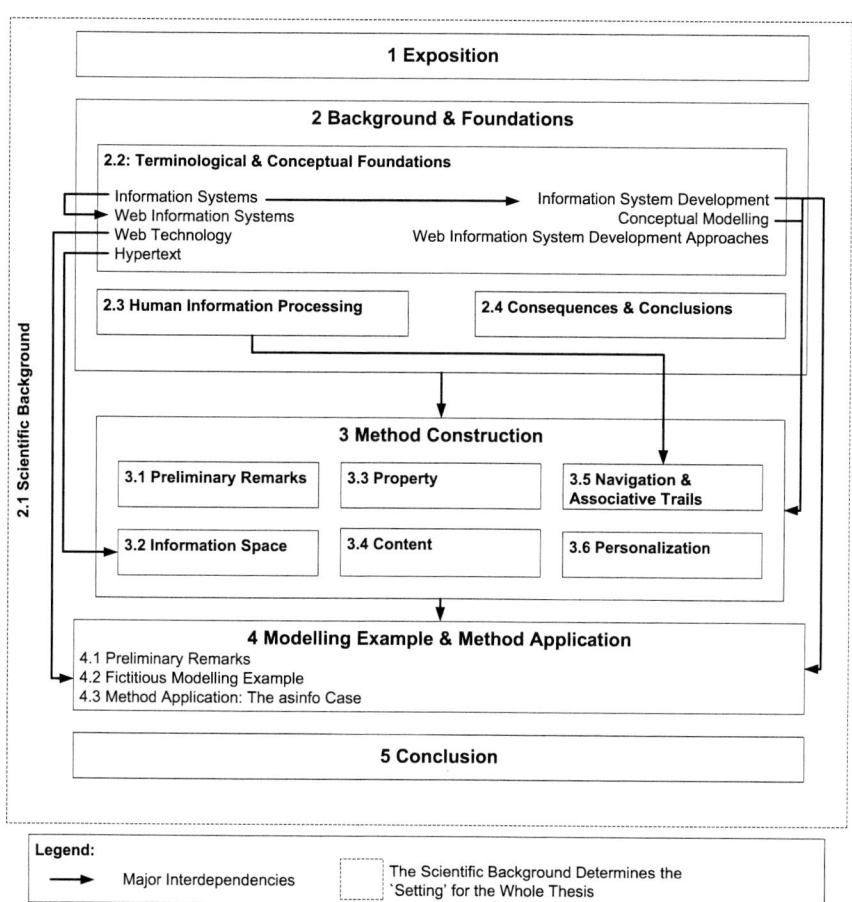

Figure 1.1: Structure of the Thesis

Chapter 2

Background & Foundations

2.1 Scientific Background

An outline of the scientific background of this thesis is essential for ensuring consistency of the approach and the methods that are used. Moreover, it is necessary to explicate presuppositions that are taken as a basis in order to ensure comprehensibility of the argumentation.[1] As the name indicates, presuppositions are suppositions which are implicitly taken as a basis and usually not outlined explicitly, which might possibly result in misconceptions and inadequate interpretations of scientific work. Although it may be arguable whether philosophical reflections are potentially useful in the information systems discipline or not, COLLIER can be assented to, who states that

> A good part of the answer to the question 'why philosophy?' is that the alternative to philosophy is not *no* philosophy but *bad* philosophy. The 'unphilosophical' person has an unconscious philosophy, which they apply in their practice – whether of science or politics or daily life.[2]

As the quote implies, philosophical considerations are vital for focusing on intended goals and the methods that are used to achieve these goals. This is especially useful

---

[1] Cf. KNACKSTEDT (2004), p. 11 and SCHÜTTE (1998), pp. 13 ff. Similarly KROGSTIE & SOLVBERG (1996), p. 280.

[2] Cf. COLLIER (1994), p. 16. Italics from the original. This thesis is written in British English. Quotes are always reproduced as closely to the original as possible (including the writing style, page breaks, italics etc.). The insertion '[sic!]' is not used. Therefore, different notations can be found in quotes (for instance, modeling versus modelling and organisation versus organization) and the text. Additionally, quotation marks are used as follows: double quotation marks indicate quotes, single ones indicate that a term is relativized or used symbolically. Unless otherwise stated, quotation marks in quotes are not adapted. Therefore, their usage in quotes may differ from their usage in the text.

if the research approach differs from the most commonly used approach in a scientific discipline. Positivistic approaches clearly dominate in journals within the IS community.[3] As a result, the underlying paradigm is usually implicitly assumed and not outlined, which causes difficulties for non-mainstream researchers since they have to explain why they refrain from using the dominant approach.[4] Finally, the scientific background motivates and defines the suitability of research methods. Therefore, it seems to be essential to describe the scientific background, its implications for the research approach and the position which is adopted in this thesis.

2.1.1 Paradigms in Social Science Research

Positioning a scientific work implies that there is a set of criteria that can be used to differentiate between different paradigms. The term paradigm is used in the sense of KUHN who uses it to suggest that some accepted examples of actual scientific practice–examples which include law, theory, application and instrumentation together–provide models from which arise particular coherent traditions of scientific research.[5] As ALVESSON & DEETZ point out, paradigms provide "taken-for-granted understandings of the nature of the world and the people in it, preferred methods for discovering what is true or worth knowing, and basic moral and aesthetic judgements about appropriate conduct and quality of life"[6]. In other words, paradigms are common sets of metatheoretical assumptions and presuppositions about scientific research which spawn independent and yet influential schools of research.[7] Some researchers argue that a dominant paradigmatic foundation of research approaches is crucial for the development of scientific disciplines.[8]

Several frameworks have been proposed over the years which use different dimensions to characterize research paradigms.[9] For the purpose of this thesis, it seems sensible to

---

[3]   For an empirical analysis of research paradigms in the IS discipline see ORLIKOWSKI & IACONO (2001). With regard to the rhetoric of positivism and interpretivism in the IS discipline refer to WEBER (2004). Likewise LEE (1999).

[4]   Cf. WALSHAM (1995), pp. 380–381.

[5]   Cf. KUHN (1996), p. 10. KUHN's model has been applied by BANVILLE & LANDRY in order to investigate the nature of the MIS discipline (cf. BANVILLE & LANDRY (1989) and BANVILLE & LANDRY (1992)).

[6]   ALVESSON & DEETZ (2000), p. 23.

[7]   KUHN names, for instance, the Copernican astronomy or Newton's physics as examples for paradigms.

[8]   For the domain of organization science, for example, refer to PFEFFER (1993) and HASSARD (1999). A radically different viewpoint, however, is taken by FEYERABEND (1975) who argues against the use of *any* method and for 'anarchistic' respectively 'paradigm-free' research approaches.

[9]   Refer, for instance, to BURRELL & MORGAN (1979); DEETZ (1996) and ALVESSON &

adopt a framework proposed by HIRSCHHEIM, KLEIN & LYYTINEN, since it is especially tailored to information system development and data modelling.[10] HIRSCHHEIM, KLEIN & LYYTINEN's approach to classify paradigms is based on a framework for social science research proposed by BURRELL & MORGAN. It has a substantial impact on social science research and has become the dominant framework for classifying different research paradigms.[11] Yet, this does not necessarily imply that the framework is not being discussed controversially.[12] In fact, it is criticized for various reasons that are discussed below.

In order to provide a sound foundation of the discussion, BURRELL & MORGAN's work will be discussed briefly before the framework is applied to the domain of information system development. As the following discussion will illustrate, the framework is considered to be suitable since information system development is seen as a social process that includes a technical one. The framework uses two dimensions in order to classify research paradigms and consequences for social science research. According to BURRELL & MORGAN, social science research can be classified by the *nature of science* and a dimension that characterizes the *nature of society*.

Following BURRELL & MORGAN, the nature of science can be characterized by four aspects which reflect the stance a researcher takes with regard to the object of his or her study and his or her means to achieve knowledge of it. Each aspect can be characterized to be within a continuum that is delimited by extreme positions (compare Figure 2.1). Firstly, an *ontological dimension*[13], which concerns the very essence of the phenomena under investigation, is relevant. In BURRELL & MORGAN's words, the aspect explicates

whether the 'reality' to be investigated is external to the individual – imposing

---

DEETZ (2000).

[10] Refer to Section 2.1.2 for references.

[11] The framework is discussed and adapted extensively in literature. Refer, for example, to ASTLEY & VAN DE VEN (1983).

[12] Refer, for instance, to HOPPER & POWELL (1985); WILLMOTT (1993); DEETZ (1996) and SCHULTZE & STABELL (2004) as well as the brief discussion below.

[13] It is important to note that the term 'ontology' is used very differently in various research disciplines. In its philosophical sense, the term refers to the philosophical discipline which is concerned with the nature of being (cf. SCHWEMMER (1995), p. 1077). Within the information systems community and particularly the computer science discipline, a different notion of ontology emerged (compare, for instance, GUARINO (1998) and the brief discussion in SCHÜTTE & ZELEWSKI (2001)). A frequently cited definition of ontology has been coined by GRUBER: "An ontology is a formal, explicit specification of a shared conceptualization." (GRUBER (1993), p. 199 and FENSEL (2001), p. 8). The proliferation of the usage to the term ontology is partly due to the emergence of the Semantic Web. A detailed discussion of different aspects of ontology is beyond the scope of this thesis. This chapter basically focuses on the philosophical understanding of ontology.

itself on individual consciousness from without – or the product of individual consciousness; whether 'reality' is of an 'objective' nature, or the product of individual cognition; whether 'reality' is a given 'out there' in the world, or the product of one's mind.[14]

Secondly, assumptions about the *epistemological nature* are relevant. Generally, epistemology is the philosophical discipline dealing with questions of how knowledge of a subject matter can be achieved. Additionally, epistemology is concerned with methods which make it possible to qualify knowledge to be 'true' or 'false'.[15] With regard to social science research, this aspects entails assumptions of how someone might be able to understand the world and how the knowledge of the world can be communicated to other human beings.[16] The question of qualifying knowledge claims as being 'true' or 'false' already implies a certain epistemological stance.[17] As BURRELL & MORGAN point out, this is a view of the nature of knowledge itself: whether, for example, it is possible to identify and communicate the nature of knowledge as being hard, real and capable of being transmitted in tangible form, or whether 'knowledge' is of a softer, more subjective, spiritual or even transcendental kind, based on experience and insight of a unique and essentially personal nature.[18]

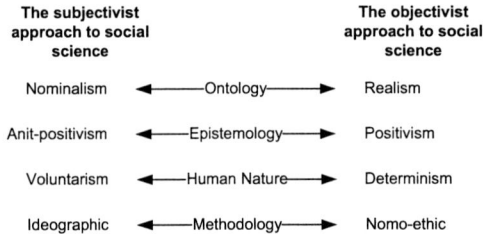

Figure 2.1: Aspects of Social Science Research (BURRELL & MORGAN (1979), p. 3)

The third aspect regarding the nature of science concerns the *human nature* and particularly the relationship between humans and their environment.[19] The extremes defining the continuum of this aspect are *voluntarism* and *determinism*. Concerning the deterministic view, BURRELL & MORGAN point out that human beings respond to

---

[14]   BURRELL & MORGAN (1979), p. 1.
[15]   Cf. MITTELSTRASS (1995), p. 576.
[16]   Cf. BURRELL & MORGAN (1979), p. 1.
[17]   Cf. BURRELL & MORGAN (1979), p. 1.
[18]   BURRELL & MORGAN (1979), pp. 1–2.
[19]   Cf. BURRELL & MORGAN (1979), p. 2 for the following.

the situations encountered in their external world in a mechanistic or even deterministic fashion. This view regards human beings and their experiences as products of their environment; one in which humans are conditioned by their external circumstances.[20] Voluntarism, on the other hand, characterizes the human nature to be more creative and free. In BURRELL & MORGAN's words

> 'free will' occupies the centre of the stage; [...] man is regarded as the creator of his environment, the controller as opposed to the controlled, the master rather than the marionette.[21]

Finally, the *methodological nature* characterizes the nature of science. BURRELL & MORGAN argue that different assumptions of ontology, epistemology and the human nature are likely to incline researches to use different methodologies.[22] If, for instance, ontological objectivity is presumed, it is likely that researchers tend to explore relationships and regularities of phenomena by means of (empirical) data analysis. Research is based on systematic protocols and techniques.[23] BURRELL & MORGAN use the term *nomoethic* in order to characterize this viewpoint. If another viewpoint, which stresses the importance of the subjective experience of individuals in the creation of the social world, is taken as a basis, the search for understanding has to be made by focusing on different issues and by approaching them in different ways.[24] The principal concern is an understanding of the way in which the individual creates, modifies and interprets the world in which he or she finds himself.[25] This *ideographic* approach to social science is based on the view that one can only understand the social world by obtaining firsthand knowledge of the subject under investigation.[26]

The second dimension of BURRELL & MORGAN's framework is their reflection on the *nature of society*. According to BURRELL & MORGAN it can be characterized by *regulation* or equilibrium on the one hand and *change* or coercion on the other. It reflects the stance that researchers adopt when studying social phenomena.[27] A sociology of regulation is concerned with the need for regulation in human affairs; the basic questions it asks tend to focus upon the need to understand why society is maintained as an entity.[28]

---

[20] BURRELL & MORGAN (1979), p. 2.
[21] BURRELL & MORGAN (1979), p. 2. Interrogative 'where' left out in order to improve readability.
[22] Cf. BURRELL & MORGAN (1979), p. 2.
[23] Cf. BURRELL & MORGAN (1979), p. 6.
[24] Cf. BURRELL & MORGAN (1979), p. 3.
[25] Cf. BURRELL & MORGAN (1979), p. 3.
[26] Cf. BURRELL & MORGAN (1979), 6.
[27] Cf. BURRELL & MORGAN (1979), pp. 10 f. for the following.
[28] Cf. BURRELL & MORGAN (1979), p. 17.

The sociology of *radical change* is essentially concerned with man's emancipation from the structures which limit and stunt his or her potential for development.[29] BURRELL & MORGAN elaborate extensively on this dimension and conclude that it is the most problematic one.[30] The dimension includes aspects of revolution and radical change as well as class conflicts between the working class and the ruling capital.[31] Obviously, these questions are interesting from a sociological perspective. For the purpose of this thesis, however, it is not necessary to elaborate on this dimension on a detailed level. Nevertheless, it is acknowledged that there are different forces with different goals at work in social systems. Since information systems are social systems, their participants may hinder or even sabotage procedures and goals that are used to improve, change or develop an information system. However, more violent changes are rather far fetched from an information systems perspective. When mapped together, both dimensions yield four dominant paradigms for social science research (compare Figure 2.2).

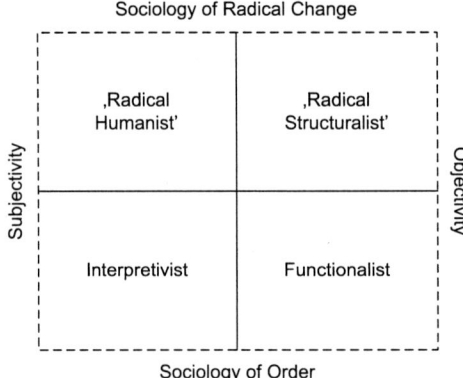

Figure 2.2: Paradigms in Social Science Research (BURRELL & MORGAN (1979), p. 22)

BURRELL & MORGAN's framework has been criticized for various reasons. For instance, DEETZ argues that the differences implied in the dimensions of BURRELL & MORGAN do not really make a difference in social science research.[32] Additionally, DEETZ argues that BURRELL & MORGAN, being sociological functionalists themselves, use their definitorial authority in order to enforce their framework on other researchers,

---

[29]   Cf. BURRELL & MORGAN (1979), p. 17.
[30]   Cf. BURRELL & MORGAN (1979), p. 16.
[31]   Cf. BURRELL & MORGAN (1979), pp. 10–16.
[32]   Cf. DEETZ (1996), p. 191.

which now have to use a language that does not fit with their own conception of science.[33] As DEETZ points out, they have to choose between misrepresenting themselves clearly through BURRELL & MORGAN or representing themselves well while being considered obscure or bad writers.[34] Additionally, DEETZ argues that the strict separations between different paradigms is of little use for social science research since all assumptions and paradigms are potentially useful to study phenomena and can contribute to the overall understanding.[35] Not only does DEETZ criticize the distinction between subjectivism and objectivism in particular, but he also qualifies them as misleading and even 'boring' since it implies artificial dichotomies that are simply not relevant.[36] Consequently, DEETZ replaces the subjectivity objectivity dimension with a local/emergent-elite/a priori dimension. As DEETZ points out, the questions this dimension addresses is where and how research concepts arise: within an established group or school of research or without.[37] It should also be noted that each attempt to classify research paradigms is necessarily simplifying the diverse reality of research disciplines and subjects. The four paradigms identified by BURRELL & MORGAN do not really constitute homogeneous 'groups' of research.[38] However, they can be interpreted as examples which correspond more or less to schools of research.

Nevertheless, the framework is considered to be appropriate for the purpose at hand due to the following reasons. The framework is used in order to explicate assumptions of different paradigms and their consequences for the research approach of this thesis. The overview is neither complete nor sufficient for a detailed philosophical discussion which is, however, not the intention of the overview. An interested reader may refer to the various references which are given for a more 'philosophical' and far reaching discussion. It is rather intended to provide a sound background and to explicate the *practical* consequences which are entailed by different paradigms. Essentially, information systems is a rather pragmatic or applied science which is concerned with the development and the usage of information systems. Mainly rooted in social science and computer science, it adopts, uses and combines methods of different disciplines in order to investigate the phe-

---

[33]   Cf. DEETZ (1996), p. 192.
[34]   Cf. DEETZ (1996), p. 192.
[35]   Cf. DEETZ (1996), p. 193.
[36]   While DEETZ's argument is comprehensible, it is not necessary to elaborate on this point on a detailed level. The reader may refer to the original publication. DEETZ's viewpoint itself, however, is not without criticism (cf. SCHULTZE & STABELL (2004), p. 553.).
[37]   Cf. DEETZ (1996), p. 195 and ALVESSON & DEETZ (2000), pp. 28 f.
[38]   Cf. for a similar point KLEIN & MYERS (1999), p. 70 and the footnote on page 49 in HIRSCHHEIM, KLEIN & LYYTINEN (1995).

nomenon of 'information systems', which are socio-technical systems.[39] However, there
are major differences in the way the information system development process is carried
out which has to be reflected by the means used to assist in this process. Additionally, it
is sensible to arrogate that the methods do 'fit' concerning their implicit assumptions. In
other words, discussing social and linguistic problems becomes senseless if requirements
can be objectively perceived and mapped to implementation artefacts. Following GAL-
LIERS & SWAN (2000), it is argued that it is suitable to view the development process
as a social process which is particularly subject to errors, misunderstandings, political
and social influences and, most importantly, constrained by the limitations imposed
by language. In other words, information system development is not a deterministic,
well defined or 'technical' process. It is a rather imprecise, creative and communicative
process which is prone to errors. Participants are trying to achieve something in terms
of mutual agreements that create incremental improvements of an information system.
This is not meant to imply, however, that other research approaches for information
systems are wrong or generally of little use. They simply focus on different aspects
of the multifaceted term information systems.[40] In analogy to DEETZ's view of social
science research, different approaches and paradigms are considered to be potentially
useful in studying the phenomenon of information systems by mutual exchange and discussion of ideas and concepts. Most importantly, the framework proposed by BURRELL
& MORGAN was used by HIRSCHHEIM, KLEIN & LYYTINEN in the context of information system development and particularly data modelling, which aligns it with the
subject matter of this thesis.[41] Therefore, this particular framework has been chosen
in order to motivate the discussion and to provide a sound basis for the analysis and
selection of a suitable research approach.

2.1.2 A Paradigmatic Foundation for Information System Development & Data Modelling

HIRSCHHEIM, KLEIN & LYYTINEN used BURRELL & MORGAN's framework with minor
modifications in order to explicate presuppositions of different research paradigms for
the domain of information system development and particularly data modelling.[42] Mod-

---

[39]   Cf. LAND (1992); GALLIERS & SWAN (2000) and HOLTEN (2004).

[40]   Refer to Section 2.2.1 for a discussion of various information system definitions.

[41]   Similar approaches can be found in NIEHAVES (2004); NIEHAVES et al. (2004); NIEHAVES (2005)
       and RIBBERT et al. (2004).

[42]   The paradigmatic foundation is based on HIRSCHHEIM, KLEIN & LYYTINEN's book from 1995.
       Briefer overviews can be found in LYYTINEN (1987b) and HIRSCHHEIM & KLEIN (1989). A
       comprehensive overview of epistemological issues in information system research is given in

ifications include different names for the paradigms (compare Figure 2.3). HIRSCHHEIM,
KLEIN & LYYTINEN name the interpretivism paradigm 'social relativism' and the radical humanist paradigm 'neohumanism'. Each pair of terms is used interchangeably in
the following. Additionally, they revert the dimension regulation versus change back
in the order versus conflict dimension. However, there are no changes concerning the
contents.[43] The framework is discussed in order to position this thesis with regard to
a scientific background that explains what and how its goals as outlined in the exposition are supposed to be achieved. Furthermore, the background implies a certain
stance about information system development and the obstacles that hinder a successful
implementation and deployment.

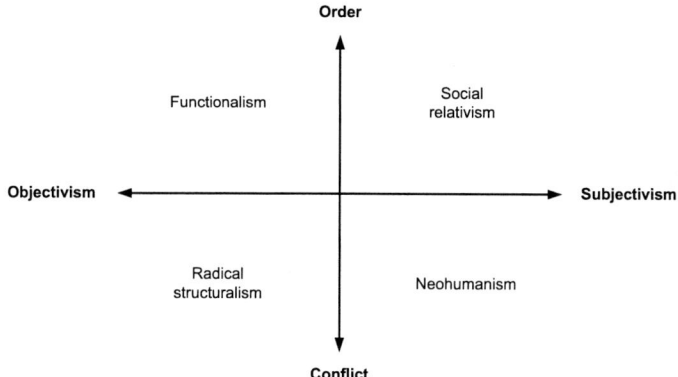

Figure 2.3: Paradigms in Information System Development & Data Modelling
(HIRSCHHEIM, KLEIN & LYYTINEN (1995), p. 48)

It is, however, not necessary to discuss in detail those paradigms that are not used
for the purpose at hand. For various reasons which will be outlined below, the social
relativism paradigm (interpretivism in BURRELL & MORGAN's terms) is considered
to be the most appropriate for the purpose at hand. This does not mean that other
paradigms are less useful, but they imply a particular world view and methodological
proceeding which is not adopted. Thus, interpretivism respectively social relativism
is selected and discussed in detail. The neohumanism paradigm (radical humanism in
BURRELL & MORGAN's terms) differs from social relativism by a sociology of change

---

HIRSCHHEIM (1985) and HIRSCHHEIM (1992). A similar foundation for action research presents
WOOD-HARPER (1985).

[43]   Additionally, HIRSCHHEIM, KLEIN & LYYTINEN have switched BURRELL & MORGAN's framework
by 180 degrees for no apparent reason (cf. Figure 2.3 and the original depicted in Figure 2.2).

among other things. Since several insights are gained from this paradigm, the discussion briefly sketches aspects of neohumanism as well.[44] However, some paradigmatic differences are outlined in order to improve the overall understanding of the interpretivistic paradigm. HIRSCHHEIM, KLEIN & LYYTINEN use a series of tables in order to oppose assumptions, principles and other characteristics of each paradigm.[45] For the purpose of this thesis, however, the discussion is mainly textual since the tables cannot be depicted in detail and only one paradigm is discussed extensively. Moreover, not all characteristics are relevant for the purpose at hand. Therefore, only a selection is reproduced in this section.

According to HIRSCHHEIM, KLEIN & LYYTINEN, *ontological assumptions* are concerned with the nature of the universe of discourse – the slice of reality to be modelled.[46] *Epistemological assumptions* are closely related to the ontological aspect. They are concerned with the appropriate approach for inquiry regarding which aspects need to be known to create the data model and with regard to the cognitive status of the result: is the data model 'true' or is it merely a convenient fiction, for instance a simplifying design assumption presumed to be valid only for a particular system at a particular time?[47] Within the domain of conceptual modelling, ontological and epistemological assumptions mainly determine the way requirements for information systems are supposed to be elicited and how their validity can be assessed. For instance, objectivism postulates that the universe of discourse is comprised of immutable objects and structures that exist as empirical entities.[48] In principle, a model from the universe of discourse ought to exist which is correct independently of the observers' appreciation of it. A data model is 'true' if it accurately depicts the underlying reality. Different opinions about the universe of discourse must be a reflection of human error and can be eliminated in principle. In interpretivism, however, subjectivism in data modelling claims that the universe of discourse is a subjective construction of the mind. Concerning this point, HIRSCHHEIM, KLEIN & LYYTINEN argue that

> A data model can at best reflect peoples' conventions or perceptions that are subject to negotiated change. Basically, the immediate social milieu of users and society at large preorder what subjectively is experienced as reality by means

---

[44]   A comprehensive treatment of a neohumanistic approach to information system research using critical theory can be found in LYYTINEN (1985).

[45]   Cf. HIRSCHHEIM, KLEIN & LYYTINEN (1995), pp. 49 ff.

[46]   HIRSCHHEIM, KLEIN & LYYTINEN (1995), p. 58.

[47]   HIRSCHHEIM, KLEIN & LYYTINEN (1995), p. 58. Similarly FALKENBERG (1983a), p. 4.

[48]   HIRSCHHEIM, KLEIN & LYYTINEN (1995), p. 58 for the following. The universe of discourse is that part of the reality which is of interest for an information system (cf. FALKENBERG (1983a), p. 3).

of socialization in the home, the educational institutions and at work. Important mechanisms by which subjective experiences take on an objective quality in the minds of individuals are the rules surrounding institutions (i.e. institutional programming), tradition as transmitted through artefacts and changing use of language and sedimentation (BERGER & LUCKMANN (1991)).[49]

The subjective nature of perception is supported by recent research results in cognitive neurobiology and related disciplines.[50] Subjective perception does not imply, however, that the existence of a certain 'reality' is neglected. It is the perception of reality that is subjective. The process of perceiving and understanding our individual world is called *sense-making*.[51] Individuals make sense of what they perceive. They sort and put away new phenomena according to prior experience and socialization. In this regard, reality is socially constructed.[52] Interpreted radically, however, communication between individuals would be impossible since they have nothing in common and live in disjoint 'worlds' which is obviously not the case in everyday life. In everyday life, certain signs (for instance, a red traffic light) or linguistic statements are 'objectified' and perceived and interpreted equally by humans, although they are socially constructed. Obviously, what can be considered objectified depends on the social background and prior experience. For instance, by nature a child is not aware of red traffic lights and their meaning. This objectification is a result of a learning process which is necessary for living together in society. BERGER & LUCKMANN illustrate the intersubjective nature of everyday life:

> The reality of everyday life further presents itself to me as an intersubjective world, a world that I share with others. This intersubjectivity sharply differentiates everyday life from other realities of which I am conscious. I am alone in the world of my dreams, but I know that the world of everyday life is as real to others as it is to myself. Indeed, I cannot exist in everyday life without continually interacting and communicating with others.[53]

An important difference between an objective and a subjective position is the role language plays in the development process. Whereas objectivism postulates that language

---

[49] HIRSCHHEIM, KLEIN & LYYTINEN (1995), p. 58. Reference to BERGER & LUCKMANN adapted to a newer version.

[50] Refer, for instance, to ROTH (1992) and ROTH (1997).

[51] Refer to ROWAN & REASON (1981) for a comprehensive introduction to sense-making and its relation to hermeneutics. For an introduction see also WEICK (1995).

[52] BERGER & LUCKMANN (1991).

[53] BERGER & LUCKMANN (1991), p. 37.

depicts reality free from distortions, subjectivism explicitly acknowledges the subjective
nature of language and perception which is influenced by cultural and social aspects.[54]
As a consequence of the subjective or objective nature of paradigms, they react differently if users or modellers construct different representations of the universe of discourse,
that is, different models of the same object system. In objective paradigms, different
models are a sign of human error whereas in interpretivism different models are simply
a logical consequence of subjective perception.[55]

The assumption of a dichotomy of subjectivism (interpretivism) versus objectivism
(positivism) exists already for a long period of time.[56] Within the information systems
community, the appropriateness of different research paradigms has been discussed controversially. It has to be noted, however, that the differences portrayed are extreme
positions, which are usually not adopted in their 'pure form'. WEBER even argues that
the alleged differences have become 'folklore' and are mainly rhetorical rather reflecting
relevant differences.[57] Additionally, it can be argued whether this dichotomy is useful
for classifying research paradigms at all. DEETZ can be assented to, who argues that
the dichotomy is mainly used for 'political' reasons.[58] Although, DEETZ's argument is
conceivable, the subjective-objective discussion concerning the ontological aspect of information system development and data modelling is included in this overview in order
to reflect its prominent stance within the discussion in IS literature.

Epistemological assumptions influence the methodological proceeding used in data
modelling. In social relativism, interpretivist reflection and hermeneutic cycles are used
in order to disseminate ideas through social interaction.[59] It is the major goal to achieve
a mutual understanding and agreement about goals and procedures of the informa-

---

[54] Cf. HIRSCHHEIM, KLEIN & LYYTINEN (1995), pp. 50 and 58.

[55] In neohumanism, conflicting representations are welcomed since they help to reveal distortions and
      unwarranted uses of power. By doing so, they contribute to the overall of emancipation from unwar-
      ranted constraints. In radical structuralism, conflict is endemic to work life. As noted above, both
      paradigms are not discussed in detail. Refer to HIRSCHHEIM, KLEIN & LYYTINEN (1995), pp. 49 f.
      and 59.

[56] Cf. DEETZ (1996), p. 193.

[57] Cf. WEBER (2004), p. iii. As a result, WEBER suggests to assign "the rhetoric of positivism versus
      interpretivism to the scrap heap" (WEBER (2004), p. xi).

[58] Cf. DEETZ (1996), p. 193 f. DEETZ argument is threefold. Firstly, the meaning of the objective-
      subjective labels are already socially contrived since the first critics of positivism argued that it is
      rather subjective than objective. Secondly, the dualism is used for political reasons by both groups
      in order to demarcate research disciplines or schools. Thirdly, the retention of the conception of
      subject-object separation has led to the continuation of rather misleading conflicts and equally
      misleading presumed relations between so-called qualitative and quantitative research.

[59] Cf. HIRSCHHEIM, KLEIN & LYYTINEN (1995), p. 50.

tion system development process within the development group. The process of data modelling becomes a series of communicative and interpretative actions which incrementally produces an output which is 'true' in sense of a mutual agreement. The notion that knowledge is gained through social constructions such as language, consciousness, documents or other artefacts is constituting for interpretative research.[60] Objectivistic paradigms tend to use empirical and analytical methods.[61] Notably, neohumanism differs in the ontological and epistemological aspects since it proposes a distinction between physical and social reality.[62] Consequently, a mixture of methods is proposed in order to gain and verify knowledge about both 'worlds'. The validity of truth claims is established through critical debate.[63]

Having outlined ontological and epistemological assumptions, the implications for the definition of object systems can be described. Object systems consist of phenomena that are perceived by members of the development group and that are supposed to be changed with regard to objectives defined by the development group.[64] Thus, object systems can be viewed as abstract representations of an information system. A data model depicts a fraction of an object system which is perceived by the development group. Depending on the paradigmatic assumptions, the role of an object system changes which influences the way representation forms are created. In interpretivism object systems emerge through shared creation of meanings rather than being 'objectively given' like in functionalism.[65] As HIRSCHHEIM, KLEIN & LYYTINEN point out

> The description of the object system reflects a shifting group consensus rather
> than an unbiased picture of reality. A data model is like an agreed upon painting,
> the usefulness of which is in the eyes of its beholders, not a depiction of reality
> which can be made more or less accurate.[66]

Additionally, language plays a critical role in interpretivism. Language mediates the construction of reality.[67] In information system development, natural languages (for instance, German or English) as well as artificial or specialized (modelling methods like

---

[60]   Cf. KLEIN & MYERS (1999), p. 69.
[61]   Cf. HIRSCHHEIM, KLEIN & LYYTINEN (1995), p. 50.
[62]   Cf. HIRSCHHEIM, KLEIN & LYYTINEN (1995), p. 50.
[63]   Cf. HIRSCHHEIM, KLEIN & LYYTINEN (1995), p. 50.
[64]   Cf. HIRSCHHEIM, KLEIN & LYYTINEN (1995), pp. 15 f. The term is explained in more detail in
       Section 2.2.5.
[65]   Cf. HIRSCHHEIM, KLEIN & LYYTINEN (1995), p. 66.
[66]   HIRSCHHEIM, KLEIN & LYYTINEN (1995), p. 66.
[67]   Cf. HIRSCHHEIM, KLEIN & LYYTINEN (1995), p. 66.

entity relationship modelling) are used to make sense of and construct reality.[68] The crucial role of language is adopted in neohumanism and extended by rational reconstruction of meanings and language critique.[69] As outlined above, neohumanism differs from interpretivism by a sociology of change. It is concerned with human emancipation from unwarranted constraints, whether they are physical or social. Since language is a social construction itself, it can enforce unwarranted constraints in social interaction which have to be addressed by means of rational reconstruction from a neohumanist's point of view.[70]

Two arguments require attention at this point. Firstly, language is subjective and, secondly, its role in the development process is crucial. A subjective notion of language and the consequences for the information system development process are rather commonsensical than philosophical and, therefore, of practical importance for the purpose at hand. There is no 'easy' and accurate transfer of information by means of language. The 'engineering' view on information systems is based on the inappropriate assumption that they are similar to projects in physical engineering.[71] Language, whether artificial or not, is ambiguous, imprecise and error-prone. Even formal grammars can be imprecise if interpreted by humans. More importantly, language ultimately determines our ability to perceive the world and exchange knowledge about it. We can only perceive and know what we can name or address. More particular, our language reflects our socialization, cultural background as well as educational background. Language shapes our perception actively.[72] We perceive what we can name rather than name what we perceive.

---

[68]   Cf. HIRSCHHEIM, KLEIN & LYYTINEN (1995), p. 66. In contrast to this view, functionalism assigns to 'language' a mere technical role. Language is a necessary requirement to exchange information, but it is equal (in terms of meaning) for anyone and information as well as the intended meaning is conveyed free of distortion and unbiased.

[69]   Cf. HIRSCHHEIM, KLEIN & LYYTINEN (1995), p. 66.

[70]   Concerning the problematic use of language from a neohumanist's point of view, HIRSCHHEIM, KLEIN & LYYTINEN note that "the processes of language use can be distorted by threatening social influences such as authority relationships, asymmetry in education and access to information, unwarranted uses of power (e.g. control of hidden agendas), and other barriers to effective communication. Along with these process distortions, the language itself can produce miscommunication through unwanted connotations, loaded terms, euphemisms, misconceptions, jargon, etc." (HIRSCHHEIM, KLEIN & LYYTINEN (1995), p. 67). In data modelling, this situation can apply if the use of a methodical procedure for information system development (for instance, a particular modelling method) is enforced, just because 'it was always done this way'. Senior employees may use their superior methodical knowledge of old methods in order to hinder the promotion of younger ones.

[71]   Cf. SUTTON (2000), p. 115.

[72]   Cf. HIRSCHHEIM, KLEIN & LYYTINEN (1995), p. 109.

This does not imply that 'reality' is totally dependent on our language. Of course, new phenomena (like the internet) appear constantly and have to be 'named'.[73] However, until something is 'named' in terms of an agreed-upon-understanding we cannot discuss meaningfully about it. We just 'feel' that there is something 'new' that requires to create appropriate linguistic means (for instance, by introducing new terms) in order to talk and exchange information about it.

This viewpoint has been introduced by a shift in philosophy usually paraphrased as the 'linguistic turn' which was mainly inspired by the works of WITTGENSTEIN.[74] In his earlier works, WITTGENSTEIN laid down the ontological presuppositions that are central to an analytical approach, for instance, correspondence between language constructs and reality, objectivity and neutrality of language and the ideals of exactness.[75] In his later works, the relationship between language and reality is turned upside down: it is through the description in language that the world is revealed to us.[76] Thus, language ultimately determines our ability to perceive the world and to exchange information in and about it. It plays an active role in our perception process.

Concerning the role of language, as it has been induced by the linguistic turn, HIRSCHHEIM, KLEIN & LYYTINEN enumerate four major consequences which substantially influence the practice of data modelling:[77]

1. Abandonment of the realist theory of linguistic meaning: phenomena of the ob-

---

[73] Only 'real' new phenomena are meant here. New terms are created and appear regularly (for instance, marketing phrases).

[74] It should be noted that the consequences of the linguistic-turn in philosophy are grave and challenge even the relevance of the objectivity versus subjectivity debate as it was outlined above. DEETZ points out that "its refutation [refutation of the objectivity-subjectivity dichotomy C.S.B] is core to the twentieth century writers (e.g., Husserl, Heidegger, Wittgenstein), who in developing a 'linguistic turn' in philosophy, have served as inspiration for many of the 'nonfunctionalists' organizational researchers (including many feminists, critical theorists, poststructuralists, postmodernist, and labor process theorists). Such research programs are not at a different place on the subjective-objective continuum; the dualism itself is disputed (see WILLMOTT (1990) and WILLMOTT (1993) for a similar point). As language replaces consciousness as central, theories of discourse and representational practices replace philosophies of science based on subject-object, idealist-realist, rationalist-empiricist, or similar contrasts. Any attempt to classify these new research programs on the subjective-objective dimension of BURRELL & MORGAN does an injustice to their conceptions and practices and leads to distorted understandings." (DEETZ (1996), p. 194) References in quote adapted to the format used in this thesis and integrated in the bibliography.

[75] Cf. HIRSCHHEIM, KLEIN & LYYTINEN (1995), p. 148 and WITTGENSTEIN (1922).

[76] HIRSCHHEIM, KLEIN & LYYTINEN (1995), p. 148 and WITTGENSTEIN (1963). Similarly WHORF (1956), pp. 246 ff.

[77] Cf. HIRSCHHEIM, KLEIN & LYYTINEN (1995), pp. 148–149 for the following.

ject system are not given independently of language. They are projections of the
linguistic structures the development uses.

2. Denial of semantic reductionism and absolutism: an object system cannot be built
   up in an unambiguous (absolutism) and definite (reductionism) manner. Therefore, it is impossible to develop an ontologically 'complete' ideal language which
   can be used to describe object systems.

3. Focus on how every day language works: natural language is the major medium
   in which meaning is revealed. Therefore, data modelling needs to investigate how
   well natural language works and which functions it has in social activity.

4. Collapse of the myth of linguistic precision: language (whether natural or artificial)
   is not exact or precise. It is more or less exact respectively suited within a specific
   context or purpose.

2.1.3 Research Approach

The paradigmatic foundation describes the 'setting' in which information system development takes place and the problems entailed if this position is adapted.[78] Moreover,
this position influences the selection of a suitable research approach that is compatible
with the position and potentially useful to achieve the intended goal.[79] Moreover, it is
necessary to outline some guidelines by which the appropriateness of the approach can
be judged. The subjective and 'vague' nature of interpretivism does not imply that interpretative research cannot be judged.[80] KLEIN & MYERS point out that interpretivism

---

[78] As this paradigmatic foundation indicates, interpretivism is similar to constructivism which
      has been used in similar works as a foundation. Examples include the brief sections in ZUR
      MÜHLEN (2002), pp. 12–18; BERGERFURTH (2004), pp. 4–7 and HANSMANN (2003), pp. 8–11.
      Constructivism as a foundation for information systems and conceptual modelling is discussed in
      more detail in SCHÜTTE (1998), pp. 13–33 and KNACKSTEDT (2004), pp. 11–32. As the name
      indicates, constructivism presupposes that every perception is essentially a subjective construction
      of the mind. The constructivistic paradigm includes a variety of different constructivistic 'flavours'
      (KNACKSTEDT (2004), p. 11).

[79] GALLIERS presents an overview of research approaches in the IS discipline. In particular, strengths
      and weaknesses are discussed (cf. GALLIERS (1992)).

[80] Cf. KLEIN & MYERS (1999), p. 69 and HIRSCHHEIM & KLEIN (2003), pp. 257 f. for a similar
      point. Since positivistic approaches are dominating in the IS discipline, there is a rich body of
      knowledge for assessing research contributions, refer, for instance, to BENBASAT, GOLDSTEIN &
      MEAD (1987) and LEE (1989).

is rooted in the philosophical discipline of hermeneutics.[81]

Hermeneutics is concerned with the human understanding of a subject matter and, in particular, the interpretation of textual documents.[82] Historically, hermeneutics was mainly concerned with the interpretation of theological documents. *Philosophical Hermeneutics* is concerned with the conditions and the possibility of understanding and tries to analyze a subject matter itself critically (usually in a fictitious dialogue with the author) instead of interpreting it in subjective terms. Thus, philosophical hermeneutics is primarily interested in the subject matter itself rather than the text.[83] Each interpretative act depends on a personal background which constitutes the *pre-understanding* of an individual. Author as well as interpret have to be willing to alter their pre-understanding if an understanding is to be achieved. A change of pre-understanding may lead to a different understanding of the subject matter and to new questions, which may be discussed subsequently. The concept of pre-understanding is central to hermeneutic philosophy.[84] On a metaphorical level, the cycle of altering pre-understanding and of re-investigating a subject matter is usually circumscribed with the notion of a *hermeneutic spiral*.[85] According to KLEIN & MYERS, the hermeneutic spiral is the fundamental principle of interpretive research.[86] The hermeneutic spiral comprises two aspects. One aspect concerns the interpretation of textual documents (intra-textual) while the other describes the general relation of knowledge acquisition and pre-understanding.[87]

According to BOLAND and WALSHAM our "everyday experience of the social world is hermeneutic and that in the world we encounter a 'text' of meanings already made and being made".[88] Obviously, this is closely related to information systems and their development since the usage as well as the development of information systems can be seen as a sequence of interpretative acts of artefacts (documents, models etc.) created by or for an information system. Consequently, BOLAND argues that

---

[81]   Cf. KLEIN & MYERS (1999), p. 71. Hermeneutics is a sub-discipline of phenomenology (cf. WALSHAM (1993), p. 9).

[82]   Cf. VERAART & WIMMER (1996), pp. 85 ff. for the following. Etymologically *hermeneutics* is derived from the Greek word $\epsilon\rho\mu\eta\nu\epsilon\nu\tau\iota\kappa\eta$ meaning 'art of interpretation'. Brief introductions to hermeneutics can be found in CAPURRO (1986), pp. 13 ff. and Cf. SEIFFERT (1996), pp. 104 ff. A comprehensive treatment of hemeneutics as a research approach in the IS discipline is presented by ALVESSON & SKÖLDBERG (2000), pp. 52–109.

[83]   Cf. VERAART & WIMMER (1996), p. 87.

[84]   Cf. VERAART & WIMMER (1996), p. 88 and CAPURRO (1986), pp. 13 f.

[85]   Cf. for a comprehensive introduction to ALVESSON & SKÖLDBERG (2000), pp. 50 ff .

[86]   They call it a "meta-principle upon which the other six principles expand" (KLEIN & MYERS (1999), p. 71).

[87]   Cf. TEICHERT (1996), p. 850 for details.

[88]   Cited after WALSHAM (1993), p. 9.

> [...] Use, study and design of information systems is best understood as a
> hermeneutic process [...]. In *using* an information system, the available output
> is a text that must be read and interpreted by people other than its author. This
> is a hermeneutic task. In *designing* an information system, the designer reads the
> organization and and its intended users as a text in order to make an interpretation
> that will provide the basis for a system design. This is also a hermeneutic task.
> In *studying* information systems, social scientists read the interaction during the
> system design and use in order to interpret the significance and potential meanings
> they hold.[89]

A hermeneutic approach to information system research investigates *what* information
systems are rather than finding out *how* they work as it is done in positive science.[90]
It does so by entering into a (fictitious) dialogue with the system respectively with the
author of the output that is generated. BOLAND clearly points out the crucial and active
role language plays in and for research on information systems.[91] Phenomenology seeks
to point out what the subject matter of a study actually is by describing it systematically
and carefully.[92] For the purpose of this thesis, this discussion applies as follows:

- The modelling method provides means for modelling web information systems with
  special regard to navigational means that allow users to satisfy their information
  needs. *Additionally*, the method describes *what* web information systems are. The
  conceptualization of the method contains an understanding of web information
  systems and how they should work. The development of the system is viewed as a
  hermeneutic process that intends to achieve a mutual understanding of the system
  at its goals.

- Likewise, the conceptualization presupposes a certain understanding of human
  information processing and seeks to facilitate it by suitable navigational means.
  Thus, the usage of the system can equally be understood as a hermeneutic process
  of conversations with a web information system.

In order to provide a sound understanding of the modelling method, the *logical
propaedeutic* proposed by KAMLAH & LORENZEN is used in this thesis. This ap-

---

[89] BOLAND (1985), pp. 195–196. First part left out due to readability. Second part referenced a
      figure. Underlined words were adapted to italics.
[90] Cf. BOLAND (1985), p. 194.
[91] Cf. BOLAND (1985), p. 195.
[92] Cf. BOLAND (1985), p. 194.

proach has been used by HOLTEN as a foundation of method construction.[93] The careful and systematic (re)construction of a language that allows to exchange information in a meaningful and scientific manner is central to the language-critic concept. KAMLAH & LORENZEN's approach aims at (re)constructing languages by analyzing the linguistic means used to speak (and write) about phenomena. According to KAMLAH & LOREN-ZEN, language is the fundamental concept in which the world is revealed to humans and which is used to disclose the phenomena in it.[94] A special language is created as a result of the (re)construction process. This language differs from natural language by its precision and the mutual understanding having been achieved concerning the meaning of its terms by the 'language community'[95].

Terms are introduced during the (re)construction process by using *predicators*[96]. A predicator represents a 'class' or group of phenomena (like 'human beings'), whereas a *proper name* is used to address a single *thing* (like 'Christian Stephan Brelage').[97] A thing represents everything about which can be spoken or written.[98] In other words, a thing is everything that can be specified by *predication*. Predication refers to the linguistic action that asserts or denies predicators to things.[99] Predication allows the construction of elementary statements like '$x \varepsilon P$' or '$x \varepsilon' P$'. P is a predicator, x is a thing and the copula ε stands for 'has' or 'is' respectively ε' for 'is not' or 'has not'.[100] Predication is a fundamental principle of all languages. Without the possibility to assign predicators to things, a language cannot disclose the world since it is impossible to 'name' new phenomena.[101] By introducing predicators for things, their 'meaning'

---

[93] Refer, for instance, to HOLTEN (2003b); HOLTEN, DREILING & BECKER (2004); HOLTEN (2004). Additionally, the language-critical approach has been applied in the information system discipline to overcome problems of system analysis and design. Refer, for instance, to WEDEKIND (1981) and ORTNER (2002).

[94] Cf. HOLTEN (2004), p. 36.

[95] KAMLAH & LORENZEN Language community is a literal translation of the German term 'Sprachge-meinschaft'.

[96] 'Predicators' is literally translated from the German term 'Prädikator'.

[97] Cf. KAMLAH & LORENZEN (1984), pp. 17–23.

[98] The introduction of terms like 'things' and predicators seems to be an attempt to 'organize' the world in an ontological way, which implies a rather positivistic world view. However, KAMLAH & LORENZEN explicitly state that an ontology for the phenomena in the world cannot exist (cf. KAMLAH & LORENZEN (1984), p. 33). Nevertheless, they argue that disclosing the world by means of language is suitable since language is used to disclose the world 'all along' (cf. KAMLAH & LORENZEN (1984), p. 33). Thus, the logical propaedeutic is a rather pragmatic than an ontological endeavour.

[99] Cf. KAMLAH & LORENZEN (1984), p. 24.

[100] Cf. KAMLAH & LORENZEN (1984), pp. 23–27.

[101] Cf. HOLTEN (2004), p. 37.

is normalized in terms of an explicit, mutual understanding in a scientific and definite manner.[102] Additionally, it is required that terms are introduced in a *context-invariant* way, that is, their meaning is not dependent on a specific context of communication.[103] The mutual understanding about the meaning of a predicator is achieved by means of discourse. Somebody proposes to use the predicator P for the phenomenon x. The language community accepts, rejects or replaces the proposal by another one.[104] This process is being iterated until an agreement is reached.[105] By using predication, more complex statements and constraints can be constructed. Constraints restrict the assignment of predicators to phenomena and, thus, clarify their usage and determine the construction of valid or invalid statements.[106]

This approach is used in this thesis as follows: the method which is constructed in Chapter 3 is supposed to describe *what* web information systems are and *how* they can be specified by developers, end users and other members of the project team. In order to do so, a special terminology is introduced that constitutes a special language for the domain of web information systems. For instance, the predicator 'Content' represents pieces of data stored in the web information system. Entity relationship modelling is used as a metalanguage to further clarify and normalize the meaning of predicators and their relationships. In contrast to natural language, the artificial ERM language is more precise and clear but less expressive.

The subjective nature of the scientific background and the research approach of this thesis render it difficult to validate and assess the results that are created. Nevertheless, it is necessary to point out some criteria by which scientific work can be judged. Obviously, the problem of validating interpretivistic work is inherent to the approach. Nevertheless, several guidelines have been proposed in the past. Yet, they cannot be applied to the approach taken in this thesis.[107] The following criteria may serve as

---

[102]   Cf. KAMLAH & LORENZEN (1984), p. 54.

[103]   Cf. KAMLAH & LORENZEN (1984), p. 58.

[104]   Cf. KAMLAH & LORENZEN (1984), pp. 57–58.

[105]   It has to be noted that such an agreement cannot be absolute or objective since there is no possibility of ultimately validating whether the meaning of the predicator is equal to all members of a language community. Thus, the mutual understanding is best viewed as a process that converges to an 'objectified' understanding. An 'objectified' understanding is theoretically unachievable since it requires that each predicator is explicitly different from a potentially unlimited number of other predicators (cf. also HOLTEN (2004), pp. 39–40).

[106]   More complex statements are not discussed in detail since they are not used within this thesis. Refer to KAMLAH & LORENZEN (1984), pp. 57 ff. for details.

[107]   For instance, guidelines for interpretivistic case studies have been proposed by KLEIN & MYERS (1999).

examples of how the results of this research approach can be assessed:[108]

- Completeness: the language that is constructed by the approach described above has to be complete with regard to its focal domain. That is, it has to contain at least a *minimal set* of terms (predicators) that are required to specify web information systems.[109]

- Correctness: according to the logical propaedeutic, the elements of the language (predicators) have to be introduced systematically and logically consistent. Therefore, the language must not contain self-describing or circular definitions.

- Suitability: the language is supposed to facilitate meaningful information exchange between developers, end users and other project participants. Therefore, while providing the necessary means to specify web information systems, it must be easy to learn for potentially large and diverse groups of people.

Obviously, these criteria cannot be assessed easily due to the subjective nature of the language. Nevertheless, it can be assessed by experts or peers. For instance, a development expert for web information systems may judge the completeness of the language.

This research approach has been chosen since it is likely to produce a useful result concerning the scientific background. The construction of a modelling method is a subjective, creative and speculative act by nature. The main goal of this kind of research is not to merely *describe* the phenomena observed. It is rather intended to create *new* phenomena and a *new* conceptualization of web information systems as well as suitable means to specify and to describe them. Other research approaches are mainly based on observation and empirical data analysis which is obviously not a promising approach for the purpose at hand since the phenomenon does not yet exist in the sense that will be outlined in the following sections.[110] According to GALLIERS, an interpretative research approach has the following characteristics:[111]

---

[108] These criteria have been adapted from the guidelines of modelling proposed by BECKER, ROSEMANN & SCHÜTTE. Refer to BECKER, ROSEMANN & SCHÜTTE (1995) and BECKER & SCHÜTTE (2004), pp. 120–133. The framework has been revised by SCHÜTTE (1998). Essentially, the modelling method itself is a model of a language.

[109] Obviously, it is always possible to introduce new predicators if new phenomena need to be introduced. Therefore, the language can never be 'complete' at a given time.

[110] Phenomenon refers to a particular understanding of web information system, the conceptual modelling method as well as the underlying conceptualization of web information systems which differs from the systems that can actually be observed in reality at the present time.

[111] Cf. GALLIERS (1992), p. 152 for the following.

- Key features: interpretative approaches are creative research which are based more on opinion/speculation than on observation. Thus, they place greater emphasis on the role/perspective of the researcher. They can be applied to an existing body of knowledge (reviews) as well as to actual/past events/situations.

- Strengths: interpretative approaches are useful in building theory that can subsequently be tested. They create new ideas and insights and recognize that the researcher will interpret what is being studied in a particular way. They contribute to a cumulative knowledge.

- Weaknesses: the research process is unstructured and subjective by nature. Although it is acknowledged that the researcher is prone to prejudices, interpretations compounded by the time the research is undertaken might well be biased.

2.1.4 Implications & Conclusion

The main objective of this thesis is the development of suitable means for developers and users that can be used to communicate about goals, procedures and artefacts during the web information system design process. Essentially, information system *development* is considered to be a social process which entails social, technical and, most importantly, linguistic problems.[112] The information system development process is intended to achieve a mutual agreement by means of discourse.[113] Moreover, it is problematic to view the development process as something that has a well defined end. It is rather an infinite process in which new (or old) requirements (re)appear, changes are made to the system and the feedback of users is gathered and allowed for. In order to do so, information system development is an iterative activity that constantly adapts to changes in the system itself induced by people and/or technology as well as changes that occur in their environment. Information systems are considered to be part of an ongoing evolutionary change.[114]

Additionally, the *usage* of the information system is mainly considered to be a social activity, which is equally subject to limitations and problems imposed by linguistic means. This holds especially true for the type of web information system addressed in this thesis. As it will be outlined in Section 2.2.2, this thesis focuses on those web information systems that are used to satisfy diverse, potentially unknown and unpredictable

---

[112] Cf. GALLIERS & SWAN (2000) and COUGHLAN & MACREDIE (2002). A detailed conceptualization of information systems as social systems can also be found in HOLTEN (2004), pp. 73 ff.

[113] Cf. LYYTINEN (1987a), pp. 13 f. for a foundation of this view

[114] Cf. HIRSCHHEIM, KLEIN & LYYTINEN (1995), p. 53.

information needs of users.[115] Thus, these web information systems are basically 'communication machines' like knowledge management portals used to convey information between users. Given the potentially large amount of information, it becomes crucial to structure the information space in order to provide efficient and effective means for information access and to ensure the accurate interpretation of information.[116] The means to design and implement this structure are information structures which are navigated by users. As it will be seen, the navigational design is essentially a linguistic problem since language is used for labels that classify and represent large amounts of information.

Thus, the background outlined above has got double impact on this thesis. Firstly, it provides insights in the nature of the development process and means to cope with problems that arise due to its vague and social nature. Secondly, the information system itself and particularly the way users are satisfying their information needs is determined by the scientific background. As a consequence, the development process as well as the usage of the system once it is deployed itself is subject to the limitations imposed by our language. The approach to conceptual modelling outlined in this work makes sense in the context of this particular background and differs from other, more 'technical', approaches that solve other aspects of web information system development.[117]

As HIRSCHHEIM, KLEIN & LYYTINEN point out, the implications of this background are manyfold. They include a certain perspective on the role of the developer as well as the nature of information systems, their goal and the characteristics of the development process. The *role* of the information system designer is that of a catalyst, who "smoothes the transition between evolutionary stages for the social system for which he is a part".[118] It is crucial to note that the IS designer is part of the information (or social) system himself. The designer cannot be excluded from the interactive and communicative process by any means and does not act independently from the system him- or herself.[119] He or she actively shapes the system and influences it by his or her actions rather than adopting an external, objective view. The IS designer mediates require-

---

[115] This lookahead is necessary at this point since different types of web information systems cannot be discussed in this section.

[116] Cf. for a similar point RASMUSSEN, PEJTERSEN & GOODSTEIN (1994), pp. 179–180 and 304–306.

[117] Refer to Section 2.2.7 for a brief overview of other modelling approaches.

[118] HIRSCHHEIM, KLEIN & LYYTINEN (1995), p. 52. Only those implications are outlined in the following that are relevant if an interpretivistic view is appropriated. Additionally, not all implications outlined by HIRSCHHEIM, KLEIN & LYYTINEN are discussed. Of course, these implications can be contrasted with those induced by other paradigms. Refer to HIRSCHHEIM, KLEIN & LYYTINEN (1995), pp. 46–67 for a detailed discussion that opposes implications of different paradigms.

[119] Obviously, this view contrasts with positivistic approaches which postulate that the designer appropriates an objective view from the 'outside'.

ments (which can be conflicting) within the group and facilitates information exchange and communication. To achieve this, conceptual models are a suitable tool acting as abstract representations of the information system to be implemented. Users and the system developer are the key actors in the development process.

Different paradigmatic assumptions imply different conceptualizations of the term 'information'. In interpretivism information is metaphorically paraphrased as a journey with a partner that emerges from reflection, interaction and experience.[120] Thus, information is neither 'static', nor well defined, nor a product. It cannot be traded or distributed easily if the recipient is not involved in the sense-making process from which information emerges.[121] Furthermore, interpretivism emphasizes a learning perspective on information systems rather than a functionalistic view.[122] Information systems are concerned with the creation of meaning, they contribute to and they are part as well as product of the sense-making process. The development process in interpretivism specifically addresses the problem of subjective perception and seeks to achieve a mutual agreement and to mitigate differences by social interaction and sense-making.[123] The IS designer fosters interaction and information exchange in order to investigate the existing basis of interaction and communication such as differing horizons of meanings of different stakeholders.[124] User languages are reconstructed (for instance, by using conceptual modelling) in order to improve communication and more efficient means for conveying meaning than every day language.[125] Thus, the development process in interpretivism focuses on communication and social interaction. Individuals are the focal point of the development process which is intended to enable 'humanly' information processing, interpretation and the creation of meaning by sense-making.[126]

---

[120] Cf. HIRSCHHEIM, KLEIN & LYYTINEN (1995), p. 53.

[121] In contrast to this, information is viewed as a product in functionalism (cf. HIRSCHHEIM, KLEIN & LYYTINEN (1995), p. 53).

[122] The functionalisitc view implies that information systems are built around deterministic laws of human behaviour and technology in 'controlled environments' and are used to control business functions (cf. HIRSCHHEIM, KLEIN & LYYTINEN (1995), pp. 52–53).

[123] Cf. HIRSCHHEIM, KLEIN & LYYTINEN (1995), p. 53.

[124] Cf. HIRSCHHEIM, KLEIN & LYYTINEN (1995), p. 53.

[125] The approach of this thesis addresses this extensively. The modelling method which is constructed in Chapter 3 is intended to provide suitable linguistic means that allow the IS designer to reconstruct the user language.

[126] In contrast to this, functionalism postulates a rather economical view (cf. HIRSCHHEIM, KLEIN & LYYTINEN (1995), p. 53). Superior performance for the organization is the main goal of the development process. Individual demands are subordinated to organizational requirements.

2.2 Terminological & Conceptual Foundations

2.2.1 Information Systems

Systems & System Theory

General system theory[127] is an approach for analyzing and describing complex phenomena from the real or imaginary world.[128] Systems theory is an abstract and general framework for the analysis of systems. Thus, it is neither restricted nor related to a specific subject or domain.[129] Although the modern system theory supposedly originated from the 1940s biology[130], the underlying idea and principles of system theory can be traced back to the greek occidental philosophy.[131]

In general, a system is a set of entities and relationships between these entities.[132] The description and analysis of the relations within a system is particularly interesting because the knowledge about the elements in a system is not sufficient for the understanding of the system as a whole.[133] Moreover, systems are always analyzed holistically in order to avoid solutions which are optimal for a subsystem but suboptimal for the system as a whole.[134] Formally, systems are defined by using set theory. A system is composed out of a set of entities (E), their relations (R), and its environment (En).[135] Thus,

---

[127] The word 'system' is derived from the Greek word συστημα which means composition (cf. SIEG-WART (1996a), p. 183).

[128] Cf. VON BERTALANFFY (1972), p. 17; Cf. TEUBNER (1999), pp. 8 f. and Cf. ZUR MÜHLEN (2002), pp. 22–27. System theory is sometimes restricted to the analysis and (mathematical) description of technical systems. *General system theory* has a broader scope and serves as an universal concept for analysis and description of phenomena (e. g. human behaviour or usage of power). Thus, organizational issues are implicitly taken into consideration as well (cf. VON BERTALANFFY (1972), p. 17 and LEHNER (1995), pp. 45–46). Since information systems have always an organizational aspect, this viewpoint is adopted for the purpose of this thesis. Systems theory is inherently positivistic (cf. BURRELL & MORGAN (1979), pp. 57 ff.), which contradicts with the scientific positioning of this thesis. Nevertheless, it is introduced in order to provide a sound terminological foundation. However, a positivistic position is not appropriated.

[129] Cf. HILL, FEHLBAUM & ULRICH (1989), p. 18; TEUBNER (1999), p. 8 and HOLTEN (1999), pp. 126 f. Accordingly, system theory is sometimes called a meta theory (cf. TEUBNER (1999), p. 8).

[130] Cf. ZUR MÜHLEN (2002), p. 22.

[131] Cf. VON BERTALANFFY (1972), p. 18.

[132] Cf. VON BERTALANFFY (1972), p. 18; LEHNER (1995), pp. 44 ff. and ZUR MÜHLEN (2002), p. 22.

[133] This position is often illustrated by ARISTOTELE's well-known statement: "The whole is more than the sum of its parts" (cf. VON BERTALANFFY (1972), p. 18 and HILL, FEHLBAUM & UL-RICH (1989), p. 21).

[134] Cf. ACKOFF (1971), p. 661.

[135] Compare ACKOFF (1971) for details on the definition of a system and its parts.

a system can be written as a triple <E,R,En>. Furthermore, entities have properties.[136]
Each entity in a system is connected to every other element directly or indirectly.[137]
A system can be (de)composed hierarchically by defining sub- and super-systems (each
entity in a system can be a system itself). The set of entities constitutes the inside of a
system.[138] The structure of a system is defined by the set of its relations.[139] The definition of the outside of a system is achieved by characterizing the strength of the relations
by which the entities are linked. Moreover, the environment of a system contains all
variables that can cause a change in the state of a system.[140] The state of a system at
a moment of time is a set of relevant properties which a system has at that time.[141] An
event is a change in at least one structural property of the system or its environment.
The changes of a system (reactions, responses, and acts) constitute its behaviour.

Furthermore, systems can be characterized by their *complexity*. Complexity itself can
be distinguished whether it is *quantitative* or *qualitative*.[142] Quantitative complexity is
caused by the number of elements and their relations within a system. Qualitative complexity refers to the inhomogeneity within a system. That is, entities differ substantially.

Data, Information & Knowledge

The terms data, information and knowledge are widely (over)used in all scientific disciplines as well as in everyday life. Since different disciplines and authors use the terms
differently, it cannot be expected that there will be widely accepted definitions and interpretations of the terms. Nevertheless, it is necessary to introduce clear and unambiguous
definitions of these terms in order to ensure scientific precision and a common as well as
a consistent understanding of the approach developed in this thesis. Therefore, rather
than providing a comprehensive discussion about the pros and cons of different definitions and origins, the following overview concentrates on definitions that are compatible

---

[136] Cf. ACKOFF (1971), p. 662 and LEHNER (1995), p. 48.
[137] Cf. ACKOFF (1971), p. 662.
[138] Cf. SIEGWART (1996b), p. 191.
[139] Cf. SIEGWART (1996b), p. 191.
[140] Cf. ACKOFF (1971), p. 663.
[141] Cf. ACKOFF (1971), p. 662.
[142] Cf. LORENZ (1996), p. 427 and BECKER & SCHÜTTE (2004), p. 32. The prefixes quantitative and
       qualitative are added in order to reflect the difference between the German words *Kompliziertheit*
       and *Komplexität* which are both properly translated with complexity in English. However, it is
       sensible to differentiate between both types of complexity. Although, a distinction between different
       types of complexity is common in literature, the definition varies. LEHNER defines qualitative
       complexity in relation to the states a system can adopt (LEHNER (1995), p. 49). ZUR MÜHLEN
       uses the terms organizational and structural complexity (ZUR MÜHLEN (2002), p. 23) and gives
       more examples of different definitions.

with the philosophical background.[143]

It is accepted to define *data* as a sequence of invariances that are potentially meaningful to someone who is able to interpret them.[144] Invariances can be transmitted in
different forms like voltage fluctuations, pheromones or letters and digits.[145] If a given
set of symbols is encoded as a standardized set the symbols are an alphabet.[146] The
rules that map invariances to symbols are called a code.[147] Data does not carry meaning
itself. As HIRSCHHEIM, KLEIN & LYYTINEN point out, the meaning of data is socially
constructed rather than 'objectively given':

> Contrary to some writings in artificial intelligence and the IS literature, we take the
> attitude that by themselves invariances have no intrinsic meaning just as 'paper'
> acquires meaning as money only through social conventions. If some invariances,
> as the letters in this book, assume meaning it is only through the interpretation
> of the human recipient. We do not follow the suggestion that the meaning of an
> invariance is identical with the behavior it produces. This does not adequately
> account for the possibility that the meaning can be freely renegotiated: as meaning
> comes first and behavior follows the former should not be equated with the latter.
> The interpretation is a creative act and no two interpretations are ever quite the
> same. Hence *meanings* are in the eye of some human beholder(s).[148]

As a consequence, human beings are able to exchange and share meanings in social
communication, albeit only imperfectly.[149] In contrast to data, *information* corresponds
to speech acts that convey intentions.[150] Thus, pieces of information, whether they are
true or not, are intended to influence other human beings in some way.[151] In this case,
'true' means that somebody accepts the information to be 'true' in terms of a bilateral
arrangement since objective truth is unattainable. *Knowledge* refers to a statement
about a subject which is supported by legitimate claims to truth or correctness.[152] The

---

[143]   More detailed discussions can be found in LANGEFORS (1980), pp. 17 ff.; DAVIS &
        OLSEN (1985), pp. 201–233; COLE (1994), pp. 456 f.; BODE (1997), pp. 449 ff.;
        EHLERS (2003), pp. 13–25 and STYHRE (2003), pp. 57 ff. GALLIERS & NEWELL discuss the
        usage of the term knowledge in the IS community (GALLIERS & NEWELL (2003), pp. 5 ff.).
[144]   Cf. HIRSCHHEIM, KLEIN & LYYTINEN (1995), p. 12.
[145]   Cf. HIRSCHHEIM, KLEIN & LYYTINEN (1995), p. 13.
[146]   Cf. HIRSCHHEIM, KLEIN & LYYTINEN (1995), p. 13.
[147]   Cf. HIRSCHHEIM, KLEIN & LYYTINEN (1995), p. 13.
[148]   HIRSCHHEIM, KLEIN & LYYTINEN (1995), p. 13. Italics from the original.
[149]   Cf. HIRSCHHEIM, KLEIN & LYYTINEN (1995), p. 13.
[150]   Cf. HIRSCHHEIM, KLEIN & LYYTINEN (1995), p. 14.
[151]   Cf. HIRSCHHEIM, KLEIN & LYYTINEN (1995), p. 14.
[152]   Cf. HIRSCHHEIM, KLEIN & LYYTINEN (1995), p. 14.

claims have to be approved of by a group of individuals and are, therefore, socially constructed like meanings.[153] Consequently, computers cannot possess knowledge since they are unable to validate truth claims.[154]

Information Systems

Having introduced the underlying terminology, a suitable, widely accepted definition of information systems can be derived which itself is the basis for a precise definition of web information systems. According to HIRSCHHEIM, KLEIN & LYYTINEN information system definitions can be subdivided by the perspective they focus on: a structural (emphasizing elements and participating entities of the system) and a functional one (concentrating on the processes and tasks carried out by the system).[155]

> From a structural perspective (DAVIS & OLSEN (1985)), an information system consists of a collection of people, processes, data, models, technology and partly formalized language, forming a cohesive structure which serves some organizational purpose or function. From a functional perspective (LANGEFORS (1973); GOLD-KUHL & LYYTINEN (1982b); GOLDKUHL & LYYTINEN (1982a)), an information system is a technologically implemented medium for the purpose of recording, storing, and disseminating linguistic expressions as well as for the supporting of inference making. Through performing these elementary functions, IS facilitate the creation and exchange of meanings that serve socially defined purposes such as control, sense-making, and argumentation (i.e. the formulation and justification of claims). In either of these two perspectives on information systems, it should be noted that humans are included within its boundaries which means that the services provided by an IS in part depend upon human capabilities and contributions.[156]

---

[153] Cf. HIRSCHHEIM, KLEIN & LYYTINEN (1995), p. 14.

[154] Cf. HIRSCHHEIM, KLEIN & LYYTINEN (1995), p. 14. Similarly, GALLIERS & NEWELL (2003), pp. 5 ff. More precisely, computers cannot achieve knowledge in terms of a mutual understanding. However, they can conclude meaningful statements (for instance, by inferencing) if 'knowledge' is encoded in a way the computer understands. However, this is not the kind of knowledge that is outlined in this section.

[155] Cf. HIRSCHHEIM, KLEIN & LYYTINEN (1995), p. 11.

[156] HIRSCHHEIM, KLEIN & LYYTINEN (1995), p. 11. References in quote adapted to the format used in this thesis and integrated in the bibliography.

Similarly, the FRISCO-report[157] differentiates at least three different groups of information system definitions that emphasize a social, a technical and a conceptual perspective:[158]

> Even the term 'information system' itself is interpreted quite differently by different groups of people. It seems to be interpreted in at least three different ways:
>
> - As a technical system, implemented with computer and telecommunications technology.
> - As a social system, such as an organisation in connection with its information needs.
> - As a conceptual system (i.e. an abstraction of either of the above).

The social dimension of the term 'information system' is equally stressed by a common definition, which defines information systems as "socio-technical, man-machine systems used to provide efficient and effective support for the provision of information and communication while maintaining economical efficiency"[159]. The technical component of an information systems provides effective means for communication in a social interaction rather than generating information or even knowledge itself.[160] Consequently, HIRSCHHEIM, KLEIN & LYYTINEN describe information systems as technically mediated social interaction systems aimed at creating, sharing and interpreting a wide variety of meanings.[161] According to AVISON & FITZGERALD a technical view in information systems was prevalent during the early days of computer technology due to the relative costs of the technical component.[162] Today, however, the social dimension is more likely

---

[157] The acronym FRISCO stands for Framework of Information System Concepts. The report was published by the International Federation for Information Processing (IFIP) and intends "to provide a suitable conceptual framework, i. e., wherever possible, simple, clear and unambiguous definitions of, and a suitable terminology for the most fundamental concepts in the information system field, including the notions of information and communication, and of organization and information systems" (FALKENBERG et al. (1998), pp. 1 ff.).

[158] Cf. FALKENBERG et al. (1998), p. 5.

[159] Cf. (WKWI) (1994), p. 80; TEUBNER (1999), pp. 19 f.; HOLTEN (2003a), p. 33; KRCMAR (2003), p. 25; BECKER & SCHÜTTE (2004), p. 33. Similar viewpoints without using this particular definition can be found in LANGEFORS (1977), pp. 207 ff.; LAND (1992); SOLVBERG & KUNG (1993), pp. 4 f.; AVISON & FITZGERALD (1995), pp. 1 ff.; LAUDON & LAUDEN (1993), pp. 8 ff. Differently, with less emphasis on the organizational aspect HARMSEN (1997), p. 7.

[160] Cf. HIRSCHHEIM, KLEIN & LYYTINEN (1995), p. 13.

[161] Cf. HIRSCHHEIM, KLEIN & LYYTINEN (1995), p. 13.

[162] Cf. AVISON & FITZGERALD (1995), p. 6.

to cause problems since, all in all, the technology is reliable and well tried.[163]

Thus, three aspects can be condensed which are crucial and suitable for defining the subject of research more precisely.[164]

- Organizational/social context: the information system view explicitly comprises a social aspect respectively an organizational setting the system is deployed in. In accordance with the FRISCO-report, the organizational context of information systems is not limited to large or commercial organizations. Instead, it is used in a more general sense for the purpose of this thesis. Any other organizational setting (small and medium sized companies, non-governmental organizations, a development team or universities etc.) can constitute a goal-defining organizational setting for an information system. [165]

- Goal-orientation and purpose: information systems are used to support the goals of an organization by providing various functions for communication and information exchange. Thus, they are designed for a specific purpose in an organizational context and have to be aligned with the social components of the information system (users and the organization as a whole). Moreover, communication and information exchange between the social components takes place with regard to economical efficiency. Communication and information exchange imply *meaningful* conversation rather than mere signal transmission. Meaningful conversation takes place between the social components of the system.

- Information technology: communication and information are facilitated by the usage of information technology including software and hardware components. In the present case, the information technology aspect focuses on web technology and, particularly, on a distinct concept of information access. Strictly speaking, an information system without any technical component (for instance two humans engaged in a conversation) is similarly conceivable like one with a technical component.

Following this discussion, it is important to note that the concept of 'information system' can be applied twofold for the purpose of this thesis.[166] The method that is to be constructed intends to support meaningful conversation between the members of an information system's development team. This team is an information system. The

---

[163] Cf. AVISON & FITZGERALD (1995), p. 6.
[164] Cf. HOLTEN (2004), p. 33.
[165] Cf. FALKENBERG et al. (1998), pp. 5 ff.
[166] Compare for a similar view BOLAND (1985), pp. 195–196.

method is supposed to provide the linguistic means necessary for meaningful conversation about the purpose at hand. The goal of this information system is the design of an information system which itself intends to facilitate meaningful conversation between users. Meaningful conversation in this type of information system is facilitated by the models and artefacts created by the development team. In other words, the development team and the means they use are a meta-information system with regard to the actual information system that is to be implemented.[167]

Several subsystems of information systems can be identified which punctuate different aspects of their design and implementation and provide a more detailed, yet holistic view on information systems.[168] The hardware system comprises tangible objects like computers and network equipment. Software systems can be divided into system software (for instance, operating systems) and application software (for instance, ERP software like SAP R/3). Both subsystems are embedded in the organizational context.

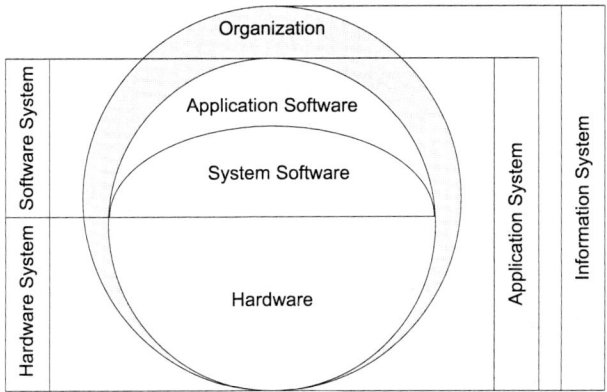

Figure 2.4: Subsystems of Information Systems (cf. HESSE et al. (1994), p. 43; TEUB-NER (1999), p. 26; BECKER & SCHÜTTE (2004), p. 33.)

2.2.2 Web Information Systems

Following the definition of information systems, a suitable definition of the term web information system can be derived: web information systems are socio-technical sys-

---

[167] Refer for a more detailed discussion to Section 2.2.6.

[168] Cf. HESSE et al. (1994), p. 43; TEUBNER (1999), pp. 26 f.; BECKER & SCHÜTTE (2004), p. 33. Some authors differentiate more levels, for instance, the hardware system is further decomposed in computer hardware and network equipment. For the purpose of this thesis, however, this differentiation is not necessary.

tems used to support the goals of an organization by facilitating information access
through web technology. They do so by providing a distinct concept of information
access enabling individuals to satisfy their information needs efficiently and effectively.
Web information systems include those systems, whose software systems comprise web
applications rather than traditional applications.[169] This definition stresses the following
two aspects in addition to the ones derived from the information system definition:

- Individuality: individuals belonging to an organization are different concerning
  their social and educational background. More particularly, information processing styles are different. It is one basic premise of this thesis that a flexible environment supporting multiple information processing styles of individuals is rather
  more efficient and effective for satisfying an individual's information needs and,
  therefore, it supports an organization's goals.

- Concept of information access: as a consequence of individuality, the means for
  information access cannot be defined uniquely and objectively by an authority.
  Instead, flexible and adaptable means have to be provided supporting individual
  differences, associative information processing and arbitrary combination of pieces
  of information.

As outlined above, web information system are supposed to facilitate meaningful communication between its users and maintainers. Concerning this communicative aspect,
it is important to note that this type of communication is *asynchronous*.[170] Authors
and readers of information stored in the system are usually spatially and temporar-
ily separated. Additionally, communicative capabilities are reduced since gestures or
moods cannot be expressed. As a consequence, asynchronous communication is subject
to various problems. As MONTOYA-WEISS, MASSEY & SONG point out

> In lean, asynchronous communication environments, the conveyance of cues is
> hindered, feedback is delayed, and interruptions or long pauses in communication
> often occur (MCGRATH (1991)).[171]

Likewise OCKER & HILTZ argue that structure becomes an important component in
asynchronous communication environments.[172] In this case, structure refers to means

---

[169] Cf. for a similar definition KAPPEL et al. (2004), p. 2. Likewise ISAKOWITZ, BIEBER & VI-
       TALI (1998), p. 79.
[170] This problem is inherent to the interpretation of textual documents.
[171] Cf. MONTOYA-WEISS, MASSEY & SONG (2001), p. 1252. Reference in quote adapted to the
       format used in this thesis and integrated in the bibliography.
[172] Cf. OCKER & HILTZ (1995), p. 129.

used to order the overall communication process. As a consequence of asynchronous communication, it is usually not possible for authors and readers to check back whether the intended meaning of a piece of information is actually conveyed or not. Thus, special precautions have to be made that help authors to convey their intentions and enable readers to grasp the intended meaning. This problem is, however, inherent for web information systems and any other asynchronous communication. Nevertheless, it is argued that a suitable navigational design which outlines the context of each piece of information can potentially improve comprehension for readers.

The bewildering variety of web information systems can be described more precisely if properties of web information systems are investigated. In contrast to characteristics, which are discussed below, properties designate subclasses and can be used to define the subject of research more precisely. Each property can be described adequately by a continuum of peculiarities rather than a strict assignment of a single peculiarity. For instance, it is neither possible nor desirable to qualify the purpose of a web information system uniquely as 'specific' or 'general'. By using a continuum, various hybrid forms are taken into account as well.

Following the discussion of web information systems, six properties suitable for defining subtypes can be identified. The *organizational focus* refers to the setting in which the web information system is to be deployed. The classification of the organizational focuses refers to the relationship of the information provider and recipient. If they belong to distinct organizational entities, the web information system is considered to be *inter-organizational*, otherwise it is *intra-organizational*. Several hybrid forms of WIS, which are operating to varying degrees inter- and intra-organizational are conceivable. Inter-organizational WIS tend to be more difficult to design since the integration of different backgrounds, special languages and cultures pose considerable challenges for the information system developer. Moreover, information needs and user characteristics are more difficult to specify since users as well as their background are unknown.[173]

Organizational stability refers to the degree of change concerning the participating organizational entities or users in the course of time. Obviously, a *low* stability requires technical as well as conceptual adjustments of the web information system. For instance, it is necessary to provide an intuitive and easy-to-use interface if users or customers change on a regular basis because training of all (new) users is neither possible nor economically feasible. In contrast to this, a *highly* stable environment can be controlled more easily so that training is possible. Typical examples of WIS with a low organizational stability are news portals such as www.independent.co.uk or www.spiegel.de.

---

[173]   Cf. GRÜNBACHER (2004), pp. 34 f.

WIS with a high degree of stability are those that are usually restricted to a small group of users (for instance, an intranet).

User diversity denotes the uncertainty about users of the system, their social, educational and cultural background and other user-related characteristics.[174] Like the organizational stability, a *high* user diversity requires adjustments and adequate precautions when designing a web information system. In contrast to the organizational stability, which focuses on the change of organizational entities in the course of time, user diversity is a complexity measure at a given time.[175] Therefore, a low organizational stability (high rate of change) can be combined with a low user diversity (users are homogenous) and vice versa. *Low* user diversity is typical for controlled and small environments like intranets, whereas large, publicly available systems like news portals tend to be characterized by high diversity.

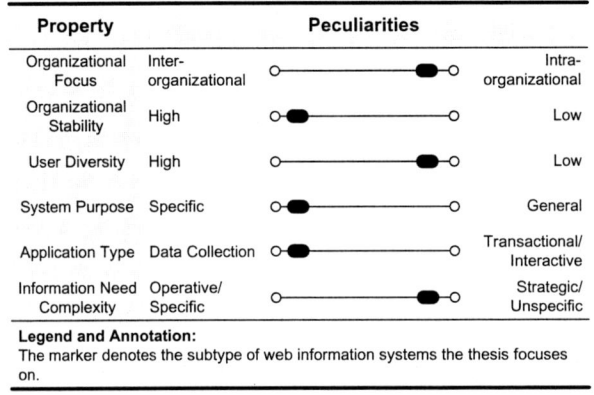

Property		Peculiarities	
Organizational Focus	Inter-organizational	○————●○	Intra-organizational
Organizational Stability	High	○●————○	Low
User Diversity	High	○————●○	Low
System Purpose	Specific	○●————○	General
Application Type	Data Collection	○●————○	Transactional/Interactive
Information Need Complexity	Operative/Specific	○————●○	Strategic/Unspecific

Legend and Annotation:
The marker denotes the subtype of web information systems the thesis focuses on.

Figure 2.5: Subtypes of Web Information Systems

The *purpose* characterizes the variety of tasks and information needs addressed by a web information system. If a broad variety of services is offered, the system can be characterized as *general*, otherwise it is *specific*. Obviously, this categorization is highly subjective and depends on the degree to which tasks and information needs are decomposed. Nevertheless, it seems reasonable to distinguish between a system that solely concentrates on one type of information and context from a news portal which offers a broad variety of information. For instance, the web information system asinfo[176]

---

[174] Cf. KAPPEL et al. (2004), p. 15 for similar characteristics.

[175] From a system theoretic point of view, users diversity measures qualitative complexity since the homogeneity of system elements is assessed (compare Section 2.2.1).

[176] The system asinfo was analyzed during a case study for this thesis. Refer to Section 4.3 for details.

focuses on information concerning maintenance of industrial health, safety standards, and provisions on labour exclusively.[177]   Obviously, this type of system differs from general purpose sites like news portals.

The *application type* classifies a system as *transactional* if it is intended to support business processes or transactions from a user perspective.[178] Transactional web information systems are characterized by a higher degree of interaction and usually allow or require input from users apart from clicking links. In contrast to this, collections of data merely allow users to traverse the information space. Typical examples of these subtypes are amazon.com (transactional) and asinfo.de (data collection).[179]

Finally, the *complexity of information needs* can be used to subclassify web information systems.[180] This criterion is especially useful for subdividing information systems in controlled environments. System like wikipedia[181] or similar encyclopaedias are called in if the information need is rather specific respectively implicitly known. They are used for confirmation purposes, whereas other system may provide support in more unspecific situations (the information need is unknown). Users start to browse information and constantly refine and reject their initial information need. Such usage patterns are typical of tasks which require a high degree of creativity (for instance, development of a new product) and which are characterized by a high degree of uncertainty. Obviously, the information requirements are more difficult to specify in such environments.

On the basis of this discussion, the subject of research can be outlined more precisely. The thesis focuses on web information systems in controlled environments (intra-organizational, high organizational stability and low user diversity). Therefore, information requirements can potentially be specified since users, their background and the tasks that have to be carried out are known. The system purpose can be characterized as rather specific. Concerning the type of application, large data pools and their usage for satisfying user information needs are investigated. Transactional systems are not discussed in detail. Finally, the complexity of information needs is unspecific (implicitly including specific information needs) which complicates information requirements

---

[177]   Compare http://www.asinfo.de/.

[178]   Obviously, every system is transactional to some degree since data has to be entered in some way (for instance, by using a content management system). Thus, the classification has to be done from a user view.

[179]   Refer to http://www.amazon.com resp. http://www.asinfo.de/.

[180]   This conceptualization of information needs intends to subclassify web information systems. A more detailed conceptualization of information needs and its role in human information processing will be outlined in Section 2.3.

[181]   Wikipedia (http://www.wikipedia.org) is an encyclopedia that allows users to write and change entries (wiki concept).

engineering although the system is deployed in a controlled environment.

Web applications have special characteristics when compared to traditional application systems and are constituted for the definition of web information systems. Web applications are based on web technology and standards. Web technologies and standards include markup languages (for instance, XML and HTML), protocols (for instance HTTP and FTP) as well as related technologies that have been developed in the context of the web.[182] The World Wide Web Consortium (W3C) and the Internet Engineering Task Force (IETF) are internationally accepted institutions for the dissemination, development and standardization of new technologies. Some characteristics are less distinctly in traditional applications (for instance, frequency of change), whereas others are mostly missing (for instance, non-linear navigation).[183] However, not all characteristics are necessarily applicable for each web application. The peculiarity of each characteristic mainly depends on the type of web application.[184]

KAPPEL et al. categorize characteristics by using four dimensions (product, utilization, development and evolution[185]) which are derived from the ISO/IEC-9126-1-standard for the assessment of software product quality.[186] Although KAPPEL et al. do not focus on a particular type of web application, their collection of characteristics clearly emphasizes commercial applications and implementation issues.[187] Therefore, the following overview concentrates on those characteristics that are relevant for the type of web application this thesis focuses on.[188]

- Product-related characteristics: the product dimension can further be subclassified in content, hypertext (resp. navigation) and presentation which is a common classification of web application systems.[189]

---

[182] Refer to Section 2.2.4 for a brief overview of web technology.

[183] Cf. KAPPEL et al. (2004), p. 10.

[184] Cf. KAPPEL et al. (2004), p. 10.

[185] Evolution encompasses characteristics like competitive pressure and rapidity of change. The aspect of evolution is excluded from the overview since it is not useful for characterizing web applications. The aspect may apply to traditional applications as well.

[186] Cf. for the following KAPPEL et al. (2004), p. 11 ff. A brief discussion of web information systems and conceptual modelling is also provided by THALHEIM & DÜSTERHÖFT (2003), pp. 80 f.

[187] For instance, KAPPEL et al. stress the importance of an attractive presentation which is an obvious and crucial requirement for commercial web applications. In controlled environments like in an intranet, however, there is usually no direct competition of different web applications. Therefore, the presentation dimension becomes less important.

[188] Compare 2.5.

[189] Cf., for instance, MERIALDO, ATZENI & MECCA (2003), pp. 50 f.; BRELAGE, EHLERS & BECKER (2002), p. 1548 and EHLERS (2003), p. 139.

– Content: the production and the publication of content is crucial for web applications and has to be planned simultaneously with the development of the actual application. Content in web application systems is usually semi- or unstructured, document-oriented and comprises multiple media like text, pictures or videos. Semi-structured data is in general more difficult to handle than structured data since content with varying data structures can represent equal or similar real world objects (semantically) and information (static irregularities).[190] Moreover, data structures are changing spontaneously or continuously in time (dynamic irregularities). Additionally, metadata information is missing or represented implicitly by content data structure (missing schema information). As a consequence of these irregularities, the *meaning* of a semi-structured piece of information cannot be anticipated.[191] This is a major difference to structured data, whose meaning is mainly determined by its structure. Transaction data processed by an ERP-system consisting of item-number, price and amount has a fixed meaning.[192] Thus, the meaning of future data entries in such a table can be anticipated. On the contrary, the *meaning* of semi-structured pieces of information like e-mail is unpredictable.

– Hypertext/navigation: the hypertext origin is the most distinctive characteristic of web applications.[193] Hypertext itself is characterized by non-linearity, that is, documents and texts do not have to be traversed in a pre-defined order. Instead, users can move freely from one document to another by using links between documents. This freedom, however, raises problems of user-disorientation and cognitive load.[194]

– Presentation: depending on the type of web application and its competitive environment, the design of the presentation level of a web application can represent a crucial success factor.[195] Design refers to aesthetic requirements as well as usability considerations.

---

[190] Cf. BENN & LANGER (2003), pp. 5 f. and BECKER et al. (2004b), pp. 25 ff. for the following. Semi-structured data is also discussed by BUNEMAN (1997) and ATZENI, MECCA & MERIALDO (1997a).

[191] Cf. BECKER et al. (2004b), p. 26.

[192] As introduced above, meaning is socially constructed rather than objectively given. Therefore, the meaning of the dataset in this example may change due to changes in the social environment. Nevertheless, it is obvious that there is a difference between structured and semi-structured data concerning its interpretability.

[193] Cf. KAPPEL et al. (2004), pp. 12 f.

[194] Both concepts are discussed in detail below.

[195] Cf. KAPPEL et al. (2004), p. 14.

- Utilization-related characteristics: this dimension comprises social, technical and natural factors influencing the usage of the system.[196]

  - Social context: users can enter and leave a system spontaneously. Customer loyalty is generally low, whereas traditional information systems are usually deployed in non-competitive environments. In this case, users have to use what is being offered and cannot use alternative solutions. Moreover, users are unknown in inter-organizational environments. Therefore, the educational, social and cultural background is unknown, too.

  - Technical context: networked environments have several characteristics (for instance, bandwidth limitations, different client platforms, data transfer latency) that influence the quality of service and have to be considered during specification and development.

  - Natural context: inter-organizational web information systems are potentially accessible on a global level and have to be available at any time.

- Development-related characteristics: the development of web applications is characterized by the project team characteristics and infrastructure.[197]

  - Project team: the development of web applications tends to be a multi-disciplinary endeavour since content editors, designers and artists have to work together. Thus, it requires corresponding adjustments in the development process since different backgrounds have to be integrated.[198]

  - Infrastructure: the infrastructure web applications are based on is inhomogeneous (for instance, various browsers and client platforms) and often immature. Therefore, the technical setting in which an application is working on the client is difficult to predict.

However, due to the quick development of web technology and its functional extension as a consequence thereof, the boundary between traditional and web application systems

---

[196] Cf. KAPPEL et al. (2004), pp. 14 f.

[197] Cf. KAPPEL et al. (2004), pp. 17 f. KAPPEL et al. mention two more characteristics: process of development and need of integration. Concerning the process of development, KAPPEL et al. argue that it is characterized by flexibility and parallelism. Likewise, they argue that web applications are characterized by a special need of integration. Both aspects are ignored since they are not special for web applications and apply in likewise manner to traditional applications.

[198] Similarly LYYTINEN, ROSE & WELKE (1998), pp. 247 f. and LANG (2003).

becomes less definite.[199] The most special characteristic of web information systems is a distinct concept of information access, which is rooted in the hypertext origin of the web. Therefore, the following pays special regard to the hypertext concept and its relation with this thesis.

2.2.3 Hypertext

Concepts & History

The origins of hypertext can be traced back to BUSH's seminal article 'As We May Think' which was published in 1945.[200] BUSH noted that the technical and scientific progress has greatly increased the knowledge base available to mankind. However, the information processing capability of the human mind remained the same.[201] Thus, efficient information storage and retrieval was becoming more and more difficult from a technical perspective. Moreover, he stated that the human mind works on the basis of association rather than on classification or indexing:[202]

> Our ineptitude in getting at the record is largely caused by the artificiality of systems of indexing. When data of any sort are placed in storage, they are filed alphabetically or numerically, and information is found (when it is) by tracing it down from subclass to subclass. It can be in only one place, unless duplicates are used; one has to have rules as to which path will locate it, and the rules are cumbersome. Having found one item, moreover, one has to emerge from the system and re-enter on a new path.
>
> The human mind does not work that way. It operates by association. With one item in its grasp, it snaps instantly to the next that is suggested by the association of thoughts, in accordance with some intricate web of trails carried by the cells of the brain. It has other characteristics, of course; trails that are not frequently followed are prone to fade, items are not fully permanent, memory is transitory. Yet the speed of action, the intricacy of trails, the detail of mental pictures, is awe-inspiring beyond all else in nature.

---

[199] For instance, the programming language Java can be used to develop fully fledged applications that are executed over the web (applets in a browser environment). There is virtually no difference to traditional applications.

[200] Cf. BUSH (1945); SIMPSON et al. (1996), pp. 47–51; LANDOW (1997), pp. 7 f.; LENNON (1997), pp. 18 f. and EHLERS (2003), pp. 36–38.

[201] Cf. SIMPSON et al. (1996), p. 49.

[202] Cf. BUSH (1945), Section 6. Paragraph break in the original.

In order to align information storage and retrieval technology with human information processing and, thus, extending the capabilities of the human mind BUSH proposed a system called *memex*.

> A memex is a device in which an individual stores all his books, records, and communications, and which is mechanized so that it may be consulted with exceeding speed and flexibility. It is an enlarged intimate supplement of [ones, C.S.B.] memory.[203]

Memex was meant to be a mechanical, photo-electric device that should be able to store different types of data (pictures, text, audio, etc.). Moreover, it should be capable of associating information by links. Thus, users can build and store associative 'trails' of thought. BUSH's *memex* vision comprised all elements of current hypertext systems and, more remarkably, even ideas that have not yet been implemented today (nearly 60 years later).[204]

The term *hypertext* was coined 20 years later by NELSON.[205] Basing his work on BUSH, NELSON investigated obstacles that hinder the realization of BUSH's *memex* vision and concludes that the obstacles costs and needs are not enduring, whereas the design of such a system is still problematic.[206] NELSON extended BUSH's work and was in particular concerned with the limitations of computer technology, user interface design and the process of writing in general. Specifically, he noted that the organization of data in files and single hierarchies, which was adapted from traditional paper-based office work, enforces unsuited structures on data and limited the capabilities of the human mind.[207] Moreover, NELSON argued that writing is a non-sequential process and that current computer technology transferred the limitations of paper into modern technology. Since NELSON was a writer himself, he was especially interested in the reuse and the archiving of documents and document parts as well as copyright issues.[208]

---

[203] BUSH (1945), Section 6; LENNON (1997), p. 18. The term *memex* is an abbreviation for 'memory extension'.

[204] For instance, the *memex* system should be capable of storing a trail used by the user persistently. Current WIS usually provide histories of visited links. However, histories do fade and are not categorized or ordered in any way. Moreover, personalized trails through information cannot be shared (efficiently) among users. Nevertheless, current computer technology provides means to implement BUSH's vision.

[205] Cf. NELSON (1965), p. 97 and more detailed NELSON (1993), pp. 1/14 ff. (there are no 'normal' page numbers in NELSON's book 'Literary Machines') and EHLERS (2003), p. 37.

[206] Cf. NELSON (1965), p. 85.

[207] Cf. NELSON (1999a), p. 4 (page numbering refers to a reprint).

[208] Cf. NELSON (1999b), pp. 1 ff. (page numbering refers to a reprint).

In order to overcome these limitations of computer technology, NELSON proposed a data structure which he called *xanalogical structure* that was supposed to be totally different to hierarchical file structures.[209] A key notion of the xanalogical structures are parallel documents.[210] Parallel documents are interconnected by links. In contrast to the link concept used in the World Wide Web today, links in the xanalogical model also incorporated the concept of the so-called *transclusion* and typecasted links. By transclusion, pieces of data appear simultaneously in more than one document without being physically copied, whereas normal links are interconnections of the information space used for navigation. Documents and data were supposed to be presented on the screen by *transpointing windows* showing the relations between documents as lines which were drawn between them. Additionally, transpointing windows were intended to provide functionality for document editing. Pieces of data were stored uniquely and were accessed by a single unchangeable address.[211] By assigning permanent addresses to pieces of data, the links between them were supposed to be unbreakable. Links between documents referred to pieces of data rather than the document's address.[212] Technically, the starting as well as ending address of a link is encoded by two numbers that address the pieces of data of the documents the link is supposed to connect. Thus, the link concept of this concept is fairly different from links known from the World Wide Web, which connect to addresses of documents rather than ranges of data and are not typecasted.

By implementing these functionalities, NELSON intended to create a hypertext system providing the following:[213]

- Unlimited storage and support of multiple media types: the system should store a(n) (virtually) unlimited amount of documents, the relationships that exist between them and comments about the documents. Moreover, the system should support various data types such as text, videos or audio files.

- Unlimited number of categories: the system provides an index of the documents that are currently stored and file documents and an unlimited number of categories.

- Dynamic outlining/indexing: texts are linked with each other. The dependent text changes with the text it is linked to.

---

[209] Cf. NELSON (1999b), pp. 1 ff. (page numbering refers to a reprint).
[210] Cf. NELSON (1999b), p. 3 (page numbering refers to a reprint); NELSON (1993), pp. 1/14 ff. and NELSON (1965), pp. 84 ff. for the following.
[211] Cf. NELSON (1999b), p. 11 (page numbering refers to a reprint).
[212] Cf. NELSON (1999b), p. 14 (page numbering refers to a reprint).
[213] Cf. NELSON (1965), p. 88.

- Versions and variants: the system should be able to store multiple versions and variants of a document while remaining its integrity with regard to links and classifications.

NELSON proposed the *Xanadu* system which was supposed to implement the functionalities mentioned above. Although several attempts have been made, the system has not been implemented up to now.[214] However, it is remarkable that BUSH as well as NELSON envisioned such complex web information systems before the technical means to build them were available. BUSH's vision was published before computers were available; NELSON's before the internet was invented. Moreover, the principles and ideas of both approaches are still relevant and, in some cases, they have not been realized today. Independently from NELSON (1965), the famous inventor ENGELBART worked early on the fulfilment of BUSH's vision and realized the first real hypertext system called oN-Line System (NLS).[215] Not unlike NELSON, ENGELBART had the vision of a conceptual framework that could 'augment' and structure cognitive processes, concepts, symbols, processes, and physical artefacts.[216]

The development of hypertext can be roughly subdivided into three eras: visions and concepts, prototypes and the World Wide Web. During the vision era, complex systems, which could not be implemented and were not commercially successful, were designed. During the prototype era numerous prototypes were developed that provided comprehensive functionality for individuals.[217] Finally, the WWW, which was developed by BERNERS-LEE, HENDLER & LASSILA, became a synonym for hypertext due to its (commercial) success.[218] It is remarkable that the functional characteristics decreased over time while the (commercial) success of the systems, particularly the WWW, increased. Additionally, the WWW-era is characterized by an ongoing diffusion of Web technology and Web based applications. More and more applications are deployed on the Web creating new types of applications and work environments. Likewise, the organizational scope of the hypertext systems changed significantly. Hypertext systems in

---

[214] Cf. NELSON (1999a); NELSON (1999b) and WOLF (1995).

[215] LENNON (1997), pp. 19 f. NELSON himself credited ENGELBART for building the first hypertext system (NELSON (1993) and LENNON (1997), p. 20). The invention of the computer mouse, word processing, the concept of windows on the screen, email and hypertext is attributed to ENGELBART (LENNON (1997), p. 22). Refer to CONKLIN (1987), pp. 22 f. for an overview of NLS. ENGELBART spoke of the augmentation of human intellect, reflecting the 'enhancing' of intellectual capabilities.

[216] Cf. LENNON (1997), p. 21.

[217] Cf. CONKLIN (1987) and LENNON (1997), pp. 17–32 for an overview of early hypertext implementations and their characteristics.

[218] Refer to BERNERS-LEE, HENDLER & LASSILA (2001) for an overview of the development of the Web.

BUSH's as well as NELSON's vision and early prototypes were meant to be supplements and additions of the human mind or, in CONKLIN's words, a computer-based medium for 'thinking and communication'.[219] Current web technology, however, was explicitly designed to provide efficient means for information exchange between spatially distributed individuals. Consequently, the design goals of both concepts are different. Earlier vision incorporated richer functionality, whereas current web information system are designed with special regard to easiness of use, the ability to be distributed and peripheral organization. Figure 2.6 comprises the history of hypertext, its origins, concepts and technologies in form of a timeline.[220]

Characteristics, Terminology & Navigation

In general, *hypertext* is a graph consisting of nodes (textual documents) and edges (links) between them. *Hypermedia* is a more general concept which also includes other media like videos, pictures and audio files.[221] Both terms are used interchangeably in the following, since there are virtually no pure hypertext applications that contain textual documents only. CONKLIN reviewed several hypertext implementations that were designed before the World Wide Web became a synonym for hypertext.[222] As CONKLIN points out, the hypertext concept simultaneously comprises three aspects:

> From a computer science point of view, the essence of hypertext is precisely that it is a hybrid that cuts across traditional boundaries. Hypertext is a *database method* providing a novel way of directly assessing data. This method is quite different from the traditional use of queries. At the same time, hypertext is a *representation schema*, a kind of semantic network which mixes informal textual material with more formal and mechanized operations and processes. Finally, hypertext is an *interface modality* that features "control buttons" (link icons) which can be arbitrarily embedded within the content material by the user. These are not separate applications of hypertext: They are metaphors for a functionality that is an essential union of all three.[223]

CONKLIN argues that the concept of links as well as nodes are the cornerstones of successful hypertext implementations.[224] Links extend the text beyond the single dimension

---

[219] Cf. CONKLIN (1987), p. 32.
[220] The abbreviations in Figure 2.6 are described in the following subsections.
[221] Cf. CONKLIN (1987), p. 18; AKSCYN, MCCRACKEN & YODER (1988), p. 820; BIEBER et al. (1997), p. 33 and EHLERS (2003), pp. 37–38.
[222] Cf. for the review CONKLIN (1987), pp. 20–32.
[223] CONKLIN (1987), p. 33. Italics in the original.
[224] Cf. CONKLIN (1987), p. 33.

Year	Visions and Concepts	Era	Products and Tools	Languages		
1945	Bush's Memex	Pre-implementation/ Visionary				
1965	Nelsons's Xanadu Internet		Engelbart's NLS			
1986		Implementation and Prototypes	Apple's HyperCard	SGML		
	Berners-Lee WWW					
1990				HTML (without version number)		
1993		World Wide Web	Mosaic			
1994						
1995				HTML 2.0	HTML 3.0	
1996			IE 3.0 NN 4.0	CSS 1	XML	
1997				HTML 3.2	HTML 4.0	
1998				CSS 2	DOM 1	
1999					HTML 4.01	
2000				DOM 2	XHTML	
2001	Berners-Lee et al. Semantic Web					
2002						
2003						
2004				RDF	OWL	DOM 3

Figure 2.6: Hypertext History: Visions, Concepts, Tools and Languages (cf. LENNON (1997), pp. 17–31; SCHARL (2000), pp. 7 f. and EHLERS (2003), pp. 63 f.)

of linear flow and provide flexible and adaptable means for information access. Nodes store the documents and can be used to build flexible networks that model his or her problem respectively solution especially when it is used as a thinking, writing or design tool.[225] The hypertext concepts reviewed by CONKLIN are obviously more interactive

---

[225] Cf. CONKLIN (1987), p. 33.

and user-centered than the ones underlying the Word Wide Web today. The implementations were intended to provide support for individuals performing creative tasks rather than mere browsing. Additionally, the concepts entailed more functionality, for instance, typecasting of links and link properties.[226] Hypertext nodes represent pieces of information and could be manipulated by users in some implementations.[227] By doing so, the user was able to model his or her own concepts with the hypertext system by joining or splitting documents. Like links, hypertext nodes can be typecasted.

The hypertext concept allows users more freedom to interact with the system than traditional applications. The act of movement within the information space that is, following of a link to another document, is called *navigation*.[228] The sum of all documents and links is called the *information space*. Users navigate this space by using links. Links can be roughly subdivided in referential (reference another document) and organizational links created by the structure used to organize pieces of information. Formally, a simple link can be described as a tuple containing a *label* and a *target*, which is the address of the target document. The label is usually indicated in textual or graphical form. Obviously, careful labelling of links is crucial for successful hypertext implementations. Users must be able to predict what kind of information they can expect when following a link. The link concept can be greatly enriched by provided bidirectional links (encoding the source as well) and cardinalities (one-to-many and many-to-one links) that link to more than on document simultaneously.[229] Additionally, links to strings can be supported, which address a whole block of text inside a document rather than the document itself.[230]

The sum of all organizational links respectively the structures they incorporate is called the overall *information structure*. It does not contain pieces of information. The strict separation of information and links is rather artificial since links (particularly their labels) are pieces of information as well. The term information structure is used, however, to denote the means used to organize the information. Consequently, only organizational links constitute the information structure. The information structure can be defined by one hierarchy, multiple hierarchies, a network of nodes or any hybrid of these.[231] The information structure mainly determines the user's ability to retrieve the desired information. Depending on the type of the information system, some information structures may be appropriate while others are not. In general, the following concepts

---

[226] Cf. CONKLIN (1987), p. 33.

[227] Cf. CONKLIN (1987), p. 35 f.

[228] Cf. NIELSEN (1990), p. 298.

[229] Cf. LANDOW (1997), pp. 11 f. Bidirectional links are not encoded in standard HTML. Nevertheless, the back-function of browsers provides this functionality.

[230] Cf. LANDOW (1997), pp. 11 f. This linking concept is similar to NELSON's transclusion.

[231] Cf. CONKLIN (1987), p. 35.

can be used to structure information:[232]

- Hierarchy: a hierarchy is the most basic concept for information structures. Hierarchies are considered to be intuitively understandable for users since they resemble a well-known concept of abstraction.[233] Hierarchies are *strict* if each document is assigned to a single node, otherwise they are *ambiguous*. A single hierarchy can be easily implemented from a technical perspective. Depending on the type of information, however, they may enforce unsuitable structures on information. It is only seldom that each piece of information can uniquely be assigned to a single element of the hierarchy. Moreover, hierarchies have a half-life: their utility and applicability fade over time.[234] Instead of a single hierarchy, multiple hierarchies can be used for different 'parts' of the information space. In order to distinguish hierarchies from multitrees (see below), pieces of information are always assigned to one hierarchy and the hierarchies differ (all elements are different) in this case.

- List: a list can be considered a special case of a hierarchy. Elements of the list are objects ordered sequentially. This concept can be used, for instance, to indicate the sequence of months or years. Lists are easy to implement and supposed to be easily understandable.

- Mutlitrees/Combined hierarchies: in contrast to hierarchies, pieces of information can be assigned to more than one hierarchy.[235] Additionally, hierarchies may be overlapping. This structures are the most flexible and comprehensive ones, but tend to be more difficult to implement. Moreover, they are more difficult to use. In contrast to a single hierarchy, combined hierarchies can be navigated *simultaneously*.[236]

- Network: finally, information may not be structured at all. Instead an arbitrary network of nodes can be used. This kind of structure can be appropriate for artistic systems.

Pieces of information are rather stored in smaller units than in traditional file systems. Therefore, users are confronted with a significant higher amount of pieces of information.

---

[232] GLOOR gives an overview of design concepts for navigation including hierarchies and related concepts (GLOOR (1997), pp. 49–139).

[233] Cf. SCHARL (2000), p. 222.

[234] Cf. NELSON (1993), p. 2/49; LANDOW (1997), p. 7.

[235] The concept of multitrees was proposed by FURNAS & ZACKS.

[236] This concept is extensively used for the modelling method, which is developed in Chapter 3.

Moreover, hypertext systems are characterized by a high degree of freedom for users. In addition with a potentially very high number of links that represent the users ability to interact with the system, this situation can lead to two major problems having been identified in early research on hypertext and navigation:[237]

1. User-disorientation: In analogy to (physical) movement in natural space, the concept of *user-disorientation* is used to describe a user's inability to define his or her own position in the information space and how to get to another place from his or her actual position.[238] It was early identified as a major problem for successful implementation of hypertext systems.[239]

2. Cognitive overhead: the term cognitive overhead denotes user's inability to keep track of a multitude of alternatives at once.[240] Since there are virtually no predefined processes a user has to carry out, he or she can select from several activities at any given time: read, create, delete, modify a document or follow, create, delete, modify a link. The multitude of possibilities can lead to cognitive overhead.[241]

Literary Theory Perspectives

The interactive nature of hypertext has caused researchers to investigate the influence of hypertext for literature in general and particularly the roles of readers and writers. AARSETH argues that the act of reading and writing of cybertext[242] respectively *ergodic literature* differs substantially from the act of reading and writing of traditional literature:[243]

> The concept of cybertext focuses on the mechanical organization of the text, by positing the intricacies of the medium as an integral part of the literary exchange.

---

[237] Cf. CONKLIN (1987), pp. 38 ff. for the following.

[238] Cf. CONKLIN (1987), p. 38 and, more detailed, LANDOW (1997), pp. 115–123.

[239] Cf., for instance, NIELSEN (1990), p. 298. Some recommendations and examples of well and poorly designed navigation can be found in NIELSEN (2000), pp. 188 ff. THENG discusses ethical and cultural usability issues and web information systems (cf. THENG (2003)).

[240] Cf. CONKLIN (1987), p. 40.

[241] Obviously, the problem of cognitive overhead particularly applies to interactive hypertext systems.

[242] The term cybertext is a combination of WIENER's term cybernetics (WIENER (1948)) and traditional text. According to AARSETH's taxonomy of text, cybertext is a superset of hypertext also including video games and other interactive media. Refer to AARSETH (1997), pp. 58 ff. for details.

[243] AARSETH (1997), p. 1. The term 'ergodic' is a neologism derived from the Greek words 'ergon' and 'hodos' which mean 'work' and 'path'. According to AARSETH, ergodic literature is not limited to artefacts created and processed by computers. Instead, several examples of non-linear texts could be identified, for instance, the Chinese text or oracular wisdom (*I Ching*) and the poems and calligrammes of APPOLINAIRE (AARSETH (1997), pp. 9 f).

However, it also centers attention on the consumer, or user, of the text, as a more integrated figure than even reader-response theorists would claim. The performance of their reader takes place all in his head, while the user of cybertext also performs in an extranoematic sense. During the cybertextual process, the user will have effectuated a semiotic sequence, and this selective movement is a work of physical construction that the various concepts of "reading" do not account for. [...] In ergodic literature, nontrivial effort is required to allow the reader to traverse the text.[244]

Similarly, LIESTOL notes that hypertext reconfigures the way we perceive texts and conjoin hypertext with the 'linguistic turn' in philosophy.[245] Thus, from a literary point of view, the development of hypertext seemed to be caused by a paradigm shift from structuralism to poststructuralism respectively deconstructionism.[246] The distinction between ergodic and traditional literature has been challenged by literature researchers.[247] Especially the notion of non-linearity, which is constituent for a definition of hyper- and cybertext, is contested. They argue that a cybertext is not different from traditional literature since each text is non-linear to some degree as readers have to make choices during the reading process of every text and, finally, a text cannot be non-linear because readers can only perceive it sequentially.[248] Contradicting this position, AARSETH argues that there is a different interpretation of what is being read and what is being read *from*.[249] When reading a drama, the reader is always aware of what he or she is reading, whereas the reader of a cybertext is constantly reminded of inaccessible strategies and paths not taken, voices not heard.[250]

The changing roles of authors and readers of hypertexts are intensively discussed by LANDOW.[251] As LANDOW argues, the boundaries between both roles are fading: reader and writer are merging. This is relevant for hypertext systems that provide interactivity, that is, users are readers *and* writers and can change or add text to the system. However, the freedom hypertext systems allow the users enables them to recreate the document by compiling it in an (probably) unforseen way. Since this thesis is particularly interested

---

[244] The omitted part of the text is a description of the term 'ergodic', which is given in the previous footnote.

[245] Cf. LIESTOL (1994), pp. 87 ff.

[246] Cf. AARSETH (1994), pp. 58 f. and LANDOW (1997), pp. 2 f.

[247] Cf. AARSETH (1997), p. 2 ff. for the following.

[248] Cf. AARSETH (1997), p. 2.

[249] Cf. AARSETH (1997), p. 3.

[250] Cf. AARSETH (1997), p 3. A more detailed essay on the nonlinearity concept in hypertexts can be found in AARSETH (1994), pp. 51–87.

[251] Cf. LANDOW (1997), pp. 90 ff.

in the conceptual specification of web information systems, the literary theory branch cannot be investigated in detail. Specifically, the role of authors is not discussed. It is, however, important to note that the hypertext concept causes the traditional role separation of author and reader to fade. Information providers as well as information recipients have to be aware of the potentials and changes in their respective roles that are facilitated by hypertext systems. Therefore, classical models of reading and writing are not appropriate for hypertext applications.

Related Work on Web Information Systems & Navigation

Related work on navigation and web information systems can be roughly divided into *empirical* and *conceptual* papers. The empirical papers present studies of content and design respectively navigation of web information systems as well as their influences on user satisfaction and the user's ability to retrieve the desired information. Conceptual papers mostly deal with modelling issues and metrics for web information systems. Although most of these papers concentrate on different subtypes of web information system, there is no reason to assume that the insights gained in these works are not applicable in a likewise manner to the systems investigated in this thesis. In particular, empirical work usually focuses on commercial web sites and factors influencing the user's satisfaction and, therefore, a web site's success. These systems can be classified as uncontrolled (inter-organizational, low organizational stability and high user diversity), they have a rather general purpose and they are frequently transactional.[252] Additionally, the empirical as well as the conceptual work clearly indicates that a suitable navigational design is a crucial success factor for web information systems.

HUIZINGH presents an empirical study on the content and design of web sites.[253] In order to describe web information systems, he distinguishes content from design. The navigation structure is one aspect among others in the design dimension of his framework and can be divided into four categories: Tree, tree with back-to-home page button, tree with horizontal links and an extensive network. The majority of systems analyzed in this study have a tree-structure or tree with back-to-home page button.[254] The complexity of web sites has been found to be correlated to the industry-type (Information industry most complex, Services and Products the least). MUYLLE, MOENAERT & DESPONTIN present an empirical study on web-site user satisfaction.[255] They introduce and define

---

[252] Refer to Section 2.2.2 for a classification of subtypes of web information systems and the positioning of this thesis.

[253] Cf. HUIZINGH (2000).

[254] Cf. HUIZINGH (2000), p. 131.

[255] Cf. MUYLLE, MOENAERT & DESPONTIN (2004).

the construct of user satisfaction and its underlying dimensions in order to provide a measure for assessing web site user satisfaction.[256] Eleven dimensions are identified to have direct influence on user satisfaction. Three of these dimensions (Entry guidance, web site structure and hyperlink connotation) are directly or indirectly linked to issues of navigation and navigational design.[257] The navigational design of a web-site is described by the measure 'web-site structure'. A more detailed description and investigation of the navigational design was not the focus of their work. Likewise, PALMER investigates success factors for web sites. Among the five hypotheses tested, one is directly related to navigation. It proposes that more navigable web sites will be associated with greater perceived success by users.[258] Empirical evidence is found in PALMER's study that confirms the hypotheses. Nevertheless, critical factors for web site success have been discussed by LIU & ARNETT, who identify system design quality as one important factor of web site success, but do not describe the navigational design quality on a detailed level either.[259] BUCY et al. have conducted an extensive study on web page complexity and its correlation with site traffic.[260] Graphical design issues (usage of colours, frames etc.) and its effect on page complexity have been investigated in detail and not the navigational design. KHAN & LOCATIS have performed a study on link display and density and their effects on information retrieval effectiveness.[261] Since their study was based on a quite simple information system, they point out that additional research is needed to investigate effects of information structuring in large, deeply structured information spaces.[262] Using HERZBERG's two factor model, ZHANG & VON DRAN clearly identify navigation as a hygiene factor.[263] Thus, the absence of a clearly defined and appropriate navigational structure is a 'dissatisfier' for users surfing the Web.

There is a vast body of conceptual research on web information systems which cannot be presented in detail. Therefore, the following overview concentrates on those contributions directly related to issues of navigation. FARKAS & FARKAS present guidelines for web navigation.[264] Specifically, they address the problem of designing hierarchies

---

[256] Cf. MUYLLE, MOENAERT & DESPONTIN (2004), p. 544.
[257] Cf. MUYLLE, MOENAERT & DESPONTIN (2004), p. 547.
[258] Cf. PALMER (2002), p. 155.
[259] Cf. LIU & ARNETT (2000).
[260] Cf. BUCY et al. (1999).
[261] Cf. KHAN & LOCATIS (1998).
[262] Cf. KHAN & LOCATIS (1998), p. 181.
[263] Cf. ZHANG & VON DRAN (2000), p. 1260. HERZBERG's model is a general approach for identifying factors that influence human behaviour positively (motivation factors) or negatively (hygiene factors). It was originally intended to investigate human motivation in work environments. Compare HERZBERG (1966), pp. 71–91 and HERZBERG, MAUSNER & SNYDERMAN (1967) for details.
[264] Cf. FARKAS & FARKAS (2000).

and optimal ratios of breadth and depth. They state that it tends to be better to favour breadth over depth.[265] However, determining optimal ratios mathematically seems to be rather useless or artificial since the objects and things in the world are ordered in themselves rather than in an arbitrary, calculated structure. Thus, a mathematically 'bad' structure may be excellent in terms of interpretability and understandability. Additionally, FARKAS & FARKAS distinguish different types of linking similarly to the traditional separation of organizational and referential linking. LARSON & CZERWINSKI surveyed several studies on optimal ratios between depth and breadth of hierarchies, too.[266] RIVLIN, BOTAFOGO & SHNEIDERMAN present algorithms for (semi)automated identification and construction of hierarchies in hypertext environments using textual analysis of contents.[267] Since hierarchies have several advantages (for instance the ability to be laid out in plain and inherent concept of abstraction), they have intensively been investigated with concern to navigational purposes in information spaces.[268] FURNAS & ZACKS have introduced the concept of multitrees allowing the use of multiple hierarchies on the same set of data simultaneously. As indicated earlier, this concept is adapted and extended in the modelling method.[269] The problem of outlying complex graphs in a flat structure is discussed by VAN DYKE PARUNAK who also correlates graphs with navigation.[270] The quantitative analysis and description of graphs in hypertext have been surveyed by DHYANI, NG & BHOWMICK.[271] NIELSEN published several articles in which navigational issues are discussed with regard to user interface design. His research culminates in his pessimistic statement that the web will suffer a severe usability melt down in the year 2000 unless some skillful maneuvering is applied.[272] In NIELSEN's point of view, reasons for inefficient information retrieval on the web are poorly designed user interfaces, which are partly caused by inappropriate navigation structures and the amount of data on the web.[273] Retrospectively, NIELSEN's vision did not entirely come true. However, the issues Nielsen describes remain unsolved. BIEBER & YOO propose the relationship navigation analysis in order to assist web information system developers in their work of creating appropriate navigational means.[274] THÜRING, HANNEMANN

---

[265] Cf. FARKAS & FARKAS (2000), p. 345.

[266] Cf. LARSON & CZERWINSKI (1998).

[267] Cf. RIVLIN, BOTAFOGO & SHNEIDERMAN (1994).

[268] Cf. FURNAS & ZACKS (1994).

[269] Cf. FURNAS & ZACKS (1994) and the description of the multidimensional information space in Section 3.2.

[270] Cf. VAN DYKE PARUNAK (1989).

[271] Cf. DHYANI, NG & BHOWMICK (2002).

[272] Cf. NIELSEN (1999), pp. 66 f.

[273] Cf. NIELSEN (1999), p. 67.

[274] Cf. BIEBER & YOO (1999).

& HAAKE focus on the reading process of hypermedia documents for learning and note that issues of cognition and human information processing are still widely neglected and barely influence hypermedia design.[275] They propose eight principles and relate them to ten cognitive design issues. Specifically, they propose visualization of the documents structure and complementary navigation facilities for location, direction as well as distance in order to reduce a user's cognitive overhead by navigational concepts.[276] SPANGLER, KREULEN & LESSLER present an approach which is similar to the one developed in this thesis.[277]

This brief overview of related works clearly indicates that an adequate navigational design is crucial for the implementation of a successful web information system.[278] However, since the focus of related research is usually broader (e.g. web site success, user satisfaction), navigational design issues are only one variable among others and are, consequently, not investigated in detail. Moreover, researchers seem to have problems to describe the navigation structure of information spaces and its characteristics in detail. In particular, the navigational structure of very complex systems containing several thousands of contents, which are quite common in the web and intranets today, seems to be indescribable. In other words, researchers lack a well defined, conceptualization of web information systems paying special regard to navigational issues. The method developed in this thesis contributes to the body of knowledge on navigation by providing suitable means for describing and specifying web information systems.

2.2.4 Web Technology, Markup Languages & Semantic Web

Although this thesis is not concerned with implementation issues, a brief overview of technical foundations is provided in this section. Moreover, the modelling approach constructed in this thesis is closely related to recent advancements in web technology which are subsumable under the term 'Semantic Web'. The modelling approach is basically intended to foster communication in the development process. In principle, the models can be used for the design process and support the semi-automated generation of implementation artefacts (for instance, database structures) for the web information system in terms of a CASE-approach. Therefore, some technical aspects of web information systems are outlined briefly.

---

[275] Cf. THÜRING, HANNEMANN & HAAKE (1995), p. 57.
[276] Cf. THÜRING, HANNEMANN & HAAKE (1995), p. 59.
[277] Cf. SPANGLER, KREULEN & LESSLER (2003), pp. 191 ff.
[278] Cf. HITZ & LEITNER (2004), p. 277 for a similar point.

Protocols & Architecture of Web Application Systems

The variety of web applications leads to various architectures which can differ substantially and are specifically suited for a given scenario. Nevertheless, some common principles of web applications can be outlined.[279] Generally, the internet contains hosts that are connected via a network. A stack of protocols organize data transfer.[280] Well known protocols include the hypertext transfer protocol (HTTP), the internet protocol (IP) and the file transfer protocol (FTP).[281] An internet hosts is uniquely identified by its IP address which is translated by the domain name system (DNS) into readable addresses (such as uni-muenster.de for 128.176.188.115). Each host can potentially act as a server and/or client. Resources (for instance, documents) are stored on a server and are uniquely identified by uniform resource identifiers (URI), for instance, http://www.uni-muenster.de/index.html where http: is the schema which describes the way documents can be accessed (in this case with the HTT-protocol) and www.uni-muenster.de/index.html the service type (WWW) and the address of the resource.[282] A client retrieves documents from the server by establishing a connection to the server. A HTTP-request containing the address of the document is sent to the server. The server answers the request by transferring the document and closes the connection afterwards. If the HTTP protocol is used, connections are not permanent and have to be re-established each time a new document is requested. Moreover, the HTTP request can contain variables which can be used, for instance, to transfer user input.

With the growth of the amount of data on the web, it became necessary to create documents dynamically from (relational) database rather than storing each document

---

[279] It is not intended to give a comprehensive overview of languages and protocols used in web environments. The reader may refer to the various resources provided by the World Wide Web Consortium (http://www.w3c.org) and the Internet Engineering Task Force (http://www.ietf.org) as well as the references given in this brief overview. Moreover, only issues that are concerned with the transfer of documents are discussed.

[280] Cf. WILDE (1999), pp. 18 f. for an overview of protocols. The ISO/OSI reference model gives an overview of different protocol layers. Compare TANENBAUM (1981) for a comprehensive overview.

[281] Refer to BERNERS-LEE, FIELDING & FRYSTYK (1996); LENNON (1997), p. 94 and GAEDKE et al. (2004), pp. 136–137 for a brief introduction in HTTP. Refer to WILDE (1999), pp. 53 ff. for a comprehensive overview. See the INTERNET ENGINEERING TASK FORCE for the internet protocol and POSTEL & REYNOLDS (1985) for the FTP specification. The Internet Engineering Task Force focuses on the development and dissemination of standards used in networked environments (particularly protocols). Each standard is discussed and published in a Request For Comment (RFC) which are consecutively numbered. For instance, the HTTP 1.1 protocol is specified in RFC No. 2068 (cf. http://www.ietf.org/rfc/rfc2068.txt?number=2068).

[282] Cf. WILDE (1999), pp. 35 f. URI's are a superset of uniform resource locators (URL).

as a static piece of HTML.[283] In this case, the server gets a request for a document containing server side scripting components that are parsed and executed each time a document is accessed by a client.[284] For instance, the personal hypertext preprocessor (PHP), java server pages (JSP) as well as the practical extraction and reporting language (PERL) are popular scripting languages which can be used to compile documents dynamically.[285] Additionally, parameters can be used to personalize the document during dynamic compilation. Client side scripting (for instance, with JavaScript) can be used to validate user input and to control the client application respectively the browser.[286]

Architecture components of web applications include at least a web server and a client (browser) which do not necessarily run on different machines.[287] The web server transfers data which is parsed and formatted on the client.[288] Additionally, a database server can be integrated in the architecture. Data is either entered manually by writing HTML documents or processed by content management systems which provide extensive functionalities for maintaining a web site.[289] The general principle of data transfer and an example for a typical architecture of a web application is illustrated in Figure 2.7. It illustrates the case of a more complex web application storing data in a relational database.[290]

Markup Languages

In contrast to traditional storage methods for data (for instance, relational databases), data which is supposed to be transferred via web environments is encoded differently. Databases structure data according to technical principles that are enforced in order

---

[283] Refer to the next subsection for a brief overview of HTML.

[284] There are various other possibilities for evoking a programmes on the server, for instance, the common gateway interface (CGI). Refer to LENNON (1997), p. 98; VOSSEN (1999), pp. 660–663 and EHLERS (2003), p. 68 for an overview.

[285] Cf. EHLERS (2003), pp. 68 f.

[286] Cf. GAEDKE et al. (2004), pp. 139–140 for a brief overview of client side technologies.

[287] Refer to KAPPEL et al. (2003), pp. 101 ff. and EICHINGER (2004), pp. 77 ff. for comprehensive overviews of architecture concepts for web information systems.

[288] Cf. LENNON (1997), p. 95.

[289] Content management systems and their functionality are not discussed in detail. Refer, for instance, to BÜCHNER et al. (2000) and EHLERS (2003).

[290] Virtually all web applications store data in databases and compile HTML documents dynamically during run-time (except of very small web sites like personal homepages). This does also include web sites maintained by a content management system that creates static HTML documents in order to increase performance and security. In this case, the content management system typically stores data in a database. Compare LU & FENG (1998) for an overview of integrated WWW and database technologies.

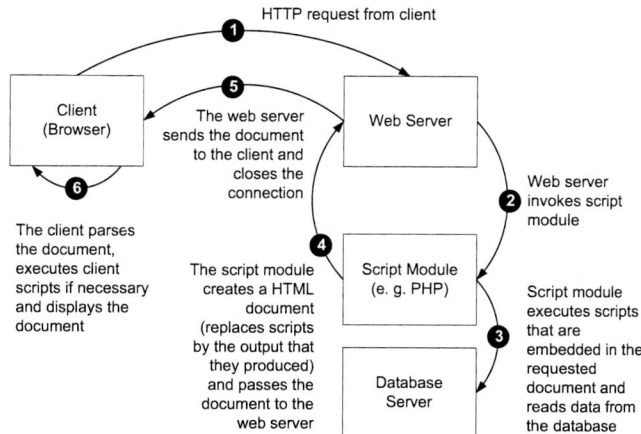

Figure 2.7: Example of a Web Application Architecture and Usage Scenario (Adapted from EICHINGER (2004), p. 86)

to improve performance and data security. Typically, users are not directly confronted with data that is stored in databases. In web environments, however, users are interacting directly with data elements of a web site. Thus, the presentation level of the application is essential. Markup languages are used in order to integrate structural information in semi-structured data.[291] The hypertext markup language (HTML) developed by BERNERS-LEE, FIELDING & FRYSTYK is based on the standard generalized markup language (SGML) that was disseminated by the international organization for standardization (ISO) as a standard in 1986.[292] The general principle of SGML and other markup languages is the separation from content and layout. As the name markup indicates, data elements are marked with 'tags' that give information about how the data element is supposed to be processed.[293] Therefore, it is possible for parsers to distinguish between data and markup although both objects are embedded in the same file.

Types of documents are specified in document classes respectively document type definitions (DTD).[294] A DTD specifies the elements (tags), the general structure and

---

[291] The World Wide Web Consortium provides a comprehensive overview of markup languages and related technologies at http://www.w3c.org which were developed and standardized under their supervision. See also STROBEL (2004) and GAEDKE et al. (2004), pp. 140–152.

[292] Cf. WILDE (1999), p. 137 ff. for a comprehensive overview of SGML.

[293] More precisely, a markup is an uniquely defined element (for instance, 'section') which is enclosed in delimiters (usually '<' and '>'). The element and the delimiters are a 'tag' (cf. WILDE (1999), p. 142).

[294] Cf. WILDE (1999), pp. 144 f.

the number and/or sequence of elements a document of this class may contain. A DTD is instantiated by documents. Parsers are able to validate documents based on their document type definitions, that is, whether they do conform with the syntax specified in the DTD. In case of HTML, version 4.0 specifies three different document types which can be used to create and validate HTML documents.[295] Since the amount of data on the web is constantly increasing, it became obvious that the embedding of content and layout in one file is difficult to maintain. If, for instance, the visual appearance of a web site which contains several documents should be changed, each document has to be updated. Therefore, cascading style sheets (CSS) were specified.[296] A CSS file specifies formatting options for a HTML document like colours and fonts that are used as well as additional visual options (for instance, the way links are displayed).[297] A HTML document references a CSS file. Thus, the visual appearance of multiple documents can be changed by updating the CSS file they refer to. Additionally, CSS can be used to provide multiple versions of documents like a print preview or a braille output for blind users. The document object model (DOM) provides a standardized interface for accessing and updating documents.[298]

The first version of the extensible markup language (XML) was disseminated by the W3C in 1996. Like HTML, it is based on SGML and represents a subset of SGML's functionality especially tailored to the information exchange needs of web environments.[299] In contrast to HTML, custom and human-readable tags can be specified in XML as the 'extensible' in its name indicates.[300] For instance, a tag $< product > ... < /product >$ can be specified. The data between these tags (indicated by the dots) is, therefore, marked to be a product. It is claimed that XML files contain the meaning of the data they represent.[301] SGML's concept of DTD's is adapted in XML and called XML-Schema. XML-Schema provides comprehensive capabilities for specifying XML data resp. documents, for instance, data types, inheritance and constraints.[302] Specifically,

---

[295] Cf. WILDE (1999), p. 178. The document types are transitional, strict and frameset.

[296] Refer to Bos et al. (2005) for an overview of CSS 2.1. Version 3.0 has not been published as a recommendation yet.

[297] Cf. EHLERS (2003), pp. 66–67.

[298] Refer to HORS et al. (2004) or BENN & LANGER (2003), pp. 24 f. for details.

[299] Cf. GOLDFARB & PRESCOD (1998), p. xli. The specification is described by BRAY et al. (2004).

[300] Cf. BENN & LANGER (2003), p. 13.

[301] Cf. GOLDFARB & PRESCOD (1998), p. xl. However, with regard to the background of this thesis and the concept of information and knowledge outlined above, a XML document cannot contain meaning. Meaning is always bound to humans. In this case, humans have to agree upon the meaning of the tag $< product >$ before they can exchange meaningful information with XML. XML provides a standardized way for specifying syntax requirements for data rather than meaning.

[302] Refer to SCHÖNING & WATERFELD (2003), pp. 33 f. and FALLSIDE & WALMSLEY (2004) for

XML-schema is itself defined in XML. Additionally, several shortcomings (for instance, missing data types and namespaces) of traditional DTD are solved by XML-schema.[303] XML documents can be validated in two ways. Firstly, a XML document can be well-formed, implying that it follows the general construction rules of XML documents. Secondly, it can be valid with regard to the syntax specified in a XML-Schema.[304] The HTML standard was reformulated in XML in order to combine the flexibility of HTML with the clearness and validity of XML. The standard is called XHTML.[305] The XML activities of the World Wide Web Consortium include various other standards and recommendations for representing, manipulating and accessing data with XML.[306] The following figure depicts some relationships between the various markup languages and standards mentioned in this paragraph.[307]

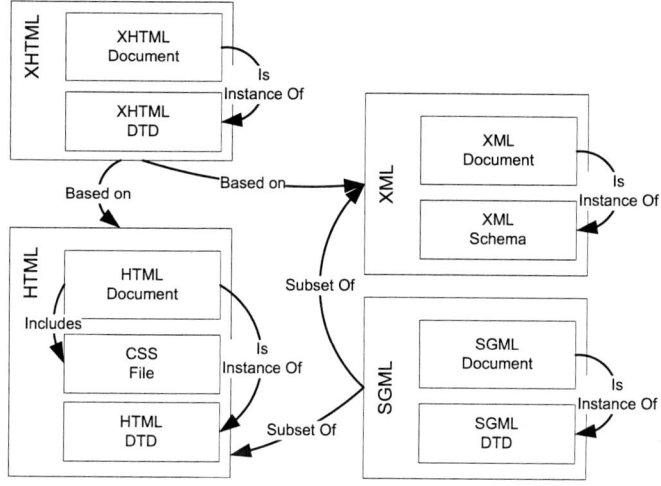

Figure 2.8: Relationships between Markup Languages

---

details.

[303] Cf. Schöning & Waterfeld (2003), p. 35–36.

[304] Refer to Goldfarb & Prescod (1998), pp. 44–45 and Benn & Langer (2003), pp. 14–15 for an explanation of the different types of validation.

[305] Refer to World Wide Web Consortium for details.

[306] For instance, XPath (specifies means for accessing parts of XML-documents) and Xlink (includes comprehensive functionality for linking). Refer to http://www.w3c.org for details.

[307] Obviously, this overview is far from complete. For instance, standards used to transform XML documents for presentation purposes are not discussed.

Semantic Web

Due to the semi-structured and vague nature of data in web environments, computers or software agents are not able to interpret data precisely. Thus, in contrast to structured data, which is usually typed and described by a schema defining elements and their relations, semi-structured data is subject to misinterpretation and cannot be processed by computers automatically in a meaningful manner.[308] Computers are 'blind' concerning the information that is supposed to be conveyed. In order to overcome these deficiencies, the 'Semantic Web' has been proposed by BERNERS-LEE, HENDLER & LASSILA in 2001. The Semantic Web is "an extension of the current web in which information is given well-defined meaning, better enabling computers and people to work in cooperation."[309]

Essentially, the various standards and languages developed in the context of the Semantic Web aim to improve the interpretability of information for computers as well as humans by annotating pieces of information with metadata and assigning them to objects that are specified in ontologies. The Resource Description Framework (RDF) provides extensive functionality for annotating metadata to pieces of information, which are not necessarily stored and distributed in web environments.[310] The general concept of RDF is that things (for instance documents on the web) have properties (for instance, a creator) which have values (for instance, Christian Stephan Brelage).[311] Each triple of thing, property and value is called a statement which can be written as <subject> <predicate> <object>.[312] Statements can be represented by graphs. Figure 2.9 contains an example of some RDF statements in graph notation.

In this case, the resource identified by the URI

`http://www.example.org/index.html`

has three predicates (properties) which are annotated at the arrows: language, creation-date and creator. The predicates language and creation-date are specified by literals[313] ('August 16, 1999' and 'en'), whereas the creator property is specified by the web resource at

---

[308] In this case, automated processing refers to any act requiring the correct interpretation of the meaning which is conveyed by a piece of information (for instance, judging the relevance for a search query) rather than simple functions like updates or deletions.

[309] Cf. BERNERS-LEE, HENDLER & LASSILA (2001). A brief overview of the Semantic Web is also provided by BEHRENDT (2004), pp. 345 ff.

[310] For an overview to RDF refer to MANOLA & MILLER.

[311] Cf. MANOLA & MILLER.

[312] The subject is the thing, the predicate a property and the value is expressed by the object.

[313] Literals are basically values for objects. In RDF, literals can only be used as objects. Literals can be typed (for instance, date) or plain. Refer to KLYNE & CARROLL for details.

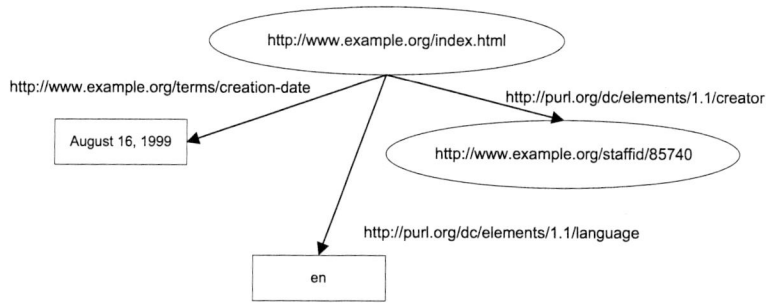

Figure 2.9: Example of a RDF Graph (cf. MANOLA & MILLER)

`http://www.example.org/staffid/85740`

The predicates itself are defined by the resources they refer to. For instance, the creator property refers to a section of the dublin core standard for metadata specification which is located at the address

`http://purl.org/dc/elements/1.1/creator`

In order to enrich the 'semantics' associated with statements, literals (or resources) can be broken down into smaller pieces of information which can be addressed separately. For instance, the creation-date property of the example above (encoded as a plain literal) can be broken down into three literals day, month and year. In this case, an 'intermediate' node is created which represents the concept of date. Three properties (day, month and year) and their values are assigned to this intermediate node.[314] In analogy to SGML and XML, RDF elements like the creator item are specified in a schema called RDF-Schema.[315] The creator definition from the example above is an example of an RDF-schema describing a predicate (property) which can be used to annotate web resources. Thus, RDF-schema specifies the vocabulary which can be used by RDF applications.[316] RDF-schema allows the specification of classes and properties. A class represents a collection of things. A web resource can be qualified as an instance of a class. For instance, a class 'person' can be defined.[317] The web pages of staff members of an institution are instances of the class 'person'. By doing so, the 'semantics' of the web

---

[314] Refer to MANOLA & MILLER for details on intermediate and blank nodes.

[315] RDF-schema itself is specified by using RDF (self-describing like XML). Refer to BRICKLEY & GUHA for an introduction.

[316] Cf. MANOLA & MILLER.

[317] Cf. MANOLA & MILLER for the following.

resource are enriched.[318] For instance, internet search engines can 'decide' whether the web page is relevant for a query or not. If a query 'find all persons in institution X whose names contain jaguar' is submitted, the searching algorithm can prune all resources from the result list which are not qualified to be 'persons' (cars and animals in this case). Additionally, properties can be defined.

RDF and RDF-schema provide comprehensive functionality for annotating web resources with metadata in a structured and yet flexible way. In order to provide more complex functionality for annotating metadata, the web ontology language (OWL) is proposed.[319] OWL is based on RDF and RDF-schema and extends the vocabulary by additional constructs that are needed to specify ontologies. Basically, OWL proides a standard syntax for specifying ontologies which can be used by reasoning algorithms (inferencing) in order to deduce meaningful statements about the things and properties that are specified. OWL comprises three subclasses which base on each other and have different functionality:[320]

1. OWL Lite: provides basic functionality like classification hierarchies and constraints.

2. OWL DL: in contrast to OWL lite, OWL DL has a much higher expressiveness but is still computational complete and decidable. That is, a reasoning algorithm like inferencing always generates a result in finite time. Although all constructs of OWL can be used, several constraints are enforced in order to ensure decidability and computational completeness.

3. OWL Full: provides the full expressiveness of OWL and RDF. Reasoning algorithms will not always generate results in finite time.

Among others, OWL Lite provides the following constructs which are derived from RDF schema:[321]

---

[318] It has to be noted again that this conceptualization of semantics is different from the one in the foundations of this thesis since the act of interpretation is always bound to the intellectual capability of humans. However, it is common to speak of semantics in this case in the computer science community.

[319] Cf. McGuinness & van Harmelen for an overview and Smith, Welty & McGuinness for a more detailed introduction on OWL.

[320] Cf. McGuinness & van Harmelen for the following.

[321] Cf. McGuinness & van Harmelen for the following. The overview concentrates on those constructs of OWL which can be depicted by the modelling method that is constructed in Chapter 3. Thus, the overview is not a complete enumeration of all constructs that are specified by the current OWL recommendation.

- Class: a class defines a group of individuals that belong together because they share some properties.

- subClassOf: subClassOf creates a hierarchy of classes. Reasoners can deduce statements about instances of classes. For instance, the class 'person' may be a subclass of the class 'mammal'. Thus, a reasoner can deduce that the person 'Christian Brelage' is also a 'mammal'.

- Property: like in RDF, properties can be used to state relationships between individuals (ObjectProperty) or from individuals to data values (DatatypeProperty).

- subPropertyOf: properties can be structured hierarchically like classes.

- Domain and Range: the construct domain is used to limit the individuals to which a particular property can be applied. For instance, the property 'hasChild' may be limited to the class 'mammal' and its subclasses. Likewise, the range of a property limits the individuals (instances of classes, see below) that a property can have as its value.

- Individual: individuals are instances of classes.

OWL provides several constructs that can be used to specify constraints between classes and properties.[322] For instance, classes and properties can be characterized to be equivalent (equivalentClass respectively equivalentProperty, all instances are identical). Likewise, two individuals can be characterized to be identical (sameAs) or different (differentFrom). The construct AllDifferent qualifies all individuals to be mutually distinct. Properties can have certain characteristics that are used to enrich the semantics of them and allow reasoners to deduce more meaningful statements. For instance, properties can be characterized to be inverse (inverseOf). For instance, the properties 'hasChild' and 'hasParent' can be declared to be inverse. Thus, if the statement 'A' 'hasChild' 'B' (B is the child of A) is made, a reasoner can deduce that 'B' 'hasParent' 'A' is also a valid statement.[323] Likewise, properties can be qualified to be transitive, symmetric, functional and inverse-functional. Moreover, cardinalities can be used to specify constraints between properties and classes.[324] In OWL Lite cardinalities can have the values zero and one. Finally, OWL Lite allows classes to be defined as intersections of two other

---

[322] Cf. McGuinness & van Harmelen for the following.
[323] Cf. McGuinness & van Harmelen.
[324] For instance, the class 'Parent' would have a minimum cardinality of one for the property 'hasOffspring' implying that each individual of the class 'Parent' has at least one child. Refer to McGuinness & van Harmelen for details and examples of other cardinality constraints.

classes. The language variants OWL DL and OWL Full extend these constructs in order to provide a richer functionality. For instance, cardinalities can have arbitrary integer values and boolean combinations (union, intersection, complement) of classes are allowed.[325]

The ideas and approaches underlying the languages of the Semantic Web are not new. They are mainly derived from earlier works from the artificial intelligence community.[326] As noted above, the enthusiasm about the Semantic Web and the claims that are made how it will influence and change data seems to be rather exaggerated. The facts that are expressed in RDF or OWL documents do not represent knowledge since knowledge is always bound to a knowing (human) individual. In order to convey meaning with documents, a prior, mutual agreement between the participating individuals has to be achieved. RDF and OWL serve as tools to specify this agreement in a flexible and yet formal way. Computers can process these documents and derive conclusions from them, but they are not meaningful to computers.[327]

2.2.5 Information System Development

In analogy to the information system definition, *information system development* consists of several subcomponents.[328] Sometimes, the terms information system engineering and information system development are used interchangeably. However, the term 'engineering' stresses a more technical role.[329] Thus, the term 'development' is preferred in this thesis. The term *software engineering* is commonly used to refer to the engineering tasks involved in the development of software systems. According to BOEHM software engineering

> is the application of science and mathematics by which the capabilities of computer equipment are made useful to man via computer programs, procedures, and

---

[325] Refer to MCGUINNESS & VAN HARMELEN for details.

[326] See, for instance, CHARNIAK & MCDERMOTT (1985); RICH & KNIGHT (1991); DUTTA (1993) and LUGER & STUBBLEFIELD (1993) for introductions to artificial intelligence. For a critique on the claims made from the AI community refer to DREYFUS (1979); DREYFUS (1989) and NEUMAIER (1989).

[327] A detailed discussion of this critique is beyond the scope of this thesis. This statement is introduced since the assumptions and approaches underlying the Semantic Web differ from the position taken in this thesis.

[328] Information systems have been defined as socio-technical systems comprising technical as well as organizational components. Compare the definition of information systems given in Section 2.2.2.

[329] Cf. for a similar point HIRSCHHEIM, KLEIN & LYYTINEN (1995), p. 53.

associated documentation.[330]

The discipline emerged as the need for a systematic and reliable design of software became apparent during the software crisis in the late 1960s.[331] The definition as well as the methods of software engineering[332] clearly indicate that the discipline is mostly concerned with the development of software systems and does usually not claim to consider sociological factors. According to the information system definition, however, the term *information system development* comprises organizational respectively sociological aspects as well which have to be taken into consideration during the development process. Therefore, the term is defined in a broader sense implying the development of organizational aspects, though the methods of software engineering are fundamental for the technical component.

A variety of information system development definitions can be found in literature reflecting the diverse use of the information system conceptualization. HARMSEN stresses an engineering and project management perspective:

> *Information system engineering* is the set of all development and project management activities related to the consistent and effective design, installation and modification of an information system.[333]

Information system development is a continuous *process* in which all tasks create artefacts that are input for subsequent tasks. It is common to divide the process into *phases* that differentiate different stages of the development process that are usually characterized by varying degrees of abstraction concerning the artefacts created and used in each respective stage: early phases are 'conceptual' (models, figures) with a high degree of abstraction, whereas later stages are less abstract or 'implementation-oriented' (for instance, source code).[334] Artefacts are gradually transformed from phase to phase until they form a working information system entailing the technical as well as the organizational aspect. Amount and naming of phases depend on the software or information system development methodology. The ordering in which phases and

---

[330] Cf. BOEHM (1981), p. 16. Similarly, RATCLIFF (1987), p. 3; SODHI (1991), pp. 3. A review of different definitions of software engineering can be found in MAYRHAUSER (1990), pp. 4 f.

[331] Cf. RATCLIFF (1987), p. 2.

[332] Well-known software engineering methods are the structured analysis method and object-oriented approaches. An overview of software engineering methods can be found in SODHI (1991), p. 63–284.

[333] Cf. HARMSEN (1997), p. 8. Italics in the original.

[334] Cf. FALKENBERG (1983b), pp. 19 f. for an early motivation of different abstraction levels in data modelling. In addition to a decreasing level of abstraction, HARMSEN notes that scope and increasing level of detail can be used to break down the engineering process.

task are carried out is determined by the development *procedure model*.[335] There are various propositions in literature of different procedure models. While some of these are linear (defined order of phases, no back-tracking), others allow back-tracking and provide more flexibility. Well-known procedure models are the waterfall model and its derivates[336], BOEHM's spiral model[337], prototyping approaches[338] and so called agile methods[339]. However, the decision which procedure model is applicable for a given task is mainly determined by characteristics of the project itself. For instance, a high degree of uncertainty in combination with a large and complex project tends to favour more flexible approaches, whereas clear and easy projects can be carried out without any support of complex procedures. Additionally, other characteristics like the foreknowledge of the project team members and the overall composition of the team have to be taken into consideration as well. An appropriate procedure model has to be selected with regard to project characteristics. Therefore, procedure models are explicitly not investigated in detail for the purpose of this thesis. The modelling approach outlined in Chapter 3 does in principle not dependent on a special procedure model.

Apart from the differentiation of phases, it is commonly accepted to break down the whole information system by using *views* in order to reduce the complexity of the development process.[340] It is widely accepted to differentiate between a *data* and *process* view, reflecting static and dynamic aspects of an information system.[341] By focussing on one view while considering integration, it is potentially possible to cope with higher complexity. Depending on purpose and scope of the development methodology, additional views are differentiated, for instance an organizational view[342] or a network view.[343]

Taken together, phases and views on information system development form a matrix which allows describing tasks and artefacts or deliverables more precisely. The thesis

---

[335] Similarly HARMSEN (1997), p. 9.

[336] Cf., for instance, BOEHM (1981), pp. 35 ff.; SOMMERVILLE (2001), pp. 45 ff.

[337] Cf. BOEHM (1988); SOMMERVILLE (2001), pp. 53 f.

[338] Cf. SOMMERVILLE (2001), pp. 46 f.

[339] Agile methods are more extensive approaches and cover more than the procedure model. For an introduction refer to COCKBURN (2002); STAPLETON (2003) and SCHWABER (2004).

[340] Complexity is used in a quantitative as well as qualitative case. Refer to section 2.2.1 for a description of complexity.

[341] Cf. Refer to 2.2.1 for static and dynamic aspects of systems.

[342] The organizational view usually depicts the organizational structure which is a static view on organization, whereas processes entail a dynamic aspect.

[343] For instance, the framework proposed by ZACHMANN & SOWA comprises the views data, function, network and people (ZACHMAN (1987) and SOWA & ZACHMAN (1992)). The ARIS (architecture for integrated information systems) architecture proposed by SCHEER distinguishes data, process, function and organization (SCHEER (1992); SCHEER (1994)).

focuses on the conceptual specification of data structures for web information systems. Concerning the process taking place in web information systems, the reading process is being focussed. The process of creating and manipulating information or content in web information systems (for instance by content management systems) and related tasks (review, follow-up, workflows) are not investigated in detail.

Information system development is a creative process carried out by a group of developers and takes place in a specific environment. The usage of (abstract) models of real or imaginary objects is an essential tool for information system development. Therefore, it is useful to adapt a definition that aligns information system development and conceptual modelling.[344] HIRSCHHEIM, KLEIN & LYYTINEN adapt a definition which was originally introduced by WELKE which defines information system development as

> a *change process* taken with respect to *object systems* in a set of *environments* by a *development group* to achieve or maintain some objectives.[345]

Object systems consist of phenomena that are perceived by members of the development group and which are supposed to be changed with regard to objectives defined by the development group (compare Figure 2.10).[346] According to HIRSCHHEIM, KLEIN & LYYTINEN and the scientific positioning of this thesis, perception is subjective and socially constructed through sense making and institutionalized conventions. Therefore, an individual's perception is neither wrong nor right, raising the question how conflicting perceptions have to be handled. A *change process* is a sequence of events in which phenomena (objects and properties of object systems) come into being as a result of a development's group's deliberate action.[347] The change of the object system is intentional rather than accidental, implying that a consensus concerning how and what has to be done has to be achieved intersubjectively by the development group. HIRSCHHEIM, KLEIN & LYYTINEN note that

> Intersubjectivity means that the change process is founded on recognition of phenomena by more than one participant and on mutual understandings and coordination of participants' actions. Systems development is not just an artificial intervention because it is always embedded in a social and cultural milieu entailing many uncertainties. Therefore, the change process is not a deterministic

---

[344] A detailed terminology of conceptual modelling is introduced below.

[345] WELKE (1983). Cited after LYYTINEN (1987b), p. 6 and HIRSCHHEIM, KLEIN & LYYTINEN (1995), p. 15. Italics in the original.

[346] Cf. HIRSCHHEIM, KLEIN & LYYTINEN (1995), pp. 15 f. for the following.

[347] Cf. HIRSCHHEIM, KLEIN & LYYTINEN (1995), p. 16.

one.[348]

Environments are webs of conditions and factors surrounding the development process.[349] They include labour, economy, technology and applications as well as external and normative environments. HIRSCHHEIM, KLEIN & LYYTINEN's notion of a *development group* illustrates that information system development is primarily a social process rather than a technical one:

> The notion of a development group entails that systems development is carried out by a formally organized group. It has similarities with social institutions (ROBEY & MARKUS (1984)): it sets mutual expectations; it punishes and gives rewards; it consists of positions and roles filled by people, and so on. A development group can organize itself in alternative ways by specifying the set-up of its positions, roles, authority structures and decision making rights (SCACCHI (1985)). Note how this view of the development group differs from the classical view of IS development which still prevails in the software engineering literature, where the nature of systems development is seen more as a technical than social process.[350]

The development of an information system takes place with regard to *objectives* expressing intentions of the development group.[351] Objectives have special features rendering them difficult to specify and to handle during the development process. According to HIRSCHHEIM, KLEIN & LYYTINEN, objectives can be

1. imposed implicitly, for instance, by the methods used or they are explicitly agreed upon through negotiation or by fiat.[352]

2. clear or vague respectively ill-defined.

3. uni- or multi-functional and conflictual or a-conflictual.

It is important to note that the components of information system development are strongly interweaved and interdependent. The outcome of the development process is unsure due to uncertainty. It is subject to various conditions and restrictions caused

---

[348] Cf. HIRSCHHEIM, KLEIN & LYYTINEN (1995), p. 16.

[349] Cf. HIRSCHHEIM, KLEIN & LYYTINEN (1995), p. 17 f. for the following.

[350] HIRSCHHEIM, KLEIN & LYYTINEN (1995), p. 17. References in quote adapted to the format used in this thesis and integrated in the bibliography.

[351] Cf. HIRSCHHEIM, KLEIN & LYYTINEN (1995), p. 17 for the following.

[352] Cf. HIRSCHHEIM, KLEIN & LYYTINEN (1995), p. 17 for the following. Similarly WAND & WEBER (2002), p. 369.

or enforced by the environment which is not controlled by the development group. As
HIRSCHHEIM, KLEIN & LYYTINEN note:[353]

> The components of the definition of systems development form a complicated
> 'web' of social, technological, and cultural phenomena. The components are not
> independent of each other, nor are they completely dependent. Rather, we can
> speak of the totality in which components' features are defined by their interactions
> with other components - they are thus emergent. A detailed specification of one
> component is a case of a constrained choice: a choice with regard to one component
> constrains our freedom to choose the others, for example, identified object systems
> are constrained largely by pursued objectives.

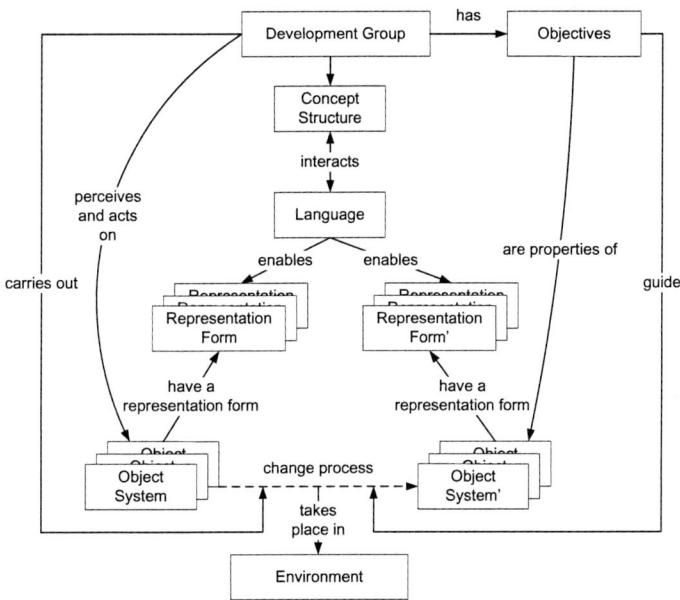

Figure 2.10: Information System Development and Object Systems (Adapted from
HIRSCHHEIM, KLEIN & LYYTINEN (1995), pp. 16 f.)

This notion of object systems and particularly their subjective nature raises the questions how they can be represented and changed. All perception of the system is mediated
by an individual's concept structures that reflect his or her foreknowledge or 'prejudices'

---

[353] Cf. HIRSCHHEIM, KLEIN & LYYTINEN (1995), p. 17.

of the world.[354] This foreknowledge is constantly refined, contradicted and renewed in an iterative cycle of interpretations.[355] Consequently, information system intervention is an open-ended, situation-dependent and cyclical process because the concept structures may change due to learning or other influence.[356] Usually, the initial change intervention is motivated by the initial perception of some deficiency in the recognized object system. This perception is strongly influenced by the language used by those articulating the deficiency.[357]

The conceptualization of information system development emphasizes two important aspects. Firstly, information system development is a *social process* carried out by participants of the development group.[358] It is not restricted to technical specification that can be objectively performed by a dedicated mechanism. Secondly, the *role of language* as a means to achieve a common understanding of object systems and objectives is stressed. Participants of the development group communicate through (natural) language, which is often imprecise and ambiguous. Therefore, appropriate linguistic means moderating confusion and misunderstanding have to be constructed as well. The exchange of meaningful information constitutes an information systems. Moreover, it is obvious that the concept of information systems (the system itself as well as the meta-information[359] system which builds it) can be applied twofold for the purpose of this thesis. Therefore, it seems necessary to provide the user and the developer with the following artefacts in order to provide efficient means for the development process:

- A language or conceptual model that provides appropriate means for specifying web information systems, entailing their technical as well as social components (model). The language focuses on data structures. More particular, it enables the specification of appropriate means that can be used by individuals to satisfy their information needs efficiently. Specification takes place on a conceptual level, that is, with a high degree of abstraction. Concerning the processes covered, the thesis concentrates on the reading process, particularly the usage of navigation for satisfying information needs.

---

[354] Cf. HIRSCHHEIM, KLEIN & LYYTINEN (1995), p. 19. As HIRSCHHEIM, KLEIN & LYYTINEN note, this insight is adapted from philosophical hermeneutics. Refer to Section 2.1.3 for details on hermeneutics.

[355] Cf. HIRSCHHEIM, KLEIN & LYYTINEN (1995), p. 20.

[356] Cf. HIRSCHHEIM, KLEIN & LYYTINEN (1995), p. 19.

[357] HIRSCHHEIM, KLEIN & LYYTINEN (1995), pp. 19–20.

[358] HIRSCHHEIM & NEWMAN (1991) stress the social nature of information system development and challenge several 'rational' beliefs about the process (cf. HIRSCHHEIM & NEWMAN (1991)).

[359] Refer to Section 2.2.1 for a disctinction of information and meta-information system and its appliance for the purpose of this thesis.

- A language or conceptual model that specifies the language used by information system developers (metamodel). The language or conceptual model created for the information system is an instance of the language used by the meta-information system (the development group). As the model provides means for the description of the actual system, the metamodel provides means for effective, efficient and meaningful information exchange between participants of the development group. It is a language specially designed and tailored for a focal domain (in this case web information system development) that helps to avoid misunderstandings, ambiguity and inefficient communication.

2.2.6 Conceptual Modelling

Overview, Perspectives & Terminology

The understanding of information system development outlined above implies that a development group constructs representation forms of object systems used to articulate thoughts, beliefs and requirements of the system and the objectives of the change process. The process of generating these representation forms is called *conceptual modelling*.[360] The representation forms are *conceptual models* usually depicted by using a graphical notation but which can be documented in any other suitable way (for instance, textually or tabularly). A bewildering variety of conceptual modelling approaches have been proposed in the past. Each supposedly better than the rest.[361] OEI et al. characterize the situation with the term 'YAMA-syndrome' (Yet Another Modelling Approach) which reflects the unsettled state of the information systems discipline as well as the lack of sound foundations of newly proposed modelling approaches.[362] This situation has caused researchers to work on the scientific foundations of conceptual modelling. For instance, OEI et al. proposed a metamodel hierarchy for ordering modelling approaches.[363] WAND & WEBER proposed the ontological evaluation of modelling methods. By mapping the language constructs to things and objects of a top-level ontology (in this case the ontology of BUNGE was used)[364], the linguistic capabilities of modelling approaches should be assessed.[365] The approach implicitly assumes that modelling languages are

---

[360] Cf. WAND et al. (1995), p. 285 as well as WAND & WEBER (2002), pp. 363 f. for the following.

[361] Cf. WAND & WEBER (2002), p. 365.

[362] Cf. OEI et al. (1992), p. 2.

[363] Cf. OEI et al. (1992), pp. 6 f.

[364] Refer to BUNGE (1977) and BUNGE (1979) for a detailed description of the ontology.

[365] More detailed descriptions of the approach and its foundations can be found in WAND & WEBER (1989); WAND & WEBER (1990a); WAND & WEBER (1990b); WAND & WEBER (1993) and WAND et al. (1995).

supposed to depict some kind of objectively perceived reality. The ontological evaluation is supposed to reveal certain deficiencies of the modelling language:[366]

- Construct overload: several ontological constructs map to one grammatical construct. The language concept is homonymous. Therefore, the correct interpretation of a language concept is not ensured. It is ambiguous. For instance, WAND, STOREY & WEBER have identified this deficiency in the modelling language entity relationship modelling since a thing can be modelled as an entity or a relationship in some occasions.[367]

- Construct redundancy: several language concepts map to one ontological construct. The concepts are synonymous.

- Construct excess: a grammatical language concept might not map to any ontological construct. Therefore, it has no 'meaning' with regard to the ontology.

- Construct deficiency: an ontological construct might not map to any language concept. Thus, the modelling approach lacks the capability of modelling a certain phenomenon.

This evaluation approach has been applied with varying results to several modelling languages in the past.[368] However, the approach is rather controversial. Particularly, its implicit assumption that some 'objectively' perceived reality exists is contested.[369] WYSSUSEK argues that the appliance of the approach potentially helps to reveal differences of a modelling language and the axiomatic system of the ontology while failing to respect the crucial role of language which constrains our ability to speak about and model the world and the phenomena in it.[370] Nevertheless, it is necessary to reflect on the justification and usefulness of newly proposed modelling approaches. Moreover, it is necessary to anchor conceptual modelling more deeply in related research disciplines in order to outline goals, objectives, commonalties and differences of various approaches more precisely. In order to do so, different perspectives on conceptual modelling can be outlined.

---

[366] Cf. WAND & WEBER (2002), p. 365.

[367] Cf. WAND, STOREY & WEBER (1999), pp. 513 ff.

[368] Refer, for instance, to WAND, STOREY & WEBER (1999); GREEN & ROSEMANN (2000); GREEN & ROSEMANN (2002).

[369] Cf. WYSSUSEK (2004). A more detailed discussion of 'ontology' and its usage in the information system discipline can be found in WYSSUSEK & KLAUS (2005).

[370] Cf. WYSSUSEK (2004), p. 4307 and HIRSCHHEIM, KLEIN & LYYTINEN (1995), p. 149.

Firstly, the philosophical background highly influences the way conceptual modelling is perceived and performed. This background is discussed extensively in Section 2.1. As HIRSCHHEIM, KLEIN & LYYTINEN point out, each paradigm entails several presuppositions that highly affect the way the development process is perceived and carried out. For instance, a functionalist perspective views the development process as a mere 'mapping' of phenomena to implementation artefacts. Interpretivism, on the other hand, presupposes that the 'reality' is constructed in terms of a mutual understanding and by social interaction.

Secondly, modelling methods can be characterized by their scope. General purpose modelling languages (like ERM and UML) found widespread use in the past and they are well documented and supported by modelling environments. They are, however, not tailored to specific requirements and environments. For instance, they do not support a specific terminology used in organizations. The adaption of modelling methods can be motivated by two aspects. Firstly, some methods are tailored to a particular type of application. The web information system development methods discussed in Section 2.2.7 are an example of modelling methods especially designed to model web information systems. Although, the entity relationship modelling language focuses on database applications, it is considered to be a general purpose modelling method since it is used for other purposes and serves as a de facto standard for modelling in general.[371] Additionally, virtually all applications contain a database component. Secondly, the domain in which the application is supposed to be deployed can influence the modelling methods. For instance, the supply chain reference model (SCOR) and its underlying modelling method are particularly tailored to model processes and data requirements in supply chains.[372] The adaption of modelling methods to project or domain specific requirements is discussed under the term *(situational) method engineering*. Some researchers argue that general purpose modelling methods have to be be tuned according to the situation at hand.[373] The method engineering process is a coordinated and systematic approach for establishing work methods. [374] General purpose modelling methods are adapted or even newly created by this process to suit specific requirements. They are, therefore, situational modelling methods. The method engineering process usually incorporates the usage of a metamodelling language and meta CASE tools.[375]

---

[371] Refer also to the brief introduction in entity relationship modelling in Section 3.1.

[372] The SCOR model depicts process on a high degree of abstraction. Therefore, it includes its own modelling method.

[373] Cf. ODELL (1996), p. 1.

[374] Cf. ODELL (1996), p. 1.

[375] Cf., for instance, GRUNDY & VENABLE (1996); ROLLAND & PRAKASH (1996) and HARMSEN & SAEKI (1996) MARTTIIN, HARMSEN & ROSSI evaluate different method engineering environments

Finally, conceptual modelling can serve different purposes. For instance, WAND & WEBER name four different purposes: firstly, supporting communication between developers and users, secondly, helping analysts to understand a domain, thirdly, providing input for the design process, and finally, documenting the original requirements for future reference.[376] Obviously, these purposes cause differences in the modelling process. If, for instance, conceptual models are intended to serve as an input for the design process (CASE approach), a more formal and unambiguous grammar has to be used in order to map concepts precisely on implementation artefacts. Support of the communication process, however, can be achieved with less formal means and even in textual form. Figure 2.11 comprises different perspectives on conceptual modelling and motivates the permanent need for developing and adapting modelling languages. Note that the demarcation between the peculiarities of each perspective is not a strict separation. Each peculiarity marks an extreme which does not mean that various hybrid or intermediate forms are equally conceivable.

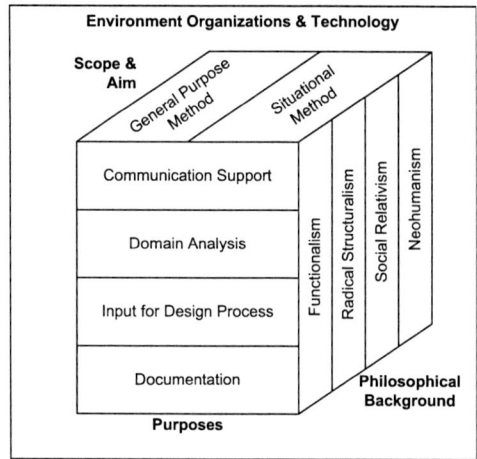

Figure 2.11: Perspectives on Conceptual Modelling (Compare HIRSCHHEIM, KLEIN & LYYTINEN (1995) and WAND & WEBER (2002))

As a consequence of this discussion of conceptual modelling, it is argued that there is a *permanent* need for developing, adapting and abolishing modelling languages – a position contrasting to WAND & WEBER, who argue that existing approaches should be evaluated first before new ones are proposed.[377] WAND & WEBER propose eight future

---

(MARTTIIN, HARMSEN & ROSSI (1996), pp. 63 ff.).
[376] WAND & WEBER (2002), pp. 363.
[377] Cf. WAND & WEBER (2002), p. 366.

research opportunities for conceptual modelling languages.[378] None is concerned with the development of new grammars or the adaption of existing grammars in order to meet changing requirements. Contrary to their position, it is argued that the environment in which conceptual modelling takes place is in constant flux: technologies, languages, social factors and goals are permanently changing. Consequently, modelling approaches have to change as well if they are supposed to serve as tools for achieving a mutual understanding. It is neither possible nor desirable to develop the 'ultimate' modelling technique. Particularly, the purpose of supporting the communication between and among developers and users motivates the need for specialized and situation specific modelling languages.

To understand the modelling mechanisms thoroughly and to ensure a consistent terminology of conceptual modelling for the purpose of this thesis, the following conventions are used (compare Figure 2.12): according to KNACKSTEDT, a modelling *method* can be conceptualized as a triple of *task types*, *document types* and a *set of rules* for a systematic proceeding.[379] Since a method can be generally applied to a multitude of problems and situations, it is terminologically consistent to describe key terms on type level. For instance, the task type 'conceptual specification of a data model' can be used to specify the steps and procedures that are required in database design. Obviously, it can be instantiated multiple times. Task types describe problems the method is supposed to solve and its general purpose. They describe what has to be done. They can be assigned to phases (for instance, conceptual specification) and views (for instance, data view) structuring the whole development process. Task types may support several views at once. For instance, object-oriented modelling approaches cover dynamic as well as static aspects of an object.[380] Phases and task types can be structured, reflecting their respective hierarchies and structures. At least one task type of the method generates a document type including the usage of a conceptual modelling technique[381] in order to create a document of the respective type.[382] Documents are artefacts that are created during the development process.[383] They are produced and used by tasks (input-output

---

[378] Cf. WAND & WEBER (2002), pp. 365 f. WAND & WEBER use the term conceptual modelling grammar.

[379] Cf. KNACKSTEDT (2004), pp. 44 ff. for the following. Similarly but less detailed TEUBNER (1999), pp. 93 f.; HOLTEN (1999), pp. 18 f.; BECKER et al. (2001). Cf. also MATHIASSEN & MUNK-MADSEN (1986).

[380] Object-oriented modelling approaches encapsulate structure and behaviour and are hybrids in this regard (cf. HIRSCHHEIM, KLEIN & LYYTINEN (1995), p. 20).

[381] The term modelling technique is specified in detail below.

[382] Cf. KNACKSTEDT (2004), pp. 44 f.

[383] Cf. KNACKSTEDT (2004), p. 45.

relation). For instance, the task type 'create conceptual data model' includes the creation of a conceptual data model, which can be depicted by using the technique entity relationship modelling.[384] The creation of documents for a given task takes place with regard to a set of of rules. Rules describe how documents are produced and used. For instance, they describe how to map concepts from the real world to their representation forms.[385] Rules can be based on general principles that are intended to increase the overall quality of conceptual models.[386] An example of systematic rules are the mechanisms used to identify entities and relationships when using entity relationship modelling.

A specific set of rules used to create documents which are conceptual models is called a *modelling technique*.[387] A modelling technique is an operational approach for the creation of conceptual models.[388] It is an essential building block for a modelling method. The differentiation between the terms 'method' and 'technique' is problematic since they are often used interchangeably.[389] However, it is quite common and more precise to separate between these terms.[390] A modelling technique contains a *language* which specifies the concepts and terms that are used to create models and *guidelines* showing how the concepts of the language can be used and combined. This notion of a modelling technique is similar to WAND & WEBER's concept of a modelling grammar which is defined as a "set of constructs and rules that show how to combine the constructs to model real-world domains"[391]. In case of entity relationship modelling, the language contains the concepts 'entity' and 'relationship'. A rule in the guidelines specifies that

---

[384]   The entity relationship modelling technique is used extensively in this thesis. It is described in detail in Section 3.1. Since this section is mainly concerned with terminological foundations, a detailed description is not useful here, although this procedure implies to accept a lookahead.

[385]   Cf. WAND & WEBER (2002), p. 364.

[386]   A detailed discussion of modelling principles and frameworks structuring them is beyond the scope of this thesis. Refer, for instance, to BATINI, CERI & NAVATHE (1992); BECKER, ROSEMANN & SCHÜTTE (1995); ROSEMANN (1996), pp. 85–152; SCHÜTTE (1998); MOODY et al. (2002) and BECKER & SCHÜTTE (2004), pp. 120 ff.

[387]   Cf. KNACKSTEDT (2004), p. 46. KNACKSTEDT differentiates four types of rule sets (modelling technique, modification rules, coordination rules and others). Similarly, TEUBNER distinguishes between two types of rule sets: representation technique and problem solving technique (TEUBNER (1999), pp. 96–98). Such a detailed differentiation is not necessary for this thesis. Therefore, the specialization construct is not disjoint and partial indicating that other rule sets may be defined.

[388]   Cf. STRAHRINGER (1996), p. 91 and KNACKSTEDT (2004), p. 46.

[389]   Cf. STRAHRINGER (1996), p. 91.

[390]   STRAHRINGER gives an overview of the usage of the terms and notes that technique is used in international literature as well, for instance, by CURTIS, KELLNER & OVER (1992) and VESSEY, JARVENPAA & TRACTINSKY (1992).

[391]   Cf. WAND & WEBER (2002), p. 364.

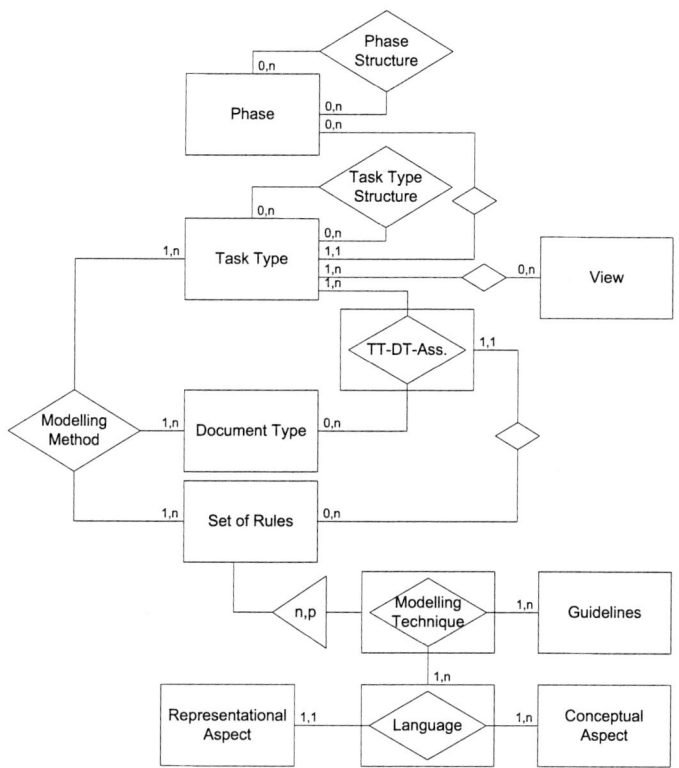

Figure 2.12: Modelling Method Conceptualization (Adapted from KNACKST-
EDT (2004), pp. 43 ff.)

two entities can be associated only via a relationship.[392] The language itself is constituted by a *conceptual* and a *representational* aspect.[393] The conceptual aspects specify
which language concepts are existent and what they 'mean'. The notion of meaning implies that a development group has to achieve an agreement upon the meaning of each
concept. Otherwise, the interpretability and appropriateness of the model cannot be ensured. Expressive power and usability of a modelling technique are mainly determined
by the language. Therefore, the language constitutes the technique.[394] Language-based
metamodels[395] can be used in conjunction with plain text descriptions in order to specify
the conceptual language aspect. This approach is applied extensively in this thesis in

---

[392]   Cf. WAND & WEBER (2002), p. 364.
[393]   Cf. STRAHRINGER (1996), pp. 18 f.; KNACKSTEDT (2004), pp. 50 f. for the following.
[394]   Cf. STRAHRINGER (1996), p. 92.
[395]   A more detailed description of language-based metamodels is given below.

Chapter 3. The representational aspects specify the notation that is used to depict the model. Obviously, multiple notations can be used to depict the same concepts. For instance, an oval can be used for depicting entities instead of a rectangle. A change of the representational aspect does not constitute a change of the modelling technique. Symbols are assigned to concepts of the language and are used to create models in graphical languages and a topology describes the overall model layout.[396]

A *conceptual model* is an abstract representation of a subject generated by a modelling process depicting facts which are supposed to be relevant by one or more modellers for a group of model users at a given time by using a language.[397] The process of model generation is characterized by subjectivity, imagination and creativity. This notion of model stresses four points.[398] Firstly, a model is a construction generated by one or more modellers. The facts that are depicted are reflecting their subjective perception. Modelling is a creative development task rather than a functional mapping of an objectively perceived reality. Consequently, a model is neither wrong nor right. Instead, it is more or less suitable for a given objective or task.[399] Secondly, model users define the purpose of the modelling task.[400] Model users can be abstract entities like organizations. The subjective perception of a problem defines the subject that is modelled. Thirdly, models are created in order to solve a problem at a given time. Thus, the validity and usefulness of models is restricted to a certain period in time since problem perception and environment are in a constant flux. Finally, models are created by using a language.[401]

Linguistic Levels & Modelling

As introduced above, models are denoted by using a language, which usually uses a graphical notation but can have any other form (for instance textual). In general, languages can be subdivided in natural (for instance, English and German) and artificial languages.[402] Natural languages are often ambiguous and imprecise and are subject to inaccuracies like synonyms or homonyms. Therefore, artificial languages are used in order to increase precision. However, any information system development process usually makes use of a combination of natural and artificial languages. A language itself can be

---

[396]   Cf. KNACKSTEDT (2004), pp. 49 f.
[397]   Cf. SCHÜTTE (1998), p. 59; HOLTEN (1999), p. 9; WAND & WEBER (2002), p. 364; KNACKSTEDT (2004), p. 36 and BECKER & SCHÜTTE (2004), p. 65. WAND & WEBER use the term script instead of model.
[398]   Cf. SCHÜTTE (1998), pp. 59–62 for the following.
[399]   Cf. HOLTEN (1999), pp. 9 f.
[400]   Cf. SCHÜTTE (1998), p. 60.
[401]   Cf. SCHÜTTE (1998), p. 62.
[402]   Cf. STRAHRINGER (1996), pp. 17 f. for the following.

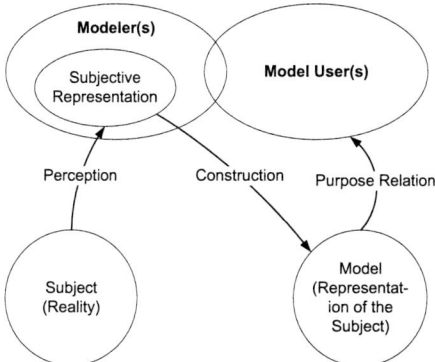

Figure 2.13: Modelling as a Process of Construction (Adapted from HOLTEN (1999), p. 9)

subject to an analysis. In this case a *metalanguage* is used in order to 'speak' about the perceptions which are stated in an *object language*.[403] If no differentiation between both language levels is made, it is not clear which language is addressed, resulting in confusion and imprecise statements. Thus, the object language (used to express statements about the world) and the metalanguage (used to express statements about the validity and truth of statements) are differentiated. By doing so, it is possible to solve antinomies that can arise in natural language. Hence, the prefix *meta* denotes the role of a language rather than classifying different types of languages. The creation of metalanguage can be iterated recursively, resulting in a infinite continuum of languages on different linguistic levels. If, for instance, a metalanguage for a metalanguage is constructed, it is called a meta-metalanguage with regard to the object-language. It is more convenient to indicate the linguistic level by an index.[404] For instance, the metalanguage can be written as $meta^1language$ and the meta-metalanguage as $meta^2language$.

The question, whether a language is a metalanguage or an object language depends on the role it is used in.[405] Rather than being a fixed property, this role is relative with regard to other languages. Thus, a language can be a metalanguage and an object-language simultaneously. STRAHRINGER illustrates this point by the example of a German dictionary:[406]

---

[403]   Cf. STRAHRINGER (1996), pp. 17 ff.; HOLTEN (1999), pp. 11 ff. for the following. LORENZ provides brief introductions on the terms on meta- and object-language (LORENZ (1995a) and LORENZ (1995b)).

[404]   Cf. STRAHRINGER (1996), p. 18.

[405]   Cf. STRAHRINGER (1996), p. 18.

[406]   Cf. STRAHRINGER (1996), p. 18. Own translation from the German original.

Subject of the German dictionary is the German language. Thus, German is the object-language of the dictionary. The dictionary itself is also written in German which serves, therefore, as a metalanguage as well. Additionally, the introduction of the dictionary contains hints how the dictionary can be used and what the German terms of the metalanguage mean.[407] As a consequence, German is used a meta-metalanguage.

As stated earlier, models are depicted by using a language. The concept of linguistic levels can be applied likewise to different levels of modelling (compare Figure 2.14). Unlike a real-world object, the modelling language itself can be modelled. It is commonly accepted to speak of a *metamodel* in this case.[408] A metamodel represents perceptions about the modelling language, whereas a model depicts perceptions of an excerpt of the real world. Thus the subject of the modelling process changes from a perceived reality to a language which is analyzed.[409] In analogy to the linguistic levels, an abbreviated notation can be used ($meta^1model$ for metamodel and $meta^2model$ for meta-metamodel). According to STRAHRINGER, metamodels can be distinguished by their construction principle: *language-based* and *process-based*.[410] Language-based metamodels normalize the linguistic means used to create models. They provide a semi-formal, compressed yet holistic and comprehensive description of concepts and their relations, and are used in conjunction with descriptions in natural language. They provide the basis for the understanding of a modelling technique. As stated previously, a development group has to achieve a mutual agreement concerning the subject which is modelled and the means that are used to create a model. If such an agreement is not achieved, the creation of meaningful and precise models is impossible. *Process-based* metamodels focus on the process that is used to create a model (for instance, the sequence in which tasks are carried out). The process of modelling is not the focus of this work. Therefore, language-based metamodels are meant whenever the shorter form metamodel is used in the following.

Having introduced the underlying terminology, the purpose of conceptual modelling for web information systems and the roles of languages on different linguistic levels can be outlined in detail. Additionally, conceptual modelling can be linked with two different types of information systems introduced in Section 2.2.1. On the information system level (level -1 in Figure 2.14), an object system is to be implemented. In this case, the

---

[407] For instance, grammatical expressions are explained in the introduction.
[408] Cf. TOLVANEN (1998), p. 82.
[409] Cf. KNACKSTEDT (2004), p. 43.
[410] Cf. STRAHRINGER (1996), pp. 24 ff. and HOLTEN (1999), pp. 12 ff. for the following.

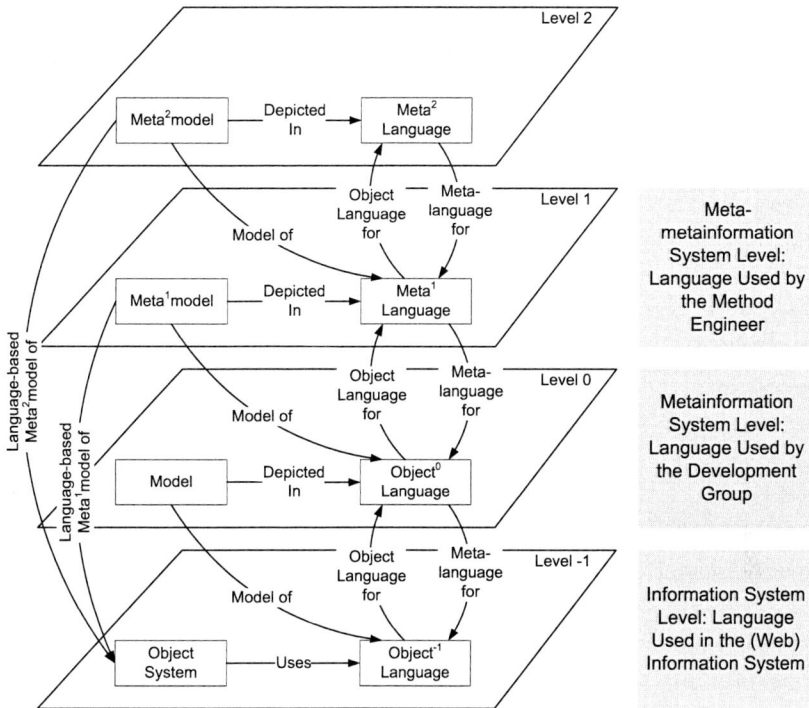

Figure 2.14: Linguistic Levels & Modelling (Adapted from HOLTEN (1999), pp. 11 f.
and STRAHRINGER (1996), pp. 19 ff. Similarly TOLVANEN (1998), p. 67)

object system is a web information system with the characteristics outlined in Section
2.2.2. As an information system, it is intended to facilitate meaningful information
exchange between its human (or technical) components.[411] It does so, by providing a
specialized language which is used to achieve a mutual understanding of a subject matter.
An example may illustrate this point: consider a complex web information system used to
organize documents and serves as an organization-wide knowledge base. Due to the vast
amount of data stored in the system, it becomes necessary to provide efficient means for
navigation within the information space. Therefore, information structures (for instance,
hierarchies) are constructed. Each element of this structure represents a potentially
large amount of data. For instance, a link 'current projects' can be created which
yields all the documents that are currently used in projects. This information structure
is used in analogy to the $object^{-1}language$ in Figure 2.14. Obviously, a meaningful

---

[411] Compare the discussion of information system definitions in Section 2.2.1.

construction of this language is of outstanding importance to the creation of an efficient web information system. If the elements of the information structure do not correspond to the concepts and terms known to the users of the system, they are not able to anticipate the information behind the link. Thus, wittingly and meaningful navigation becomes impossible. This statement can be supported by a simple thought experiment: consider a web information system organizing all pieces of information alphabetically. Elements of the information structure would contain 'A', 'AA', 'AB', 'B', 'BA' and so on. Obviously, a user would be unable to decide whether the information behind a link in this structure can potentially satisfy his or her information need or not.[412] Therefore, it seems indispensable to explicate the linguistic means used to structure information. This thesis is concerned with a methodical approach facilitating this explication process.

The web information system is created by a development group which can be conceptualized as an information system as well. It is a meta information system with regard to the web information system. Again, the meta-information system is intended to facilitate meaningful communication between participants of the development group. The development group achieves a mutual understanding of the subject matter and the problem domain by formalizing it by means of conceptual models (*Model* in Figure 2.14). The model is expressed in a language (*object⁰language*). The object-language serves as a metalanguage with regard to the *object⁻¹language* used in the actual application. The meta-information system has to provide suitable linguistic means allowing information system developers to specify the web information system effectively and efficiently. One of the tools applied in this task can be a modelling method. In case of this thesis, the model can contain the representational elements of the modelling method which is constructed in Chapter 3. The modelling method is specified by method engineers, who form a metameta-information system with regard to the web information system. They construct a language which can be used by information system developers. In order to do so, the concepts of the language have to be introduced carefully and precisely. Within this thesis, language-based metamodels are used in conjunction with descriptions in natural language in Chapter 3 in order to specify the modelling method. The method contains proposals which can be used by information system developers. The language constructs specified by the method engineer might well be insufficient or unsuited for a given task. In this case, the method has to be adapted to specific requirements. Following this understanding of information systems, languages and conceptual modelling, a

---

[412] Of course, there is an exception to this rule. Alphabetical structures are well-known and accepted navigation mechanisms for encyclopedias. Nevertheless, it is obvious that the information in other systems has to be organized differently.

hierarchy emerges. Each level seeks to support an information system for a specific task. Meaningful conversation is facilitated by semi-formal languages which are constructed by sense-making with regard to the target domain.

The role and importance of suitable linguistic means in conceptual modelling of web information systems is of outstanding importance and differs fundamentally from other modelling approaches. A conceptual database model depicted in entity relationship notation is usually hidden from the user's view. A user *does not* interact directly with the concepts represented in the model. The model clearly has a pure technical view and can, therefore, abstract from individual differences and problems of user interaction with the system. Conceptual models of web information systems, however, are directly transformed and represented in the user interface. Hierarchies and structures which are used to organize information obviously determine a users ability to retrieve the desired information. If these structures are poorly specified, the system will not achieve the organization's goals.

2.2.7 Web Information System Development Approaches

It is sensible to review existing modelling approaches in order to position the approach of this thesis and to outline differences and commonalities. Moreover, fruitful insights can thus be gained on characteristics and concepts of web information systems. There has been a controversial debate whether web information systems differ from 'traditional' information systems and whether they require alternative modelling methods or not. Recently, a discipline known as *web engineering* emerged, which presupposes that special characteristics of web information systems have influences on the development process.[413] Their viewpoint is supported by researchers who are not directly concerned with web engineering. For instance, VIDGEN argues that differences are caused by the content the web information system displays.[414] BASKERVILLE & PRIES-HEJE analyzed information system development in 'internet time'[415] and concluded that a metamorphosis is on the way concerning traditional methodological assumptions.[416] They constructed causal

---

[413] Cf., for instance, DESHPANDE & GINIGE (2001); DESHPANDE et al. (2002); GINIGE & MURUGE-SAN (2001); GINIGE (2002) and BAHLI (2003). Likewise BANSLER et al. (2000) and LANG (2003).

[414] Cf. VIDGEN (2002), p. 257.

[415] The term 'internet time' has been coined by Netscape and publicized by CUSUMANO & YOFFIE (cf. BASKERVILLE & PRIES-HEJE (2001), p. 50). It refers to the tremendous speed by which technological innovations are adopted in networks.

[416] Cf. BASKERVILLE & PRIES-HEJE (2001), p. 50.

chains containing ten factors[417] influencing the development of web information systems.
Time pressure and vague requirements are dominant and lead to a different conception
of methodology. BASKERVILLE & PRIES-HEJE conclude that methodologists have to
rethink what being a methodology implies.[418] The difficulty of specifying complex web
information systems is noted by BALASUBRAMANIAN & BASHIAN. They were unable
to apply existing methodologies to a large-scale, unstructured, document-oriented web
information systems and decided to derive their own methodology by extending an existing one.[419] LYYTINEN, ROSE & WELKE argue that information system development
skills have to change significantly in what they call the 'internet-network computing
architecture', which also includes web information systems as they are conceptualized
in this thesis.[420] For instance, IS development has to be more multidisciplinary in these
environments implying changes in the methods that are used.[421] There are, however,
other authors who claim that the problems in web engineering are not different from
those known from traditional software engineering.[422]

Table 2.1 gives a chronological overview of specialized modelling approaches for web
information systems that were proposed in the past.[423] Only modelling approaches
including a graphical notation have been integrated in the overview. More formal and
technical approaches are beyond the scope of the thesis. Consequently, the overview
is far from complete. It only concentrates on the most common approaches that are
frequently cited in publications.

Following RETSCHITZEGGER & SCHWINGER, the modelling approaches for web information systems can be roughly classified according to their origin.[424] In general, three

---

[417] The factors do not have to be discussed in detail at this point. They are time pressure, vague
requirements, prototyping, release organization, parallel development, fixed architecture, coding
ones way out, the fact that quality is negotiable, the dependence on good people and the need for
structure. Cf. BASKERVILLE & PRIES-HEJE (2001), pp. 54 f. for details.

[418] Cf. BASKERVILLE & PRIES-HEJE (2001), p. 65.

[419] Cf. BALASUBRAMANIAN & BASHIAN (1998), p. 109.

[420] Cf. LYYTINEN, ROSE & WELKE (1998), pp. 247 f.

[421] Cf. LANG (2003) for a similar point.

[422] Cf., for instance, KAUTZ & NØRBJERG (2003).

[423] The overview is based on publication date. Additional references for the approaches: HDM
(GARZOTTO, PAOLINI & SCHWABE (1993)), eW3DT (SCHARL (2000)), W3I3 (CERI, FRATER-
NALI & PARABOSCHI (1999)), WebML (CERI, FRATERNALI & MATERA (2002)). Less frequently
cited approaches that are not included in the overview are, for instance, SiteLang (THALHEIM
& DÜSTERHÖFT (2001)); OODM (SHAH (2003)), THALHEIM & DÜSTERHÖFT (2003)) as well
as the modelling approaches presented by TROYER & DECRUYENAERE (TROYER & DECRUYE-
NAERE (2000)); CHRISTODOULOU, ZAFIRIS & PAPATHEODOROU (CHRISTODOULOU, ZAFIRIS &
PAPATHEODOROU (2001)) and EHLERS (EHLERS (2003)).

[424] Cf. RETSCHITZEGGER & SCHWINGER (2000). A similar overview can be found in SCHWINGER &

Author(s)	Year	Approach
GARZOTTO, PAOLINI & SCHWABE	1991	Hypertext Design Model (HDM)
HALASZ & SCHWARTZ	1994	Dexter Hypertext Reference Model
ISAKOWITZ, STOHR & BALASUBRAMANIAN	1995	Relationship Management Methodology (RMM)
BICHLER & NUSSER	1996	World Wide Web Design Technique (W3DT)
SCHWABE, ROSSI & BARBOSA	1996	Object-oriented Hypermedia Design Model (OOHDM)
SCHARL	1998	Extended World Wide Web Design Technique (eW3DT)
MECCA et al.	1998	Araneus
CERI et al.	1998	WWW Intelligent Information Infrastructure (W3I3)
CONALLEN	1999	N/A (Derived from the Unified Modelling Language)
FRATERNALI & PAOLINI	2000	Autoweb/HDM-Lite
CERI, FRATERNALI & BONGIO	2000	Web Modelling Language
GÓMEZ, CACHERO & PASTOR	2001	Object-oriented Hypermedia (OO-H)

Table 2.1: Chronological Overview of Web Information System Engineering Approaches

origins can be distinguished. Firstly, some approaches (for instance RMM and Araneus) are rooted in the database community and are, therefore, based on entity relationship modelling (ERM) or are influenced by the approach (for instance, HDM). The Dexter hypertext reference model represents the hypertext origin of modelling approaches and has virtually influenced all modelling approaches.[425] The Dexter model has been de-

---

KOCH (2004), p. 70.

[425] RETSCHITZEGGER & SCHWINGER term the Dexter reference model as the origin of the hypertext branch although it was published after the modelling technique HDM, which leads to the inconsequential conclusion that HDM is based on Dexter. Therefore, HDM and Dexter are considered to be the root of hypertext modelling.

veloped in order to provide a sound basis for comparing systems as well as to develop interchange and interoperability standards. The provision of a standardized terminology of hypertext systems was the focus of the model. Although the Dexter model is a reference model rather than a conceptual modelling approach, it is included in the discussion for the sake of completeness and its significance. Finally, object-oriented approaches like the Object Modelling Technique (RUMBAUGH et al. (1991)) or the Unified Modelling Language (RUMBAUGH, JACOBSON & BOOCH (1998)) have been adapted or extended (for instance, OOHDM or OO-H) in order to meet specific requirements of web information systems. Figure 2.15 gives an overview of origins and relations of the modelling approaches.

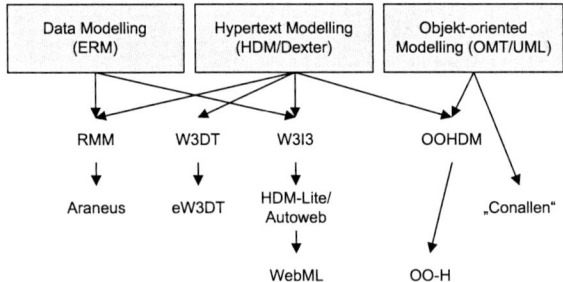

Figure 2.15: Relations of Web Information System Engineering Approaches (Adapted from RETSCHITZEGGER & SCHWINGER (2000) and SCHWINGER & KOCH (2004), p. 70)

The modelling approaches differ substantially, which renders a comparison rather difficult. However, depending on scope and type of the implementation project, a suitable method has to be selected. Several modelling approaches have been compared in the past. Like the modelling approaches themselves, the comparisons also differ in scope and aim. FRATERNALI provides an overview of modelling approaches as well as related web technology.[426] The modelling capabilities of the approaches are investigated by RETSCHITZEGGER & SCHWINGER and GU, HENDERSON-SELLERS & LOWE as well as SCHWINGER & KOCH.[427] EHLERS has analyzed the applicability of the approaches for the specification of content management systems.[428] SCHELLHASE has surveyed their

---

[426] Cf. FRATERNALI (1999).
[427] Cf. RETSCHITZEGGER & SCHWINGER (2000); GU, HENDERSON-SELLERS & LOWE (2002) and SCHWINGER & KOCH (2004).
[428] Cf. EHLERS (2003), pp. 74–104.

capabilities to model personalization and adaptability.[429] Table 2.16 gives an overview of the surveys and the approaches covered. As representatives of their respective line of development the approaches Araneus, (e)W3DT, WebML and OO-H are briefly examined in the following. The comparison mainly intends to scrutinize the modelling capabilities of the approaches. Particularly, the navigational capabilities of the approaches are investigated. A more detailed discussion of the other modelling approaches is not necessary since they follow the same modelling paradigm as the ones analyzed. As the comparison will reveal, these approaches are different from the method which will be constructed in Chapter 3. The comparison is based on a brief description of each approach in natural language. Additionally, language based metamodels are constructed in order to normalize the modelling concepts in a semi-formal and uniform way (refer to A). Finally, the approaches are analyzed and compared with regard to a set of criteria developed in the discussion.

Author(s)	Approaches Covered											
	HDM	Dexter	RMM	W3DT	OOHDM	eW3DT	Araneus	W3I3	"Conallen"	Autoweb/HDM-Lite	WebML	OO-H
Fraternali (1999)	✓	✓	✓		✓		✓	✓		✓		
Retschitzegger, Schwinger (2000)	✓		✓		✓		✓	✓	✓	✓		
Schellhase (2001)	✓			✓	✓	✓	✓			✓		
Gu, Henderson-Sellers, Lowe (2002)					✓					✓	✓	✓
Ehlers (2003)	✓			✓	✓	✓					✓	
Schwinger, Koch (2004)	✓		✓		✓				✓	✓	✓	✓

Figure 2.16: Surveys of Web Information System Modelling Approaches

Araneus Overview

The Araneus approach has been proposed by MECCA et al.. The approach aims at developing a new kind of data repository that allows managing web data in the database style.[430] It concentrates on data-intensive sites that publish significant amounts of data stored in a back-end database.[431] The Araneus approach is a complex framework for

---

[429] Cf. SCHELLHASE (2001), pp. 44–94.
[430] Cf. MECCA et al. (1998), p. 544.
[431] Cf. MERIALDO, ATZENI & MECCA (2003), p. 50.

designing, implementing and maintaining web information systems rather than a mere conceptual modelling method. It comprises the following concepts:[432]

- Separation of levels: the design of a web information system is clearly separated in the levels data design, hypertext design and presentation design. According to MERIALDO, ATZENI & MECCA, these levels are largely independent of each other and can be specified separately. As MERIALDO, ATZENI & MECCA point out, web information system engineering is different from database engineering since it explicitly encourages redundancy in the representation of content and associations (links) between them. In contrast to this, database design is generally interested in a non-redundant normalized representation of data.[433] Therefore, it seems appropriate to separate between different levels and apply suitable tools for modelling and implementation at each level.

- Model-based design and development: each of the three levels is modelled on a conceptual level with an appropriate modelling technique. The data level is modelled by using common data modelling techniques, whereas new modelling concepts are proposed for the hypertext and presentation level.

- Design methodology: the design methodology structures the overall design process and integrates the artefacts created on different levels. The design methodology covers the following steps: 1. requirements analysis 2. site content design with a conceptual database schema in entity relationship notation 3. logical database design (relational model) 4. site structure and site presentation design with newly developed modelling approaches and 5. implementation.[434]

- A CASE tool for web site development: in order to support information system engineers in a efficient manner, a CASE tool is provided allowing to create models and implementation artefacts for different levels and perspectives.

- A formal framework: the framework describes products and transformations of the design process without regard to implementation details by using extensions of the nested algebra and the nested relational model.

The following overview concentrates on the conceptual modelling aspects of Araneus in order to compare it with other modelling approaches and with the method to be

---

[432] Cf. MERIALDO, ATZENI & MECCA (2003), pp. 50 f. for the following.
[433] Cf. MERIALDO, ATZENI & MECCA (2003), pp. 64 f.
[434] Cf. MERIALDO, ATZENI & MECCA (2003), p. 53.

designed in this thesis. As mentioned above, Araneus differentiates three perspectives (content, navigation and layout) which are modelled separately. The content level is specified by using an entity relationship modelling notation with min-max cardinalities (compare Figure 2.17).[435] The conceptual data model serves as a basis for the database and site structure design. The relational database schema is derived from the conceptual model.[436]

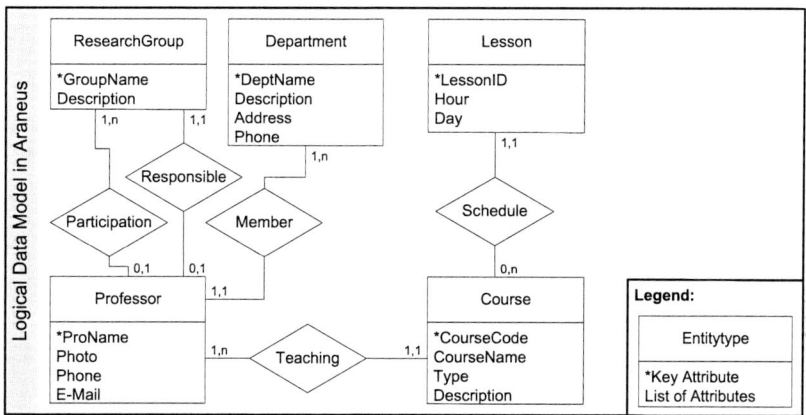

Figure 2.17: Modelling Example Araneus: Logical Data Model (Adapted from MERIALDO, ATZENI & MECCA (2003), p. 53)

Navigation and the structure of the system are modelled in the ADM-d model (compare Figure 2.18 for the following).[437] MERIALDO, ATZENI & MECCA propose a two-step approach in order to create a ADM-d model based on the conceptual database model. Firstly, the hypertext design is modelled.[438] The information system developer models nodes and navigation paths which are conceptualized as views on the database model. A view is based on entities which represent nodes in the hypertext model and relationships that correspond to navigation paths. Only some, not necessarily all, entities are mapped to n-entities.[439] An n-entity can contain multiple entities which provide

---

[435] Cf. MERIALDO, ATZENI & MECCA (2003), pp. 52 ff. for the following. The entity relationship modelling technique is introduced in detail in Section 3.1.

[436] The derivation of a relational model out of a conceptual data model is well documented in literature. Compare, for instance, VOSSEN (1999), pp. 125 ff.

[437] ADM-d is an abbreviation of Araneus data model design. Compare MERIALDO, ATZENI & MECCA (2003), pp. 60 f.; ATZENI & PARENTE (2003), pp. 127 f. and ATZENI, MECCA & MERIALDO (1997b) for details of the model.

[438] Cf. MERIALDO, ATZENI & MECCA (2003), pp. 64 ff.

[439] Cf. MERIALDO, ATZENI & MECCA (2003), p. 68. An n-entity is a navigational entity.

a complex view on the original data model. Navigation paths are derived from relationships. They are directed relations with a cardinality between two n-entities or hypertext nodes. A hypertext node is not based on an entity and is depicted by an oval. Hypertext nodes can be structured and are depicted by ovals. Navigation paths are depicted by arrows. The result of the hypertext design process is a variant of the entity relationship schema with some navigational features called N-ER model.[440] As MERIALDO, ATZENI & MECCA note, this idea of deriving navigational functionality is inspired by the notion that entities and relations in the ER model are quite suitable to describe content and navigation of web pages.[441] ER models, however, represent a technical view on data, intended to provide a sound basis for the subsequent implementation. They do not necessarily correspond to the mental structures of the human being. This is a major difference to other modelling approaches. The hypertext concept implicitly encourages redundancy and nontechnical views on data. Consequently, MERIALDO, ATZENI & MECCA note

> However, we observe that when the site offers a rich information content, the task of designing an effective structure becomes a complex problem. In fact, a conceptual representation of data always separates the various concepts in several entities (this is the conceptual counterpart to database normalization), whereas in a Web site it is reasonable to show distinct concepts together (denormalizing or adding nested structures, in database terms) for the sake of clarity and effectiveness in the presentation of information to the final user. [...] Similarly, a conceptual schema aims at avoiding transitive dependencies among relationships (TEOREY, YANG & FRY (1986)), which occur whenever different paths can be associated with the same semantics; in contrast, in a Web site redundant paths are often very useful for improving navigation. For example, it might be useful to have a direct navigation path between the departments and the courses they provide, despite the fact that there is no relationship that directly connects them. Another important issue is that a Web site must provide an access structure; starting from the home page, the access to the information offered by the site must be carefully organized in order to ease the site browsing.[442]

---

[440] Cf. MERIALDO, ATZENI & MECCA (2003), p. 54.
[441] Cf. MERIALDO, ATZENI & MECCA (2003), p. 64.
[442] MERIALDO, ATZENI & MECCA (2003), p. 65. References in quote adapted to the format used in this thesis and integrated in the bibliography. The part left out referred to examples given in the publication.

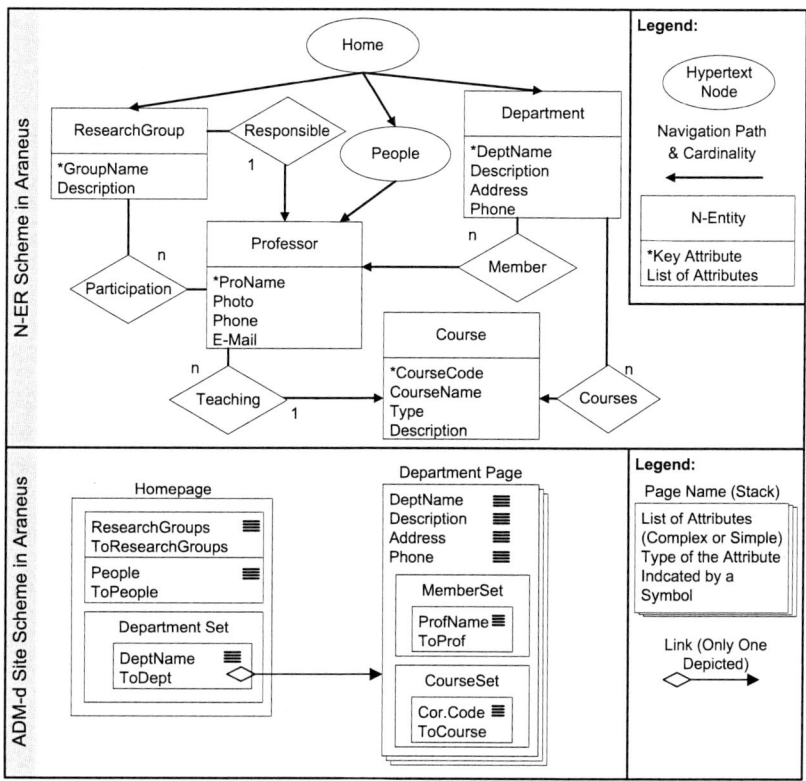

Figure 2.18: Modelling Example Araneus: Hypertext and Page Structure Design (Adapted from MERIALDO, ATZENI & MECCA (2003), pp. 54–55)

Secondly, the page structure design, which is also based on the entity relationship model, defines pages and their content (entities and attributes).[443] As MERIALDO, ATZENI & MECCA point out, the N-ER schema describes how concepts can be navigated in the target hypertext, whereas the actual web site is a graph of pages.[444] Both ways of organizing information can be rather different. Thus, two approaches are used to specify the navigational design of a web information system. Page structure design is carried out in two steps: (1) the initial ADM-d schema is derived from the N-ER model and (2) this schema is restructured if necessary. A page schema is derived from an n-entity. The name of the page as well as the originating links are derived automatically by the case tool. It represents a web page that displays the attributes of the n-entity it is based on.

---

[443] Cf. MERIALDO, ATZENI & MECCA (2003), pp. 72 ff. for the following.
[444] Cf. MERIALDO, ATZENI & MECCA (2003), p. 72.

The attributes are the pages content. Attributes can be complex and have a type (like picture or text). For instance, an attribute can be nested containing other attributes of different types. Links are special attributes that link the page schema to another one. Page schemes can be unique or non-unique. Non-unique page schemes correspond to a stack of pages indicating structural and semantical similarity.[445] Araneus contains a modelling approach for the design of the presentation level. The focus of the analysis, however, is on navigation rather than presentation. Therefore, a detailed discussion is omitted.[446]

WebML Overview

WebML (formerly named Autoweb/HDM-Lite and W3I3) has been proposed by CERI, FRATERNALI & MATERA with special regard to data intensive web applications.[447] It features a CASE tool that implements WebML and automatically generates websites (at least partially).[448] Basing their work on several other conceptual modelling approaches (for instance, HDM and RMM), CERI, FRATERNALI & MATERA focus on the construction of an easy-to-use yet, powerful modelling technique with regard to model driven application development. WebML differentiates between two orthogonal dimensions: data model and hypertext model (compare Figure 2.19 for the following). The data modelling technique is similar to the entity relationship model. It specifies a logical data structure on which the web application is based on. The data structure provides a technical view on the application. Entities are depicted by rectangles. Attributes are denoted below the entity's name. Relationships are depicted by lines and min-max-cardinalities are used. The hypertext model describes content and operation units and hypertext interconnections between them. Units are the central constructs of the modelling approach. They represent pieces of information and are usually linked to a database table for dynamic content generation. Additionally, interactive units (operation units) are used to gather information from users or customers (for instance, in an ordering process). Table 2.2 gives an overview of the different types of units and their usage.

Web pages are composed of content units. One content unit or more are assigned to a web page in the hypertext model. The web page represents an addressable object the user can view. Interconnections respectively links are depicted by arrows which conjoin

---

[445] Cf. MERIALDO, ATZENI & MECCA (2003), p. 60.

[446] Refer to MERIALDO, ATZENI & MECCA (2003), pp. 78 ff. for details on the specification of the presentation level.

[447] Cf. CERI, FRATERNALI & BONGIO (2000) and CERI, FRATERNALI & MATERA (2002) for the following brief description of WebML. Autoweb is described by FRATERNALI & PAOLINI (2000).

[448] Refer to the web site http://www.webratio.com/ for details.

Unit	Description
Data Unit	Shows data about a single entity instance.
Multidata	Shows data about several entity instances.
Index	Shows a list of properties (also called descriptive keys) of a given set of entity instances. A user clicks on an index entry to select and display one instance.
Scroller	Provides commands for scrolling through objects in a list – for example, the sequence of all the instances of an entity. Scrolling commands let the user move to a set's first, last, previous, and next elements and select and display one instance of the set.
Data Entry	Shows a form with several fields for collecting user input. Input might be conditions used for searches over entity instances or parameters for operations such as content updates, logins, and generic external operations.
Create	Establishes a new instance of an entity.
Delete	Removes an instance of an entity.
Modify	Changes an instance of an entity.
Connect	Creates an instance of a relationship.
Disconnect	Drops an instance of relationship.
Generic	Invokes a generic operation, possibly implemented by externally available Web services.

Table 2.2: Content and Operation Units in WebML (cf. CERI, FRATERNALI & MATERA (2002), pp. 22–23)

operation or content units. Links are neither named nor typed. Operation units are not assigned to web pages since they are invisible from a user's perspective.[449] They represent functionality which is, for instance, implemented by small scripts that are invoked and executed during run-time.

eW3DT Overview

The extended World Wide Web Design Technique (eW3DT) was proposed by SCHARL with special regard to reference modelling of commercial web applications. The approach provides a user-centric view on the application.[450] It is based on the work of BICHLER

---

[449] Cf. CERI, FRATERNALI & MATERA (2002), p. 23. The example depicted in Figure 2.19 does not contain operation units.

[450] Cf. SCHARL (1998) and SCHARL (2000), p. 85.

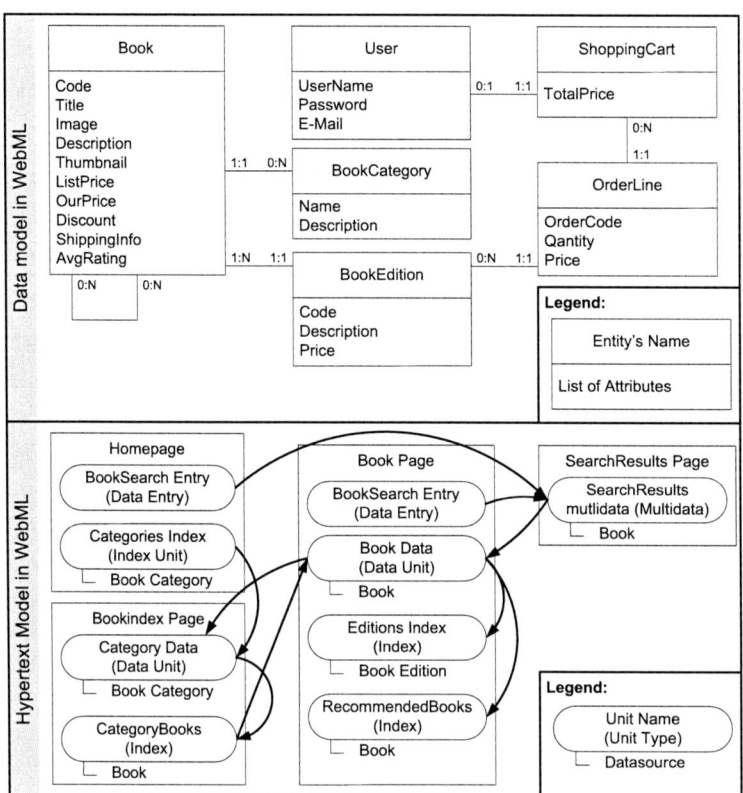

Figure 2.19: Modelling Example WebML (Adapted from CERI, FRATERNALI & MAT-
ERA (2002), pp. 21–22)

& NUSSER who have introduced the World Wide Web Design Technique (W3DT) which
was formerly called Structured Hypermedia Design Technique (SHDT).[451] According to
SCHARL, eW3DT is characterized by a higher degree of abstraction.[452] SCHARL argues
that it can be used for reference modelling of commercial applications and serves as a
basis for implementation models in other notations (for instance, OOHDM or HDM).[453]
A web application is modelled in eW3DT by using a single diagram with refinements
on different levels. It does not contain special model types for different views on the
application (for instance, data view and hypertext view). A site represents the WWW

---

[451] Cf. BICHLER & NUSSER (1996). A brief introduction to W3DT can also be found in SCHELL-
      HASE (2001), pp. 86–94.
[452] Cf. SCHARL (2000), p. 95.
[453] Cf. SCHARL (2000), p. 95.

application to be modelled (for instance, a web shop). A site consists of a number of information objects that are used for static as well as dynamic web pages (compare Table 2.3 and Figure 2.20 for the following). Information objects are the core constructs of eW3DT. The classification of an information object as static or dynamic refers to the content it represents rather than to the (technical) generation mechanism of the information object. All in all, eW3DT offers six information object types that are graphically illustrated by a symbol in the upper right corner. Each information object can represent static or dynamic pieces of information. Dynamic information objects are depicted by ovals.

Information Object	Description
Page	A page is used to model standard hypertext documents, which usually represent the logical end of a hierarchical tree.
Menu	A menu is frequently found on a higher hierarchical level as it symbolizes alternative, manually created navigational paths and access mechanisms.
Index	An index represents a complete enumeration of links, for example a list of available products or staff members.
Interaction	Interaction includes various interactive elements in order to process user inputs.
File	File visualizes mechanisms to transfer data of various formats and sizes (for instance, downloads).
Database	The database construct represents information that is compiled dynamically from databases.

Table 2.3: Information Objects in eW3DT (cf. SCHARL (2000), pp. 87–88)

Moreover, information objects comprise several additional constructs that represent the hierarchical level (by means of two digits in x.y notation), the maintenance intensity (illustrated via one to three stars ranging from low to high), and the organizational as well as the technical responsibility unit that allow eW3DT to distinguish content-specific from technical responsibilities for designing, implementing and maintaining the web information system.[454] Besides information objects, eW3DT provides structuring objects and navigation objects. The primary structuring element represents hierarchical relationships between information models in eW3DT (model decomposition). Moreover, external links are used to symbolize hyperlinks to external information sources. Multiple

---

[454] Cf. SCHARL (2000), p. 86.

sources facilitate reducing redundancy within the models as they can be used where multidimensional selections (for instance, out of an index) offer access to large amounts of data. The navigational design of a web information system is modelled by four different types of links.[455] Static links are implemented permanently and change only if the overall structure of the web site is redesigned. Dynamic links are created during run-time and address automatically generated documents. Representative links are a sub-type of dynamic links. They refer to different versions of static information which are delivered depending on the user's behaviour (for instance, the selection of an item in a drop-down list) or other conditions. Horizontal links are adapted from the Dexter hypertext reference model. They do not provide navigational functionality to users but allow the information system engineer to structure heterogenous documents. Figure 2.20 illustrates the usage of eW3DT.

OO-H Overview

The modelling approach Object-Oriented Hypermedia (OO-H) has been proposed by GÓMEZ, CACHERO & PASTOR.[456] The approach is aims at extending existing object-oriented software engineering approaches with special modelling capabilities which are needed for web applications. GÓMEZ, CACHERO & PASTOR argue that behaviour in web applications should be addressed rigorously by applying well-known and tested principles from object-oriented software development. Moreover, they note that the presentation level of web applications is fundamentally different from other applications. OO-H proposes a user centered view on the system, that is, requirements should be specified regarding the interactions users make with the system.[457] The approach is supported by a CASE tool which allows to model OO-H models and generates code segments automatically.[458]

   The OO-H approach is based on object-oriented modelling and provides a complete framework and design process which leads from the conceptual specification to the implementation of the application. For the purpose at hand, only the conceptual specification is discussed in detail. The specification process in OO-H involves the following steps: Firstly, a conceptual UML class diagram is constructed that represents the content of the application as well as the functionality which is hidden from the user. Since object-oriented modelling is hybrid by nature, structural as well as behavioural aspects are

---

[455]   Cf. SCHARL (2000), p. 90 for the following.

[456]   Cf. GÓMEZ, CACHERO & PASTOR (2000), pp. 79 f.; GÓMEZ, CACHERO & PASTOR (2001), pp. 26 ff. and GÓMEZ & CACHERO (2002), pp. 144 f. for the following.

[457]   Cf. GÓMEZ, CACHERO & PASTOR (2000), p. 90.

[458]   Cf. GÓMEZ, CACHERO & PASTOR (2001), p. 27.

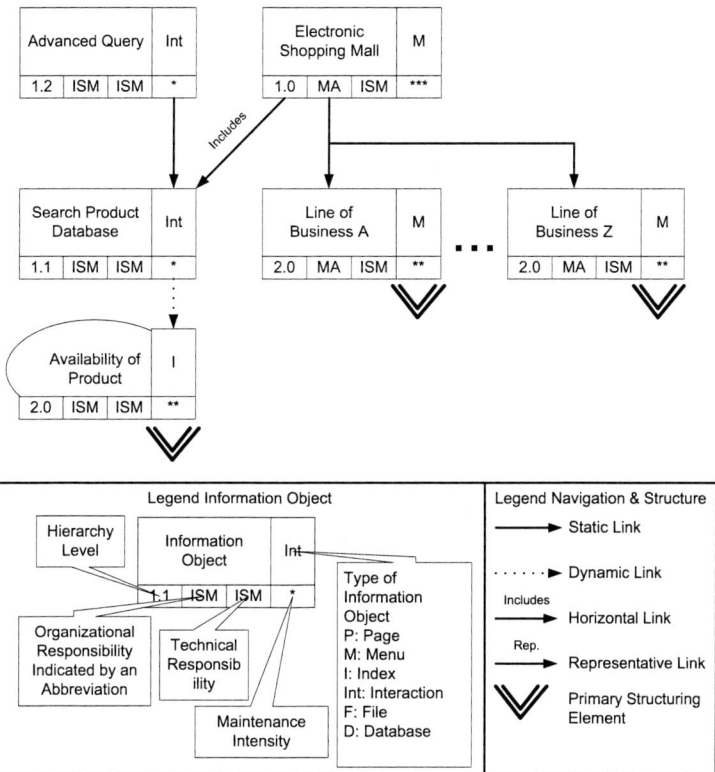

Figure 2.20: Modelling Example eW3DT (Adapted from SCHARL (2000), p. 93)

covered by the model. Secondly, the navigation structure is specified. Finally, the presentation level is modelled. In order to model the steps two and three, the approach introduces two new diagrams.

The *navigational access diagram* (NAD) is based on a class diagram which is modelled in UML notation (compare Figure 2.21[459] for the following).[460] Multiple NADs can be

---

[459] The diagrams of OO-H are fairly complex and, consequently, difficult to depict and explain. Thus, only a portion of the diagrams is depicted here. The reader may refer to the original publications for more detailed diagrams.

[460] Cf. GÓMEZ, CACHERO & PASTOR (2001), pp. 28 f. and GÓMEZ, CACHERO & PASTOR (2000), pp. 81 f. for the following. Only a brief overview of the approach is given in the following. OO-H is rather complex and the language concepts of the approach are usually not presented in detail in the publications of GÓMEZ, CACHERO & PASTOR. Therefore, only the main concepts are described in order to avoid misinterpretations and inaccuracies.

created for each class diagram. Each NAD instance reflects the information, services, and required navigation paths for the associated user's navigation requirements.[461] Navigation requirements represent processes users execute in the system. Therefore, GÓMEZ, CACHERO & PASTOR's notion of navigation strongly correlates to processes. One NAD has to be constructed for each view that is required on the system.[462] At least one should be constructed for each user group. An NAD contains navigational classes which represent views on the UML class diagram. Attributes and services of the UML class are derived and extended by additional information. For instance, attributes of a navigational class are either visible for the user, displayed on demand or hidden.[463] Thus, the amount and type of information as well as the behavioural aspects of the web application are specified by navigational classes. Navigational targets group navigational classes into 'packages' that cluster related navigational classes in a meaningful manner. The navigation structure is specified by navigational links connecting navigational classes. OO-H differentiates five different link types.[464] Internal links define the navigation path within the boundaries of a given navigational target. Traversal links are defined between navigation classes belonging to different navigational targets. Requirement links point at the starting navigation point inside each navigational target. Finally, service links show the services available to the user type associated to that NAD. Links can be associated with navigational patterns or filters. A navigational pattern specifies the operation that takes place if a user traverses the link. For instance, an internal link can be associated with the 'showall' pattern, indicating that all associated elements are to be displayed on the next page.[465] Navigation filters can be used in order to specify the quantity of links, their order or the characteristics of the target object. Collections are (hierarchical) structures that are defined on navigational classes and/or navigational targets. They provide additional navigational functionalities for users. For instance, they focus on a certain aspect of an NAD and can be assigned to navigation patterns and/or filters.

The *abstract presentation diagram* represents templates that illustrate and depict the specification of the interface. Multiple APDs can be derived for each NAD. Since the presentation level is not the focus of this thesis, a detailed discussion is omitted.

---

[461]   Cf. GÓMEZ, CACHERO & PASTOR (2001), p. 28.
[462]   Cf. GÓMEZ, CACHERO & PASTOR (2001), p. 30.
[463]   Cf. GÓMEZ, CACHERO & PASTOR (2000), p. 83.
[464]   Cf. GÓMEZ, CACHERO & PASTOR (2001), p. 31. for the following.
[465]   Cf. GÓMEZ, CACHERO & PASTOR (2001), p. 32.

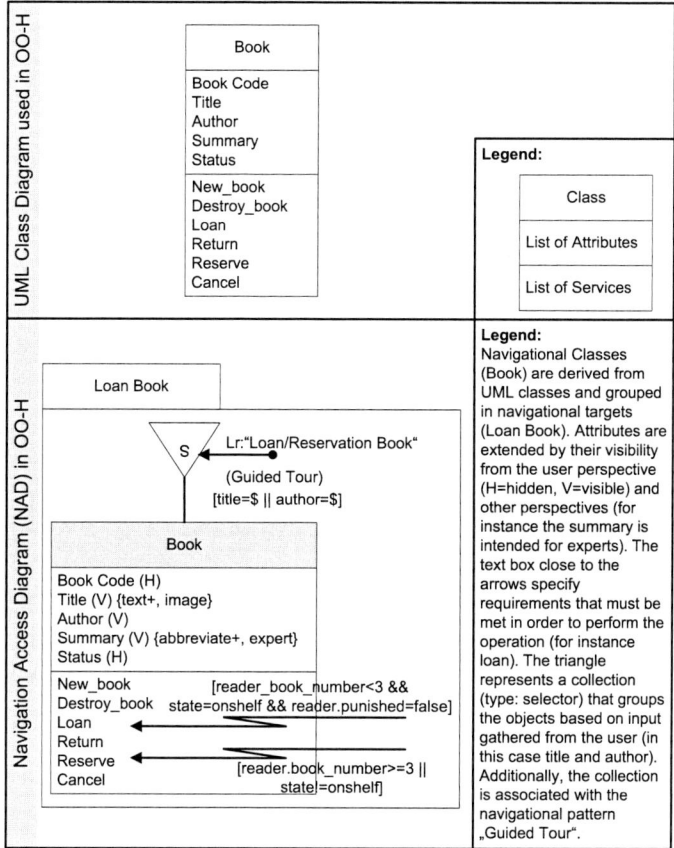

Figure 2.21: Modelling Example OO-H (Adapted from GÓMEZ, CACHERO & PAS-TOR (2000), pp. 82 f.)

Comparison & Discussion

Having briefly introduced the modelling approaches, a comparison framework can be constructed. Obviously, the construction of relevant criteria and the positioning of each modelling approach is subjective by nature. However, it is useful to outline common-alities and differences of the approaches. Thus, the comparison framework is intended to characterize the approaches rather than qualifying them. According to the focus of the thesis, special regard is given to navigational issues and the means that are used to model navigation. Additionally, means and concepts for modelling content are also investigated. The presentation dimension is not investigated. Moreover, the comparison allows to position the approach constructed in this thesis in relation to previous work. The comparison is based on the overview of the modelling techniques and the language-based metamodels.

Firstly, some general characteristics including *origin* and *application focus* of the approaches can be collected. The application focus of the approaches has already been identified in the brief discussions. Additionally, the *abstraction level* which corresponds roughly to different phases of the development process varies. Although all approaches claim to model web information system on a conceptual level, there is obviously a difference on the degree of abstraction. For instance, OO-H is close to the implementation level since it models conditions and variables on a detailed level, whereas eW3DT has explicitly been designed for reference modelling and is characterized by a higher degree of abstraction.[466] Since the demarcation of abstraction levels is not strict, the approaches are most adequately characterized by assigning them to a continuum that is limited by the conceptual specification on the one side and the implementation on the other. Thus, the approaches can be roughly characterized as 'more technical' and 'mainly conceptual'. In general, modelling approaches that are rooted in computer science (like OO-H, WebML and Araneus) and follow a CASE approach are 'more technical', whereas the information system's community focuses mainly on other issues like complexity reduction, general description and communication (like in eW3DT). Without a definite terminology, the classification of the modelling approaches has to be done subjectively by a pair wise comparison of the approaches. The *modelling focus* characterizes the dominant approach used to create models. Data-centric approaches model the application from the data perspective including aspects and content which is hidden from the user and only used internally. In contrast to this, user-centric approaches adopt the user's viewpoint on the application and its usage for satisfying a user's information needs. Again, the demarcation between the extremes 'data-centric' (Araneus, WebML) and 'user-centric' (OO-H and eW3DT) is not strict. However, each approach features characteristics of both extremes.

Secondly, the modelling characteristics of the navigation perspective can be compared. As outlined in the discussion on hypertext, the following aspects should be supported by a modelling approach for web information systems:[467]

- *Link types*[468]: it seems reasonable to postulate that modelling techniques should support different types of links. By doing so, the semantics of the conceptual

---

[466] Compare also SCHARL (2000), p. 95.

[467] Refer also to Section 2.2.3.

[468] Cf. BIEBER et al. (1997), pp. 37 f. for a comprehensive discussion of link types.

models as well as the applications can be enriched. For instance, the difference between a link referring to a related document and a part of the actual document can be visualized. Additionally, the difference between organizational and referential links can be outlined.[469] OO-H and eW3DT differ link types while Araneus and WebML do not. However, Araneus derives links from relationships. Links inherit the name of the relationship which roughly corresponds to types of links in case appropriate names for the relationship are used.

- *Link labelling*[470]: since links provide the basic functionality of web information systems, it is interesting to see whether each link is explicitly labelled by the modelling approach or not. Some modelling methods depict links as arrows while others specify the name of the link that has to appear in the web information system. It is reasonable to assume that a careful labelling and naming of links highly increases the user's abilities to retrieve the desired information. The approaches eW3DT, OO-H and WebML do not provide explicit labelling of links. Just like link types, the labels of links are derived from relationships in Araneus. Therefore, relationship names can potentially be used as link labels. However, this is not an explicit labelling of links in information structures, as it is intended in this thesis.

- *Information structures*: the information structure organizes all pieces of information which are stored in the system. It provides the main navigational functionality. As argued in Section 2.2.3, a sound engineering of an appropriate information structure is considered to be crucial for the successful implementation of a web information system. None of the approaches proposes a specific information structure (like a hierarchy or multi-tree). However, it should be possible to model a suitable information structure with all the approaches. Yet, there is no distinct concept showing how information structures are to be constructed and which types are to be differentiated.

Finally, modelling of the content perspective can be investigated. The approaches eW3DT and WebML differ between static and dynamic *content types*, whereas the other approaches model content with one language concept which is derived from data modelling or object modelling. In Araneus, the data type (for instance, picture or text) of content is modelled explicitly. Since OO-H is based on the object-oriented paradigm, concepts like inheritance and composition can be used which resemble content

---

[469] Refer to Section 2.2.3 for a classification of links.
[470] Cf. BIEBER et al. (1997), pp. 40 f.

types. *Metadata* is used to describe and enrich the specification of content. Additionally, automated processing of content can be achieved if metadata is annotated. For instance, a web information system can withdraw content automatically if its expiry date is reached.[471] Content metadata is not modelled explicitly in WebML, Araneus and OO-H. However, the approaches are based on a data model or object model which potentially allows the specification of suitable metadata annotations. The approach eW3DT integrates language constructs in order to specify some metadata elements (hierarchy level, technical and organizational responsibility as well as maintenance intensity). A flexible specification of metadata, however, is not supported. Figure 2.22 summarizes the characterization of the modelling approaches.

	Criterion	Araneus	WebML	eW3DT	OO-H
General	Origin	Data Modelling	Data & Hypertext Modelling	Hypertext Modelling	Object Modelling
	Application Focus	Data-intensive Web Sites	Data-intensive Web Applications	Web Applications	Web Applications
	Level of Abstraction	Rather Conceptual	Rather Conceptual	Conceptual	Design
	Modelling Focus	Data-centric	Data-centric	User-centric	User-centric
Navigation	Link Types	Not explicitly modelled (can potentially be derived from relationships)	No (difference between operation and content link hidden from user)	Four different types	Four different types
	Link Labelling	None explicitly modelled (potentially derived from relationship name)	None	None	None
	Information Structure	None explicitly proposed but potentially all	None explicitly proposed but potentially all	None explicitly proposed but potentially all	None explicitly proposed but potentially all
Content	Content Types	No, but content data types are modelled	Five content and six operation units	Six content types (each static or dynamic)	Possibly types derived from the UML class diagram
	Metadata	Not explicitly modelled	Not explicitly modelled	Selected metadata	Not explicitly modelled

Figure 2.22: Comparison of Modelling Approaches for Web Information Systems

The modelling approaches provide comprehensive modelling concepts for the conceptual specification of web applications. However, as indicated by the term 'web application', they concentrate mostly on the specification of the technical component of the web information systems and follow a CASE approach. Especially OO-H and WebML

---

[471] Refer to Section 3.4.1 for a more detailed description of metadata and its usage in web information systems.

are clearly tailored to develop web applications with complex functionality. Thus, the type of web information system addressed by the approaches is different from the one in this thesis. They focus on commercial applications like web-shops and systems that substitute traditional applications through the usage of web technology. These systems are usually characterized by a high degree of interactivity that goes beyond navigation (application type is transactional). Additionally, all approaches are rooted in the computer science discipline which implies a certain view on the world and the task of web information system development as outlined in the previous chapters. Requirements are considered to be 'hard' facts, which have to be mapped to suitable representation forms. The approaches are concerned with the technical aspects of web information systems. It is implicitly assumed that problems like achieving a mutual understanding of the linguistic means for retrieving information take place 'outside' the modelling process. This, however, is not a deficiency. It reflects different assumptions and approaches for specifying web information systems.

To conclude the discussion, it might well be argued that all approaches provide means for modelling navigation and information structures. However, they do not elaborate on the linguistic means used for navigation in detail (information structures and link labelling). Instead of substituting other approaches, the method constructed in this thesis is complementary to other existing approaches. It focuses on an earlier stage of development and pays special regard to achieve a mutual understanding of the subject matter and navigational means to foster human information processing.

2.3 Human Information Processing

Having outlined the scientific background and foundations of web information systems, different models of human information processing can be reviewed and a conceptualization of information needs can be derived. This section aims at the derivation of a model that explains the process individuals use to satisfy their information need. In order to do so, some models of human information processing are briefly reviewed and their contribution to this goal is outlined. On the base of this overview, a model of its own is constructed depicting the position and understanding of human information processing for the purpose of this thesis. It has to be noted that the following overview is highly selective and far from complete. It basically covers those approaches frequently used in the information science community. Additionally, this overview does not elaborate on the complex issue of human information processing on a detailed level. It is mainly intended at outlining an understanding of how individuals use web information systems in order to satisfy their information needs and the problems that are entailed in this process.

2.3.1 Overview

Contributions of Communication Theory

SHANNON and WEAVER addressed the *technical* problem of information transmission from an engineering perspective. Their sender-receiver model (compare Figure 2.23) is a fundamental communication model and has found widespread use and several extensions in various research disciplines. For instance, a feedback mechanism has been integrated in order to enable participants to check whether the meaning of a message has been correctly transmitted. However, SHANNON explicitly states that they are *not* concerned with *meaning*:[472]

> Frequently the messages have *meaning*; that is they refer to or are correlated according to some system with certain physical or conceptual entities. These semantic aspects of communication are irrelevant to the engineering problem.[473]

Thus, semantical and pragmatical aspects of information are excluded by the model.[474] Likewise, the applicability of the model in literary theory is contested and, at the present time, negated.[475] Therefore, SHANNON and WEAVER's work, though seminal, applicable and useful from the engineering perspective, does *not* provide useful insights in the phenomenon of human information processing with regard to the background of this thesis.[476]

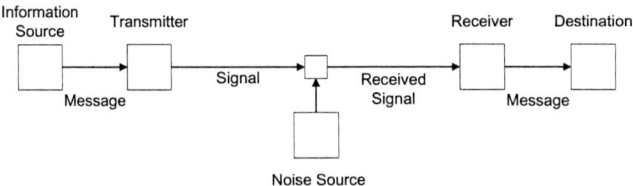

Figure 2.23: Sender-Receiver-Model (SHANNON (1949), p. 34)

---

[472] Cf. SHANNON (1948), pp. 1 (the page information refers to a reprint); SHANNON (1949), p. 49; WEAVER (1949), p. 8 and DREYFUS (1979), p. 165.
[473] SHANNON (1948), pp. 1 (page information refers to a reprint). Italics in the original.
[474] Cf. CAPURRO (1986), p. 84.
[475] Cf. AARSETH (1997), p. 58.
[476] Cf. for a similar argument CAPURRO (1986), p. 84.

Likewise, several models propose an objective view on information and human information processing.[477] For instance, STONIER argues that information exists *physically* in an objective sense and that meaning can be embodied in a non-human information processor.[478] The human brain is regarded as a complex and powerful, yet deterministic, machine that determines the meaning of information and its consequences by calculating it with an (unknown) algorithm. Thus, the phenomenon of human information processing has been reduced to the problem of finding the 'correct' algorithm. If this algorithm is found, intelligent behaviour is supposed to be implementable in artificial agents like computers. Since these assumptions contradict with the metatheoretical assumptions stated in Section 2.1, these viewpoints are neither adapted nor are they analyzed in detail.[479]

Contributions of Poppers Three Worlds Model

POPPER's three worlds model has found widespread use within the *information science*[480] discipline.[481] Although POPPER is mainly concerned with scientific knowledge acquisition and although his work is, therefore, basically of philosophical nature, the model is included in the discussion due to its popularity and widespread appliance. The notion that epistemological problems should and can be addressed by viewing them from different perspectives is central to POPPER's philosophy.[482] According to POPPER the world consists of at least three ontologically distinct sub-worlds. The first world is the physical realm of objects and states. The second is the mental realm or the world of mental states. The third world is the world of ideas in the objective sense. The second world (the realm of mental states and minds) acts as a mediator between the other worlds. There is no direct interaction between the physical world and world of objective knowledge.[483] Thus, indirect links between physical entities and theories exist.

---

[477] Compare, as a representative for this research direction, NEWELL & SIMON (1972).

[478] Compare the philosophical preface in STONIER (1997), p. 2 and the definition of meaning on page 124. Similarly STONIER (1992).

[479] The reader may refer to the references given in the works mentioned above. A critical perspective on this research direction is taken by DREYFUS.

[480] Refer to BROOKES (1980a) and INGWERSEN (1992), pp. 1–14 for an introduction to information science.

[481] POPPER (1979), p. 154. POPPER's three worlds model has been discussed and applied in the context of information science extensively. Compare, for instance, ABBOTT (1997), pp. 131 f.; COLE (1999), pp. 547 f.; BAWDEN (2002), pp. 52 f. and ABBOTT (2004), pp. 97 f. as well as the articles from BROOKES for brief introductions and discussions.

[482] Cf. POPPER (1979), pp. 153 ff. for the following.

[483] Cf. POPPER (1979), p. 155.

POPPER claims that traditional epistemology is mistaken since it is concerned with the question how *individuals* gain knowledge.[484] On the contrary, POPPER argues that the study of scientific knowledge acquisition has to be concerned with the third world respectively with knowledge in an *objective* sense.[485] According to POPPER's philosophy, knowledge in the third world is knowledge without a knowing subject and, therefore, it transcends an individual's mind.[486] Although man-made, the third world is largely autonomous implying that theories in the third world may develop a 'life' or create new problems on their own.[487] They may surpass their creators. Additionally, POPPER points out the role and importance of language for the achievement of knowledge.[488] Without appropriate language means, there can be no object for critical discussion. Therefore, epistemological questions in a scientific sense have to be concern with pieces of knowledge in the third world rather than with the study of individual processes of knowledge acquisition.

Following POPPER, the theory of understanding should be anchored in the third world and, thus, concentrate on the understanding of objective pieces of knowledge rather than on subjective understanding of a subject matter.[489] Concerning individual understanding, POPPER remarks that it can be more thoroughly described by its relation to third world objects than by mere subjective means.[490] The process of understanding consists of a sequence of different states of understanding rather than a single, unique activ-

---

[484] Cf. POPPER (1979), p. 108 and POPPER (1979), p. 225.

[485] It should be noted that the objectivity of the third world is relative in a certain sense. Knowledge embodied in the third-world is the 'best guess' or the 'best theory' that has been developed so far. Therefore, the derivation of knowledge is a historical process by which new and better theories are proposed, tested and accepted or refuted by the scientific community. Humans are prone to error and may for various reasons sabotage testing and verifying or simply refuse to accept 'better' theories. Thus, the process by which knowledge is generated is not continuous even if this issue could be judged objectively. There are several examples in human history (for instance, the Middle Ages) showing, retrospectively, a decline in human knowledge and its embodiment in the third-world. The reason for this downturn is that the 'function' that measures the superiority of a theory against another one is subjective. For instance, the 'superiority' of the Copernican model of planet movements was rejected due to ideological reasons. Thus, the superiority of a theory may be judged wrongly at a certain time for various reasons. Thus, objective knowledge does not have to be 'true' in a god-views sense. It represents knowledge which proved, on a historic level, best or most appropriate to explain phenomena.

[486] Cf. POPPER (1979), p. 109 and 111.

[487] Cf. POPPER (1979), p. 111 and particularly pp. 115–119 and 146–150.

[488] Cf. POPPER (1979), p. 120.

[489] Cf. POPPER (1979), pp. 162 f.

[490] Cf. POPPER (1979), p. 163.

ity.[491] Although the process itself is subjective, it consists of operations with third world-objects.[492] Therefore, a general schema of problem solving called the method of conjecture and refutation can be derived:[493]

$$B \rightarrow P_1 \rightarrow TT \rightarrow EE \rightarrow P_2$$

P_1 denotes the initial problem which is picked from the third world against a personal background B.[494] Particularly, the background contains a language which is crucial for the perception of a problem. The tentative theory TT is the first conjectural solution of the problem, which is examined critically and errors are pruned (error elimination EE).[495] The examination can encompass experiments, the analysis of documentary evidence or the critical reflection of the theory in comparison to competing ones. Finally, a new problem situation P_2 is reached that leads to subsequent attempts for problem solving using the same schema. Finally, a solution can be derived which may create new problems by giving deeper insights or solve several sub-problems at once.[496]

POPPER's philosophy and, in particular, his claim that knowledge can be objective and can exist independently of a knowing subject has been criticized by several authors.[497] However, this model is used extensively in the information science community which is especially concerned with theories and models of human information processing and comprehension. Although essentially objective by nature, the model is used in a variety

---

[491] Cf. POPPER (1979), p. 164.

[492] Cf. POPPER (1979), p. 164.

[493] Cf. POPPER (1979), p. 164 f. Concerning the appliance and extension of the model in the informa-
       tion science discipline compare, for instance, COLE (1999), pp. 547 f. and FORD (2004b), pp. 771 f.

[494] The concept of background is not integrated in POPPER's original model although it is mentioned in
       the text (cf. POPPER (1969), p. 164–165). Since it is used in subsequent models of this section, it is
       integrated in the problem solving schema for the sake of completeness. Moreover, the background
       concept supports the statement that a shared understanding respectively the foundation of a
       language community is crucial as noted by POPPER: "The background consists at least of a
       language, which always incorporates many theories in the very structure of its usages [...], and
       of many other theoretical assumptions [...]. It is only against a background like this that a problem
       can arise." POPPER (1969), p. 165.

[495] Usually, more than one tentative theory can be formulated or imagined for a given problem.
       Cf. POPPER (1979), p. 243.

[496] Cf. POPPER (1979), p. 165.

[497] For instance BUNGE (1974), pp. 186 f.; CAPURRO (1986), pp. 88 ff. and the critic as well as the
       references mentioned by BAWDEN (2002), pp. 53 f. BUNGE and CAPURRO argue that knowledge
       is always bound to a knowing subject respectively to the capability of being grasped by somebody
       by means of language. Thus, there can be no objective knowledge in the sense of POPPER. POP-
       PER's philosophy is rooted in the natural sciences which differs from assumptions, methods and
       approaches used in social sciences (cf. KOERTGE (1997), pp. 365 f.).

of other research 'branches' particularly subjective ones.[498]

Contributions of Hermeneutical and Cognitive Approaches

Hermeneutics and cognitive approaches are closely related concerning the general principle how information is perceived by individuals.[499] Therefore, both approaches are discussed within one section. As outlined in Section 2.1, interpretivistic research approaches are closely related to the philosophical discipline of hermeneutics.[500]

CAPURRO presents a hermeneutical approach to information retrieval.[501] Particularly, CAPURRO investigates the phenomenon of information in professional communities.[502] CAPURRO's approach is founded on three assumptions which constitute hermeneutics of information in conjunction.[503] Firstly, professionals are coexisting in professional communities in which information exchange takes place. CAPURRO does explicitly *not* differentiate between an individual and a 'realm' of information.[504] Both, the individual and its environment are inseparable. Secondly, subjects are disclosing the world. Subjects are problems or problem domains rather than categories of science. Most problems are interdisciplinary. The information in a problem domain is called 'Fachinformation',

---

[498]   Cf., for instance, ABBOTT (1997); ABBOTT (1999); ABBOTT (2004); FORD (2004b). This incompatibility issue of applying an objective theory to subjective approaches, however, is usually not addressed. POPPER's work has been proposed as a foundation for information science by BROOKES (cf. BROOKES (1980a); BROOKES (1980b); BROOKES (1980c) and BROOKES (1981)). BROOKESs articles are considered to be seminal for the information science community and may explain the prominent stance of POPPER's work. It should be noted that the figure depicting POPPER's worlds model is inaccurate since the circles are overlapping (cf. BROOKES (1980a), p. 127). As POPPER points out, however, the first and the third world do not interact directly.

[499]   INGWERSEN discusses similarities and differences of hermeneutics and cognitive approaches and concludes that they share essential concepts but differ by the degree of 'individuality' (cf. INGWERSEN (1992), pp. 41–47).

[500]   According to KLEIN & MYERS, the hermeneutic spiral is the fundamental principle for interpretive research. They call it a 'meta-principle' (KLEIN & MYERS (1999), p. 71).

[501]   Cf. CAPURRO (1986).

[502]   CAPURRO uses the German term *Fachinformation*. It can be roughly translated with 'information related to specific subject' which is cumbersome to write as well as to read. Thus, the more generic form information is used in to following synopsis of CAPURRO's approach. Likewise, CAPURRO uses the prefix 'Fach' for other concepts, for instance, 'Fachgebiet' (subject), 'Fachkommunikation' (communication related to a specific subject), 'Fachleute' (professionals or specialists) and 'Fachgemeinschaft' (professional community). CAPURRO focuses on a specific type of information and a specific 'setting' in which information exchange takes place.

[503]   Cf. CAPURRO (1986), pp. 119 f. for the following.

[504]   This view is the main reason why CAPURRO, following BUNGE, rejects POPPER's philosophy as a 'Platonic fantasy' (cf. CAPURRO (1986), p. 91).

that is, information related to a community respectively to a subject. The information
is encoded in a technical terminology.[505] The ability to understand the technical terminology constitutes the foreknowledge of a specialist and differentiates him or her from
a layman.[506] Thus, the body of knowledge for a specific subject is a combination of a
professional community and a language rather than an autonomous realm of knowledge
in POPPER's sense.[507] Thirdly, communication related to specific subject takes place in
the professional community. Communication includes speech as well as documents or
images.

CAPURRO investigates information retrieval from this hermeneutical perspective.
Concerning classification, CAPURRO notes the impossibility of representing information contents in hierarchical structures.[508] The assignment of information changes over
time or has to be classified differently when viewed from different perspectives. Moreover, a classification schema represents and imposes a *single* view of *objectified pre-
understanding*. Similarly, indexing is problematic.[509]

According to MEY, cognitive science deals with the study of knowledge, its nature,
representation and handling.[510] Thus, cognitive science is the application of cognitive
approaches respectively their consequences to science.[511] Following MEY, the development of the cognitive view on information processing can be seen as a result of the
limitations of classical models of information processing. According to MEY

> the central point of the cognitive view is, that *any* such *information process-
> ing*, whether perceptual (such as perceiving an object) or symbolic (such as
> understanding a sentence) *is mediated* by a *system of categories or concepts*

---

[505] Cf. CAPURRO (1986), p. 128.

[506] Cf. CAPURRO (1986), p. 130.

[507] Cf. CAPURRO (1986), p. 130.

[508] Cf. CAPURRO (1986), pp. 146 f. ABBOTT investigates the problem of classification with regard
to a different background (POPPER's three-worlds model) and draws the same conclusion (cf. AB-
BOTT (2004), p. 100). The problem is seen differently, for example, by LANCASTER who adopts a
rather pragmatic approach (cf. LANCASTER (1991), pp. 10 f.).

[509] Cf. CAPURRO (1986), pp. 151–161. CAPURRO discusses some approaches that were intended to
provide more efficient and accurate indexing algorithms. For a comprehensive overview of indexing
compare LANCASTER (1991).

[510] Cf. MEY (1982), p. 3. Similarly MEY (1980), pp. 48 ff. It should be noted that MEY does not
position himself clearly concerning metatheoretical assumptions nor is his work intended to do
so. He discusses positivistic approaches as well as cognitive ones, which are subjective by nature
(compare the next quote). He aims mainly at explaining the development of the cognitive view
and its consequences for science in general. Cf. FORD (2004a) for a discussion of objectivity versus
subjectivity in information science.

[511] Cf. MEY (1982), p. 3.

which for the information processor constitutes a *representation* or a *model* of his *world*.[512]

Each individual has a multiplicity of world views or models which represent systems of concepts that mediate every information perception.[513] The fact that users *actively* shape what they perceive rather than processing externally given input passively, is central to the cognitive view on information processing.[514] As a consequence, human information processing entails many uncertainties and unpredictabilities and there are no means that can assess the question whether the intended meaning is actually conveyed or not.[515] The concept of world view corresponds to the hermeneutical concept of pre-understanding which guides and determines the interpretation of a document or a particular situation. World models are changed unknowingly and frequently. As a result, different phenomena are perceived or remembered depending on the requirements of the actual situation. As a consequence for the purpose at hand, an individual may search for the same piece of information in the same problem situation differently, depending on his or her actual 'world view'. Likewise, the same piece of information can be interpreted differently. Thus, neither information needs nor the means to satisfy them can be encoded statically and user independently in an application system. On the other hand, phenomena may be perceived which are not existent like a missing word in a sentence.[516] Likewise, other visual stimuli are sometimes ignored.[517]

Individual patterns used to organize and process information which are referred to as *cognitive styles* are the consequence of the cognitive view of human information processing.[518] Several experiments on information processing were conducted yielding different cognitive styles for groups of individuals that were faced with the same problem situation. As SADLER-SMITH points out, cognitive styles are likely to influence the form and content of individual's mental models:[519]

> For example, individuals with a wholist style may have global and inclusive mental
> models with more nonhierarchical interlinkages than analytic individuals (akin

---

[512] MEY (1982), 4. Italics in the original.

[513] Cf. MEY (1982), p. 20. For a comprehensive treatment of information processing strategies and cognitive styles compare also RASMUSSEN, PEJTERSEN & GOODSTEIN (1994), pp. 70 f.

[514] Cf. INGWERSEN (1996), p. 5. Obviously, the notion of an active information recipient corresponds to understanding of language as outlined in Section 2.1.

[515] Cf. INGWERSEN (1996), p. 8.

[516] Cf. MEY (1982), pp. 182 f.

[517] Cf. MEY (1982), p. 184.

[518] Cf. DRIVER (2000), p. 41.

[519] Cf. SADLER-SMITH (2000), p. 202.

to a "web" form). Conversely, analytics are more likely to have mental models characterized by linear and logically consistent hierarchical relationships (akin to a "tree" form). Verbalizers' mental models are likely to be replete with verbal and semantic associations, whereas imagers are more likely to have mental models rich in pictorial and graphical information. The form and content of an individual's mental models may influence the ways in which others interpret and are able to understand them. When different individuals have models that are congruent in form and content the process of surfacing and sharing models may be more effective than if the individual' mental models are incongruent (perhaps as a result of differences in style).[520]

Obviously, these differences in cognitive style as described in the quote are closely related to the purpose at hand. Information structures in a web information system may or may not correspond to mental models of individuals. While some may view a single hierarchy that organizes the information space as sufficient, others may not. It seems reasonable to assume that adaptive and flexible information structures which support different types of mental models and, therefore, different preferences for information processing are likely to have a positive influence on an individual's ability to retrieve the desired piece of information.[521] INGWERSEN stresses the relevance of cognitive approaches for information science and, in particular, information retrieval:

> The task of IR is to bring cognitive structures of authors, system designers and indexers into accord with those of the information worker [intermediary mechanism] and the user, in order to cope with the actual information need (HARBO, INGWERSEN & TIMMERMANN (1977)).[522]

The modelling method of this thesis is intended to provide operational means for this task. It is supposed to explicate mental structures in order to facilitate the achievement of a mutual understanding about their meaning and usefulness.

---

[520] SADLER-SMITH (2000), pp. 203–204. Concerning the dimensions (wholist vs. analytic and verbal vs. pictoral) of cognitive style see RIDING (2000), pp. 315 f.

[521] Depending on the situation, however, it can be sensible to confront individuals with 'unsuitable' information structures in order to initiate learning processes. Refer, for instance, to SADLER-SMITH (2000), p. 190. Concerning this matching hypotheses compare also HAYES & ALLINSON (1996).

[522] INGWERSEN (1992), p. 18. Italics in the original. References in quote adapted to the format used in this thesis and integrated in the bibliography.

2.3.2 Discussion and Model Construction

The discussion provides several insights into human information processing that can be used to create a new model depicting relevant aspects for the purpose at hand. As already stated in the background section, each interpretative act is essentially subjective by nature and can, therefore, not be planned, anticipated or calculated. Human information processing and its mediation by cognitive models is, essentially, unpredictable and beyond the scope of scientific investigation. Cognitive models are shaped by episodic, semantic and emotional experiences in the past and are, in this sense, socially self-constructed.[523] Moreover, they change dynamically. Thus, human information processing is significantly different from information processing by machines or agents.[524]

POPPER's Three Worlds Model is not directly applicable for the purpose at hand. The basic assumptions are different than the ones outlined in Section 2.1. Thus, although the model is applied in the information science community extensively, it is not used in its 'pure' form in this thesis. However, the general knowledge acquisition process described by POPPER is not affected by incompatible metatheoretical assumptions. Knowledge acquisition is an iterative process. For each given problem or information need, several conjectures are created and assessed by an individual. A reformulation of the information need or the problem can be the result of the assessment. Thus, information needs as well as the original problem definition are not static. They are subject to changes caused by newly acquired knowledge.

Hermeneutical and cognitive approaches provide valuable insights into the nature of human information processing. Each act of perception is based on a pre-understanding (respectively world view) that influences which phenomena are perceived and how. Each act of perception alters the pre-understanding and can, therefore, lead to a different interpretation of the original information. Cognitive science suggests that pre-understanding is not a static concept. Instead, each individual possesses a multiplicity of pre-understandings (world-views) that mediates information perception. Structures or systems that are used to systematize information (information structures like indexes, hierarchies or other classification schemas) represent an objectified pre-understanding which is, in case of web information systems, defined by the author of a piece of information or the information system developer.[525] This objectified pre-understanding does

---

[523]   Cf. INGWERSEN (1996), p. 6.

[524]   Cf. INGWERSEN (1996), 7. INGWERSEN points out that "in case of a machine as recipient the problem space and state of uncertainty may indeed, exists, but it's cognitive state is predefined and fundamentally static, and similar comments apply in the cases of neural networks or other seemingly dynamic structures" (INGWERSEN (1996), p. 7).

[525]   Information structures can be defined dynamically, that is, elements of hierarchies can be changed,

not necessarily correspond to an individual's pre-understanding (world view) which can lead to problems during the information retrieval process since pieces of information are organized differently than expected by the information seeker. Cognitive styles also influence the preferred method for navigation in web information systems.[526] While some users (so called 'holists') prefer concept maps that depict the overall organization of information, others ('serialists') prefer key word indexes that give access to particular pieces of information.[527]

In order to derive a model explaining the processes and problems entailed in human information processing, the term information need needs some clarification. As indicated in the discussion of web information systems, *information needs* can be rather specific (well-defined) or general/vague (ill-defined). Following INGWERSEN, the concept of information need can be conjoined with the stability of a user's cognitive state. Both dimension yield four different forms of information needs (compare Figure 2.24).[528]

		Characterization of Information Need	
		Well-defined	**Ill-defined**
Characterization of Cognitive State — **Stable**	1	**Rich, stable, cognitive state** Conceptual `throwness' Limited uncertainty Topical relevance assessment: yes Curiosity: low Confined navigation	4 — **Weak, stable, cognitive state** Conceptual `breakdown' High uncertainty Topical relevance assessment: no Curiosity: low Marching on the spot (dead ends)
Variable	2	**Rich, variable, cognitive state** Conceptual `throwness' Controlled uncertainty Topical relevance assessment: yes Curiosity: high Exploratory navigation	3 — **Weak, variable, cognitive state** Conceptual `breakdown' High uncertainty Topical relevance assessment: no Curiosity: high Browsing

Figure 2.24: Conceptualization of Information Need (Adapted from INGWERSEN (1996), p. 15)

---

deleted or added during run-time (adaption of navigation structures). Each new 'term' can potentially be used to classify new (or old) pieces of information.

[526] Cf. FORD (2000), p. 548. COLE & LEIDE conducted a case that assessed the usage of a user's mental model (cf. COLE & LEIDE (2003)).

[527] Cf. FORD (2000), p. 548. The terms 'holists' and 'serialists' refer to general cognitive styles. This classification of information processing strategies has been introduced by PASK. In general, 'holists' apply a 'broad' search strategy and work on several subject matters at once, whereas 'serialists' seek and use information in a more serial manner. Refer to PASK (1975) for a comprehensive discussion of these different cognitive styles and the cybernetic communication theory that serves as a basis for his work. Overviews of the concept can be found in SCOTT (2001a) and SCOTT (2001b). Refer to FORD (2004b) for an application of this theory for the domain of information retrieval.

[528] Cf. INGWERSEN (1996), pp. 14 f.

The cognitive state of a user can be stable or variable during the information retrieval process. If it is variable, the background and principles by which information is perceived and assessed changes during the process. Thus, the same piece of information may be interpreted differently. The information need forms two and three (compare Figure 2.24) are typical of problem situations requiring a high degree of creativity (for instance 'inventing a new product' or 'brainstorming'). Thus, information seeking behaviour is undirected and follows a trial-and-error approach (exploratory navigation or browsing).

Having outlined models of human information processing and a conceptualization of information need, a model that serves as an illustration of the processes entailed in human information processing can be constructed. The model outlines the process of human information processing and the means that can be used to facilitate it. Special regard is given to navigational means as a tool to foster the information perception process.

The model can be subdivided into a *static* and a *dynamic* component. The static model depicts the elements and phenomena involved in human information processing (compare Figure 2.25 for the following). An *information seeker* has a multiplicity of world views (indicated by rectangle-, circle- and triangle-systems in Figure 2.25). Each information processing takes place with regard to a particular pre-understanding (world view) which may or may not be stable during the retrieval process (stability of cognitive state). Likewise, an *information provider* has world-views that determine and mediate his or her provision of information. For instance, depending on his or her background, an author may or may not decide to publish an article in an intra-organizational knowledge portal. The 'world views' of seeker and provider will usually not 'fit', which results in differences of information perception and misunderstandings. The *information structure* (the hierarchy ABCD in Figure 2.25) organizes the pieces of information (*documents*) that are stored in the system. This structure represents an 'objectified pre-understanding' in CAPURRO's sense. The way words are used and organized in this structure already implies a particular 'world view' (pre-understanding). The information structure represents the information seeker's means by which information can be retrieved. In case of web information systems, the usage of information structures is called *navigation* (in this case to traverse the hierarchy). The act of navigation consists of a series of 'queries' that are constructed by simple point-and-click operations on the elements of the information structure. However, this is *not* identical to 'normal' searches on the Web with search engines, since the elements of the information structure are explicated. It is well documented that users are unable to formulate 'correct' search queries for their particular information need, especially if the information need is vague and unclear. In this regard, the information structure represents a *set of pre-formulated* queries which may guide users into the right direction.[529] Thus, it is obvious that the *linguistic means* as they are *embodied* in the *information structure* have to be constructed in terms of a *mutual understanding* if *meaningful* information exchange should be facilitated by the information system.

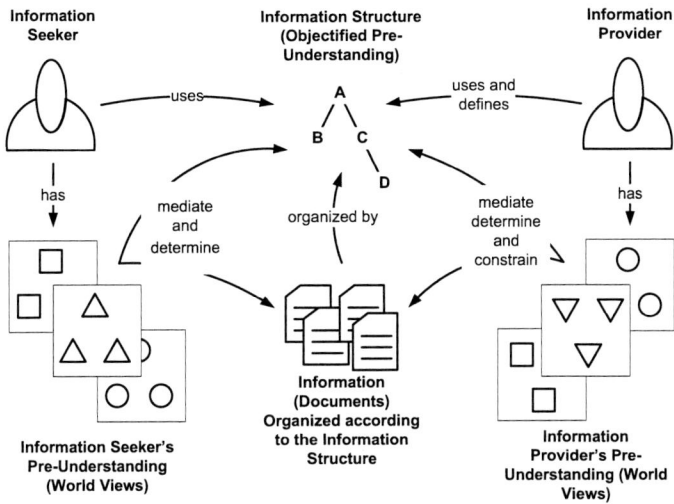

Figure 2.25: Human Information Processing (Static Model)

The *dynamic* model of human information processing focuses on the process that takes place if a user approaches an information system in order to satisfy a specific information need (compare Figure 2.26 for the following).[530] *Information needs* arise due to *problem situations.* The perception of a problem and the information need is mediated by the users' *'world view'.* Basing the search on his or her perception of the situation, the user formulates a *tentative theory* ($TentativeTheory^1$ in Figure 2.26) and navigates the information space in order to retrieve pieces of information that are associated with the term the tentative theory represents (in this case the term A). The tentative theory represents the user's guess how his or her information need can be satisfied. Information structures (navigational means) are viewed as linguistic means allowing a user to formulate tentative theories that are supposed to solve his or her problem. Technically, each tentative

---

[529] If the information structures are properly defined, users should be able to anticipate the information content behind a link.

[530] Only the processes entailed in information retrieval are discussed. A detailed investigation of the author's view on the system is not necessary for the purpose at hand.

theory corresponds to a search term that yields a specific set of documents from the information space. The information system 'processes' the query by compiling a *result set* that contains all documents associated with the classification term A (in this simple example two documents are retrieved). The interpretation of this potential solution alters the world view (pre-understanding) of the information seeker in a hermeneutic sense (indicated by changes in the world views). In case the information need of the user is not satisfied by the first result set, the user reformulates his or her information need on the base of a 'higher' level of understanding which reflects the learning process induced by the interpretation of the result set (in this case $InformationNeed^2$). Of course, it might well be that the user has a 'lower' level of understanding, if he or she has been directed in the 'wrong' direction by the first result set. The information need may be refined (extending the 'query' by adding new classification terms) or it may be reformulated. The $TentativeTheory^2$ is processed by the information system and the corresponding result is reinterpreted by the user which results in an altered pre-understanding. This process is iterated until the user has satisfied his or her personal information need or until he or she thinks that the information need is satisfied. At any given time a user may dismiss his or her tentative theory, for instance, if the information retrieval has altered his or her information need. Such situations are typical of vague problems. During the information retrieval process, the user begins to understand his or her problem, which may even render the problem different. Thus, neither the information need nor the original problem are necessarily static during the information retrieval process. The *process* of information retrieval in *web information systems* can be interpreted as a sequence of *interactions* by which tentative theories ('queries') are generated by the user. The perception of the *problem situation*, the construction of an *information need* as well as the *interpretation of a result set* is mediated and determined by a user's *'world view'* (pre-understanding). The information retrieval process is ultimately *constrained* and *determined* by *means of language* since the documents as well as the information structure are *linguistic artefacts*.

Following COLE, information systems providing this functionality are called 'enabling' information retrieval systems. An 'enabling' information retrieval "[...]'stimulates' the user's 'grasping' for a higher level of understanding of the problem, task or information need that brought the users to the IR system in the first place"[531]. When applied to the purpose at hand, the information structures defined by conceptual models are supposed to enable a user's grasping of the information space and the documents embedded in it.

---

[531]   COLE (1999), p. 545. Quotation marks adapted. Some parts of the sentence are left out in order to improve readability.

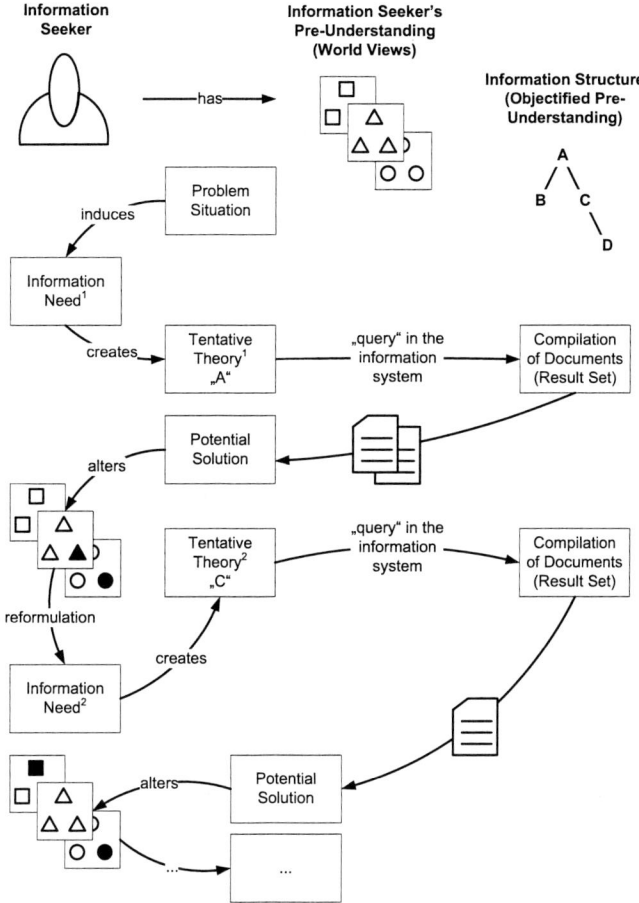

Figure 2.26: Human Information Processing (Dynamic Model) (Adapted with major changes from FORD (2004b), p. 774)

It is a basic premise of this thesis that a suitable definition of the navigational means can improve user's ability to retrieve information.

2.4 Consequences & Conclusions

This chapter comprises a discussion of issues influencing the web information system development process as well as characterizing web information systems and their usage. This chapter aims at laying the foundation of an understanding which motivates the construction of the conceptual modelling approach in the following chapter. The method is supposed to facilitate the development process and to provide suitable navigational means for human information processing outlined in this chapter. The discussion can be summarized as follows:

- Information system development is a social as well as technical activity: the development process consists of a complex and complicated set of activities that comprise social as well as technical aspects. Information system developers facilitate the creation of a mutual understanding within the development group by using linguistic artefacts like conceptual models.

- Role of language: language plays a crucial role during the development and the usage of a web information system. The subjective nature of language determines and mediates the perception of reality and users' ability to retrieve the desired information. Since information structures are basically linguistic artefacts, it is sensible to postulate that they have to be 'engineered' carefully in order to provide efficient and effective means for information retrieval.

- Characteristics of web information systems: web information systems are social as well as technical systems. They are supposed to facilitate a meaningful information exchange. They are based on web technology and are characterized by a distinct concept of information access (associative linking) which is derived from the hypertext concept.

- Conceptual modelling: conceptual modelling serves as a tool for creating mutual understandings of the development process, the methods used and the objectives that are to be achieved. Essentially, conceptual models are linguistic artefacts and, therefore, subject to the same limitations like natural language. Conceptual models are depicted by using an artificial language: a conceptual modelling method.

- Modelling approaches for web information systems: over the years, several conceptual modelling methods providing suitable means for the development process have been proposed. However, as the brief discussion has outlined, the methods focus on other aspects of the development process.

- Human information processing: due to its vagueness and complex nature, human information processing cannot be described easily or holistically. Moreover, it seems unsuitable to equate human information processing with mechanical information processing. It is crucial to acknowledge the subjective and vague nature of human information processing. As a consequence, it is impossible to 'define' information needs. Instead, suitable means have to be provided to facilitate an individual's sense-making activity. It can be argued that suitable information structures (navigation) can potentially improve human information processing and, therefore, foster the sense-making process.

Subsequently, a conceptual modelling method is proposed facilitating the development process in terms of mutual understanding within the development group. Special regard is given to the explication of the linguistic means that are used for navigation.

Chapter 3

Method Construction

3.1 Preliminary Remarks, Metalanguage and Conventions

Entity Relationship Modelling as a Metalanguage

In order to illustrate and describe the modelling language that is constructed in the following sections, a brief introduction in the metalanguage used is necessary.[1] The usage of a semi-formal metalanguage enables a more detailed and precise introduction of concepts than plain English. The Entity Relationship Modelling (ERM) language proposed by CHEN in 1976 is one of the most popular and well-known modelling languages.[2] Originally, it was used for modelling data structures that can be implemented using relational database systems. Due to its simplicity as well as expressive power it became the lingua franca of database design. Moreover, it has been used frequently as a standard language for describing architectures and application systems.[3] Additionally, it was the origin of several dialects that extend the modelling technique or vary its representation form.[4]

Besides the modelling of data structures for implementation purposes, the ERM lan-

---

[1] Cf. SOWA (1999), p. 20 for a brief description of the term metalanguage.

[2] Cf. CHEN (1976).

[3] For instance, the architecture for integrated information systems (ARIS) (SCHEER (1992)) or the reference model for retailing respectively wholesaling information systems 'Handels-H' (BECKER & SCHÜTTE (2004)).

[4] For instance, SINZ has proposed the structured Entity Relationship Modelling language (SINZ (1988)) which has been the basis for the development of the modelling dialect used by SAP, one of the largest ERP-software producers. An overview of modelling techniques based on the ER model is given in (FERSTL & SINZ (2001) and KNACKSTEDT (2004), Footnote 475. The dialect used in this thesis has been proposed by SCHEER (cf. SCHEER (1992), pp. 52 ff.; Cf. SCHEER (1999), pp. 70 ff.).

guage has been established as a *de facto* standard for modelling in general. In particular, it can be used as a metalanguage for describing modelling languages or complex sets of concepts and their relations.[5] Therefore, entities and relations depicted by an ERM are linguistic concepts or phenomena rather than data structures designed for storing information in a relational database. Although the expressive power of the ERM language is restricted, it is more precise and clear for describing concepts than plain English.

An ER model contains entities (depicted by rectangles) and relationships (symbol: rhombus) between these entities.[6] Entities represent a concept that resembles a set of phenomena that are considered to be similar in the given context. Relationships link entities or one entity with itself. They represent relations between the participating entities. Hierarchies and structures are depicted by using a relationship that links an entity to itself (recursion). In addition to the traditional ERM language, reinterpreted relationships are introduced which are depicted by a rectangle that contains a rhombus. A reinterpreted relationship represents an object which is a composition of (at least) two other objects. The resulting object can be used as an entity afterwards. Only those objects which are attached to the rhombus constitute the new object.[7]

Moreover, the ERM languages provides constructs that depict generalization respectively specialization (symbol: triangle).[8] A specialization can be specified whether it is disjoint or non-disjoint and total or partial. The categorization of the specialization is depicted by an entry of the form [d|n,t|p] in the triangle. Attributes are depicted by ovals that are linked to an entity.[9] Cardinalities depict the number of entities that have to or can join the relation. They are denoted with min-max-cardinalities. A cardinality

---

[5]   The ERM language has been used by HOLTEN in order to illustrate the concepts of the modelling language MetaMIS and subsequent variants and extension of the technique (cf. HOLTEN (1999) and the references cited in Footnote 28). Likewise, it has been used by ROSEMANN & GREEN for building a metamodel of the Bunge-Wand-Weber ontology (cf. ROSEMANN & GREEN (2002), pp. 75 ff.). This kind of 'dual' usage (implementation models and meta modelling) of the ERM language has also been noted by SCHEER (cf. SCHEER (1992), p. 52).

[6]   Since the ER modelling language is well-known, only a brief overview of the language is given. A more detailed introduction can be found in CHEN (1976); OLLE (1983), pp. 35 ff.; VOSSEN (1999), pp. 80 ff.; BECKER & SCHÜTTE (2004), pp. 85 f.; SPECK (2001), pp. 148 ff. and the references that are cited in Footnote 4 in this chapter. HOLTEN and KNACKSTEDT also use the ERM as a metalanguage and provide brief introductions (HOLTEN (1999), pp. 23 ff. and KNACKSTEDT (2004), pp. 139 ff.) as well.

[7]   For a more detailed description of reinterpretation of relationships refer to SCHEER (1999), pp. 74 f.

[8]   The concept of specialization is always double-sided – the difference depends on the direction in which it is read. One entity is specialized into one or more other entities. These entities are generalized into one entity

[9]   Attributes are not used in the following models.

of 1,n means that each entity has to be related to the other entity at least once or multiple times.[10] It is sometimes necessary to annotate restrictions that cannot be expressed by using the language constructs provided by the ERM language. In this case, textual annotations are given in the metamodel (symbol: text box). The modelling language ERM can be conceptualized by itself (Figure 3.1).

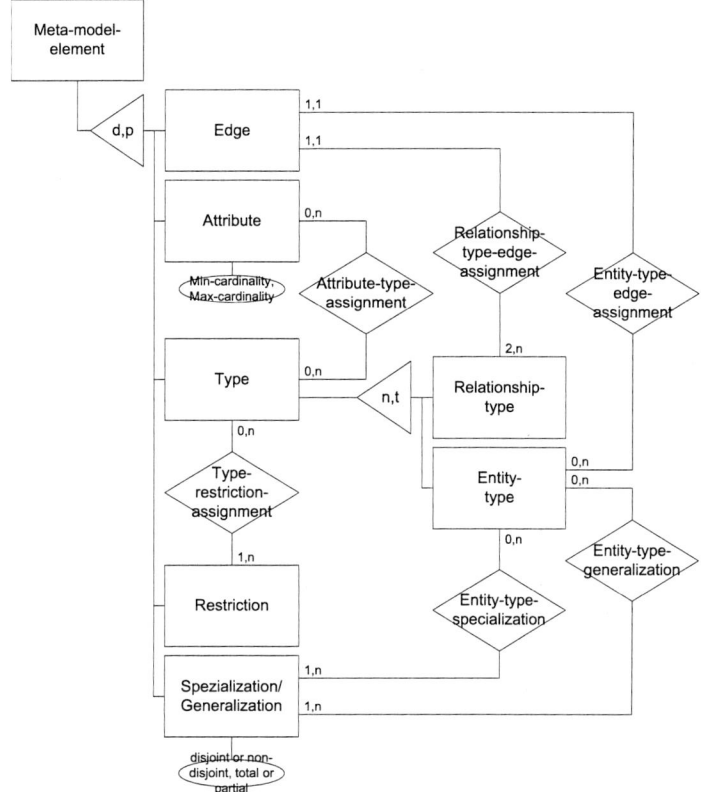

Figure 3.1: Entity Relationship Modelling Language (Meta Meta Level) (Cf. KNACK-
            STEDT (2004), p. 140)

In general, a modelling language seeks to provide linguistic means by which information system developers can describe the complex environment and requirements in cooperation with users, project stakeholder and other project team members. Following the logical propaedeutic as described in Section 2.1.3, the linguistic means by which people communicate have to be introduced precisely and well-defined in order to ensure a

---

[10]   Cf. KNACKSTEDT (2004), p. 139.

consistent and correct interpretation by all participants. In order to achieve this common understanding of concepts, the ERM language is used as a metalanguage in conjunction with descriptions of the concepts in plain English. Therefore, the expressiveness and flexibility of plain English is combined with a more formal and precise grammar.

Having specified the languages to be used, it is necessary to point out the method that is used in order to identify and create concepts. That is how concepts are identified in the focal domain and how these concepts are represented respectively built in the conceptualization. Following the method engineering approach proposed by HOLTEN, the object type method by WEDEKIND can be used in order to identify and create concepts.[11] WEDEKIND proposes the object type method in order to overcome deficiencies of traditional database engineering. According to WEDEKIND inappropriate meta-theoretical assumptions in the computer science community cause implementation problems.[12] WEDEKIND argues that data models have to be created by a systematical, language-critical reconstruction of an issue they depict and the purpose they are designed for. Although the metamodels in this chapter are not implementation models, the mechanism by which their applicability and validity can be ensured remains the same. The issue and subject of research is a conceptual modelling approach enabling information system developers to design information system that allow humanly, associative information processing. The modelling approach, which is a language itself, is true (in other terms appropriate, correct and functional with regard to the focal domain) if a language community achieves an agreement upon it. In order to do so, the linguistic means that induced the development of the approach are to be constructed language-critically and systematically. The language-critic approach and the object type method are the means used for this purpose in this thesis. The representation of the

---

[11]   Like the ERM language, the object type method was originally designed for the conceptual modelling of relational data models. However, the method is a general approach and not limited to database design. For details on the object type method compare WEDEKIND (1981).

[12]   Cf. WEDEKIND (1981), pp. 34 f. WEDEKIND notes that the computer science community has its roots in the logical empiricism which presupposes that truth about an issue can be achieved by mere observation. In contrast to this, WEDEKIND, following the interpretivistic paradigm and the logical propaedeutic from KAMLAH & LORENZEN, argues that a systematic reconstruction of appropriate language means has to precede the achievement of truth about an issue. From a interpretivists's point of view, the act of perceiving the world is elusively and subjectively since perception is a construction of an individual. Thus, truth cannot be achieved at once by observation. The achievement of truth is rather a process in which members of a language community agree upon an issue and truth by its systematic reconstruction through language. They obtain truth if they achieve an agreement about the issue respectively its representation. For a more detailed discussion of this issue, compare Section 2.1.

reconstruction is accomplished by plain text descriptions and ER models.

Moreover, the object type approach aligns the usage of the ERM language with the logical propaedeutic since it contains basic linguistic actions which can be represented by using the ERM language. Thus, this method combination can be used to achieve a profound introduction of concepts and phenomena that constitute the modelling technique on a conceptual level.[13] For instance, web information systems are usually built in order to display content respectively data. Therefore, there is a phenomenon (in this case content) in the focal domain that is important for the specification of web information systems. Thus, information system developers must have a corresponding concept in a modelling technique which allows to depict that phenomenon. However, it is usually not necessary to model all contents of a web information system. Hence, a concept 'Content' can be introduced by subsumption acting as a representation for all Contents on instance level.[14] Since Content is a complex thing in itself it is described in plain English as well as conceptualized using the ERM language. The language construct 'entity' in the ERM language stands for the linguistic action of subsumption. Thus, the real world phenomenon content is conceptualized as an entity 'Content' which subsumes all contents on instance level.[15] The appliance and mapping of linguistic actions to elements of the ERM language is illustrated in Table 3.1. Additional design principles which cannot be directly represented by the ERM language are enforced by naming conventions in the following Section.

Conventions: Metalanguage

In order to introduce a sound terminology for the modelling method, it is necessary to differentiate between language concepts and natural language. Thus, the following naming conventions are used in order to ensure a consistent naming and addressing of concepts in the metamodels and the text. Entitytypes are named in singular and the first letter is capitalized (for instance, Content). If the name contains more than one term, they are concatenated by a hyphen and subsequent terms begin with a lower case letter (Content-relation). If one term is an adjective (for instance, Atomic Element) no hyphen

---

[13]   It is important to note that this method combination is used in order to specify the conceptual language aspect. The representational aspect is not the focus of both methods. Compare Section 2.2.6 for a differentiation of both aspects of modelling languages.

[14]   The term Content is intentionally capitalized in the following since the concept Content is addressed with it. Refer to Section 3.1 for details on naming conventions.

[15]   Note that this example is not aligned with the following conceptualization which formalizes Content differently. It is meant to illustrate the usage of the object type method and corresponding conceptualization with the ERM language.

Linguistic Action	Description	Example
Subsumption	Subsumption classifies one or more objects that are considered to be equal in the given context (typecasting of objects). Depicted by the entity symbol (rectangle).	
Subordination	Subordination characterizes entities that are related by a generalization/specialization relationship like those known from object orientation (a mammal is a special animal, animal is the general term). Symbol: Triangle.	
Composition (Aggregation)	Composition allows the creation of new entities (objects) by combining existing ones. The originating object is dependent on the constituting objects. Symbol: Rhombus.	
Composition (Reinterpretation)	Reinterpretation of relationships allows the aggregation of entities and the reuse of the resulting construct as a new entity. Symbol: Rectangle-Rhombus.	
Hierarchy and Relation (Structure)	Recursions are used to depict hierarchies or structures (depending on the cardinalities) of objects. Symbol: Self-reflective relationship (rhombus).	
Dependency	An entity is dependent on another one. Depicted by min-max-cardinalities. A minimum cardinality of 1 indicates existential relationship.	

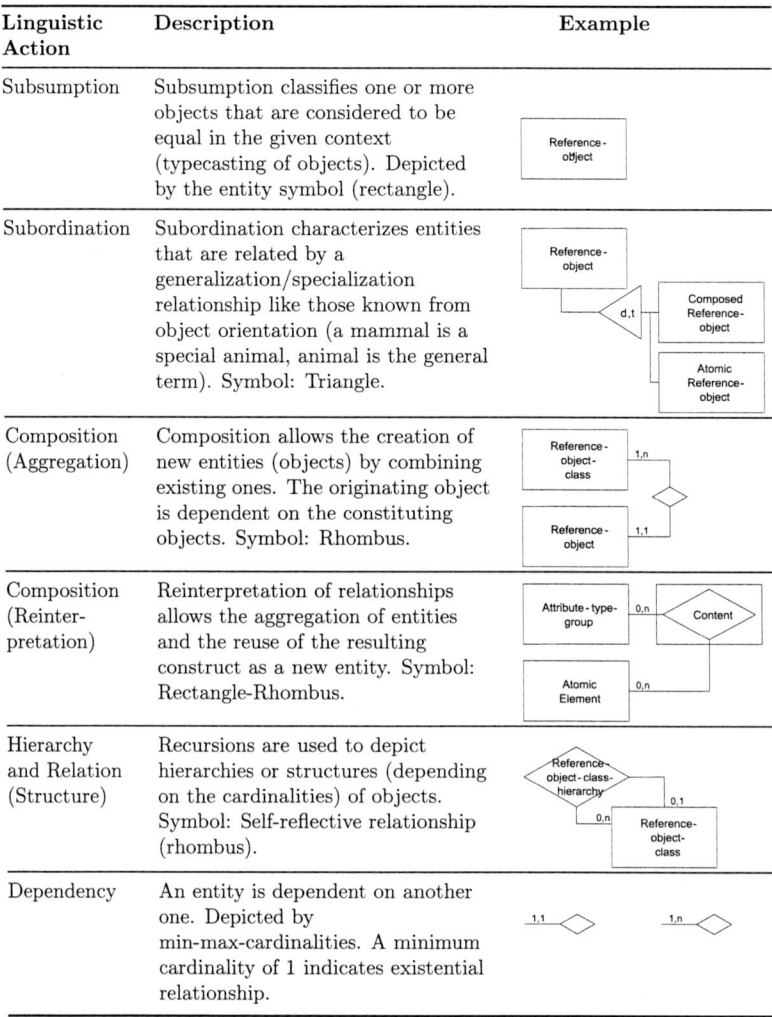

Table 3.1: Linguistic Actions and ER Models (Cf. HOLTEN (1999), pp. 23 ff.)

is used and the adjective is capitalized as well. Relationshiptypes are not named if they are trivial (for instance, the relationship between Attribute-type and Attribute-type-group) and depicted by a small rhombus.[16] In case the relationshiptype represents an

---

[16]   Unnamed relationshiptypes represent the linguistic statement 'X-Y-assignment' where X and Y represent the participating entitytypes. The naming of trivial relationships does not provide additional information and is omitted due to readability and clarity reasons.

important concept of the modelling technique that cannot be derived directly from the metamodel it may be named according to the conventions that apply to entitytypes. Occasionally, a reinterpreted relationship type is named in a short form (like P-PS-ass. for Property-Property-system assignment) containing the abbreviations of the participating entitytypes and the short form 'ass.' for assignment. This is particularly necessary if the relationship is reinterpreted and the tuple it represents constitutes a new concept. Abbreviations are ordered alphabetically if more than one is used in a name. They are derived by the first letters of the words in the name of a concept. Parentheses around cardinalities are omitted since they do not carry meaning and decrease readability.

Moreover, the conceptualization uses the following suffixes in order to indicate common principles that are used for building concepts. These principles cannot be represented by the ER modelling grammar graphically. The concepts of composition can be subdivided into the following design principles:

- Class: a class indicates a type-instance-relationship. A class represents a common concept instantiated by objects. All objects of one class share a common set of properties. The concept is well-known from object orientation. A (static) class description describes the general structure and behaviour of all objects that are instantiated during run time. Although the differentiation between run-time and design-time does not apply to the conceptualization, the general principle of the object-class-relation is the same.

- Group: in contrast to a class, the assembling of objects in a group does not imply a type-instance-relation or any other kind of meaningful composition. Grouping is a general concept of building supersets of objects.

- System: the assembling of objects in systems indicates that the structural composition of the objects implies meaning and is part of the phenomenon the system represents. Thus, a set of objects is ordered in a meaningful manner.

Additionally, the conceptualization uses the principle of trimming compositions. Accordingly, a subset of a composition is being defined provided it comprises only a portion of the objects which have been assembled within one concept. In order to indicate this, the keyword 'scope' is used in the ER models. It is important to note that the structural composition of the set that is being trimmed remains unchanged when scopes are build.

These naming conventions are also used in the text in order to ensure a sound differentiation between concepts of the modelling technique and ordinary language.[17] Abbreviations for language constructs (like ATG for Attribute-type-group) are rarely used

---

[17]   Some terms (like content and attributes) represent elements of the modelling method as well as

because they decrease readability of the text. In relationships, however, or in case the term becomes to long they are used (Refer to chapter Abbreviations for explanations). Sometimes it is necessary to use a language concept that has not yet been defined. Since the language concepts are prone to be cyclic by nature and since it is difficult to introduce them completely independent from each other, this concession cannot be omitted. In this case references to the description of the concept are given.

Conventions: Representation Form and General Model Layout

As described in Section 2.2.6, conceptual modelling methods have a conceptual aspect as well as a representational aspect. In order to ensure correct appliance and ease of communication of the models, the following conventions concerning the construction of appropriate representation forms are applied. Therefore, it is useful to define patterns for representation forms that ensure a consistent interpretation of conceptual models. That is, representation forms should be constructed similarly if similar construction principles are meant by them. Otherwise, an inappropriate construction of concepts can lead to misinterpretation. Thus, the following conventions apply to the representation forms. Table 3.2 gives an overview of the concepts of the modelling language that have representation forms.

Representation forms of the same model type are characterized by the same colour.[18] Reference-objects are depicted by rectangles. Dimensions are indicated by three arrows that resemble a multidimensional space. Properties are attributes of Reference-objects. Thus, the symbol shows two properties of an object. Property-relation-systems are depicted by a hierarchy of Property symbols. Content is depicted by a small document symbol. Attribute-types represent metadata of Content and are depicted by an attribute that is assigned to a Content. The symbol of a Personalization-object resembles the shape of the torso of a human. Access-objects are illustrated with a lock. The symbol for a Navigation-path (a double-sided arrow) indicates that two things are linked by it. The Navigation-path is annotated with a Qualifier using the same symbolism as in Attribute-type (an oval annotated to a line).

On the basis of these representation forms, the construction of appropriate symbols of the general principles described above is achieved as follows. If concepts are assembled

---

phenomena in ordinary language. The author is well aware of the problematic consequences this kind of double-usage can have. However, this problem can be solved only by introducing artificial concepts. By doing so, the relation to real world phenomena may get lost. Therefore, these conventions are enforced in order to ensure clarity as well as understandability and readability.

[18]   Although the representation forms are coloured they can be printed out in black and white. They are designed to be uniquely identifiable in this case.

Model	Concept	Symbol
Information Space Models	Reference-object	
	Dimension	
Property Models	Property	
	Property-relation-system	
Content Models	Attribute-type	
	Content	
Navigation Models	Navigation-path	
	Qualifier	
Personalization Models	Personalization-object	
	Access-object	

Table 3.2: Representation Form: Symbols of Concepts

in classes, the representation forms for classes contain a smaller version of the original in a box. The outer box corresponds to the symbols of the same model type. The principle of grouping is indicated by three smaller versions of the concept which is grouped. The smaller versions overlay themselves. Systems are illustrated by three smaller versions of the original concept. They are ordered hierarchically (indicating that the structure of the system is important and meaningful). Scopes have a cut-out in form of a triangle on the right side. The different principles of building representation forms are combinable (for instance, the concept Dimension-scope-group). Table 3.3 gives an overview of aggregated and trimmed representation forms.

The general layout of the conceptual models is derived from previous works.[19] As hierarchies are intuitively understandable for humans as well as well-known from other applications[20], a considerable part of the models is modelled using hierarchies. A tree

---

[19]   Refer to the references given in Footnote 28 in this chapter.

[20]   For instance, the structure of folders and files of hard drives is similar to the layout of the repre-

Model	Concept	Aggregation			Scope
		Class	Group	System	
Information Space Models	Reference-object	▣			
	Dimension		▣		◁
	Dimension-scope		▣		
Property Models	Property			▦	
	Property-system				◁
Content Models	Attribute-type		▣		
	Content	▣			
Navigation Models	Navigation-path	▣			
	Qualifier-class	▣			

Table 3.3: Representation Form: Aggregation and Trimming

node is indicated by a small plus-sign (hierarchy is collapsed) or a minus-sign (hierarchy is expanded). Leaves of a tree do not have these symbols. As described in Section 2.2.6, the representation forms serve as propositions. They can be replaced easily if other representations are requested or become necessary.

Scope of Meta Modelling

The metamodels in this section represent the language constructs of a modelling technique as well as a model of an information system (dualism of the metamodel). Consequently, the metamodels contain constructs that have no representation form in the conceptual modelling technique. These language constructs improve the understandability and explicate implicit assumptions of the modelling technique. Moreover, they represent propositions of implementation models of a web information system. For instance, the construct 'Attribute-datatype' (compare 3.4) is not modelled on a conceptual level. For implementation purposes, however, the differentiation between different types

---

sentation forms.

of metadata becomes important, since functionality of the system depends on the correct interpretation of the dataset.[21] Thus, these constructs are illustrated and explained although they have no direct representation in the modelling technique.

Reference Point of the Metamodels

It is obvious that the meaning of qualifiers like 'meta' or 'type' always depends on the point of view because they are relative qualifiers by nature. A specific dataset may be data if it is viewed from one perspective or metadata if it is viewed from another one. Accordingly, the interpretation of the qualifier type depends on the point of view. Thus, the characterization of a dataset as metadata must clearly identify the reference point that is used. In this case, the reference point is content respectively the information that is processed by the information system during run-time. All qualifiers refer to a real world content.

Metamodel Segmentation & Syntactical Correctness

The metamodels designed in the following sections are segments of the whole metamodel. Thus, these models may contain syntax errors or inaccuracies regarding the ER modelling technique when interpreted without considering the whole model. These syntax errors are not corrected in order to improve the overall understanding and to conserve the relationships between the model types. If the errors were corrected, the same language concepts would have to be illustrated with different constructs of the ERM language, which would cause confusion and inappropriate interpretation of the model segments. Additionally, the ER modelling language is used as a metalanguage and provides a semi-formal description of concepts in the modelling method that is to be constructed. Therefore, the strict adherence to syntactical correctness can be partially omitted because the models are not intended to be implemented. Figure 3.2 illustrates the problem and the approach used in this thesis (variant 1).

Level of Abstraction

When designing a conceptual modelling approach, it is difficult to identify a suitable level of abstraction by which language concepts should be introduced. In general, conceptual

---

[21] For instance, a system may withdraw content that has reached its expiry date. In order to perform this operation, the content has to be annotated with an Attribute-set 'Expiry Date' of Attribute-datatype 'Date'. The instantiation of this Attribute-set is given by the author or determined automatically by the system (for instance, 10 days after publication). Consequently, the system must be able to interpret the data given in the field 'Expiry Date'. Thus, it has to be typecasted.

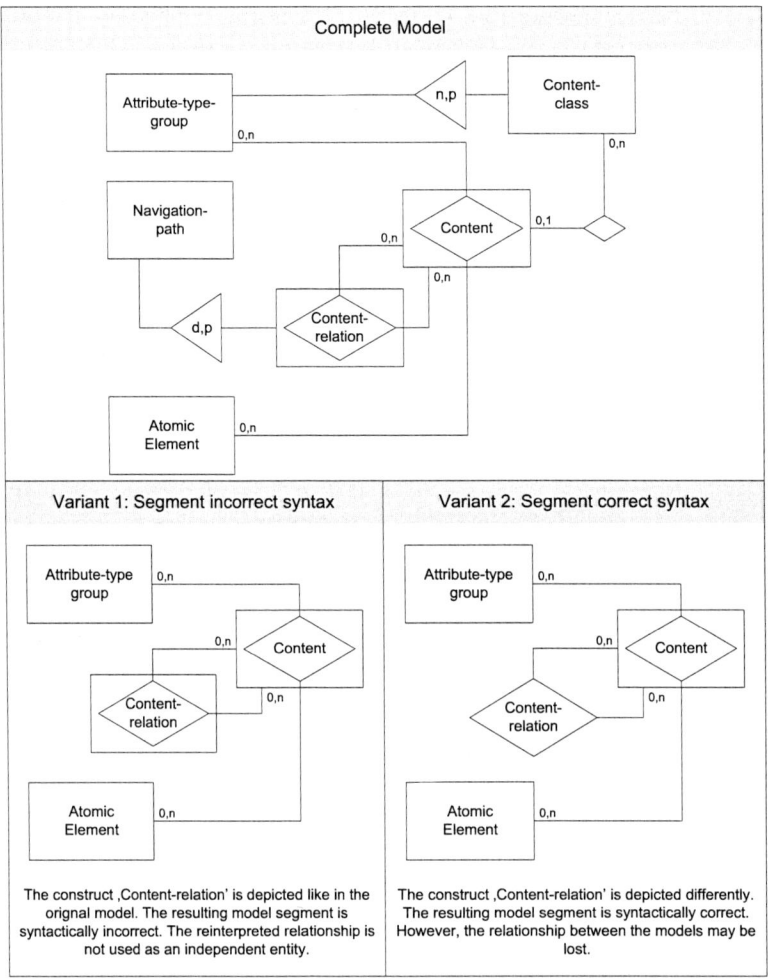

Figure 3.2: Segmentation of Models: Syntactical Correctness vs. Interpretability

modelling is not concerned with concrete instances during run-time. It is rather the type-level being specified.[22] Thus, the models created by using the conceptual modelling approach are usually limited to type-level. Consequently, only concepts of modelling on type-level are needed in modelling projects.

---

[22]   For instance, an entitytype 'customer' in an entity relationship model subsumes datasets that are structurally and semantically similar. It is usually instantiated several times (customers 'John Doe' and 'Norma J. Baker').

For the sake of completeness and clarity, however, this restriction has to be omitted at least partially. Several concepts are only understandable and more precisely specified if instances of concepts are illustrated and explained as well. Moreover, type-level modelling may only be sufficient in certain projects while it is not in other ones. A suitable level of abstraction depends on specific project characteristics (for instance, quantitative and qualitative complexity) and characteristics of the subject that is modelled.[23] A very complex and important content may be specified explicitly, whereas a well structured and simple Content (for instance, an entry in a news-feed) can be specified on type level (using the language concept Content-class). Thus, a more detailed view is useful in order to describe and analyze information systems holistically and appropriately.

Additionally, this thesis is particularly interested in navigational issues and their role in satisfying information needs of users. Some navigation structures are modelled explicitly on a conceptual level, whereas others are defined during run-time by user interactions with the system.[24] Thus, navigation structures have to be discussed on a conceptual as well as on an implementation level. Therefore, the approach also comprises concepts that are not necessarily modelled on a conceptual level.

Model Types & Subsequent Proceeding

A conceptual modelling method for web information systems is constructed systematically in the following sections by using the method engineering approach described in Sections 2.1.3 and 2.2.6. Each language construct is introduced briefly, described textually in plain English as well as modelled conceptually by using the ERM language. Additionally, representation forms are constructed that allow the creation of conceptual models using the modelling method.[25] Naming conventions for the representation forms

---

[23] Refer to Section 2.2.1 for the difference of quantitative and qualitative complexity.

[24] For instance, the information space described in Section 3.2 constitutes one aspect of navigation and is modelled implicitly on a conceptual level, whereas the relations between contents are usually defined explicitly during run-time. Modelling of the information space takes place implicitly, since the visualization of the multidimensional space is achieved by using multiple hierarchies. A multidimensional space cannot be laid out in a two-dimensional environment like a screen or paper. Thus, information system developers have to imagine the composition and shape of the information space. In contrast to the information space, the relations between two contents are explicitly modelled during run-time. For instance, a Content-composition (refer to Section 3.4.3) is created by an editor during run-time by assigning one content to the other. The implications of the assignment is an edge that can be navigated. Moreover, it implies that a Content contains the other one. These implications can be seen explicitly during run-time.

[25] Earlier version of the following conceptualization can be found in BECKER et al. (2003d); BECKER et al. (2003c); BECKER et al. (2003b) and BECKER et al. (2004b).

are given in order to increase model quality and comparability.

The order of the conceptualization is as follows: firstly, the concept of information space is introduced. It constitutes the information space and defines analytic trails through information which can be used for navigational purposes. Secondly, property models are defined. Property models define analytic trails through subsets of information and are used likewise for navigation. Content models are used to specify the data in the system and provide navigational patterns within a particular piece of information. Personalization models are used to trim the whole information space in order to decrease information overload and to increase usability of the system. Finally, different types of navigation are discussed. Navigation paths enable users to build statements about the information in the system and provide means for efficient information processing for humans by aligning analytic trails through information to associative trails used by humans. The different aspects of the modelling approach are conceptualized by metamodels that are conjoined by identical concepts. In fact, the metamodels represent a single model which is segmented. The relations between the different model types are illustrated in Table 3.4. Since information space models are fundamental for the modelling approach, they do not use concepts from other model types.

3.2 Information Space

Information space models are used for identifying a subset of data that is relevant for the person who seeks to derive information from the information space.[26] The underlying idea of the information space concept is the notion that pieces of data respectively information can be classified by multiple Dimensions which span a multi-dimensional information space. Each piece of information is characterized by the elements of the Dimensions and, thus, embedded in the information space. Subsequently, pieces of information can be accessed by defining a subset of the whole information space that is relevant for an individual in a given context. Furthermore, information space models are used to specify analytic trails. An analytic trail represents a specific purpose by which data is analyzed. If, for instance, the turnover in a retailing company has to be analyzed on shelf-level, the shelf has to be modelled as an independent construct which can be used to specify and aggregate data.[27]

The conceptualization of information space is derived from HOLTEN who has intro-

---

[26]   Compare for the following KNACKSTEDT (2004), pp. 144 ff.
[27]   In this case, shelves would be modelled as Reference-objects in a Dimension 'Shelve after Retailing Outlet'. Compare Section 3.2.2 for details.

Concept Used in	Property Meta-model	Content Meta-model	Navigation Meta-model	Personal-ization Meta-model
Reference-object	✓	✓	✓	
Reference-object-class	✓			
Reference-object-relation			✓	
Reference-object-relation-qualifier			✓	
Dimension-object			✓	
Dimension-object-hierarchy			✓	
Dimension-object-relation			✓	
Dimension-object-relation-qualifier			✓	
Dimension-scope-group				✓
Property		✓	✓	
Property-relation			✓	
Property-relation-qualifier			✓	
Property-system-scope-group				✓
Content			✓	
Content-relation			✓	✓
Content-relation-qualifier			✓	
Content-class				✓
Navigation-path-class				✓
Qualifier-class				✓
User			✓	

Table 3.4: Metamodel Relations

duced this concept for the specification of information warehouse development projects.[28]

---

[28] The conceptualization is the foundation of the MetaMIS modelling technique which was designed for information warehouse projects and has been published frequently. For a general overview of the method and its history refer to BECKER & HOLTEN (1998); HOLTEN (1999); HOLTEN (2001);

Additionally, HOLTEN has laid the foundation of the method engineering approach used in this thesis. KNACKSTEDT has extended the conceptualization considerably by introducing several additions for modelling.[29] In particular, KNACKSTEDT has integrated several modelling techniques in order to provide extensive modelling capabilities that can be used for modelling management information systems holistically and adequately. For instance, KNACKSTEDT has integrated modelling techniques for processes[30], organizational structures[31], web applications[32] and competence.

The conceptualization of information space itself is based on the works of RIEBEL who developed an approach for cost accounting which is based on a purpose neutral calculation of costs.[33] Following RIEBEL, the calculation of costs is subdivided into two phases. Within the first phase, costs are assigned to real or imaginary objects according to the principle of identity. The principle of identity postulates that costs can be assigned to cost units if, and only if, the cost unit can clearly be identified as the cause of the costs. Cost units are conceptualized as Reference-objects[34] which have a complex, multi-dimensional structure. Since Reference-objects can be aggregated

---

HOLTEN & DREILING (2002); BECKER et al. (2003e); HOLTEN (2003b); HOLTEN (2003a) and HOLTEN, DREILING & BECKER (2004). The method has been applied successfully in several real world cases, for instance, HOLTEN, DREILING & SCHMID (2002) and BECKER et al. (2003e). The method and the method engineering approach developed by HOLTEN were the starting point for the development of similar modelling techniques that extend the concept. In particular, approaches for modelling qualitative data have been integrated, for instance, BECKER, KNACKSTEDT & SERRIES (2001); BECKER, KNACKSTEDT & SERRIES (2002); BECKER et al. (2003d); BECKER et al. (2003c); BECKER et al. (2003b); BECKER et al. (2003f); SERRIES (2004); KNACKSTEDT (2004) and BECKER et al. (2004b).

[29] Cf. KNACKSTEDT (2004).

[30] KNACKSTEDT has integrated the modelling technique Event-driven Process Chains (EPC). Cf. KNACKSTEDT (2004), pp. 187 ff. EPCs have been proposed by SCHEER (cf. SCHEER (1994); SCHEER (1998) and SCHEER (2001)). A similar approach of integrating the MetaMIS approach and EPCs can be found in BECKER et al. (2003a) and BECKER et al. (2004a).

[31] Organizational charts as proposed by SCHEER (SCHEER (1994); SCHEER (1998) and SCHEER (2001)) are integrated in the modelling approach developed by KNACKSTEDT (cf. KNACKSTEDT (2004), pp. 191 ff.).

[32] Web applications are modelled by using the enhanced World Wide Web Design Technique (eW3DT) proposed by SCHARL (cf. SCHARL (1998) and Cf. SCHARL (2000)). KNACKSTEDT integrates the technique in his approach (cf. KNACKSTEDT (2004), pp. 184 ff.). For details on the eW3DT modelling technique refer to Section 2.2.7.

[33] Compare RIEBEL (1979a); RIEBEL (1979b) and RIEBEL (1992) for details on the cost accounting approach. RIEBEL's approach was the basis for the MetaMIS modelling technique as proposed by HOLTEN. Compare HOLTEN (1999), pp. 76 ff. for details. The conversion of the approach with data warehouses or relational database is discussed by RIEBEL & SINZIG (1981) and SINZIG (1990).

[34] Refer to 3.2.2 for the introduction of the concept *Reference-object*.

arbitrarily (resulting in new reference objects), it is always possible to define Reference-objects that are abstract enough and suffice the principle of identity. Thus, all costs can be assigned as individual costs. The second phase defines analyses on the data defined in phase one. Of course, the data specified in phase one determines possible pathes of aggregation and analytic trails. Thus, the specification of the data in phase one has to be aligned with the intended purpose of the analysis.[35]

RIEBEL's usage of the abstract concept Reference-object for cost accounting is adopted in this thesis as it is used in the works by HOLTEN. Reference-objects are used to structure the world and the objects in it and provide classification systems for large data sets. Specifically, Content is assigned to at least one Reference-object which renders it easier to interpret and understand the Content since it is linked to a specific, well-known concept for which a shared understanding has been achieved between users of the system. Therefore, information processing quality for humans is supposed to increase as data is embedded in a common and meaningful framework.

3.2.1 Reference-object

As indicated earlier, the concept *Reference-object* is introduced in order to represent objects from the real or imaginary world.[36] A Reference-object is a concept designed by humans that allows to structure the world and the objects in it in a meaningful as well as effective and efficient manner. Humans have to share a common understanding of the concepts they define in order to use them effectively and efficiently. Given the purpose of modelling it is required that all users of the information systems as well as its developers share a common understanding of Reference-objects and the things and objects they represent. If this shared understanding is not given, the goal which is to be accomplished by the information system cannot be achieved efficiently. Users would expect different data sets when talking or when using a particular Reference-object. Therefore, the models interfere with the goals they were meant to achieve.[37] For the purpose of this thesis, a distinction between qualitative and quantitative Reference-objects is omitted. A quantitative Reference-object is characterized by the type of data that is classified and analyzed with it. Qualitative Reference-objects cannot be used in

---

[35] The MetaMIS modelling technique from HOLTEN is designed specifically for this purpose. Refer to the references in Footnote 28 for details.

[36] Compare HOLTEN (1999), pp. 78 ff., HOLTEN (2003b) and KNACKSTEDT (2004), pp. 144 ff. for the following. The conceptualization of the modelling language is illustrated in Figure 3.3.

[37] Compare Section 2.2.6 for details on the purpose of modelling.

order to construct quantitative statements.[38] Rules that define valid combinations of data, property and object are described in the conceptualization of Property.[39] In this thesis, however, both types are conceptualized identically.

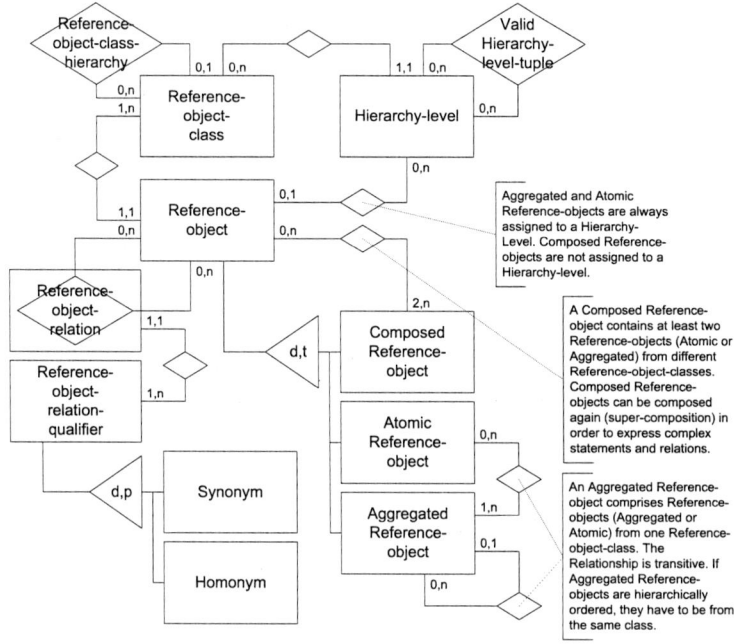

Figure 3.3: Reference-object Metamodel (Conceptual Aspect)

Following this conceptualization of Reference-objects and their structure, the resemblance to ontologies is obvious.[40] However, Reference-objects are usually defined by using natural language and are, therefore, less strictly and formally specified than ontologies, which are defined using logic and algebra.[41] These differences, however, are caused by varying foundations of the computer science and IS discipline.

Reference-objects structure quantitative and qualitative data, which state or describe something about the phenomenon the Reference-object represents. Common examples

---

[38]   The distinction between both types of Reference-objects is proposed by KNACKSTEDT (cf. KNACK-STEDT (2004), pp. 151 f.).

[39]   Refer to Section 3.2.

[40]   GRUBER's well-known ontology definition illustrates this point. GRUBER defines an ontology as follows: "An ontology is a formal, explicit specification of a shared conceptualisation." (GRUBER (1993), p. 199 and FENSEL (2001), p. 8).

[41]   Cf. GRUBER (1993) and SOWA (1999) for examples of formal ontology specifications.

for Reference-objects are:

- Products, customers and suppliers: since objects which are commonly used in organizations are usually known to members of the organization, they are good candidates for designing Reference-objects and hierarchies (for instance, assortments of products) correspondingly.

- Time: time is a mandatory dimension and the elements of it are Reference-objects like '2005' or '2005-02'. Aggregates in this Dimension are weeks, months or quarters. A hierarchy of time after weeks does not toe with months and quarters, since weeks are usually overlapping with the end of the year. Thus, a Dimension-group containing two Dimensions is built (time after week and time after month).

- Regions: companies usually divide their operations into regions. Similarly, governmental structures like districts or counties are used by official authorities.

- Organizational structure: reference-objects from organizational structures include entities like departments or divisions as well as roles (for instance, 'Project Manager') or individuals (for instance, 'John Doe').

Moreover, Reference-objects include aggregates of other Reference-objects. For instance, products can be aggregated to assortments (for instance, food) and customers to customer-groups (for instance, private customers).[42] *Aggregated Reference-objects* assemble objects assigned to the same class. They represent self-contained concepts as well as the objects for which they are used as aggregates. The year '2004' is a concept itself. Additionally, it represents the sum of the months from January to February which itself represents specific dates. The concept of *Reference-object-class* itself is not modelled. However, it is useful to introduce classes of Reference-objects in order to illustrate constraints that have to be enforced whenever groups or aggregates of Reference-objects are built. Classes of Reference-objects can be composed of hierarchies (*Reference-object-class-hierarchy*) building sub- and super-classes of Reference-objects.

Additionally, Reference-objects can be composed (*Composed Reference-object*) of complex vectors of Reference-objects such as <Private Customers, 2005, Germany> or <Politics, 2005, Europe>. In contrast to aggregates, the elements of a composed Reference-object do not have to be assigned to the same class. Thus, different types of objects can be composed. In conjunction with dimensions, a Composed Reference-object represents a coordinate in a multi-dimensional space. Finally, Reference-objects can be

---

[42]   Cf. KNACKSTEDT (2004), p. 144.

related to each other (*Reference-object-relation*) regardless of their type (atomic, aggregated or composed). The type of the relation is characterized by a *Reference-object-relation-qualifier*. Relations between Reference-objects constitute one type of navigation. Reference-objects classify the documents that are stored in the information system and are directly used by users for navigational purposes.[43] Thus, each relation between reference objects can be typed in order to state different things about the objects they connect.[44] In particular, Reference-objects can be *Synonyms* or *Homonyms*. The introduction of both concepts is particularly useful when qualitative data is to be processed by the information system. For instance, an information system can contain research papers that are written in different languages but cover the same subject areas. If users of the system are multilingual as well it is suggestive to use bilingual Reference-objects, too (for instance, the English term 'modelling' and the German equivalent 'Modellierung').

All Reference-objects, except compositions, have to be assigned to a *Hierarchy-level*. For instance, Reference-objects of the class 'Time' can be assigned to Hierarchy-levels like year, quarter and month. Hierarchy-levels can be seen as an orthogonal dimension to classes since they specify the Reference-object of one class on a more detailed level. Moreover, Hierarchy-levels give information about valid hierarchies respectively structures of Reference-objects since not all combinations of Hierarchy-levels are sensible (*Valid Hierarchy-level-tuple*). For instance, weeks are usually overlapping with years. Thus, they cannot be used within one hierarchy.

Although Reference-objects are supposed to represent a shared understanding of a concept for all users, this restriction cannot be omitted. It is impossible to rule out the existence of synonyms or homonyms since a natural language, which comprises numerous words of both types, is used to represent concepts. Instead it is reasonable to assume that the usability of the information system can be improved by allowing synonyms because the same dataset can be found by using different concepts. Furthermore, some Reference-objects can be derived automatically by applications. For instance, the author of a document[45] can be set automatically by the operating system. The operating system usually uses the account name instead of the real name of a person. Thus, it is useful to use both terms as synonyms.[46] Homonyms, however, pose a greater challenge to

---

[43]   Reference-objects are links which can be clicked within the information system.

[44]   Refer to Section 3.5 for a detailed description of pathes of navigation and typed links.

[45]   Author is a standard metadata field in Microsoft Windows operating environments.

[46]   For instance, a word processor (like Microsoft Word) automatically sets the author information by using the account name chbr which is defined by the domain controller. Thus, the real name Christian S. Brelage can be mapped to the term chbr as a synonym. By doing this, the system is able to decide that information which is associated with the term chbr has to be displayed whenever information about the Reference-object 'Christian S. Brelage' is requested.

information system developers since the datasets they represent are different, whereas the concept is the same. Thus, designers of the information system have to ensure that users are clearly able to identify the different concepts associated with homonymous Reference-objects.[47]

3.2.2 Dimension

The number of Reference-objects might well be high and their relations complex. Therefore, it is reasonable to provide a concept that allows to structure subsets of Reference-objects in a meaningful and efficient manner. The concept of *Dimensions*, which are essential for the modelling method, is introduced for this purpose. Dimensions represent an analytic path that can be used in order to retrieve or aggregate information in the information space. Dimensions span the multi-dimensional information space and constitute its structural composition. They subsume Reference-objects of the same class and order them hierarchically by using aggregates of Reference-objects.[48] Hierarchies have traditionally been used as a means to structure concepts and, therefore, they are well-known and easy to use for users. The concept *Dimension-criterion* represents the criterion by which a Dimension is constructed. A Dimension-criterion specifies the design principle used to build the Dimension. It is annotated after the name of the Dimension using the infix 'after', for instance, 'Time after Week' or 'Product after Colour'.[49] Reference-objects of the same class are assigned to Dimensions (further referred to as *Dimension-objects*) and structured hierarchically (*Dimension-object-hierarchy*).[50] A *DO-node* is superior to at least one *DO-leaf*. The design of Dimensions depends on the type of analysis or navigational structure needed. Consequently, the same set of Reference-objects can be structured and used differently in two Dimensions. Retail stores may be structured according to their location (for instance, city versus outskirts) and products may be structured according to different attributes (for instance, colour versus prize-level).[51] Corresponding Dimensions can be built in either case. Since the concept of Dimension-object-hierarchies plays a vital role in satisfying

---

[47] For instance, the distinction can be achieved visually by a suitable interface design.

[48] Apart from the requirement that Dimensions are based on Reference-objects of the same class, no further constraints are enforced. In particular, Dimensions do not necessarily have to be balanced. Cf. KNACKSTEDT (2004), p. 148 and footnote 492.

[49] Cf. KNACKSTEDT (2004), p. 145.

[50] For the sake of simplicity, it is assumed that only Atomic and Aggregated Reference-objects are used in Dimensions. Composed Reference-objects are not permitted in Dimensions. Otherwise, consistency control and complexity become hard to handle.

[51] Cf. KNACKSTEDT (2004), p. 145.

information needs of users and constitutes the layout of the information space structurally, it is introduced independently from the other relations that may exist between Dimension-objects.

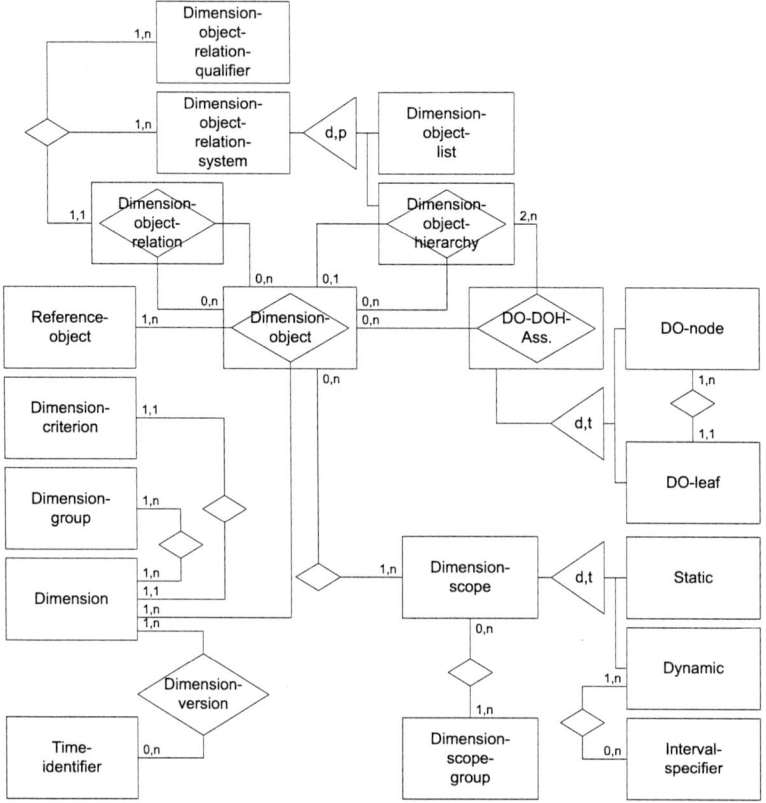

Figure 3.4: Dimension Metamodel (Conceptual Aspect)

It is possible to design general relations between Dimension-objects (*Dimension-object-relation*). The concept is used to create arbitrary structures of objects that are aggregated in *Dimension-object-relation-systems*. A qualifier specifies the type of the relation (*Dimension-object-relation-qualifier*). For instance, the qualifier 'sequence' can be used if *Dimension-object-lists* are defined. A Dimension-object-list can be considered as a special form of a hierarchy where each element has one subordinate item at the most. Since lists imply a different statement (structural (de)composition versus sequence) about the objects they assemble, it is essential to differentiate between the concepts Dimension-object-hierarchy and Dimension-object-list as indicated by the metamodel in Figure 3.4. Other variants of the information space conceptualization explicitly exclude lists.[52] For the purpose of this thesis, however, lists are introduced in order to provide more flexible and holistic means for modelling. Reference-objects can be chained in a special relation which gives the model user information about the order of objects. In particular, it is useful to indicate that one object preceded another one. For instance, preceding year, preceding month, prior versions of a product and so on. Moreover, Dimensions can be used to create arbitrary structures that are considered to be meaningful in the given context.

Dimensions based on the same set of DO-Leaves respectively Atomic Reference-objects are comprised in one *Dimension-group*.[53] As indicated earlier, Reference-objects can be structured according to different needs and analytic trails. Thus, the set of Aggregated Reference-objects may differ, whereas the set of Atomic Reference-objects is the same in two or more Dimensions. For instance, Dimension A structures retail stores according to their location and Dimension B structures them according to their size in square meters. Obviously, the set of stores (Atomic Reference-objects) is identical in both dimensions. The aggregates (for instance, the size 'Supermarket' and the location 'Neighbourhood'), however, differ. Thus, both Dimensions can be subsumed in a Dimension-group. The group is named according to the class of Reference-objects it comprises, which is, in this case, 'Retail Store'. In contrast to Reference-object-class, groups subsume Dimensions based on the same set of Leaves. This set does not necessarily comprise all the Reference-objects from one class.

In order to provide effective and efficient means for navigation and information retrieval it is reasonable to demand that the information space is structurally stable and changes slowly over time. However, Dimensions depict the structural composition of the objects that are considered to be relevant for information system developers and users. Since the phenomena they depict as well as their (perceived) structural composition are subject to change over time, it is reasonable to build versions of Dimensions. For instance, the regions an organization operates in may change. Likewise, products and their assortments can change. It is possible to track changes in the structural composition of the information space by *Dimension-versions*. The concept of *Time-identifier* depicts

---

52 Indicated by the cardinalities in the metamodel in KNACKSTEDT (2004), pp. 147 ff. Although lists are (conceptually) possible in the works of HOLTEN (cf. HOLTEN (1999), pp. 85 f.), they have never been used.

53 Cf. HOLTEN (2001), pp. 8 f.; Cf. KNACKSTEDT (2004), p. 146. This concept is similar to a navigational concept called multitrees, which was developed by FURNAS & ZACKS (cf. FURNAS & ZACKS (1994); Cf. GLOOR (1997), pp. 86–87).

points in time as well as time frames.[54] Each Dimension has at least one Dimension-version. Otherwise it cannot exist. It is important to note that the version information of Dimensions also applies to concepts directly derived from or associated with Dimensions (for instance, Dimension-scope).

3.2.3 Dimension-scope & -combination

The information space contains all pieces of information and all Reference-objects used in order to characterize and classify information. As a consequence, the quantity of information users are confronted with can be very high, resulting in the user's confusion and in decreased information retrieval efficiency. Additionally, not every piece of information is relevant in a given context. Instead, subsets of information are needed for specific tasks or individuals. In order to avoid information overflow and to increase information retrieval efficiency, the concept of *Dimension-scope* is introduced.[55] A Dimension-scope reduces the set of Reference-objects relevant in a given context by defining suitable subsets of Reference-objects assigned to one Dimension. Thus, the amount of information displayed to users is reduced indirectly by blinding out irrelevant Reference-objects. In order to achieve uniqueness and clarity, only Dimension-objects from one Dimension can be composed to a Dimension-scope. Furthermore, it is important to note that the Dimension-scope maintains the original structure of the Dimension. Thus, the general ordering of Dimension-objects remains untouched. That is, no subordinate Dimension-object can become superior to Dimension-objects that were hierarchically superordinate in the original Dimension-object-hierarchy.[56] This restriction applies likewise to sequences (Dimension-object-list). The segmentation of Dimension can take place horizontally or vertically or in combinations of both. A horizontal segmentation implies that layers of the hierarchy are cut out. Branches of the hierarchy are removed by vertical segmentation. The disposition of dimension segmentation refers to visions of Dimensions that have the root node at the top. Subordinated elements are depicted in layers below

---

[54] KNACKSTEDT provides a more detailed conceptualization of Dimension-versions by introducing additional concepts like transaction time and validity time (cf. KNACKSTEDT (2004), pp. 145 f.). Moreover, KNACKSTEDT differentiates between Dimension-scopes originating from Dimension-versions and Dimension-scopes which do not. For the purpose of this thesis, however, a more detailed investigation of this concept is not necessary.

[55] Dimension-scopes are also constituent for the definition of personalized information access. Refer to Section 3.6 for details on personalization.

[56] Of course this restriction also applies to arbitrary Dimension-object-relations.

the root node.[57]

Additionally, a Dimension-scope can either be *Static* or *Dynamic*. A Static Dimension-scope is explicitly defined and does not change, whereas a Dynamic Dimension-scope is defined relatively and its boundaries respectively the subset of Dimension-objects it contains can change. Thus, the actual composition of the Dimension-scope is defined during run-time. The concept *Interval-identifier* represents the condition that applies when the composition of the Dimension-scope is determined. This concept is particularly useful when scopes on a time Dimension are built. For instance, a Dimension-scope 'Time after Month: 2002 - Present[' is specified using the Interval-identifier 'Present[', which indicates that the interval is open to the right. In this case the identifier 'Present' which is not a Dimension-object represents an open interval. Furthermore, a bracket is added in order to avoid misinterpretation. Likewise, a Dimension-Scope 'Product after Assortment: Food[]' can be specified. The brackets indicate that the composition of the Dimension-objects in this particular scope is dynamic. Dimension-objects are assembled at the moment the scope is used by somebody. Thus, products in the assortment food added after the Dimension-scope has been specified are also included. Therefore, the Dimension-scope is glided over the set of Dimension-objects in the Dimension.

A Dimension-scope is always defined by trimming exactly one Dimension. Given the multi-dimensional nature of the information space, it is useful to combine Dimension-scopes from different Dimensions (concept *Dimension-scope-group*). As a result, a sub-space of the whole information space is specified. The concept is particularly useful for personalization purposes. The underlying idea of trimming the information space is derived from the OLAP-concept in data warehouse environments.[58] 'Multidimensional' storage of data is central to the OLAP-concept. This kind of storage is usually visualized by a cube.[59] In order to analyze the data, the information space is collapsed or expanded concerning one or more dimensions (operations drill-down respectively -up). Moreover, the view on data can be restricted (operations slicing and dicing). These operations are reflected by the concepts Dimension-scope and their combinations that have been introduced.

---

[57] The representation form of Dimensions is switched by 90 degrees. The root node is depicted in the top-left corner and subordinated layers are ordered to the right.

[58] Cf. INMON & HACKATHORN (1994); INMON (1996) and INMON (2002) for details on the data warehouse concept. For OLAP compare VOSSEN (1999), pp. 679 ff. and HOLTEN (1999), pp. 49 f.

[59] Usually normal relational databases are used for storing 'multi-dimensional' data. The attribute multi-dimensional is mainly used for marketing purposes. A 'multi-dimensional' storage is achieved by annotating metadata to datasets. Thus, each piece of data is embedded in a 'multi-dimensional space'.

3.2.4 Reference-object & Dimension Representation Form

As stated in Section 2.2.6 the construction of modelling methods includes a conceptual aspect as well as a representational aspect. Concepts of the modelling approach are constructed systematically in the preceding sections. During the discussion of conventions for the representation forms and the mechanism by which they are built, symbols for concepts were already introduced.[60] In contrast to similar conceptualizations constructed by HOLTEN and KNACKSTEDT, an independent representation form for Reference-objects is proposed. Prior approaches specified Reference-objects indirectly by using Dimensions. However, the amount of Reference-objects can be very high and their relations complex and unclear.[61] Additionally, not all Reference-objects which are conceivable or specified have to be used in Dimensions. Moreover, it is reasonable to support the modelling process by modelling environments. Reference-objects can be derived automatically at least partially from other applications like ERP-systems. For instance, products and customers, which are prone to be good candidates for Reference-objects, can be extracted. Additionally, the concept of Reference-object-classes can be used to enforce additional constraints when Dimensions are built. Thus, it is possible to help information system developers. Therefore, the following steps are proposed for the specification of Reference-objects.

Firstly, Reference-objects are modelled by using a table that depicts differences between Atomic and Aggregated Reference-objects and assigns them to classes (Compare Figure 3.5). As much information as possible is derived from data sources if Reference-objects can be derived or created automatically like those from the class 'Time'. As a result, a pool of Reference-objects exists which is partially structured. It can be used as a building set for the design of Dimensions. Reference-object-classes are named in the singular and all letters are capitalized. Reference-objects on different Hierarchy-levels are indicated by using columns of the table. The Hierarchy-level identifiers are the column heads and are underlined. A small plus or minus symbol indicates whether a table is expanded or collapsed.

Secondly, Dimensions and the concepts that are related to them are introduced. In order to increase model quality and comparability the following naming conventions

---

[60] The representation forms used in this thesis with minor changes were originally proposed by HOLTEN. Refer to the references given in Footnote 28. Naming conventions are mostly derived from KNACKSTEDT (KNACKSTEDT (2004), pp. 149 ff.).

[61] For instance, a time Dimension specifying quarters, month and days contains 381 objects (4 + 12 + 365). The amount of products can be very high, too (especially retailing). Therefore the amount of Reference-objects that are actually in use can easily add up to several thousands.

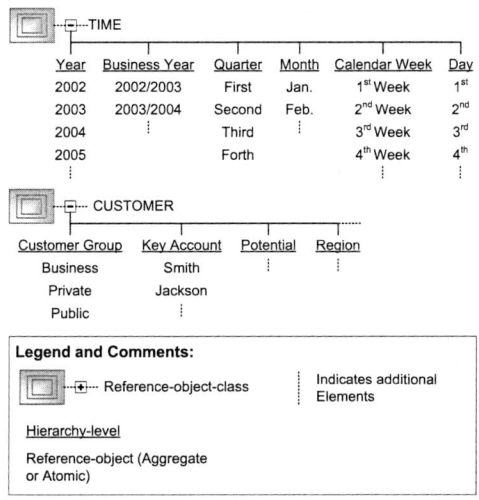

Figure 3.5: Representation Form Information Space Part 1

are proposed (compare Figure 3.6).[62] Dimensions are named with their class identifier in the plural[63] followed by the infix 'after' and the Dimension-criterion by which the Dimension is constructed (for instance 'Customers after Customer-group'). In case of a list, the key-word 'Sequence' is added. Dimension-groups are named according to the class from which they aggregate objects. Dimensions-scopes add to the name of the Dimension the interval specification (for instance 'Private Customers' or '2002/2003 to]Present') after a colon. Dimensions-scope-groups contain the interval specifications of the scopes they assemble concatenated by an 'and'.

3.3 Property

The main goal of the conceptualization is to provide extensive means of modelling meaningful and efficient navigation structures on data. Reference-objects represent concepts that can be investigated by using the system. In order to conceptualize statements more precisely and to bring together Reference-object and Content, the concept of *Property* is introduced (compare Figure 3.7 for the following).[64] In the original modelling technique by HOLTEN, properties are conceptualized as measures and measure-systems which are

---

62 Compare KNACKSTEDT (2004), pp. 163 f. for the following.
63 If a plural form cannot be built (for instance, for the class 'TIME'), the singular is used .
64 The conceptualization is partly based on the works by KNACKSTEDT and HOLTEN (KNACKSTEDT (2004), pp. 153 ff. and HOLTEN (1999), pp. 100 ff. as well as the succeeding works by HOLTEN

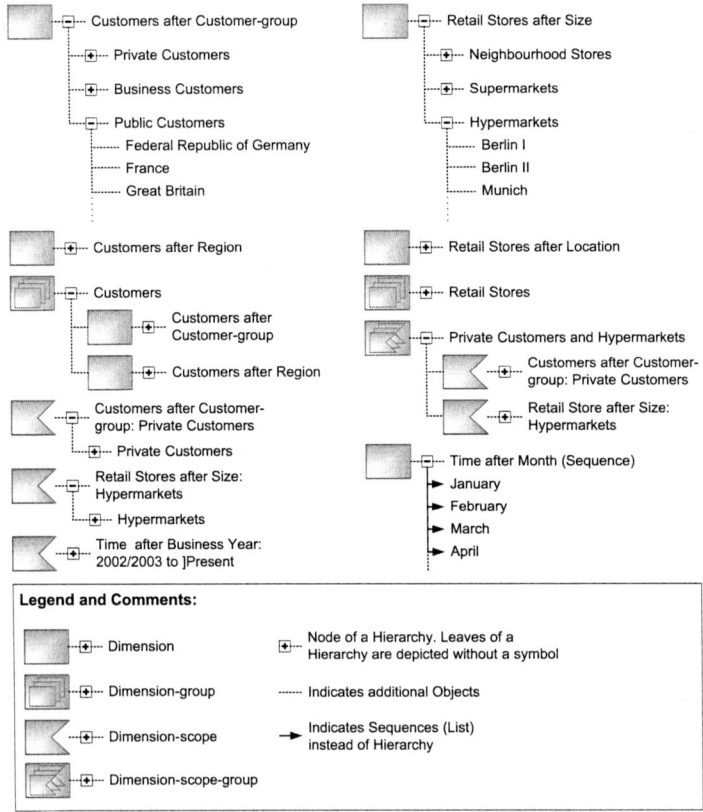

Figure 3.6: Representation Form Information Space Part 2

mainly used to characterize quantitative data (for instance, costs, turnover and profit). Basing his approach on HOLTEN's work KNACKSTEDT extended it and introduced valuation as a generalization of properties. This approach corresponds to KNACKSTEDT's introduction of qualitative Reference-object as a generalization of Reference-objects used for qualitative data. For the purpose of this thesis, however, no distinction between quantitative and qualitative data is made. Instead, both types of Properties are conceptualized under one common framework. Moreover, the naming of measures as Properties indicates that Properties of objects in general are of interest for information system developers and users. The Content used to describe the Property defines whether the value of a Property is qualitative or not. Certain Properties, however, can be derived automat-

---

and many other authors cited in Footnote 28).

ically. Therefore, some special characteristics for those Properties are conceptualized as
well.

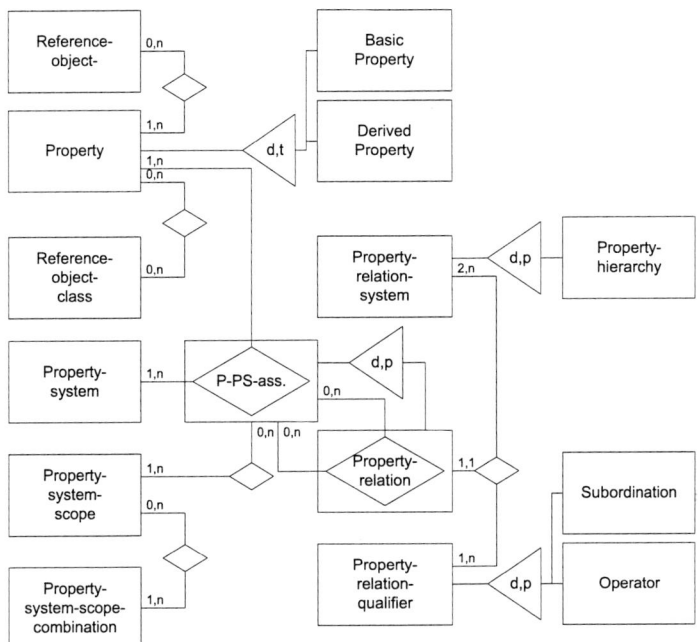

Figure 3.7: Property Metamodel (Conceptual Aspect)

3.3.1 Properties of Reference-objects

Reference-objects have Properties. Properties and Reference-objects are orthogonal to
each other and provide different views on data. Properties categorize different pieces
of information that are available for Reference-objects. Reference-objects are used to
classify all pieces of information stored in the system. Users navigate to a set of information by selecting one or more Reference-objects. Properties are used in order to
identify a particular piece of information within the set of information that is assigned
to a Reference-object. Therefore, the definition of the concept Property corresponds to
the concept Reference-object. Reference-objects define analytic trails through the information space and represent relevant objects from the real or imaginary world. Similarly,
Properties define analytic trails through pieces of information that are assigned to a particular Reference-object. It is useful to assign Properties to a class of Reference-objects.

By doing so, it is indicated that all elements of that class share the same set of Properties. Moreover, inadmissible combinations between Reference-objects and Properties are
foreclosed (for instance Property 'Photo' for the class 'Time'). Examples of Properties
are the following:

- Financial measures: turnover, costs, profits as well as margins. These measures
  are usually comprised in mathematical Property-(relation)-systems that depict the
  derivation of Properties by formulas.

- Correspondence: correspondence with customers and suppliers may include e-mail,
  fax, voice mail, letter and various other formats. Customers can use different
  channels when contacting organizations (for instance, general inquiry via e-mail,
  ordering over the Web and complaint by phone). In order to process customer or
  supplier inquiries, different types of correspondence have to be accessed efficiently
  and under one common framework. Moreover, legal regulations demand that information is stored persistently over a long period of time and that it can be accessed
  by authorities like auditing organizations or revenue authorities.

- States of documents: documents can have different statuses (for instance, in prepa-
  ration, submitted, under review and accepted). By conceptualizing these statuses
  as Properties, it is possible to explicate the cause for the generation of versions
  and variants of Content. However, this approach implies that conferences (for instance, ECIS or ICIS) and journals (for instance, MISQ or ISR) are conceptualized
  as Reference-objects. A document status is not a Property of a conference or a
  journal. Therefore, this example is not fully aligned to the definition of Properties
  which depend on Reference-objects. From the perspective of the author of a scientific publication, however, the successful submission of a paper for a conference or
  journal is generally a prerequisite for attendance or his or her career. Therefore,
  the document status is important and becomes a Property of the conference or
  journal.

Moreover, a Property can be characterized whether it is derived or not. A derived
Property can be determined automatically by the system if raw data used for the calculation respectively composition are given. If, for instance, turnover figures for the
last ten years are given, the system can automatically determine the *Derived Property*
'Average Turnover'. Consequently, Derived Properties can be defined if, and only if, the
data that characterizes this Property is purely quantitative. Application systems are

not able to derive meaningful information from qualitative data.[65] However, qualitative data can be composed automatically by the system. A property 'Construction Plan' can consist of several other Properties, which are composed in a meaningful and structured manner. Thus, Derived Property can include simple compositions of other Properties while the derivation of a qualitative Content is still impossible.

Of course, qualitative data can be used to represent quantitative data. For instance, different turnover levels can be characterized as 'good', 'excellent', 'bad' or 'improvable'. An application would be able to identify the average turnover level as 'good'. However, this representation is merely a variant of a quantitative data. Therefore, this is no exception to the rule. Thus, all Properties represented by qualitative data are *Basic Properties*.

3.3.2 Property-system & Property-relation-system

Properties can be aggregated in *Property-systems*. A Property-system comprises Properties into a set considered to be used meaningfully in conjunction. For instance, quantitative data in management information systems is usually aggregated according to financial measures defined in mathematical Property-systems like the DuPont-schema.[66] The DuPont-schema calculates the return on investment based on the stock turn rate and turnover profitability which are based on other measures as well. Users can use these Property-systems for navigating to the piece of data that explains a decline of the return of investment. Other controlling concepts (like the balanced scorecard) are based on similar measurement systems. Similar Property-systems can be constructed for qualitative data. For instance, the correspondence of customers and suppliers can be conceptualized within a Property-system 'Correspondence' that contains Properties like e-mail, voice-mail, letters and fax.

Within a Property-system, Properties can be related to each other by various relations (*Property-relation*). The concept *Property-relation-system* characterizes a specific set of Property-relations (for instance, a *Property-hierarchy*). The construction of Property-relation-systems is optional. Hierarchies are commonly used in order to assemble Properties which are based on other ones. The previously mentioned DuPont-schema

---

[65] Within the information retrieval community, several attempts have been made in order to develop algorithms that are able to process qualitative data with a high level of accuracy and as 'semantically' as possible. Given the metatheoretical assumptions stated in Section 2.1 applications system will never be able to process information like humans do, although current developments (in particular the Semantic Web) are connoting a 'semantic' information processing by machines.

[66] Cf. CONENBERG (1999), p. 592.

is an example of such a hierarchy. However, the hierarchical visualization of the measures in the DuPont-schema is only useful for navigational purposes. It does not reflect the mathematical relations between the Properties accurately. Thus, the concept of Property-relation-systems is needed in order to create subsystems of Property-systems depicting different aspects (in this case hierarchical visualization and mathematical calculation). In other words, Property-relation-systems embody representation variants of Properties. The concept *Property-relation-qualifier* specifies the type of the relation between two Properties within a Property-system. Apart from *Subordination*, which is used for hierarchical relations, and *Operators*, which are used for mathematical Property-relation-systems, several other types of relations are conceivable (the specialization is partial).

In order to create arbitrary sequences of Property-relations needed for the construction respectively calculation of complex mathematical relations between properties, a specialization of the reinterpreted relationship 'P-PS-ass.' is introduced. As a consequence, all elements of the relation 'Property-relation' are elements of the relation 'D-PS-ass.' as well. An element (a pair of two properties) of 'Property-relation' can be reused as an element in a new relation. Therefore, arbitrary sequences of Property-relations can be built. The approach is illustrated in Figure 3.8.

3.3.3 Property-system-scope & -combination

Corresponding to the conceptualization of Reference-objects and Dimensions, not all Properties are needed in every case, and the usage of Properties can be prohibited due to security reasons. Consequently, a trimming mechanism like the one introduced with Dimension-scopes is needed for Property-systems as well. Thus, the concept *Property-system-scope* is introduced. It represents a subset of a Property-system including its Property-relation-systems and Relation-qualifiers correspondingly. If Property-systems are trimmed, the resulting subsystem can get senseless and useless. In particular, mathematical relations between Properties may get lost resulting in a decreased interpretability of the system and the aspect it represents. However, the approach does not provide mechanisms that prevent the construction of inappropriate Property-system-scopes. The information system developer has to design Property-system-scopes carefully and considering usability and interpretability concerns. Similar to Dimension-scopes, Property-system-scopes can be aggregated to *Property-system-scope-groups*. The concept comprises one or more Property-system-scopes. It is used for personalization purposes.

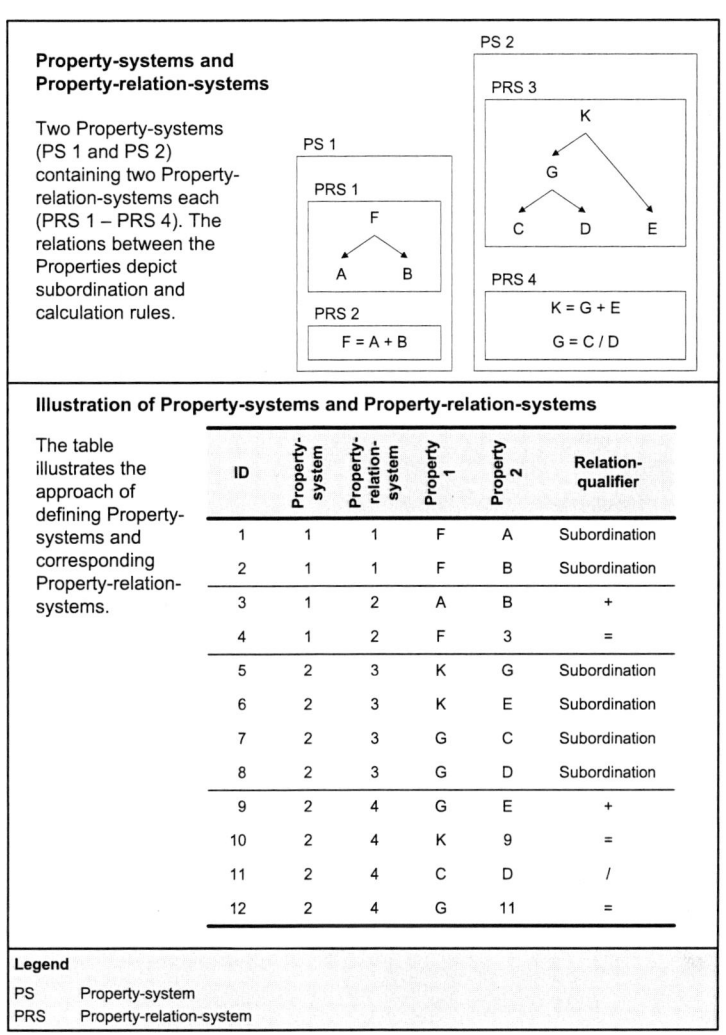

Figure 3.8: Complex Property-relations

3.3.4 Property Representation Form

The representation form of Properties is constructed in the style of Dimensions (compare Figure 3.9). An identifier classifies a Property-system (like 'Financial Measures' or

'Correspondence').[67] The name of the Property-system is given after a colon. Each Property-system can contain one or more relation systems, which adopt the name and qualify the relation (for instance, hierarchy and calculation). Scopes are named like the system itself with the colon left out followed by a specification of the trimming mechanism that was used. In case the scope is used to specify one relation system the name of the trimming mechanism is adopted from the relation qualifier (for instance, 'Financial Measures DuPont: Hierarchy').

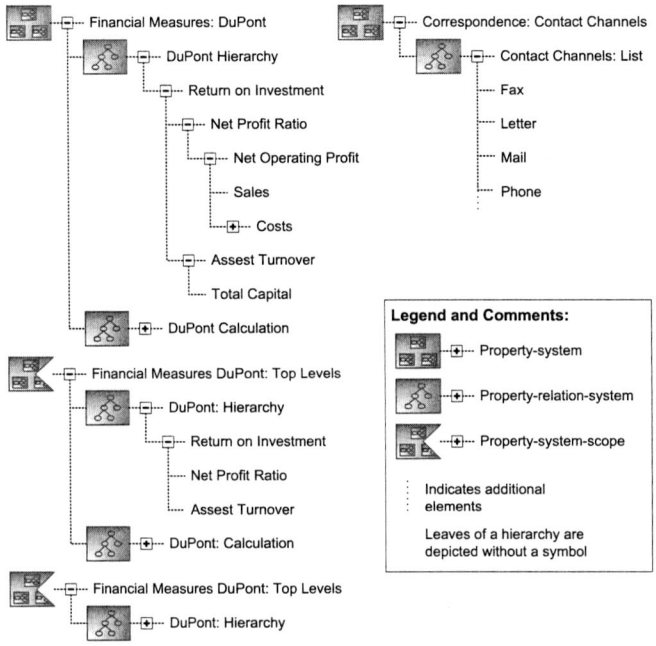

Figure 3.9: Property Representation Form

3.4 Content

Although the concepts of Reference-object and Property are central to the modelling technique, they have been introduced independently from each other up to now. Both model types are used in order to span a multidimensional space of concepts used for

---

[67] Although a concept like Property-system-class has not yet been introduced, it is useful to enforce this naming convention in order to increase model quality.

navigational purposes. Information space models define the whole solution space and provide analytic trails through the entirety of information, whereas Property models define trails through the information associated with a Reference-object. In order to unite both model types and to specify data on a more detailed level, Content models are introduced in this section.

Content models are used in order to conceptualize the data that is processed by the information system. Since the thesis is particularly concerned with semi-structured data which has special characteristics that complicate efficient processing and easy access, the Content conceptualization has to provide flexible means allowing to expatiate navigational capabilities over data. Moreover, data can be linked by numerous different relations which can be used by users to navigate more efficiently and consciously within the information system. Therefore, the following conceptualization investigates data more deeply than previous conceptual modelling approaches.[68] The Content metamodel is illustrated in Figure 3.10.

3.4.1 Attribute-type & Attribute-type-group

Metadata is used in order to annotate information processed by an information system. The understandability and interpretability of information can be enhanced by attributing each piece of information with additional data that give information on the semantics or the correct processing of the information.

If semantics of the information is illustrated, additional data about a dataset is given supporting the understanding of the dataset. For instance, a dataset in the database describes a specific person 'John Doe'. An attribute of this dataset may be 'Head of Marketing Department'. With regard to the dataset 'John Doe' this additional information represents metadata since it describes the role of 'John Doe'. Thus, the interpretation of the dataset regarding the amount of information that can be derived by a human is increased. Moreover, application systems need metadata in order to process data accurately. For instance, pictures may be stored in different resolutions and sizes. Applications need these metadata in order to ensure a correct representation of pictures on the screen.

Moreover, metadata can be characterized whether it is *inherent* or *coherent*. Inherent metadata is directly embedded in the data itself or can be derived automatically by

---

[68] In particular, the approach that serves as the basis for the following conceptualization is mainly concerned with structured data. Thus, an in-depth investigation of data itself is not necessary since each data element is conceptualized as a fact in a data warehouse environment. Refer to Footnote 28 in this chapter for references to previous work.

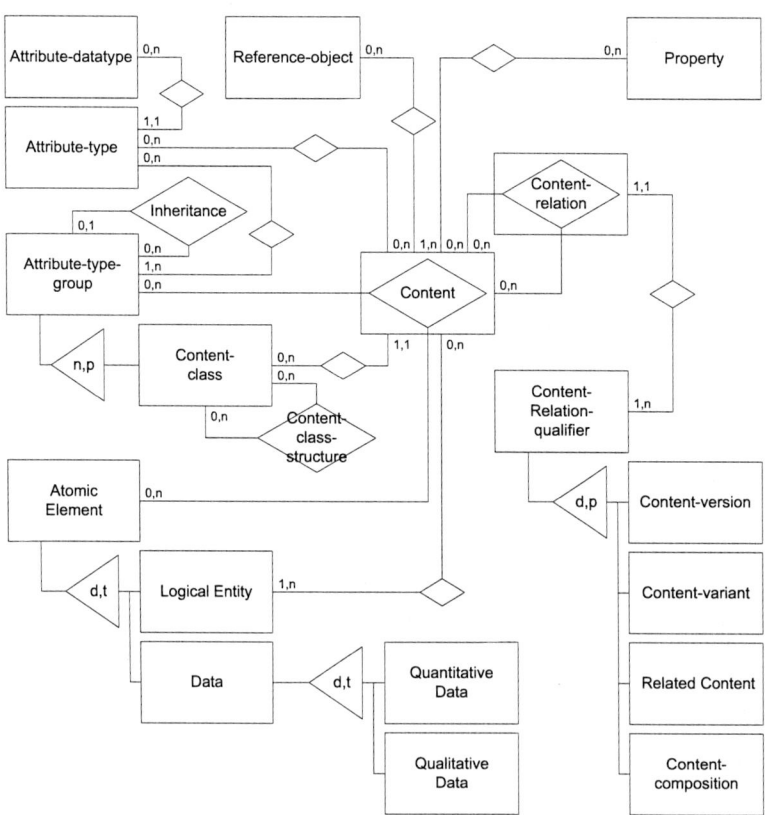

Figure 3.10: Content Metamodel (Conceptual Aspect)

applications. Thus, inherent metadata does not have to be modelled. Coherent metadata, however, cannot be determined automatically and needs to be edited by humans. Thus, only coherent metadata has to be modelled if it is considered to be useful by the information system developer. Some examples of inherent and coherent metadata can be taken from Table 3.5.

The modelling method adapts the metadata concept by introducing the concept of *Attribute-type*.[69] An Attribute-type is instantiated during run-time and represents any kind of metadata that is considered to be useful by the information system developer. Attribute-types are specified on type level. That is, the instantiations of an Attribute are not modelled on a conceptual level. For instance, the Attribute-type 'Author' specifies

---

[69]   Compare Figure 3.10 for the following.

Content Class	Inherent Metadata	Coherent Metadata
Text	number of words	author subject language
Picture	size in pixel colourdepth datatype (e. g. JPEG, BMP)	photographer subject of the photo
Video	length in minutes resolution	director production year language actors

Table 3.5: Coherent and Inherent Metadata

metadata that can be used to annotate any piece of information. During run-time that piece of information is annotated by the instantiation 'John Doe'. As stated earlier, the concept Attribute-datatype is not modelled on a conceptual level. For the sake of completeness, however, it is introduced and represents the datatypes of attribute-types. Common datatypes are string, data, number and memo. Moreover, it can be useful to define complex Attribute-datatypes like lists in order to subsume similar attributes.[70] Attribute-types may be compiled to one or more Attribute-type-sets, which comprise at least one Attribute-type. Moreover, the inheritance of Attribute-type-sets allows the efficient construction and reuse of complex sets of Attribute-types.

3.4.2 Atomic Element

An *Atomic Element* represents any kind of semi-structured or unstructured data (*Qualitative Data*) and structured data (*Quantitative Data*). The distinction between quantitative and qualitative data is important for the purpose at hand since they can be processed differently in an information system and, on top of that, different operations are possible with them. For instance, quantitative data can be aggregated.[71] Atomic Elements can include texts, pictures and videos as well as scripts that compile data dynamically during run-time. The adjective 'Atomic' indicates that elements are the

---

[70] For instance, an Attribute-type 'Authors' of Attribute-datatype 'List' may be defined. Thus, a vector of one or more authors may be defined during run-time.

[71] Aggregation is a typical operation in data warehouse environments. Compare VOSSEN (1999), pp. 669 ff. for details on the data warehouse concept.

smallest entities that can be processed by the information system and cannot be decomposed any further. No restrictions concerning the granularity of the data are made.
That is, a single word can be conceptualized as an Atomic Element as well as an entire book. Since each Atomic Element can constitute Content if it is combined with an
Attribute-type-group, a single word (Atomic Element) can be annotated extensively with
metadata and can be made accessible by creating appropriate navigation structures.[72]
If an entire book is defined as an Atomic Element it is not possible to annotate chapters
or paragraphs of the book with metadata. A (potentially) large amount of information
is viewed as a single entity within the system. Moreover, navigation structures can be
defined only for the entire book. It is not possible to access chapters or paragraphs
of the book directly. The choice of an appropriate level of granularity depends on the
decision of humans and has to be made with regard to the trade-off between economical
efficiency and efficient information processing. If higher levels of granularity are used,
efficient information processing may be reduced since only large pieces of information
are accessible directly. If lower levels of granularity are used, the effort of data creation,
maintenance and metadata management increases.

By encapsulating database queries, the datasets they represent can be annotated with
metadata. Thus, it is possible to maintain the flexibility of dynamic content generation as well as the extensive usage of metadata annotation. It is important to note
that the dataset may be dynamic, that is, the actual data displayed during run-time is
subject to change. However, the dynamic dataset is used as a container and annotated
with metadata. Thus, it can be made accessible using complex navigation structures.
Moreover, the information derived from the dataset does not change from a conceptual point of view. Although the data generated by a dynamic database query may
change, it conveys the same 'meaning'. In this case, the amount of information represents the knowledge that can be derived by humans. Since database queries usually
output structured datasets, the amount of information that is carried by the dataset can
be anticipated for future datasets as long as the dataset remains its structure. However,
humans may perceive that information differently and may derive different actions from
the data. This approach of embedding dynamic content within the conceptualization
maintains consistency regarding navigation structures and content conceptualization.
Figure 3.11 illustrates the conceptualization of database queries as dynamic pieces of
Content. A small PHP-script represents a sales report that is dynamically created during run-time. The script creates a list of products, the amount being sold and sales
value. In conjunction with an Attribute-type-group the script is conceptualized as Con-

---

[72]   Refer to Section 2.2.3 for the definition and usage of navigation structures.

tent and can be embedded in the information space. By embedding the Content in the information space it becomes trackable. Due to the dynamic nature of this query, however, the dataset actually retrieved during run-time is different (indicated by two different Content representations in Figure 3.11).

Content `Sales Report' Conceptualization

Atomic Element	```
	<?php
	  $result=dbx_query("
	    SELECT product_id, product_name, amount, value
	    FROM product_sales;");
	?>
	``

Attribute-type-set	Author = John Doe Publish Date = 2005-01-01 Expiry Date = 2005-12-31

Content `Sales Report' Representation 1 (run-time at 2005-05-01)

Product_ID	Name	Amount	Value
4711	Product A	34	7.854,23 €
4712	Product B	179	45.789,12 €
4713	Product C	15	4.589,23 €

Content `Sales Report' Representation 2 (run-time at 2005-10-01)

Product_ID	Name	Amount	Value
4711	Product A	114	26.789,11 €
4712	Product B	289	65.879,12 €
4713	Product C	45	15.042,78 €
4714	Product D	15	4.589,23 €

Figure 3.11: Dynamic Content

Additionally, Atomic Elements include Logical Entities used to annotate Content-compositions with metadata. Thus, Logical Entities serve as hulls for additional metadata annotation. For instance, a book is composed of several chapters.[73] Each chapter is conceptualized as Content. Thus, it contains the text itself as well as Attribute-type-group (for instance, an author). In order to annotate the book as a whole, a Logical Entity is needed. This logical entity and the Attribute-type-group 'Editors' constitute the Content 'Book'. Although, the Logical Entity does not carry information itself, it symbolizes that the composition of chapters represents a more complex and richer piece of information than its assembled parts alone. In other words, the composed Content is more than the sum of its parts. In order to conceptualize the added value derived from the composition of contents, it is necessary to give more information on the compilation

---

[73] Refer to Section 3.4.3 for an explanation of Content-composition.

as a whole. This can be done by using additional metadata as it is conceptualized within this approach.[74]

3.4.3 Content, Content-class & Content-relation

Having defined Attribute-types and Atomic Elements, the *Content* concept can be derived. Content is constituted by a tuple of an Attribute-type-group and an Atomic Element. Thus, it represents raw data (Atomic Elements) that is annotated with at least one Attribute-type. As soon as raw data is combined with metadata, it becomes Content and is considered to be meaningful and useful. Therefore, it may be processed by the information system and displayed to the user. Raw data alone as well as metadata itself are not useful and cannot be interpreted and processed meaningfully by humans or application systems. The Attribute-types that are assigned to the Content in the Attribute-type Atomic-Element relationship are constituent for Content. Thus, this set defines the *Content-class*. Content-classes are characterized by a common Attribute-type-group. That is, all instances of a Content-class contain the same set of Attribute-types. Therefore, they are specializations of Attribute-type-sets. Not all Attribute-type-sets constitute a Content-class (a partial specialization).[75] In order to define complex compilations of Content, Content-classes can be structured. For instance, an annual sales report contains several tables with revenues, multiple figures and some pieces of text. Consequently, the Content-class 'Annual Sales Report' is constituted by several other Content-classes.

In order to provide more flexibility, additional Attribute-types can be assigned to Content (relationship between Attribute-type and Content). These Attribute-types do not constitute the Content-class. Usually, Content is not to be modelled on a conceptual level. Instead, Content-classes are defined that characterize the type of information potentially processed by the information system. Thus, only Content-classes are specified. Under certain circumstances, however, Content may be modelled on a conceptual level. If Content, for instance, a sales report, is considered to be very important and if its placement in the information space is crucial, this Content may be modelled on a conceptual level in order to ensure a suitable handling and specification of that Content. Furthermore, the Content itself can be the subject of interest in the information system, especially if it is a complex Content like a book or a the documentation of a project.

---

[74]   This approach can be motivated by system theory. System theory states that a system cannot be characterized holistically by its elements. The relations between elements have to be analyzed as well in order to fully comprehend a system. For details on system theory compare Section 2.2.1.

[75]   Compare the specialization construct in Figure 3.10.

If the documentation of a project is done by using a web information system, certain guidelines concerning the structure and composition of contents may be defined prior to the start of the project. Thus, the Content 'project documentation' may be specified conceptually.

Content can be structured, that is, Content may contain other contents or, otherwise, it is related to other Content. Thus, the concept *Content-relation* is introduced. Content-relations constitute a navigational structure within this approach.[76] A Content-relation is classified by using a *Content-relation-qualifier*, which can be partially distinguished into the types *Content-version*, *Content-variant*, *Content-composition* and *Related Content*. A Content-version indicates prior versions of a specific Content. Thus, users can navigate to prior versions of that Content. Only one version can be valid at a given moment, whereas more than one valid variant may exist simultaneously. Prior versions can be kept for archiving purposes and documentation. Content-variants originate from the same ancestor Content. Therefore, Content-variants conjoin contents that are strongly related.

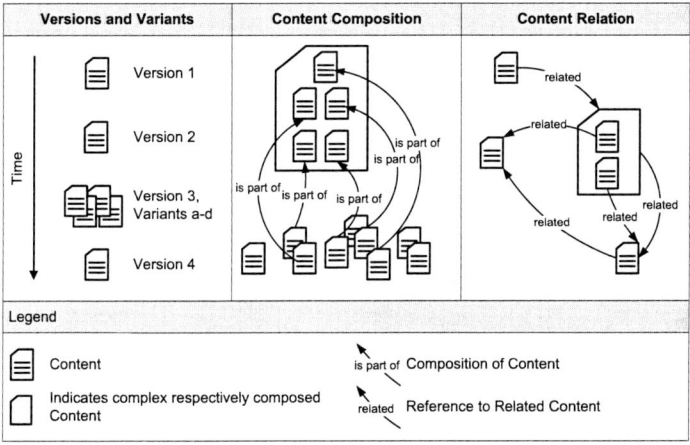

Figure 3.12: Content-relations: Versions, Variants, Compositions and Relations

In contrast to Content-variants the concept Related Content conjoins contents that are more loosely coupled. A Related Content may be totally different concerning type (for instance, pictures and text) and data (for instance, news article and scholarly paper). Related Contents may either be related thematically or in a different way and do not descend from the same ancestor Content. Finally, Content-compositions are introduced.

---

[76] Compare Section 2.2.3 for details on navigational structures as well as the example in Section 4.2.

Content-compositions are used in order to compose complex contents. Consider, for instance, a book. A book contains chapters which themselves contain paragraphs. Each element itself can be conceptualized as Content. The relations between variants, versions, Content-hierarchies and related Content are illustrated in Figure 3.12.

The conceptualization that has been introduced so far implies a differentiation of two different kinds of metadata that should be addressed briefly.[77] From the Content point of view, the concepts Attribute-type, Reference-object as well as Property represent metadata. Reference-objects and Properties classify the information contained in the system. They depict phenomena from the real or imaginary world that exist independently from Content. Thus, they contain information value themselves. Additionally, it is required that both concepts are changing slowly over time if they do so at all. Otherwise, usability and interpretability of the information classified by them is reduced. In contrast to these concepts, Attribute-types represent metadata with Content-specific values. Attribute-types cannot or should not be part of the information space. In contrast to the information space constituting concepts, a particular instance of an Attribute-type cannot be interpreted meaningfully on its own. For instance, a Content may have an Attribute-type 'Version' with the run-time value '1.0'. The run-time value has no information value and cannot exist independently from Content. Moreover, Attribute-types neither have a structural order nor are they embedded in structures in any other way except their constituting role for Content-classes.

Theoretically, the difference between both types of metadata can be explained by the logical propaedeutic of KAMLAH & LORENZEN.[78] Reference-objects and Properties are predicators. Predicators are attributed to concepts, phenomena or 'things'. Attribute-types are labels respectively proper names which are attributed to instances of things. The predicator 'dog' is attributed to a particular subspecies of mammals. 'Lassie' is an instance of the 'thing' that is meant by the predicator 'dog'. Thus, 'Lassie' is a label. Since this label could be attributed to any other animal which is not a 'dog', the label itself does not represent a concept.

3.4.4 Content Representation Form

As stated earlier, Contents are usually not modelled on a conceptual level. Instead, Content-classes and Attribute-types can be specified. Both concepts are particularly useful for implementation purposes. For instance, an Attribute-type-group can be used for configuring forms on content-management-systems automatically. Each Attribute-

---

[77]   Compare also BECKER et al. (2004b), 30 f. for the following.
[78]   Compare BECKER et al. (2004b), p. 31 and Section 2.1.3 for the following.

type represents a metadata field that editors have to fill out in order to create a new Content of a specific Content-class. Figure 3.13 illustrates the modelling of Attribute-type-(groups) and Content-classes.[79]

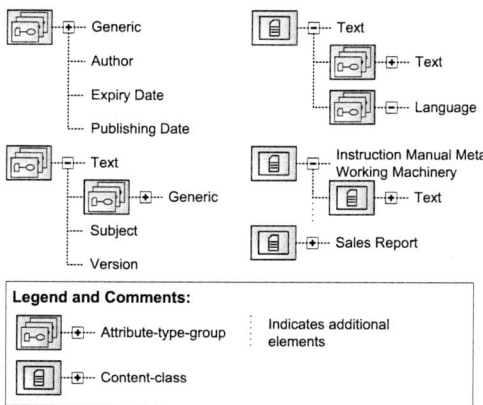

Figure 3.13: Representation Form Content

3.5 Navigation and Associative Trails

As stated above, this thesis is particularly interested in a sound investigation and conceptualization of navigation in large data pools. The modelling approach presented in the previous chapters provides extensive, implicit and explicit means for modelling navigational structures through and for data. Navigation itself is not modelled by information system developers. Instead, navigational structures arise as a by-product of the specification of the information space, Properties and Content. By combining the three model types, extensive navigational structures for navigation through the data pool are defined. Moreover, it is possible to use navigation structures in order to express statements about the concepts they combine. Therefore, associative information processing is facilitated.

In general, the act of navigation can be defined as a change the web information system is undergoing if users are interacting with it. By following links, users are changing the state of the system which results in a different collection of data that is displayed to them. Thus, each act of navigation changes the set of data considered to be rele-

---

[79] Compare BECKER et al. (2003b), pp. 119 f. for similar representation forms of Content and Attribute-types.

vant in that particular moment. Although, the mechanism of Content selection is the
same, users are interacting with different objects respectively concepts of the system
(Reference-objects, Properties or Content). Therefore, different types of navigation can
be distinguished. The usage of Reference-objects by users implies that they are using
concepts for which a shared understanding has been achieved. Reference-objects and
Properties exist independently from data that is actually stored in the system, whereas
Content represents data itself. Thus, the meaning associated which the concepts is
different and so are the navigational structures associated with them.

3.5.1 Navigation-path

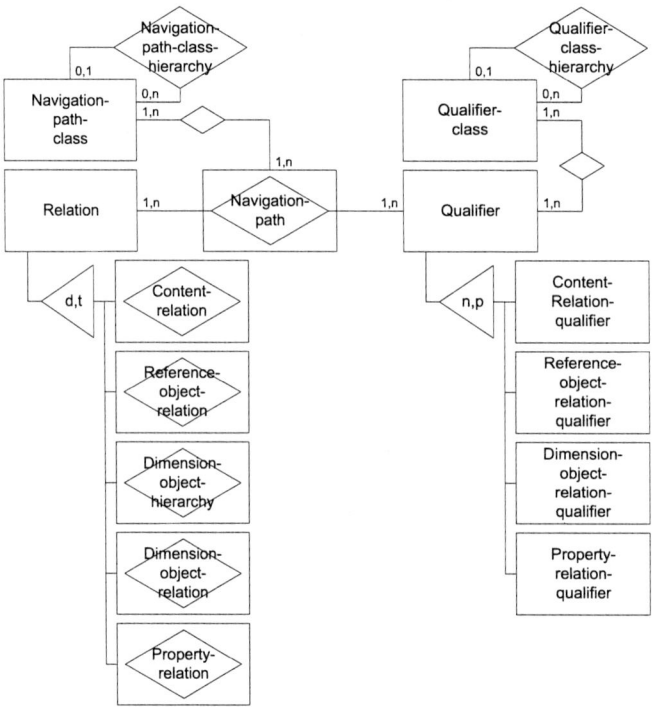

Figure 3.14: Navigation-path Metamodel (Conceptual Aspect)

The navigation metamodel (Figure 3.14) is used in order to illustrate the navigational concept introduced by this modelling approach. Several relations between objects
have been introduced in the preceding sections. Some link Contents, while others link

Reference-objects or Properties. All types of relations are generalized by using the concept *Relation*. Each Relation is specified by using a *Qualifier*, which is also derived from the other conceptualizations. The specialization of Qualifiers is not disjoint and partial because some Qualifiers (like subordination) are used for several concepts and additional Qualifiers can be introduced.[80] A tuple of one Relation and one Qualifier constitutes a *Navigation-path*. Navigation-paths as well as Qualifiers can be aggregated in classes (*Navigation-path-class* and *Qualifier-class*). Both concepts can be ordered hierarchically and are used for personalization purposes.[81]

3.5.2 Statement

Navigation-paths cannot only be used for navigational purposes but also for the sake of expressing *Statements* about the participating things in the relation. The construction of elementary statements is a core concept of approaches that are concerned with knowledge representation, appliance and modelling.[82] Not all Navigation-paths are statements and some function as Statements and Navigation-paths (non-disjoint, partial specialization). An elementary Statement has the form <subject, predicate, object>.[83] Obviously, such relations can be created by the concepts that have been introduced. The elements of the statement are defined by their relation to each other. The predicate is defined by a Qualifier. Thus, a triple like <Element A, Qualifier, Element B> resembles an elementary Statement. The usage of Navigation-paths as Statements can be illustrated with the help of the following example:

$$
\begin{pmatrix} Bread \\ Germany \\ 2005 \end{pmatrix} \quad \begin{matrix} Complementary \\ Product \end{matrix} \quad \begin{pmatrix} Milk \\ Germany \\ 2005 \end{pmatrix}
$$

Reference-object A   Qualifier   Reference-object B

---

[80]   Additional qualifiers are needed in order to express Statements whose objects have a different type. Compare next paragraph for an introduction to the construction and usage of Statements.

[81]   Compare the following Section.

[82]   SOWA provides an extensive overview of knowledge representation including logical, philosophical and computational foundations (SOWA (1999)) as well as numerous examples of statements in different representation forms. Although this thesis is *not* concerned with knowledge management and its various sub-disciplines, the author is convinced that the modelling approach presented in this Chapter provides elementary means to gather and express 'knowledge' and, thus, to improve knowledge management.

[83]   The resemblance to the concept of the Semantic Web is obvious and will be addressed briefly in Chapter 4. Compare Section 2.2.4 for a brief overview of the Semantic Web.

A Reference-object-relation relates two Reference-objects. The Qualifier 'Complementary Product' qualifies the relation between both objects. Thus, the statement can be expressed as follows in natural language: the products milk and bread are complementary in Germany in the year 2005. That is, they are usually sold in conjunction with each other. The triple of objects and a qualifier acts as a Navigation-path as well as a Statement. For instance, users can follow the Navigation-path from one object to another in order to investigate a downturn in sales of bread that might be explained by data assigned to the Reference-object milk. A comparison of different milk brands in a magazine might have documented poor quality of the company's milk brand. A copy of the article is assigned to the Reference-object milk. Since bread and milk are complementary products, the downturn in sales of bread can possibly be explained by the result of the comparison in the magazine. This example also illustrates the necessity of enriching the information space by using metadata and qualifiers as well as the problems that arise if qualitative data is integrated in the analysis. Without the qualitative data element (the article), a reason for the downturn in sales could probably not be found. Moreover, algorithms or application systems are useless in this particular case since the qualitative data cannot be interpreted meaningfully by computers. However, a large portion of the data that is currently processed in organizations is qualitative. Therefore, it is reasonable to include qualitative data and to provide means for analyzing it efficiently.

Following the conceptualization so far, statements can be built only if its subject and object are of the same type (for instance, two Reference-objects, two Contents or two Properties). In order to provide more flexible means for construing statements, the conceptualization is extended. The four different objects are generalized in the concept *Statement-element*.[84] A recursion on Statement-elements links two elements. Moreover, the relationship is constituted by a Qualifier which serves as a predicate again. Thus, a tuple of two objects and a Qualifier is build. Sometimes, it is necessary or useful to built statements about statements. That is, a (previously constructed) statement becomes subject or object in a new statement. In order to illustrate this, statements are generalized in the concept Statement-element as well. Therefore, a Statement can be used in new statements. If, for instance, somebody checks the validity of the statement of the example above he or she can predicate the statement to be valid. Finally, a Statement can become a Content (non-disjoint, partial specialization). In this case, user

---

[84]   The addition (subject or object) is added for clarity reasons. It is not part of the name of the concept. Otherwise, two concepts would have to be built resulting in decreased readability of the metamodel.

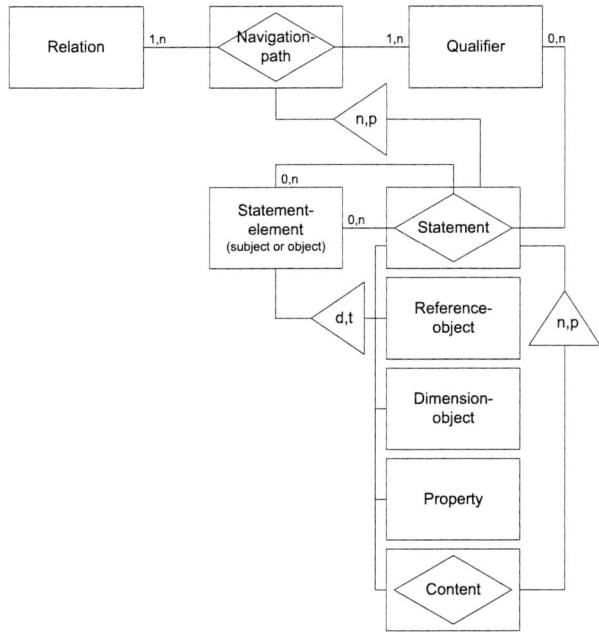

Figure 3.15: Statement Metamodel (Conceptual Aspect)

would be able to access and discuss the statement in the system.

$$\underbrace{\begin{pmatrix} Bread \\ Germany \\ 2005 \end{pmatrix} \begin{matrix} Complementary \\ Product \end{matrix} \begin{pmatrix} Milk \\ Germany \\ 2005 \end{pmatrix}}_{\text{Statement}} \quad valid \qquad (\text{John Doe})$$

Statement   Qualifier   Reference-object

3.5.3 Associative Trail

The main advantage of web information systems is the ability to enable associative information processing and, thus, to align human information processing more accurately with application systems. Although *Associative Trails*[85] are not modelled during design time, it is useful to illustrate the capabilities conceptual models can provide for associative information processing. Therefore, the usage of a web information system for associative information processing is discussed briefly. *Users* have *Information needs*

---

[85]   Compare Figure 3.16 for an illustration of the conceptualization.

when they are faced with a problem in a given context. That is, they use the information system in order to find a solution or a given problem. The example illustrated above can potentially provide a solution respectively explanation for a downturn in sales of bread. The information space is the solution space which is traversed by the users. By following links and interpreting statements about concepts and data in the system, users are enabled to map their own associative information processing to the data stored in the system. In fact, the information system is particularly designed for this purpose and the user's associative trails are analyzed and implemented in the system.[86] Thus, a web information system is potentially able to enable more efficient information processing by users.

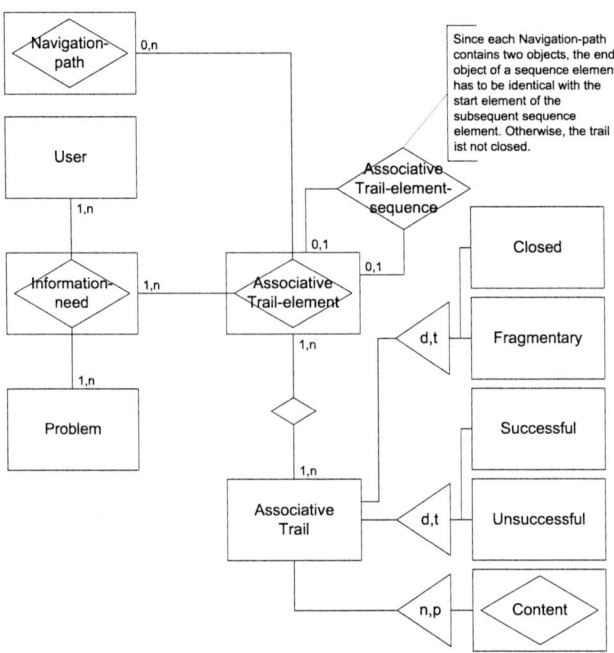

Figure 3.16: Associative Trail Metamodel (Conceptual Aspect)

An *Associative Trail-element* is constituted by at least one Navigation-path used by a User for a given Problem. Associative Trail-elements are ordered in sequences that depict

---

[86]   Of course, it is impossible to predict all information needs that can potentially arise and all Associative Trails that may be appropriate for all users of the system. The appliance and the maintenance of the system is a cyclic process by nature and requires continuous improvement of the system.

the traversing of the solution space by a user. An Associative Trail contains at least one Associative Trail-element. If a sequence is *Closed*, there are no gaps in the sequence.[87] A Closed sequence indicates that the users has successfully and efficiently traversed the information space and has satisfied his or her information need (or thinks so). Otherwise, it is *Fragmentary*. This indicates that a solution might have been found but the trail that was used was not efficient. The user had to restart his or her search or the user jumped within the information space. Such search patterns are typical for vague and imprecise information needs.[88] Accordingly, an Associative Trail can be characterized by checking whether it was *Successful* or not. In order to share Associative Trails between users, each trail can become a Content. Therefore, an Associative Trail that provides a solution for a certain problem can be easily distributed between users. It is important to note that the *whole* trail is stored in the system rather than the address of the last Content the user retrieved. The Associative Trail depicts *how* a user was able to satisfy his or her information need and which associations directed his or her search. Thus, the trail gives insight in the a user's 'thoughts'. Of course, the trail can be unsuccessful. In this case, it can be analyzed in order to evaluate why the user was not able to satisfy his or her information need. Additionally, an Associative Trail can be used in Statements. This possibility provides powerful and extensive means for creating complex statements about the information space and the data in it. As indicated earlier, Navigation-paths, Statements and Associative Trails are modelled implicitly by the other model types. Therefore, it is not necessary to create representation forms for Navigation-paths.

Obviously, this conceptualization of associative information processing does not account for the complex and vague nature of human 'thinking' and 'problem solving' in every detail. Human information processing is vague and unpredictable by nature and, therefore, difficult to conceptualize and 'implement' in information systems.[89] Given the assumptions that are outlined in Chapter 2 a 'full' and 'adequate' understanding of human information processing is currently beyond the scope of research. Nevertheless, it is crucial to outline a conceptualization and to sketch a web information system that facilitates human information processing as adequately as possible. It can not be expected that it is possible to account for every subtle difference of individual information processing and the problems that are entailed in this process. However, it is one of the basic premises of this thesis that the conceptualization outlined above gives valuable insights into human information processing and provides suitable means for information

---

[87]   The end object of a preceding sequence entry is the start object of the succeeding entry. Compare the constraint in Figure 3.16.

[88]   Cf. Section 2.3 for a discussion of information needs and human information processing.

[89]   Refer to Section 2.3 for an overview of human information processing.

system developers to describe and to implement 'efficient' and flexible web information systems. It is essential to view the interactions of users with web information systems as a sequence of navigational acts that are linked to specific information needs and associations.

3.6 Personalization

Personalization models are used for multiple purposes. Firstly, the selection of Contents can be personalized (concept *Selection-personalization*). It can take place by using Reference-objects or Properties. In this case, personalization models provide macro navigation capabilities since they can be used to switch between large amounts of information. Secondly, Content itself can be personalized (*Content-personalization*). Thirdly, the navigational capabilities of users can be personalized (*Navigation-personalization*). Finally, the restriction of information access as special kind of personalization is introduced (*Access-object*). The four different fields of application of personalization are introduced in the following Sections. The conceptual language aspect of personalization is illustrated in Figure 3.17.

The personalization mechanism is based on the definition of *Personalization-objects*. Personalization-objects are based on organizational entities or other organizational constructs that are usually modelled in organizational charts (organizational structure) or processes. However, organizational entities are used slightly differently in the following conceptualization than they are in traditional organizational models.[90] Moreover, the general layout of the representation forms (hierarchical trees) can be retained, which increases model interpretation and ease of use.[91] Therefore, Personalization-objects are introduced independently from other conceptual models which may be used by an organization.

A Personalization-object is a generalization of a *Role*, a *Task*, an individual (*User*) or an *Organizational Entity*. The relationships between the four different subtypes of Personalization-objects are not intended to illustrate the approach. A User can be assigned to Organizational Entities, performs Tasks and can take Roles. Examples for Roles include apprentice, manager, referee or head of department.[92] Tasks are em-

---

[90]   For instance, it is not necessary to model the organizational structure or business process in detail. The models are not intended to provide a comprehensive overview of business processes or other organizational aspects.

[91]   KNACKSTEDT used a different approach and intergrated well-known modelling languages like organizational charts and event-driven process chains. Cf. KNACKSTEDT (2004), pp. 139 ff.

[92]   Cf. KNACKSTEDT (2004), p. 192.

bedded in a complex task structure defined by the business processes.[93] Organizational Entities are departments, division or other units that describe the general organizational structure of an organization. Different types of relations (like 'reports to' or 'disciplinary subordinate') can exist between Organizational Entities (*OE-relation-qualifier*).[94] All different types of Personalization-objects are modelled by using a single symbol. The differentiation of the four types is achieved by naming conventions rather than by particular modelling constructs.

Finally, *Access-objects* are introduced. In contrast to Personalization-objects the appliance of Access-objects *cannot* be overruled by users. In general, users are not able to select access objects, nor are they able to ignore them.[95] Both concepts are defined for the same components (like roles or individuals) and differ merely by the interpretation of the restriction, which is strict in the case of Access-objects and optional in the case of Personalization-objects. Thus, Access-objects are a variant of Personalization-objects. In order to illustrate the difference, however, a new symbol is introduced. Personalization-objects as well as Access-objects are generalized in the concept *Delimiter-objects* in order to improve the readability of the following metamodels. Moreover, Delimiter-objects can be structured in order to compose more complex sets of them. The restriction implies that only Delimiter-objects of the same type (Personalization or Access) can be composed.

3.6.1 Selection-personalization

It is possible to reduce the amount of information considered to be relevant for an individual, a task, an organizational entity or a particular role by assigning subspaces of the information space (Dimension-scope-group) to Personalization-objects. Information overload can be prevented and the usability of the system can be increased. Likewise, Property-system-scopes can be linked to Personalization-objects in order to decrease the amount of information. The specialization of Selection-personalization is not disjoint since both constructs can be used simultaneously. For instance, a Personalization-object 'Top Management' is linked to a subspace of the information space that contains mea-

---

[93] The modelling approach does not include capabilities for modelling business processes. Event-driven process chains can be used for modelling business processes. Cf. SCHEER (1992); SCHEER (1999), in particular 102 ff. or BECKER & SCHÜTTE (2004), pp. 106 ff. for an introduction of process modelling using event-driven process chains.

[94] Cf. KNACKSTEDT (2004), pp. 192 f. The concept is integrated in order to illustrate the approach. It is not modelled on a conceptual level.

[95] Of course, this restriction does not apply to system administrators who usually have the access rights to change access objects in order to test their reliability and operativeness.

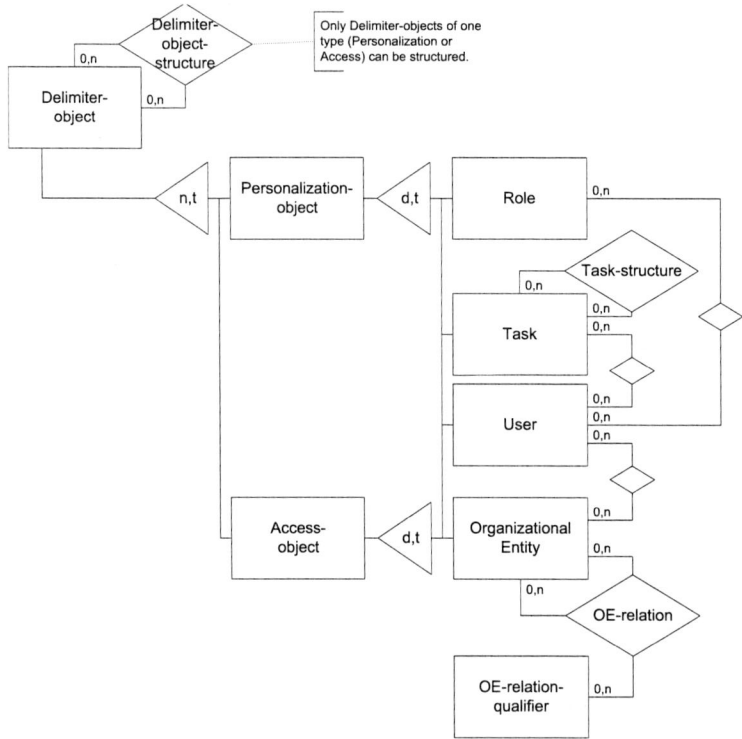

Figure 3.17: Personalization-object Metamodel (Conceptual Aspect)

sures and figures for the whole organization. Thus, other information is not displayed by default for users that belong to top management. The selection can be overruled by user interaction. During run-time, Users are able to switch or combine Personalization-objects assigned to them or inherited due to their affiliation to an Organizational-entity. Additionally, it is conceivable that users are able to define an operation (like intersection or union) if they combine Personalization-objects.

3.6.2 Content-personalization

Since the modelling approach is also concerned with the conceptual specification of the data used within a system, the concept of *Content-personalization* is introduced (compare Figure 3.19). Personalization of Content can have two effects. Firstly, data that

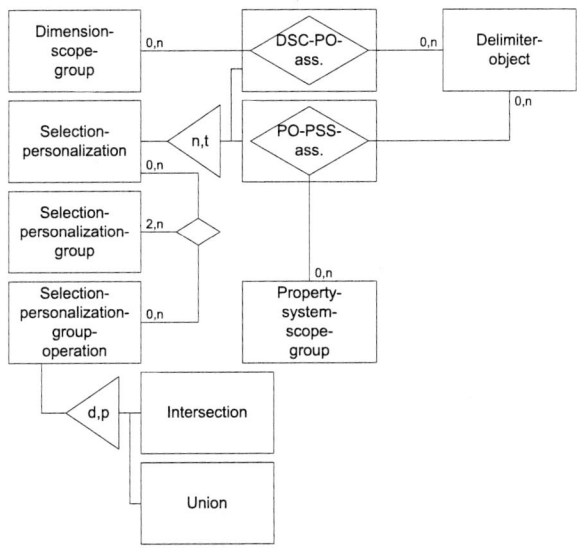

Figure 3.18: Selection-personalization Metamodel (Conceptual Aspect)

is embedded in the Content can be selected with regard to a Personalization-object.[96] Depending on the complexity of Content, the resulting Content can be totally different concerning its information content.[97] This kind of personalization is modelled using the concept of Content-class. A Personalization-object that is assigned to a Content-class indicates that instances of the Content-class are created due to requirements defined by a personalization object. Secondly, the structural composition of Content can be personalized by using Personalization-objects and associating them with Content-relations.

3.6.3 Navigation-personalization

Although no representation forms for Navigation-paths which would be needed in order to depict *Navigation-personalization* are constructed in this thesis, the approach should be illustrated for reasons of clarity and completeness (compare Figure 3.20). Like the other personalization models, Navigation-personalization can apply to a restriction in using *Navigation-path-classes* and *Qualifier-classes*. Thus, the relationships between

---

[96]   For instance, the account balance in online-banking systems. From the system's point of view the Content 'Account balance' is identical for all users (a single template) and is individualized during run-time by selecting the actual account balance for the user that has been identified during log-in.

[97]   In particular, Content that is dynamically created by complex database queries can change structurally and with regard to information content.

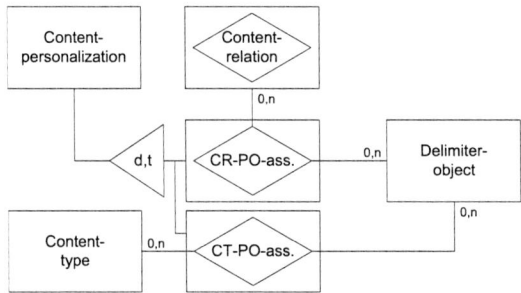

Figure 3.19: Content-personalization Metamodel (Conceptual Aspect)

both concepts and the Delimiter-object can be generalized to Navigation-personalization. If this kind of personalization was implemented in an information system, selection and display of links (Navigation-path) and Qualifiers could be accommodated to user's needs. If, for any reason, the usage of certain Navigation-path-classes is to be restricted, an Access-object can be assigned accordingly.

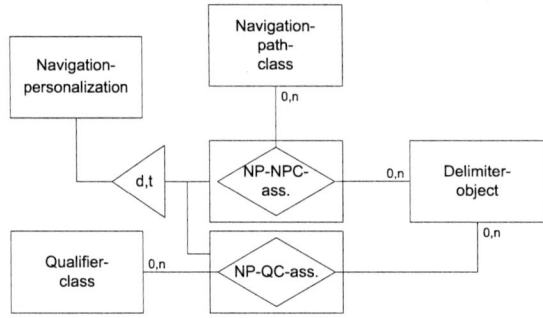

Figure 3.20: Navigation-personalization Metamodel (Conceptual Aspect)

3.6.4 Personalization Representation Form

As indicated by the metamodels in this section, personalization is a general operation that can be applied to several other concepts like Content or subspaces of the information space. Whenever a concept is assigned to a Delimiter-object, objects that are represented by the concept are pre-selected (personalization) or can be accessed only by a specific user group (access restriction). Figure 3.21 illustrates some examples for the usage of Delimiter-objects. Since independent representation forms for User, Tasks, Roles and

Organizational Entities have not yet been introduced, the type is indicated by using a naming convention. An abbreviation (U, T, R, OE) followed by a colon is used for this purpose.

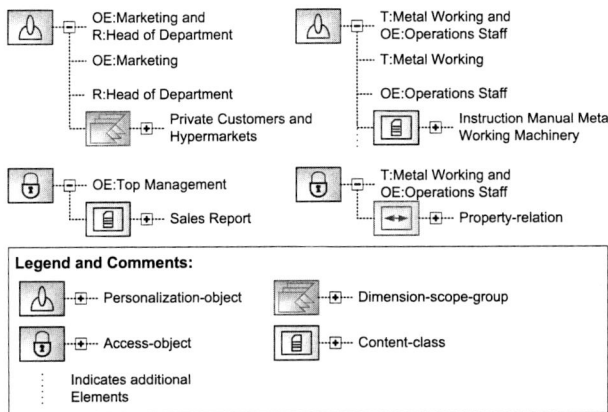

Figure 3.21: Representation Form Personalization

Chapter 4

Modelling Example & Method Application

4.1 Preliminary Remarks

On the base of the background outlined in Chapter 2, a conceptual modelling method for web information systems is constructed in Chapter 3. The research approach is essentially interpretivistic respectively hermeneutic and, therefore, speculative by nature. Additionally, this thesis does not provide empirical data that allows evaluating the modelling approach according to suitable criteria. The speculative nature is, however, an inherent problem of interpretivistic research.[1] Nevertheless, the applicability and usefulness of the approach should be substantiated with the help of examples and a case study that has been conducted. Thus, the validation of the research result is carried out by means of an 'informed argument'.[2] By doing so, the modelling approach can be evaluated by peers with regard to evaluation criteria (for instance, completeness, correctness and suitability).[3]

The discussion proceeds as follows: firstly, a fictitious scenario is described that illustrates how the conceptual modelling method can be used to specify web information systems. As stated in the exposition, this thesis is *not* concerned with the process of modelling as such. Thus, the example does not elaborate on the requirements gathering process or the means used to achieve a mutual understanding of objectives and artefacts. Additionally, the fictitious example elaborates on the usage of navigation structures for

---

[1]   Cf. GALLIERS (1992), p. 152.

[2]   'Informed arguments' is a descriptive evaluation method that "uses the information from the knowledge base to build a convincing argument for the artefact's utility" (cf. HEVNER et al. (2004), p. 86). Since the design science approach presented by HEVNER et al. is inherently positivistic, it is not discussed in detail.

[3]   Refer to Section 2.1.3 for some criteria that can be used to evaluate interpretative research.

human information processing and illustrates the relation of the modelling approach with emergent technologies of the Semantic Web.

Secondly, a case study is described that illustrates the analysis of an existing web information system with the modelling approach *ex post*. Although the modelling approach is essentially intended as a tool for the conceptual specification, it proved to be useful for the description of web information systems. Additionally, the case study substantiates the completeness of the approach since all elements of a web information system could be described and conceptualized with the means provided by the approach.

4.2 Fictitious Modelling Example: Illustration of the Modelling Approach

Example Outline

The fictitious case used for this example is a research institution like a department for information systems at university. Such organizations typically work document centered (for instance, writing and reading publications, preparing lectures, writing research proposals and supervising diploma theses'). Thus, a considerable amount of time is spent on gathering, organizing, reading as well as writing semi-structured data. This fictitious scenario assumes that a web information system is supposed to be developed which supports the members of the organization in their daily work. The system should help to integrate and to organize various documents. It serves as a tool for managing internal information. The system is not publicly accessible (for instance, by students). Moreover, flexible and comprehensive navigational means have to be constructed allowing to find pieces of information efficiently.

With regard to the web information system classification schema developed in Section 2.2.2, this system can be characterized as follows:

- Organizational focus: the organizational focus is intra-organizational since it is not intended to provide access for externals.

- Organizational stability: the organizational stability is medium or even high since members (for instance, PhD students) change regularly but stay in the organization for several years.

- User diversity: the user diversity is rather low. It is assumed that all users have a similar educational and social background. However, user diversity can increase quickly. The 'degree' of user diversity depends on the environment. For instance, foreign PhD students will have a different socialization as well as a different educational background and are, therefore, not familiar with the procedures and the terminology used.

- Systems purpose: The system purpose is rather specific although tasks and information needs are diverse. All information needs come from research and teaching.

- Application type: the application type is data collection. It is not intended to provide transactional functionalities like student registration. The web information system is supposed to serve as a knowledge base for the organization.

- Information need complexity: the information need complexity is rather vague and complex since research necessarily involves a wide variety of creative tasks.

Obviously, these criteria do not characterize the system in full detail and do not necessarily reflect the complex nature of the system in every detail. Some tasks carried out by members of the organization may be relatively easy for while others may not. However, for the purpose of this fictitious scenario a more detailed analysis is not necessary.

Model Construction

The information system developers use conceptual modelling as a tool in order to achieve a mutual understanding with the organization's members about objectives, procedures and navigational means. The conceptual modelling process can be subdivided into different phases.

Firstly, an agreement about the information structures to be used has to be achieved. In order to do so, information space models are constructed that depict the superstructure of the web information system. Reference-objects and Dimensions are identified during this stage of the conceptual specification.[4] It has to be noted again that users as well as developers have to have a shared understanding of the phenomena represented by References-objects and their structure defined in Dimensions. For the sake of simplicity this fictitious scenario assumes that the following Reference-objects and Dimensions have been identified (compare Figure 4.1).[5]

Since the models are mostly self-explaining, only a few specifics are briefly outlined.[6] As introduced in Section 3.2, information space models are defined in two steps. Firstly,

---

[4]   Cf. Section 3.2 for details on Reference-Objects and Dimensions.

[5]   For an overview of the language concepts and their representation forms compare Section 3.2.

[6]   The example is intentionally kept simple since it intends to illustrate the approach rather than to provide a complete reference model. The number of (potential) relations grows exponentially with the amount of Reference-objects defined. Thus, more complex examples get confusing easily.

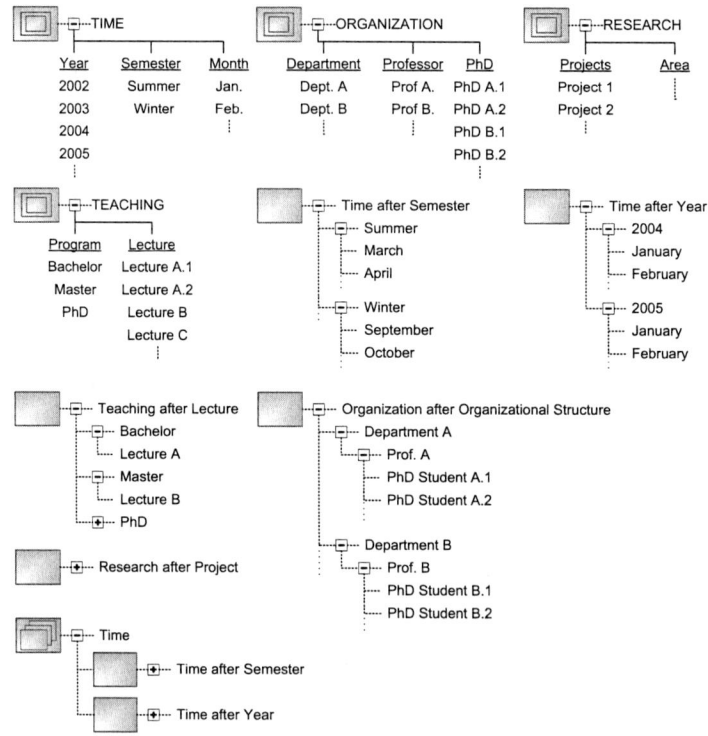

Figure 4.1: Modelling Example: Reference-objects and Dimensions

a set of Reference-objects that are *potentially* useful is collected in Reference-object-classes. It is assumed that four Reference-object-classes that represent phenomena of the target domain are defined: TIME, ORGANIZATION, RESEARCH and TEACHING. The second step of the modelling process of the first phase comprises the construction of the Dimensions based on the Reference-objects. As stated in Section 3.2.2, the construction of Dimensions is purpose-driven because Dimensions represent analytic respectively associative trails that are potentially useful for users. Thus, they are constructed with regard to a specific understanding and background of the development process. In this case, five Dimensions are identified that resemble the 'natural' order of real phenomena. For the sake of simplicity, it is further assumed that all months are assigned as leaves in the Dimension 'Time after Semester' even if semesters do not cover the whole year. Given this assumption, it is obvious that the Dimensions 'Time after Semester' and 'Time after Months' have an identical set of leaves. Thus, they can be grouped into a Dimension-group.[7] Both Dimensions represent *alternative* trails that can be used to traverse the information space.

The second step in the modelling process is the definition of Properties and their relations.[8] Properties structure the information assigned to a Reference-object. For the sake of simplicity, Properties are not structured by Property-relation-systems in this example.[9] Thus, Property-systems are basically 'lists' that 'categorize' information concerning a particular Reference-object. For instance, the Properties 'General Description', 'Financial Plan' and 'Deliverable 1' can be defined for Reference-objects of the class 'RESEARCH' (compare Figure 4.2).

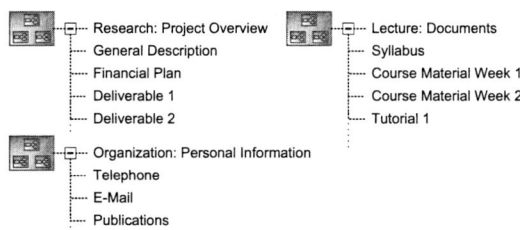

Figure 4.2: Modelling Example: Properties

The specification of Attribute-types and Content-classes is the third step of the modelling process. Attribute-types represent metadata used to annotate raw data. The combination of raw data and metadata is called Content. Thus, only those pieces of information that are annotated with metadata are considered to be useful. Only this kind of information can be processed meaningfully by humans as well as computers. The specification of Attribute-types allows configuring the interface used to maintain the web information system since they correspond to input fields on the computer screen. Content management systems usually provide an editorial workflow that structures and guides the entry of new pieces of information in the system. A basic editorial workflow has the following form: firstly, the type of Content to be entered is specified (corresponds to Content-class). Secondly, the system generates an input screen with various metadata fields (Attribute-types) necessary to process Content of the class specified in step one.

---

7   Refer to Section 3.2.3 for a detailed description of this constraint.

8   Refer to Section 3.3 for an overview of Properties.

9   This example focuses on semi-structured data like documents. Documents represent values for Properties. It is usually not possible to create meaningful Property-relation-systems for Properties that are instantiated by semi-structured data. Refer to Section 3.3 for a description of Property-relation-systems.

Thirdly, the Content itself is entered. Finally, the Content is published.[10] Additionally, common sets of Attribute-types are constituent for the definition of Content-classes that represent 'similar' Content. Figure 4.3 illustrates the specification of Attribute-types and Content-classes.

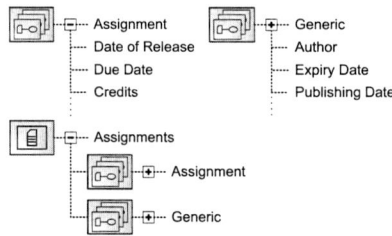

Figure 4.3: Modelling Example: Attribute-type and Content-class

As outlined in Chapter 3.4, Contents themselves are usually not specified on a conceptual level since they are created and integrated in the web information system during run-time. Likewise, Navigation-paths are defined indirectly by the information space models and by the Content-relations defined during run-time. In order to illustrate the approach, however, some fictitious Contents are 'invented' and embedded in the information structure defined by information space models and property models. Each Content is assigned to a Reference-object. The assignment to a Property is not mandatory. Additionally, the exact separation of Content-Classes and Properties is difficult in the given scenario due to its simplicity. Content-classes 'group' Content from a rather technical perspective. Contents belong to the same class if they share a common set of metadata. Properties, on the other hand, provide a rather conceptual view on data unless they represent metadata from the Content perspective as well.[11] Whether Properties provide useful means to structure information or not depends on the complexity of the system and, particularly, the amount of data. Thus, the assignment of Content to Properties is omitted for the sake of simplicity. The following table gives an overview of Contents that may be stored in the system as well as their assignment to Reference-objects and Properties:

The assignment of Content to elements of the information space can be illustrated graphically (compare Figure 4.4). Three Dimensions used to structure information span a three-dimensional space in which Contents are embedded.[12] Reference-objects define

---

10   More complex content management workflows are discussed by EHLERS (2003), pp. 105 ff.
11   Refer to Section 3.4 for details of different conceptualizations of metadata.
12   The other Dimensions are left out in order to improve interpretability.

(Combined) Reference-object	Content
<Lecture A.1>	Code of academic conduct
<Lecture A.2>	Code of academic conduct
<Lecture B>	Code of academic conduct
<Prof. A.; Lecture A.1; Winter>	List of readings for lecture A.1
<Prof. A.; Lecture A.1; Winter>	Syllabus lecture A.1
<PhD A.2; Lecture A.1; Winter>	Tutorial 1 lecture A.1
<Prof. B.; Lecture A.2; Winter>	Syllabus lecture A.2
<PhD B.1; Lecture A.2; Winter>	Tutorial 1 lecture A.2
<Prof. B.; Lecture B; Summer>	Syllabus lecture B
<PhD B.2; Lecture B; Summer>	Tutorial 1 lecture B
<PhD B.2; Lecture B; Summer>	Tutorial 2 lecture B

Table 4.1: Modelling Example: Content and Assignments

coordinates in the information space. Each Content has to be assigned to (at least) one Reference-object or any valid combination of Reference-objects (Combined Reference-objects). For instance, the Content 'Codes of academic conduct' is assigned to three different Atomic Reference-objects.[13] This assignment implies that the Content is relevant for all lectures that are represented by their respective Reference-objects (Lecture A.1, Lecture A.2 and Lecture B). Thus, whenever an individual seeks information concerning lectures he or she will find the Content 'Codes of academic conduct'. If interpreted from the author's perspective of the Content, the author has perceived the Content to be relevant whenever somebody tries to retrieve information on lectures. It is important to note that the Content is *not* physically copied. Each Content is stored only once in the repository in order to ensure data consistency. The display of Content in different places or even different web information systems is defined by its assignment to Reference-objects. Thus, if a Content is supposed to appear in a different or additional place of the system, its assignment to Reference-objects has to be changed. The other Contents of this example are assigned to a single Reference-object. For instance, the Content 'List of readings lecture A.1' is assigned to the Combined Reference-object <Prof. A.; Lecture A.1; Winter>. In this case, the Combined Reference-object contains an Aggregated Reference-object (Prof. A). The assignment can be interpreted as follows: professor A provides a 'List of readings for lecture A.1' which is to be held during the

---

[13]   Refer to Section 3.2 for an explanation of the different types of Reference-objects.

winter semester. The usage of Aggregated Reference-objects is indicated by black bars in Figure 4.4. The bar indicates that a Reference-object on a higher Hierarchy Level is used to categorize Content. In this case, the bar can be interpreted to represent a chair of the university (the chair of 'Prof. A'). A black circle is used to indicate that a Content is assigned to a single coordinate of the information space.

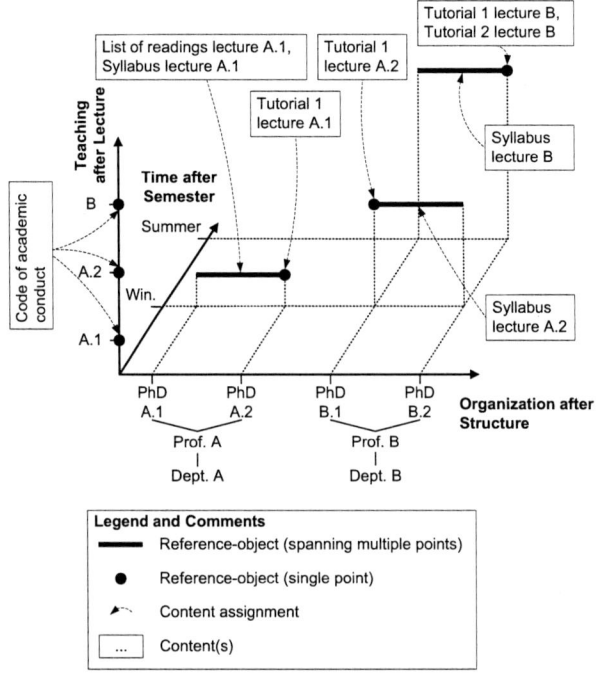

Figure 4.4: Modelling Example: Illustration of Content Assignment

It may be necessary or desirable to restrict information access or to provide personalized views on data. The construction of personalization models is the final step of the modelling process. As outlined in Section 3.6, the modelling proceeds as follow: firstly, Dimension-scopes and Property-system-scopes are defined that represent subspaces of the information space respectively the property space (compare Figure 4.5 for the following). It is assumed for the sake of this example that 'Prof. B.' is particularly interested in Contents concerning 'Lecture B' which is to be held in the 'Summer'. Therefore, a subspace of the information space is defined by a Dimension-scope-group that contains the Dimension-scopes for the Reference-objects 'Summer' and 'Lecture B'. By combining the Dimension-group with a role identifier (in this case 'Professor B'), a Personalization-object is created that represents a subspace of the whole information space. It has to be noted that the role identifier of the Personalization-object is conceptually different from the Reference-object 'Prof. B'. The person represented by the Reference-object 'Prof. B' may have multiple Personalization-objects. The selection of Content that is initially displayed before the user starts to traverse the information space can be changed quickly and efficiently by switching Personalization-objects. The second example in Figure 4.5 illustrates the usage of Access-objects. In this case, the financial information concerning 'Project 1' is only accessible by the person that is represented by the role identifier 'Professor A'.

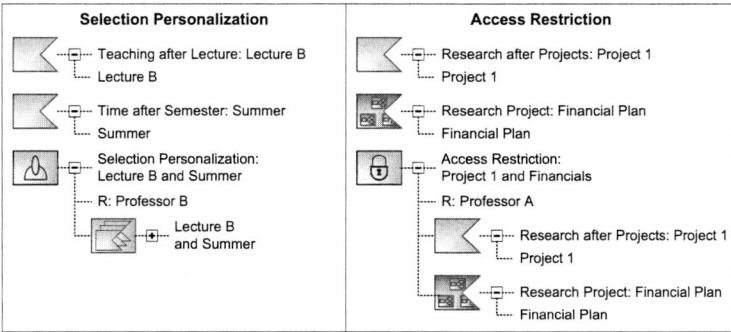

Figure 4.5: Modelling Example: Selection Personalization and Access Restriction

Navigation Concepts and Human Information Processing

Having constructed the modelling example, the concept of navigation implied by the approach and its relation to human information processing can be described. In general, five different types of navigation can be differentiated.

Firstly, users can navigate by using a single Dimension (*Dimension navigation*). Since hierarchies depict the concept of abstraction, descending a hierarchy implies a refinement of the 'search query' constructed by point-and-click operations.[14] With regard to the example outlined above, Dimension-level navigation can be illustrated as follows: the starting point of a user's information retrieval process is the whole information space. Since the user has not specified what he or she wants to see, Content is not displayed to him or her. The user decides to traverse the Dimension 'Organization after Structure' (compare Figure 4.4 for the following). The user's view is restricted to all Contents

---

[14]   Refer to Section 2.2.3 for details on navigation structures.

assigned to Reference-objects of this Dimension. In this case, this restriction applies to all Contents.[15] Therefore, all documents are displayed to the user. Subsequently, the user selects the Reference-object 'Dept. A'. Accordingly, only the Contents 'List of readings lecture A.1', 'Syllabus lecture A.1' and 'Tutorial 1 lecture A.1' remain in his or her result set and are displayed to him or her. Finally, the user selects the Reference-object 'PhD A.2', which results in a single Content ('Tutorial 1 lecture A.1'). This type of navigation is well-known and used extensively in web information systems.

Secondly, users can navigate multiple Dimensions simultaneously (*combined Dimension navigation*). In contrast to Dimension navigation this type of navigation is rarely used in current web information systems.[16] The concept of 'multi-dimensional' navigation can be illustrated as follows. A user selects the Reference-object 'Winter' from the Dimension 'Time after Semester'. His or her view is restricted to the Contents assigned to this Reference-object (refer to Figure 4.4). Subsequently, the user selects the Reference-object 'PhD B.1' in addition to the first Reference-object. Both Reference-objects resemble the search query 'Winter AND PhD B.1' which returns the Content 'Tutorial 1 lecture A.2' as a result. Obviously, this type of navigation allows to prune 'irrelevant' Contents from the 'result set' very efficiently. The selection of Reference-objects from different Dimensions creates subspaces of the whole information space. The resemblance of this approach to the OLAP-concept is obvious. The information space resembles a 'data cube' and the operations resemble actions used to 'navigate' a data cube (for instance, slicing, dicing, roll-up and drill-down).[17]. Navigation efficiency can be further improved if users are allowed to concatenate Reference-objects with boolean operators like NOT or OR. By doing so, more complex 'search queries' can be constructed by using *pre-defined* terms (Reference-objects). Thus, the flexibility of arbitrary search queries can be combined with the advantages of a well-defined and explicit navigation structure. Accordingly, it is reasonable to assume that users increase the ability to formulate their information need since Reference-objects 'point' them into the right direction.

Thirdly, users can navigate the result set by using Properties (*Property navigation*).

---

[15] This 'inefficiency' is caused by the construction of this example. Usually, not all Contents are assigned to all Dimensions. Thus, the selection of a single Dimensions can significantly reduce the amount of Contents displayed.

[16] ThyssenKrupp, one of the largest companies for industrial goods and services in the world is an exception. The ThyssenKruppBase contains several thousand documents and is structured by several Dimensions. Refer to http://base.thyssenkrupp.com/ and select 'Products' respectively 'Produkte' for an example.

[17] Cf. VOSSEN (1999), pp. 679 ff.

As outlined in Section 3.3, Properties subdivide pieces of information assigned to a Reference-object. In order to illustrate this approach, the following extension of the example is constructed. The Properties 'Telephone', 'E-Mail' and 'Publications' are used to subdivide personal information assigned to Reference-objects of the class 'Organization' (compare the modelling example of Figure 4.2). For the sake of simplicity, only the 'Organization after Structure' Dimension is considered in the following. The Dimension in conjunction with Properties forms a two-dimensional space which is illustrated in Table 4.2.

Reference-object			Property		
Level 1	Level 2	Level 3	Telephone	E-Mail	Publications
Dept. A			+49 251 8338100	info@depta.org	–
	Prof. A		+49 251 8338110	profa@depta.org	list of publications
		PhD A.1	+49 251 8338111	phda1@depta.org	list of publications
		PhD A.2	+49 251 8338112	phda2@depta.org	–
Dept. B			+49 251 8338200	info@deptb.org	–
	Prof. B		+49 251 8338210	profb@deptb.org	list of publications
		PhD B.1	+49 251 8338211	phdb1@deptb.org	–
		PhD B.2	+49 251 8338212	phdb2@deptb.org	list of publications

Table 4.2: Modelling Example: Property navigation

Content can be assigned to each cell of this table and each cell can potentially contain an unlimited number of Contents. For instance, the cell with the coordinates 'Dept. A' and 'E-Mail' contains a Content with the value 'info@depta.org'. Users traverse the information space until they reach the Reference-object on which information is requested. Since the amount of information assigned to a Reference-object is potentially large, it is useful to provide navigational means to subdivide the information of the information space at this coordinate by means of Properties. Reference-objects, Dimensions and Properties constitute the structural composition of the information space.

Fourthly, the relation between Contents can be used for navigational purposes as well (*Content navigation*). Content relations include variants, versions as well as compositions and general relations. Since each Navigation-path is qualified, that is, a 'description' of the meaning of the path is given, complex relations between Contents can be constructed. Relations are usually defined during run-time by authors. In order to illustrate the approach, the following extension of the example is constructed (compare Table

4.3). The Content 'Tutorial lecture A.2' consists of two Contents ('Exercise 1' and 'Exercise 2') that are assigned to the Reference-object '<PhD B.1; Lecture A.2; Winter>'. Thus, it is a composed Content and the exercises are subordinated to the tutorial. It is important to note that Content-relations can link Contents that are assigned to different Reference-objects. Thus, the Navigation-path created by a Content-relation can cross the information space. For instance, a Navigation-path between 'Syllabus lecture A.1' and 'Syllabus lecture A.2' can state that both Contents are closely related to each other although they are assigned to different Reference-objects. Likewise, several versions of a Content can be linked. For instance, several versions of an exercise can be stored in the system.[18]

Content 1	Content 2	Content-relation-qualifier
Tutorial 1 lecture A.2	Tutorial 1 lecture A.2 Exercise 1	Subordination
Tutorial 1 lecture A.2	Tutorial 1 lecture A.2 Exercise 2	Subordination
Syllabus lecture A.1	Syllabus lecture A.2	Related Content
Tutorial 1 lecture A.2 Exercise 1	Tutorial 1 lecture A.2 Exercise 1 (Version Winter 2004)	Prior Version
Tutorial 1 lecture A.2 Exercise 1 (Version Winter 2004)	Tutorial 1 lecture A.2 Exercise 1 (Version Winter 2003)	Prior Version

Table 4.3: Modelling Example: Content Relations

Finally, the relations between Reference-objects can be used to provide navigational means as well. The information space is constituted by Dimensions and Properties. Both concepts resemble structures supposed to be meaningful for human beings. The process of joining Dimensions results in the construction of Combined Reference-objects that represent objects from the 'world' users perceive. In this case, the Reference-objects represent concepts of an academic environment. Since (Combined) Reference-objects represent real or imaginary phenomena, their materialization as navigation components in the information space can be used to express statements about the 'real' phenomena. This can be illustrated with the help of an example. The Combined Reference-object

---

[18]   Note that the relation Content-version is used as a navigational concept in this case. As stated in Section 3.4, a version identifier is a typical example of a metadata entry (Attribute-type). Since this 'type' of metadata is not used for navigational purposes, it is necessary to differentiate between both types of metadata. Refer to Section 3.4 for a detailed discussion of different types of metadata.

<Prof. A.; Lecture A.1; Winter> represents a lecture held by 'Prof. A' in the winter term and <Prof. B.; Lecture B; Summer> a different lecture held by 'Prof. B.' in the summer. A relation (Reference-object-relation) between these Reference-objects can be constructed. This relation can be qualified as 'Prerequisite for' (Reference-object-relation-qualifier) indicating that students have to attend 'Lecture A.1' before they are allowed to enrol for 'Lecture B'.[19] The relation can be used for navigation in the information space. If a user requests information on <Prof. A.; Lecture A.1; Winter>, a *qualified* link can be displayed to him or her signalling that this lecture is a prerequisite for a different lecture. Likewise, the link can be shown if information on <Prof. B.; Lecture B; Summer> is requested.

The example allows to illustrate the concept of Associative-trails as well as the model of human information processing derived in Section 2.3. It is assumed that a student asks the PhD student B.2 the question 'Why can I not enrol for Lecture B?'. As a consequence, PhD student B.2 has an information need which he intends to satisfy by using the web information system.[20] The PhD student starts to traverse the information space as described above. As outlined in Section 3.5, an Associative Trail is any valid sequence of objects (Reference-objects, Properties and Contents). Validity means that the objects are linked by a relation. Table 4.4 depicts the Associative Trail of the PhD student.[21]

Step	Associative Trail-element
(1)	START → Dept. B.
(2)	Dept. B. → Summer
(3)	Summer → Lecture B
(4)	Lecture B → Syllabus lecture B
(5)	Syllabus lecture B → <Dept. B; Summer; Lecture B>
(6)	<Dept. B; Summer; Lecture B> → <Prof. A; Lecture A.1; Winter>

Table 4.4: Modelling Example: Associative-trail

The PhD student starts to traverse the information space by using Dimension navigation (steps one to three in Table 4.4) in order to answer the student's question. The PhD student examines the Content 'Syllabus lecture B'. It is assumed that the doc-

---

[19] The relation between both objects is directed.
[20] It is assumed that the PhD student does not know the answer to the question.
[21] Qualifiers for each Navigation-path are left out for the sake of simplicity.

ument does not contain the answer. Therefore, the PhD student backtracks his trail
to the 'coordinate' <Dept. B;Summer; Lecture B>. Finally, he recognizes the relation
between the Reference-objects <Dept. B; Summer; Lecture B> and <Dept. A; Winter;
Lecture A.1>. Since this relation is qualified ('Prerequisite for'), the PhD student will
be able to answer the student's questions. Obviously, there are a lot of possibilities to
'navigate' to this particular piece of information. This trail resembles a particular information processing strategy used by the PhD student. This strategy is determined and
mediated by the PhD student's 'world view' or pre-understanding (refer to Section 2.3
for details). Information processing strategies are subjective and different by nature. If
a student asks PhD student A.1 the same question, he or she would probably use the sequence <Dept. A> → <Winter> → <Lecture A> → <Dept. B; Summer; Lecture B> in
order to answer it. Different 'paths' to information are viewed as 'potential world-views'
of users. They reflect different information perception strategies, different educational
backgrounds or 'knowledge levels'. Obviously, this conceptualization of web information
systems provides a *multiplicity* of potential world-views respectively pre-understandings
and, thus, is supposed to support human information processing more efficiently than
other approaches.

The different types of navigation can be used in conjunction with each other. Additionally, all objects may be linked with several Navigation-paths. Thus, there is a
potentially unlimited number of ways to navigate from object 'x' to object 'y'. Different navigation possibilities represent different statements and user perceptions of the
system.

Implementation Issues

As described in Section 2.2.5, the information system development process comprises
several phases. The conceptual specification by means of conceptual models is the first
step in this process. It intends to provide a sound specification in order to structure
and describe the complex environment of the web information system as well as the
system itself. This thesis focuses on this phase of development. Nevertheless, some
implementation issues are outlined briefly in order to illustrate the applicability and
efficiency of the conceptual specification. Additionally, the relation of this approach to
emergent technologies like the Semantic Web (refer to Section 2.2.3) can be described.

The construction of conceptual models is a complex and difficult task. Depending
on the scope and the complexity of a project, the number of objects to be defined
can be very high and their relations complex. Modelling environments can be used in
order to increase model quality as well as the efficiency of the modelling process as a

whole. Modern modelling environments usually store conceptual models in a database in order to provide more comprehensive means for model construction and analysis. The modelling approach constructed in this thesis can be implemented in a metamodelling environment that is specialized on handling hierarchical representations of phenomena. In general, two major advantages of database-based modelling environments can be identified:

- CASE-support: in contrast to graphic programs, the models stored in a database-based modelling environment can be analyzed and processed automatically. For instance, the repository of the web information system can be created automatically (at least partially). The conversion of Dimensions to navigation structures in the actual web information system is obviously trivial. Likewise, other models can be used to configure other components of the web information system.[22]

- Model quality and modelling efficiency: database-based modelling environments provide means to ensure model quality. For instance, naming conventions can be enforced and conceptual models can be checked according to their adherence to the syntax specified. Additionally, modelling environments help information system developers during the modelling process (for instance, automated model layout, naming proposals or import of existing models). Thus, the model quality as well as the modelling efficiency is increased.

Recent developments that are subsumable under the term Semantic Web aim at improving the interpretability of semi-structured data in web environments (compare Section 2.2.3). The modelling approach can be implemented efficiently by using markup languages from the Semantic Web. Thus, possible mappings of model elements to implementation artefacts are presented in order to illustrate the applicability of the approach in the context of the Semantic Web.

The metadata specification (Attribute-type) obviously corresponds to statements that can be expressed by using the Resource Description Framework (RDF). The example outlined above contains metadata specifications for the Content-class 'Assignment' (compare Figure 4.3). Metadata elements for assignments include, for instance, author, publishing date and the number of credits. With regard to the RDF terminology, a Content represents the subject, an Attribute-type the predicate and the run-time value of an Attribute-type the object of a RDF statement. Thus, the assignment as specified

---

[22] For instance, the Attribute-type definitions can be used to configure the workflow of content management systems as stated above.

in the Content modelling example above can be represented by using an RDF-graph
(compare Figure 4.6).[23]

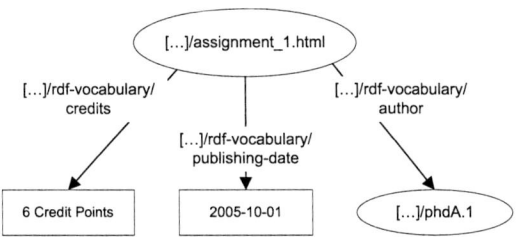

Figure 4.6: Modelling Example: RDF Graph

This representation of metadata that describes an assignment can be represented by
RDF as follows.[24]

```
<?xml version="1.0"?>
    <rdf:RDF xmlns:rdf="http://www.w3.org/1999/02/22-rdf-syntax-ns#"
        xmlns:rdf-vocabularly="[...]/rdf-vocabulary/">
    <rdf:Description rdf:about="[...]/assignment_1.html">
        <rdf-vocabularly:credits>
            6 Credit Points
        </rdf-vocabularly:credits>
    </rdf:Description>
    <rdf:Description rdf:about="[...]/assignment_1.html">
        <rdf-vocabularly:publishing-date>
            2005-11
        </rdf-vocabularly:publishing-date>
    </rdf:Description>
    <rdf:Description rdf:about="[...]/assignment_1.html">
        <rdf-vocabularly:author rdf:resource="[...]/phdA.1"/>
    </rdf:Description>
</rdf:RDF>
```

The metadata elements 'credits' and 'publishing-date' are defined by literals in this
case. They correspond to the data that has been entered by the author of the Content.

---

[23]   The URLs are abbreviated by using the suffix '[...]' in order to improve readability. The physical
       address of a document is irrelevant for the purpose at hand.

[24]   Compare MANOLA & MILLER for a brief description of RDF.

The author itself is described by a resource rather than a literal. In this case, the metadata annotation of the assignments states that information about the author can be found at [...]/*phdA*.1.

As stated in Section 3.2 Reference-objects and their ordering in Dimensions represent an ontology from the user's point of view. According to the understanding outlined in Chapter 2, the modelling approach is essentially a tool that allows to achieve a mutual understanding of the project, its objectives and suitable means to achieve them. Thus, information space models can be mapped to Web ontology specifications. For instance, Reference-object-classes correspond to OWL classes. The Hierarchy-levels are representing subclasses of a Reference-object-class (compare Figure 4.1 as well as the description of OWL in Section 2.2.3). Thus, the model depicted in Figure 4.1 might well be represented in OWL as follows:[25]

```
<owl:Class rdf:ID="TIME">
    <rdfs:label xml:lang="en">TIME</rdfs:label>
    <rdfs:label xml:lang="de">ZEIT</rdfs:label>
</owl:Class>


<owl:Class rdf:ID="Year">
    <rdfs:subClassOf rdf:resource="#TIME" />
    <rdfs:label xml:lang="en">Year</rdfs:label>
    <rdfs:label xml:lang="de">Jahr</rdfs:label>
</owl:Class>


<owl:Class rdf:ID="Semester">
    <rdfs:subClassOf rdf:resource="#Year" />
    <rdfs:label xml:lang="en">Semester</rdfs:label>
    <rdfs:label xml:lang="de">Semester</rdfs:label>
</owl:Class>


<owl:Class rdf:ID="Month">
    <rdfs:subClassOf rdf:resource="#Year" />
    <rdfs:label xml:lang="en">Month</rdfs:label>
    <rdfs:label xml:lang="de">Monat</rdfs:label>
```

---

[25] It is assumed that semesters and months can be uniquely assigned to a year. Thus, they can be conceptualized as subclasses of the class 'Year'. Refer to SMITH, WELTY & McGUINNESS for a description of OWL.

```
</owl:Class>
```

. . .

Having defined classes in OWL, individuals of OWL classes can be described. An individual is an instance of a class.[26] More precisely, an individual has a property (for instance, 'is a') that links it to a class. Individuals can be specified as follows:[27]

```
<Year rdf:ID="2004"/>
<Year rdf:ID="2005"/>
. . .
<Semester rdf:ID="Summer"/>
. . .
<Month rdf:ID="January"/>
. . .
```

This representation of the Reference-object definition states that the 'thing 2004' is a 'Year'. Likewise, all other elements are assigned to classes. Similarly, other model types of the approach can be mapped to languages of the Semantic Web. Note that this mapping is intended to illustrate the general applicability of the approach with emergent technologies of the Semantic Web. It is neither intended to be complete nor functional.

4.3 Method Application: The asinfo Case

The modelling approach has been applied to a web information system ex post in order to analyze the navigational means provided for users. This case study has been conducted during a research project concerned with the conceptual specification of information systems. The main goal of the case study is the analysis of an existing web information system and the derivation of suggestions for further improvements of the system.

Case Outline

The web information system asinfo (http://www.asinfo.de/) provides a comprehensive overview of documents concerning the maintenance of industrial health, safety standards and provisions on labour. For instance, asinfo contains regulations on wearing

---

[26]   Cf. Smith, Welty & McGuinness for details.

[27]   An abbreviated syntax is used in the following. Refer to Smith, Welty & McGuinness for details.

helmets on construction sites and handling information about explosives or chemical substances. The system integrates information from more than 130 web-sites of external information providers. Their documents are scanned on a regular basis by the system, indexed and integrated (via linking) in the system. The indexing algorithm works like common web search engines (that is, document similarities and key word occurrences). Asinfo itself does not provide any information. The system can be accessed without registration or any payment by the public. It is the most comprehensive library of its kind in Germany. The users of the system are mainly security appointees of companies who do not necessarily have an appropriate training (for instance, a university degree in chemistry or in medicine) or they are experts (especially in small and medium sized companies). Information providers are specialized institutions with numerous experts in chemistry, industrial engineering, medicine as well as other disciplines. Consequently, users are not always familiar with expert terminologies used by information providers. Thus, matching information demand and information supply is rather difficult. Information providers are using different classification schemas which may be redundant or even inconsistent if they are integrated. Integrating all information resources under one common classification schema is the greatest benefit of asinfo. A typical usage scenario for asinfo is a security appointee of a small and medium sized company who has to find out whether new regulations from the European Union require to take action in his or her company or not. Faced with this problem situation, he or she uses asinfo in order to find information on the regulation of the European Union as well as documents concerning the implementation of the regulation.

With regard to the web information system classification schema (compare Section 2.2.2), asinfo can be characterized as follows:

- Organizational focus: the organizational focus is inter-organizational. The system is accessed by externals. Since it is not necessary to register, the maintainers of asinfo are not able to determine personal data of users that can help to tailor the system to their specific information needs. For instance, the educational and the personal background as well as position in a company of a users is generally unknown. Thus, information retrieval efficiency tends to be lower since different 'world views' have to be matched. Thus, there is a potential mismatch between the 'world views' of domain experts (information maintainers), on the one hand, and those of (potential) laymen (users of the system), on the other.

- Organizational stability: the organizational stability is obviously low. Users change regularly.

- User diversity: the user diversity is (potentially) high. The users are unknown. Additionally, the system is not restricted to a specific subject. Subjects are chemistry, engineering as well as law and many others. Thus, the users are very diverse concerning their degree of training as well as the subject for which they seek information.

- Systems purpose: the system purpose can be characterized as being rather specific. Although the system is not restricted to a subject, all documents are concerned with the maintenance of industrial health, safety standards and provisions on labour.

- Application type: data collection.

- Information need complexity: the information need complexity can be characterized as medium. Users may have vague and complex information needs if they are untrained and do not know which information they actually seek. A trained user, on the other hand, may use the system as a work of reference in order to prove a specific piece of information (for instance, a date on which a regulation goes into effect).

Given these characteristics, it is obvious that suitable navigational means are essential for the system. The users may neither have an appropriate training nor are they familiar with expert terminology. Thus, the navigational design has to 'lead' users into the right direction. Furthermore, it has to explicate the potential meaning of information that can be accessed by following a link. The discussion of asinfo is included in this thesis in order to illustrate the suitability of the modelling approach and its underlying conceptualization for the description and analysis of complex web information systems.

Model Construction

Conceptual models have been constructed in order to investigate the navigational means of asinfo. The models are 'as is'-models of the system as it is currently available for users. The models have been constructed as representations of the system like it is shown in the browser since the repository of the system could not be accessed.[28] Asinfo comprises six Dimensions:[29]

---

[28]   If access to the repository of a web information system is provided, it is potentially possible to create models automatically.

[29]   The following description of asinfo contains German terms that are not translated to English which is intentional. Asinfo does not provide an English version of the system at the moment since it

- Endangerment factors (German 'Gefährdungsfaktoren'): this Dimension contains endangerment factors like heat, cold, mechanical endangerment, noise and electricity. Thus, it comprises factors that threaten an employee's health and well being.

- Single topics ('Einzelthemen'): this Dimension contains a selection of special topics like screen handling or working with heavy objects. It resembles 'frequently asked questions' since it covers the most common topics.

- Employment protection laws ('Arbeitsschutzrecht'): This Dimension contains regulations and legal information.

- Research ('Forschung'): this Dimension is a rather unstructured collection of research documents concerning industrial health.

- Economic sector ('Branche'): this Dimension structures the information according to economic sectors like agriculture, mining, building trade and retailing.

- Processes for maintenance of industrial health and safety standards ('Arbeitsschutzprozesse'): this Dimension is concerned with processes and procedures allowing organizations to implement current regulations and laws.

These Dimensions can be illustrated with the help of the modelling technique. Figure 4.7 depicts an excerpt of all Dimensions.

Data has been gathered in order to analyze the Dimensions in more detail.[30] In particular, the number of Reference-objects in each Dimension, their breadth and width and the number of Contents assigned to Reference-objects have been measured. On the base of the analysis on this data, several measures have been calculated in order to describe asinfo and the 'shape' of the information space more precisely. It has been

---

is restricted to a German speaking audience and the subject is national by nature (for instance, national regulations). A translation of the German terms is omitted in order to make the argument understandable. By using German terms, the reader is able to reproduce this analysis on asinfo's web site at http://www.asinfo.de//.

[30] Cf. BECKER et al. (2004b), pp. 24 ff. and JANIESCH, BRELAGE & HOLTEN (2005) for the following. Similar work on quantitative analysis of web information systems can be found in BOTAFOGO, RIVLIN & SHNEIDERMAN (1992) and DHYANI, NG & BHOWMICK (2002). Data gathering took place manually which is not feasible in every case. However, measures can be calculated automatically in case the models are stored in a database-based modelling environment. Data has been collected in Spring 2004. The database is updated regularly. Thus, the amount of Contents in the system is different now. The structural composition of the information space, however, is stable and does not change in the course of time.

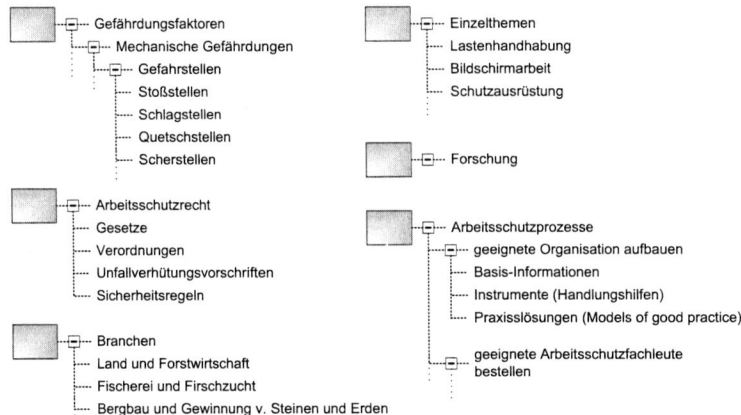

Figure 4.7: Dimensions in asinfo

claimed that it is better to favour breadth before depth when designing Dimensions.[31]
This viewpoint is explicitly *not* appropriate for the purpose at hand. Phenomena of the
real or imaginary world are ordered by 'themselves' respectively by the perception of
an individual. Enforcing arbitrary structures on information which are optimal from a
theoretical, mathematical point of view does not reflect the 'nature' of things and the
'world views' of individuals. Thus, the measures that are calculated in the following
are intended to describe asinfo as it is designed today rather than defining 'better'
navigation structures by means of a quantitative analysis. The analysis can hint at
potential problems users of the systems will face. It does not replace the need to achieve
a mutual agreement on the navigational means used to structure information.

Firstly, the Dimensions of asinfo can be described. Width and depth of Dimensions
are basic measures which can be used to describe their shape. The absolute width of a
Dimension corresponds to the number of leaves of the hierarchical tree. The maximal
depth of a Dimension is defined by the 'deepest' Hierarchy-level of a leaf. For instance,
the dimension 'Gefährdungsfaktoren' contains 185 reference objects (42 nodes, 143 leafs),
whereas the dimension 'Forschung' contains only the root node. Thus, 'Gefährdungsfaktoren' is more broadly and deeply structured than 'Forschung'. Having defined breadth
and width, it is interesting to analyze the colonization of Reference-objects with Contents. The colonization reflects the 'usage' of Reference-objects. Moreover, the relative
share of the total amount of Reference-objects for each Dimension can be opposed with
the relative share of Contents assigned to Reference-objects in one dimension (Content

---

[31]   Cf. FARKAS & FARKAS (2000), p. 345.

Ratio and Element Ratio). The result gives insights into the distribution of Content and Reference-objects in the information space. These measures are comprised in the following table:[32]

Dimension	Depth maxi- mal	Width ab- solute	Nodes ab- solute	Element Ratio	Content Ratio	Content Ass. average
Gefährdungsfaktoren	5	143	42	74.3 %	54.2 %	554.3
Einzelthemen	2	6	1	2.8 %	5.0 %	1,376.4
Arbeitsschutzrecht	2	4	1	2.0 %	5.3 %	2,022.2
Forschung	1	1	0	0.4 %	2.7 %	5,040.0
Branchen	2	17	1	7.2 %	29.0 %	3,045.9
Arbeitsschutzprozesse	3	24	9	13.2 %	3.8 %	215.7

Table 4.5: Dimension Measures asinfo

The dimension 'Gefährdungsfaktoren' comprises nearly 75 percent of all reference objects used by the system (Element Ratio) but contains only 54 percent of all content assignments (Content Ratio). The dimension 'Branchen', on the other hand, contains 29 percent of all content assignments but comprises only 7 percent of all Reference-objects. On average, each node in the Dimension 'Branchen' contains over 3000 documents, whereas the average in 'Gefährdungsfaktoren' is 554. The information at each coordinate of the information space is not structured (for instance, by Properties). Thus, the Dimension 'Branchen' contains nodes that display a list of 3,000 Contents. It is reasonable to assume that users are not able to retrieve information efficiently if they are confronted with a result as large as it is in 'Branchen'.

With regard to the conceptualization developed in this thesis, these measures imply that more linguistic means are used to structure information in 'Gefährdungsfaktoren' than in 'Branchen'. Thus, information retrieval in 'Gefährdungsfaktoren' *may* be better since users retrieve a smaller result set after they submit their 'query'. It is not possible to qualify a Dimension as 'bad' or 'unsuited' by this analysis. Different amounts of Contents may reflect a richer knowledge base in certain areas.

Reference-objects are used to structure the information space. Each Content is assigned to at least one Reference-object. At the moment data has been gathered, asinfo

---

[32] Cf. BECKER et al. (2004b) for details on the measures and their calculation. The following measures are rounded. Thus, they do not necessarily add up to 100 percent.

contained nearly 97,000 Contents and nearly 190,000 Content assignments.[33] Thus, on average, each Content was assigned to 1.9 Reference-objects. Therefore, on average, each Content can be found by using two Navigation-paths. A randomized sample of Contents has been collected in order to gather data about characteristics of Content. Each Content respectively document contains 42 pages on average. Thus, the 'amount' of information contained in each document is rather large. The Content length variance coefficient is 1.45 which indicates that Contents differ substantially concerning their lengths.[34]

In order to evaluate the assignment of Contents to Reference-objects, the measure variation coefficient of Contents can be used. It measures the relative standard deviation in relation to the mean value of Contents assigned to Reference-objects in a Dimension. A 'high' variation coefficient indicates that the amount of Contents assigned to Reference-objects differs substantially, whereas a 'low' value indicates an even distribution of Contents. In other words, 'high' values may imply that the means used to structure information are not 'balanced': some Reference-objects may categorize thousand Contents while others represent only ten Contents. Figure 4.8 depicts variation coefficients for Contents for each Dimension.

Variation coefficient (contents)

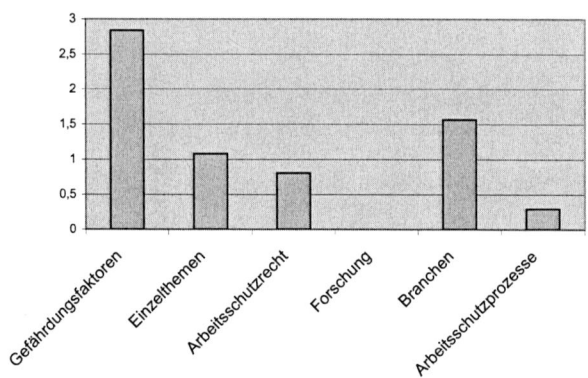

Figure 4.8: Variation Coefficient of Contents in asinfo

---

[33] Since the system is updated on a regular basis, the amount is subject to change.

[34] The randomized sample contains 240 Contents. The smallest length in pages is 1 while the largest length is 439.

It has to be noted that high values of the variation coefficient may indicate that more documents are available for a particular Reference-object. Thus, a high value does not necessarily imply that the navigational means of a Dimension are unsuited. These measures demonstrate the suitability of the conceptualization for analyzing complex web information systems. Obviously, the analysis can be extended by using more detailed measures.[35]

Analysis of asinfo

Since the dimensions mainly determine the users' ability to retrieve the desired information efficiently, some suggestions for further improvement may be derived from the analysis. The dimension 'Forschung' organizes many thousand contents, but it is not structured at all. Thus, a refinement of this dimension may improve user information retrieval efficiency substantially. On the other hand, the dimension 'Gefährdungsfaktoren' is deeply and broadly based structured. The users may get confused when navigating 'Gefährdungsfaktoren'. This dimension may be divided into two smaller ones. However, the reorganization of dimensions requires the inclusion of a domain expert in order to ensure consistency and adequacy of the resulting information structures.

The construction of subspaces and personalized information delivery is a promising approach for improving the system. Usually, only a small portion of the documents is relevant for the users (for instance 'everything concerning universities and chemistry'). The construction of subspaces for personalized information delivery can surely improve information retrieval efficiency and effectiveness while the structure of the information space remains unchanged. Furthermore, Combined Reference-objects may be used for navigation that allow users to build complex search 'queries' by selecting Reference-objects from more than one dimension. While the structure of the information space remains unchanged, too, the amount of information that is considered to be relevant for a user's 'query' decreases significantly. In general, users retrieve a large result set after having selected a Reference-object in asinfo. Thus, it is questionable whether this kind of navigation is suitable or not. If users are enabled to use more than one Dimension at once (combined Dimension navigation), the size of the result set can be decreased substantially.

---

[35] Cf. BECKER et al. (2004b) for a more detailed analysis of asinfo.

4.4 Discussion

The modelling approach is intended to provide suitable means for the conceptual specification of web information systems. As the fictitious example illustrates, various models can be used to specify different aspects of web information systems on a conceptual level. Models serve as abstract representations of the system. They are used by developers and users to discuss the development process, its goals and the phenomena involved. Additionally, the approach entails a specific understanding of 'web information systems' which differs from current implementations and practices.[36] In particular, a specific understanding of navigation is 'embedded' in the approach. It is argued that navigation structures should reflect the users' 'world views' in order to increase information retrieval efficiency. Additionally, navigational means should not be restricted to single hierarchies or arbitrary webs. Instead, more flexible means should be constructed allowing users to use different 'world views' when using the system.

The approach has the following characteristics with regard to the evaluation criteria for interpretative work:[37]

- Completeness: the approach provides a minimal set of concepts that are required in order to specify web information systems holistically.[38]

- Correctness: given the background of the research approach, the concepts introduced are specified precisely and logically consistent.

- Suitability: the models are relatively easy to understand, to create and to communicate to users as well as to developers. The method can be learned and used easily. Thus, it is considered to be suitable for the conceptual specification of web information systems.

It has to be noted that the usage of each model type is not mandatory. That is, the modelling approach can and should be tailored to specific requirements of projects. Likewise, it can neither be expected nor is it intended that the approach provides means for every conceivable situation. In fact, the conceptualization method used in this thesis is a general framework that allows to adapt and to extend the modelling approach easily if necessary. Thus, the modelling approach intends to provide a starting point and common set of concepts that are useful for the conceptual specification of web information systems. Additionally, the research approach provides means to integrate

---

[36]   As stated earlier, a multidimensional navigation is usually not provided by current systems.
[37]   Cf. Section 2.1.3.
[38]   The notion of a minimal set does not imply that each model type is necessarily required.

new concepts and to extend the modelling approach while maintaining consistency. New concepts are integrated in the approach by extensions of the metamodel. By doing so, the concept gets a well-defined 'meaning' and its relations to other language concepts are explicated. Thus, the metamodels are a tool to achieve a mutual understanding of the linguistic means between method engineers and information system developers. The different 'layers' of method construction and appliance are information systems. Thus, the specification of new concepts is a metameta-information system with regard to the actual application.[39]

The asinfo case demonstrates the applicability and usefulness of the approach for related research on web information systems. The conceptualization by the approach proved to be well-suited and applicable to analyze and to describe asinfo on a detailed level. All elements of the web information system could be mapped to their respective representation forms. In fact, the conceptualization provides more means than necessary to describe asinfo. Thus, the result indicates that the approach is complete and suitable for describing web information systems. Additionally, the approach can be used as a starting point for other types of research as demonstrated with the measurement framework for asinfo. The analysis of web information systems depends on the availability of a suitable framework allowing to 'name' and identify objects and phenomena of the system. In other words, a sound terminology is needed in order 'to make sense' of the complex socio-technical phenomenon 'web information systems'. The discussion of related work on navigation in Section 2.2.3 indicates that such a conceptualization or reference terminology has not yet been developed. Thus, empirical and conceptual work is difficult to compare since their respective authors have a different understanding and conceptualization of web information systems. For instance, some may differ between linking-types while others do not.

Given the example and the case outlined in this section, it is argued that the modelling approach provides suitable means to model and conceptualize web information systems *holistically* and *precisely*. Thus, it provides the means to specify web information systems on a conceptual level as well as it can be used to improve comparability and reproducibility of other research in this area.

---

[39] Refer to Section 2.2.5 for details.

Chapter 5

Summary, Reflection and Outlook

The specification of web information systems is a complex and complicated endeavour including technical as well as social aspects. Web information systems are a cornerstone of IT architectures in organizations. Despite considerable research efforts, the development of web information systems consistently fails to achieve the intended goals (for instance, budget overruns or time delays). In order to overcome these problems, this thesis proposes an IS perspective on web information systems that is not restricted to technical aspects and explicitly acknowledges the subjective nature of human perception. Information systems are social systems that are subject to several influences that may hinder a successful implementation. In particular, language ultimately determines the abilities of users and developers to exchange meaningful information on procedures and objectives of the project. The 'problem' of subjective perception and language usage applies twofold in the given case.

Firstly, the web information system is a social system which is constrained by the linguistic means used to convey 'meaning' respectively information from user to user. In case of web information systems, linguistic means refer to information structures used to 'organize' vast amounts of data in a meaningful manner. These structures are used for navigation and ultimately determine the user's ability to retrieve the desired information. Hence, it is crucial to postulate that these structures are 'designed' carefully and properly in terms of a mutual understanding. Otherwise, efficient navigation and, therefore, the satisfaction of an individual's information need become impossible. The sound specification of navigation is a crucial success factor for web information systems.

Secondly, the development group is an information system itself. In particular, it is equally constrained by the linguistic means used by the development group. The development group needs a suitable language enhancing the process of 'talking' and exchanging meaningful information about web information systems. Conceptual modelling languages are artificial languages that can be used as a 'tool' in the design process.

Such a modelling language has to be constructed systematically in order to ensure a mutual understanding of its terms and concepts among the development group and other project participants. From a IS development perspective, it is necessary to provide a sound modelling method allowing to specify suitable navigation structures.

The thesis addressed these issues by proposing a conceptual modelling approach based on a particular conceptualization of web information systems that implies a particular understanding how they can and should be developed. Additionally, it includes concepts indicating how large amounts of information are to be handled. The conceptualization is 'encoded' in metamodels and serves as a basis for the specification of the conceptual modelling approach. This modelling approach represents the linguistic means that can be used by developers. The research approach ensures a consistent and systematic construction of concepts. Additionally, it provides a general framework for the specification of concepts as well as their relations to each other and allows to extend the modelling approach easily and consistently. By using the conceptual modelling approach, developers specify information structures in collaboration with users of the system. These structures are used for navigation and represent the language used for information retrieval by the users. Furthermore, it is argued that a multidimensional navigation can potentially increase the efficiency and usability of web information systems. The navigation concepts 'encoded' in the conceptualization provide comprehensive means allowing to enrich the navigational means considerably (for instance, links are qualified, Navigation-paths are aligned with Associative-trails of users and the derivation of Statements about linked objects). These concepts extend current practices of web information system development considerably and systematically.

As scientific research is never finished, a thesis like this one raises in particular usually more questions than it solves. Thus, some prospects for further research on web information systems in general and the approach of this thesis in particular should be mentioned. The conceptualization as outlined in this thesis implies that different 'world-views' of users are integrated in a single, consistent information space. Given the vague and subjective nature of 'knowledge' and human information processing, it is interesting to investigate means by which *different* and potentially *conflicting* world-views of user can be mapped to the information space. The repository-grid-technique seems to be a rather beneficial approach for identifying and describing a user's 'world-view'.[1] It can be used to 'explicate' a user's world view which can be interpreted as a personal ontology respectively a 'filter' that mediates an individual's perception of the world. Personal

---

[1]   Cf., for instance, to BANNISTER & MAIR (1968); BANNISTER & FRANSELLA (1980); BANNISTER (1981) and BEAIL (1985).

ontologies are inherently different from each other and have to be mapped in order to ensure a consistent interpretation of information. Within the computer science community, this issues is discussed in the context of the Semantic Web.[2] Interpretative research approaches such as the one used in this thesis are inherently speculative by nature and, therefore, difficult to validate and assess. Further research is needed in order to validate the usefulness and applicability of the modelling approach as well as the conceptualization of web information systems and human information processing entailed by it. Such a validation can be achieved by empirical approaches accompanying real world projects and gathering data that validates or corrects assumptions of this thesis. An empirical validation of the approach has not been intended and is beyond the scope of this thesis, Thus, it remains a research prospect for subsequent works on web information systems. Likewise, the usefulness of multidimensional navigation for satisfying information needs can be evaluated empirically. The conceptualization of web information systems provides a sound terminology that helps to ensure a consistent terminology for this type of research. Finally, the general applicability of the conceptualization has been shown prototypically. Further research is needed in order to ensure the question whether the approach is functional with regard to implementation issues (for instance, mapping of conceptual models to implementation artefacts) or not.

---

[2]   Cf., for instance, NOY & MUSEN (2002); DOAN et al. (2002) and DOAN et al. (2003).

Bibliography

Aarseth, Espen J. (1994): Nonlinearity and Literary Theory. In Landow, George P., editor: Hyper Text Theory. Baltimore: Johns Hopkins University Press, pp. 51–86.

Aarseth, Espen J. (1997): *Cybertext: Perspectives on Ergodic Literature*. Baltimore: John Hopkins University Press.

Abbott, Robert (1997): Information transfer and cognitive mismatch: a Popperian model for studies of public understanding. *Journal of Information Science*, Vol. 23, No. 2, pp. 129–137.

Abbott, Robert (1999): *The World as Information*. Exeter: intellect.

Abbott, Robert (2004): Subjectivity as a concern for information science: a Popperian perspective. *Journal of Information Science*, Vol. 30, No. 2, pp. 95–106.

Ackoff, Russel L. (1971): Towards A System of System Concepts. *Management Science*, Vol. 17, No. 11, pp. 611–622.

Akscyn, Robert M., McCracken, Donald L. & Yoder, Elise A. (1988): KMS: a distributed hypermedia system for managing knowledge in organizations. *Communications of the ACM*, Vol. 31, No. 7, pp. 820–835.

Akyildiz, Ian F., Sankarasubramaniam, Yogesh & Cayirci, Erdal (2002): Wireless sensor networks: a survey. *Computer Networks*, Vol. 38, No. 4, pp. 393–422.

Alvesson, Mats & Deetz, Stanley (2000): *Doing Critical Management Research*. London: SAGE Publications.

Alvesson, Mats & Sköldberg, Kaj (2000): *Reflexive Methodology: New Vistas for Qualitative Research*. London: Sage.

Angeles, Rebecca (2005): RFID Technologies: Supply-Chain Applications and Implementation Issues. *Information Systems Management*, Vol. 22, pp. 51–65.

Arasu, Arvind, Cho, Junghod, Garcia-Molina, Hector, Paepcke, Andreas & Raghavan, Sriram (2001): Searching the Web. *ACM Transactions on Internet Technology*, Vol. 1, No. 1, pp. 2–43.

Astley, W. Graham & Ven, Andrew H. Van de (1983): Central Perspectives and Debates in Organization Theory. *Administrative Science Quarterly*, Vol. 28, No. 2, pp. 245–273.

Atzeni, Paolo, Mecca, Giansalvatore & Merialdo, Paolo (1997a): Semistructured and Structured Data in the Web: Going Back and Forth. *ACM SIGMOD Record*, Vol. 26, No. 4, pp. 16–23.

Atzeni, Paolo, Mecca, Giansalvatore & Merialdo, Paolo (1997b): To Weave the Web. In VLDB '97: Proceedings of the 23rd International Conference on Very Large Data Bases. San Francisco, CA, USA: Morgan Kaufmann Publishers Inc., pp. 206–215.

Atzeni, Paolo & Parente, Alessio (2003): Specification of Web Applications with ADM-2. In Bommel, Patrick van, editor: Information Modeling for Internet applications. Hershey: Idea Group, pp. 127–143.

Avison, David E. & Fitzgerald, Guy (1995): *Information systems development. Methodologies, techniques and tools*. 2nd edition. London: McGraw-Hill/Irwin.

Bahli, Bouchaib (2003): Web Engineering: An Assessment of Empirical Research. *Communications of the Association for Information Systems*, Vol. 12, pp. 203–222.

Balasubramanian, V. & Bashian, Alf (1998): Document Management and Web Technologies: Alice Marries the Mad Hatter. *Communications of ACM*, Vol. 41, No. 7, pp. 107–115.

Bannister, D. (1981): Personal construct theory and research method. In Reason, Peter & Rowan, John, editors: Human Inquiry: A Sourcebook Of New Paradigm Research,. New York: John Wiley & Sons Ltd, pp. 191–199.

Bannister, D. & Fransella, F. (1980): *Inquiring Man: The Psychology of Personal Constructs*. 2nd edition. Harmondsworth. England: Penguin.

Bannister, D. & Mair, J.M.M. (1968): *The Evaluation of Personal Constructs*. London: Academic Press.

Bansler, Jorgen P., Damsgaard, Jan, Scheepers, Rens, Havn, Erling & Thomesen, Jacob (2000): Corporate Intranet Implementation: Managing Emergent Technologies and Organizational Practices. *Journal of the Association for Information Systems*, Vol. 1, No. 10, pp. 1–41.

Banville, Claude & Landry, Maurice (1989): Can the field of MIS be disciplined? *Communications of the ACM*, Vol. 32, No. 1, pp. 48–60.

Banville, Claude & Landry, Maurice (1992): Can the Field of MIS be Disciplined? In Galliers, Robert D., editor: Information Systems Research: Issues, Methods and Practical Guidlines. Oxford: Blackwell, pp. 61–88.

Baskerville, Richard & Pries-Heje, Jan (2001): Racing the E-Bomb: How the Internet Is Redefining Information Systems Development Methodology. In Proceedings of the IFIP TC8/WG8.2 Working Conference on Realigning Research and Practice in Information Systems Development. Deventer, The Netherlands: Kluwer, B.V., pp. 49–68.

Batini, Carlo, Ceri, Stefano & Navathe, Shamkant B. (1992): *Conceptual Database Design. An Entity-Relationship Approach.* Redwood City, California: Benjamin-Cummings Publishing Co., Inc..

Bawden, David (2002): The three worlds of health information. *Journal of Information Science*, Vol. 28, No. 1, pp. 51–62.

Büchner, Heino, Zschau, Oliver, Traub, Dennis & Zahradka, Rik (2000): *Web Content Management - Websites professionell betreiben.* Bonn: Galileo Press, p. 253.

Beail, N. (1985): An introduction to repertory grid technique. In Beail, N., editor: Repertory Grid Technique and Personal Constructs. Cambridge, MA: Brookline Books, pp. 1–26.

Becker, Jörg, Brelage, Christian, Crisandt, Jens, Dreiling, Alexander, Ribbert, Michael & Seidel, Stefan (2003a): *Methodische und technische Integration von Daten- und Prozessmodellierungstechniken für Zwecke der Informationsbedarfsanalyse.* Institut für Wirtschaftsinformatik, Working Paper 106, Universität Münster Institut für Wirtschaftsinformatik – Technical report.

Becker, Jörg, Brelage, Christian, Dreiling, Alexander & Ribbert, Michael (2004a): Business Process-driven Information Requirements Engineering. In 15th International

Conference of the Information Resource Management Association (IRMA). New Orleans, Louisana, USA.

Becker, Jörg, Brelage, Christian, Gebhardt, Hansjürgen, Recker, Jan & Müller-Wienbergen, Felix (2004b): *Fachkonzeptionelle Modellierung und Analyse web-basierter Informationssysteme mit der MW-KiD Modellierungstechnik am Beispiel von ASInfo*. Westfälische Wilhelms-Universität Münster, Institut für Wirtschaftsinformatik, Working Paper 103, Universität Münster Institut für Wirtschaftsinformatik – Technical report.

Becker, Jörg, Brelage, Christian, Klose, Karsten & Thygs, Michael (2003b): Conceptual modeling of semantic navigation structures. The MoSeNa-approach. In Proceedings of the 5th ACM international workshop on Web information and data management (WIDM'03). New Orleans: ACM Press, pp. 118–125.

Becker, Jörg, Brelage, Christian, Thygs, Michael & Klose, Karsten (2003c): MetaWeb. Fachkonzeptionelle Spezifikation WWW-basierter Informationssysteme. In Proceedings of the Wirtschaftsinformatik 2003. Medien - Märkte - Mobilität. Band II. Dresden: Physica-Verlag, pp. 393–413.

Becker, Jörg, Brelage, Christian, Thygs, Michael & Ribbert, Michael (2003d): Conceptual Design of WWW-Based Information Systems. In Proceedings of the 11th European Conference on Information Systems (ECIS 2003). Naples.

Becker, Jörg, Dreiling, Alexander, Holten, Roland & Ribbert, Michael (2003e): Specifying Information Systems for Business Process Integration - A Management Perspective. *Information Systems and e-Business Management*, Vol. 1, No. 3, pp. 231–263.

Becker, Jörg & Holten, Roland (1998): Fachkonzeptuelle Spezifikation von Führungsinformationssystemen. *Wirtschaftsinformatik*, Vol. 40, No. 6, pp. 483–492.

Becker, Jörg, Knackstedt, Ralf, Holten, Roland, Hansmann, Holger & Neumann, Stefan (2001): *Konstruktion von Methodiken: Vorschläge für eine begriffliche Grundlegung und domänenspezifische Anwendungsbeispiele*. Westfälische Wilhelms-Universität Münster, Institut für Wirtschaftsinformatik, Working Paper 77, Universität Münster Institut für Wirtschaftsinformatik – Technical report.

Becker, Jörg, Knackstedt, Ralf & Serries, Thomas (2001): *Gestaltung von Führungsinformationssystemen mittels Informationsportalen - Ansätze zur Integration von*

Data-Warehouse- und Content- Management-Systemen. University of Münster: Working Paper 80, Institut für Wirtschaftsinformatik – Technical report.

Becker, Jörg, Knackstedt, Ralf & Serries, Thomas (2002): Informationsportale für das Management: Integration von Data-Warehouse- und Content-Management-Systemen. In Proceedings of the Data Warehousing 2002. Friedrichshafen, Germany, pp. 241–261.

Becker, Jörg, Knackstedt, Ralf, Serries, Thomas & Stewering, H. (2003f): Requirements Definition for Enterprise Information Portals. In Proceedings of the 9th Americas Conference on Information Systems (AMCIS 2003). Tampa, Fl, USA, pp. 425–437.

Becker, Jörg, Rosemann, Michael & Schütte, Reinhard (1995): Grundsätze ordnungsmäßiger Modellierung. *Wirtschaftsinformatik*, Vol. 37, No. 5, pp. 435–445.

Becker, Jörg & Schütte, Reinhard (2004): *Handelsinformationssysteme.* 2nd edition. Landsberg/Lech: Moderne Industrie, p. 845.

Behrendt, Wernher (2004): Semantisches Web - Das Netz der Bedeutungen im Netz der Dokumente. In Kappel, Gerti, Pröll, Birgit, Reich, Siegfried & Retschitzegger, Werner, editors: Web Engineering: Systematische Entwicklung von Web-Anwendungen. Heidelberg: dpunkt, pp. 345–367.

Benbasat, Izak, Goldstein, David K. & Mead, Melissa (1987): The Case Research Strategy in Studies of Information Systems. *MIS Quarterly*, Vol. 11, No. 3, pp. 368–386.

Benn, Wolfgang & Langer, Oliver (2003): Semistrukturierte Datenmodelle und XML. In Vossen, Gottfried & Rahm, Erhard, editors: Web & Datenbanken: Konzepte, Architekturen, Anwendungen. Heidelberg: dpunkt-Verlag, Web & Datenbanken: Konzepte, Architekturen, Anwendungen, pp. 3–32.

Berger, Peter L. & Luckmann, Thomas (1991): *The Social Construction of Reality - A Treatise in the Sociology of Knowledge.* London, GB: Penguin Group.

Bergerfurth, Jörg (2004): *Referenz-Informationsmodelle für das Produktionscontrolling - Nutzerspezifische Analyse- und Auswertungssichten für produktionsbezogene Aufgaben.* Berlin: Logos.

Berghel, Hal (1997): Cyberspace 2000: dealing with information overload. *Communications of the ACM*, Vol. 40, No. 2, pp. 19–24.

Berners-Lee, Tim, Fielding, R. & Frystyk, H. (1996): *Hypertext Transfer Protocol –
HTTP/1.0 (Request for Comments No. 1945)*. ⟨URL: http://www.ietf.org/
rfc/rfc1945.txt?number=1945⟩ – visited on 2005-07-15.

Berners-Lee, Tim, Hendler, James & Lassila, Ora (2001): The Semantic Web. *Scientific
American*, Vol. 2004, No. 2004-03-24, p. N/A.

Bertalanffy, Ludwig von (1972): Vorläufer und Begründer der Systemtheorie. In Systemtheorie. Berlin: Colloqium, pp. 17–28.

Bichler, Martin & Nusser, Stefan (1996): Developing structured WWW-sites with
W3DT. In Proceedings of the World Conference of the Web Society (WebNet'96).
San Francisco: AACE, pp. 7–12.

Bieber, Michael, Vitali, Fabio, Ashman, Helen, Balasubramanian, V. & Oinas-
Kukkonen, Harri (1997): Fourth generation hypermedia: some missing links for
the World Wide Web. *International Journal of Human-Computer-Studies*, Vol. 47,
No. 1, pp. 31–65.

Bieber, Michael & Yoo, Joonhee (1999): Hypermedia: a design philosophy. *ACM Computing Surveys*, Vol. 31, No. 4es, pp. 29–34.

Bode, Jürgen (1997): Der Informationsbegriff in der Betriebswirtschaftslehre. *Zeitschrift
für betriebswirtschaftliche Forschung (ZfbF)*, Vol. 49, No. 5, pp. 449–468.

Boehm, Barry W. (1981): *Software engineering economics*. Englewood Cliffs, NJ:
Prentice-Hall.

Boehm, Barry W. (1988): A spiral model of software developement and enhancement.
IEEE Computer, Vol. 21, No. 5, pp. 61–72.

Boland, Richard J. (1985): Phenomenology: A Preferred Approach to Research on
Information Systems. In Mumford, Enid, Hirschheim, Rudy, Fitzgerald, Guy &
Wood-Harper, Trevor, editors: Research Methods in Information Systems. Ams-
terdam: Elsevier, pp. 193–201.

Borriello, Gaetano (2005): RFID: Tagging the World. *Communications of ACM*, Vol. 48,
No. 9, pp. 34–37.

Bos, Bert, Çelik, Tantek, Hickson, Ian & Lie, Håkon Wium (2005): *Cascading Style
Sheets, level 2 revision 1*. ⟨URL: http://www.w3.org/TR/CSS21/⟩ – visited on
2005-07-26.

Botafogo, Rodrigo A., Rivlin, Ehud & Shneiderman, Ben (1992): Structural Analysis of Hypertexts: Identifying Hierarchies and Useful Metrics. *ACM Transactions on Information Systems*, Vol. 10, No. 2, pp. 142–180.

Bray, Tim, Paoli, Jean, Sperberg-McQueen, C. M., Maler, Eve & Yergeau, François (2004): *Extensible Markup Language (XML) 1.0 (Third Edition).* ⟨URL: http://www.w3.org/TR/2004/REC-xml-20040204/⟩ – visited on 2005-07-27.

Brelage, Christian, Ehlers, Lars H. & Becker, Jörg (2002): Modelling and Implementing Macro Web Navigation Structures. In Proceedings of the European Conference on Information Systems (ECIS). Gdânsk: Uniwersytetu Gdanskiego, pp. 1547–1557.

Brickley, Dan & Guha, R.V.: *Resource Description Framework (RDF) Schema Specification.* ⟨URL: http://www.w3.org/TR/1999/PR-rdf-schema-19990303/⟩ – visited on 2005-07-28.

Brookes, Bertram C. (1980a): The foundations of Information Science. Part I. Philosophical aspects. *Journal of Information Science*, Vol. 2, No. 3-4, pp. 125–133.

Brookes, Bertram C. (1980b): The foundations of information science. Part II. Quantitative aspects: classes of things and the challegene of human individuality. *Journal of Information Science*, Vol. 2, pp. 209–221.

Brookes, Bertram C. (1980c): The foundations of information science. Part III. Quantitative aspects: objective maps and subjective landscapes. *Journal of Information Science*, Vol. 2, pp. 269–275.

Brookes, Bertram C. (1981): The foundations of information science. Part IV. Information science: the changing paradigm. *Journal of Information Science*, Vol. 3, No. 1, pp. 3–12.

Bucy, Erik P., Lang, Annie, Potter, Robert F. & Grabe, Maria Elizabeth (1999): Formal Features of Cyberspace: Relationships between Web Page Complexity and Site Traffic. *Journal of the American Society for Information Science*, Vol. 50, No. 13, pp. 1246–1256.

Buneman, Peter (1997): Semistructured data. In PODS '97: Proceedings of the sixteenth ACM SIGACT-SIGMOD-SIGART symposium on Principles of database systems. New York, NY, USA: ACM Press, pp. 117–121.

Bunge, Mario Augusto (1974): *Treatise on Basic Philosophy, Vol. 2: Semantics II: Interpretation and Truth*. Dorderecht: D. Reidel Publishing Company.

Bunge, Mario Augusto (1977): *Treatise on Basic Philosophy, Vol. 3: Ontology I: The Furniture of the World*. Volume 3, Dordrecht: D. Reidel Publishing Company.

Bunge, Mario Augusto (1979): *Treatise on Basic Philosophy, Vol. 4: Ontology II: A World of Systems*. Volume 4, Dordrecht: D. Reidel Publishing Company.

Burrell, Gibson & Morgan, Gareth (1979): *Sociological Paradigms and Organisational Anlysis: Elements of the Sociology of Corporate Life*. Brookfield, Vermont: Ashgate Publishing.

Bush, Vannevar (1945): As We May Think. *The Atlantic Monthly*, Vol. 176, No. 1, pp. 101–108.

Capurro, Rafael (1986): *Hermeneutik der Fachinformation*. Freiburg: Alber.

Ceri, Stefano, Fraternali, Piero & Bongio, Aldo (2000): Web Modeling Language (WebML): a modeling language for designing Web sites. In Proceedings of the 9th international World Wide Web conference on computer networks. Amsterdam: North-Holland Publishing Co., pp. 137–157.

Ceri, Stefano, Fraternali, Piero & Matera, Maristella (2002): Conceptual Modeling of Data-Intensive Web Applications. *IEEE Internet Computing*, Vol. 6, No. 4, pp. 20–30.

Ceri, Stefano, Fraternali, Piero & Paraboschi, S. (1999): Data-Driven One-To-One Web Site Generation for Data-Intensive Applications. In Very Large Databases (VLDB). Edinburgh, Scotland.

Ceri, Stefano, Fraternali, Piero, Paraboschi, S. & Pozzi, G. (1998): *Consolidated specification of WWW intelligent information infrastructure (W3I3)*. Milano, Italy: Politecnico di Milano – Technical report.

Charniak, Eugene & McDermott, Drew (1985): *Introduction to Artificial Intelligence*. Reading, MA: Addison-Wesley.

Chen, Peter Pin-Shan (1976): The Entity Relationship Model - Toward a Unified View of Data. *ACM Transactions on Database Systems (TODS)*, Vol. 1, No. 1, pp. 9–36.

Christodoulou, Sotiris P., Zafiris, Paris A. & Papatheodorou, Theodore S. (2001): *Web Engineering: The Developers' View and a Pracitioner's Approach.* Volume 2016, Web engineering: managing diversity and complexity of web application development. Berlin u. a.: Springer, pp. 170–187.

Cockburn, Alistair (2002): *Agile Software Development.* Boston: Addison-Wesley.

Cole, Charles (1994): Operationalizing the Notion of Information as a Subjective Construct. *Journal of the American Society for Information Science and Technology*, Vol. 45, No. 7, pp. 465–476.

Cole, Charles (1999): Acitivity of Understanding a Problem during Interaction with an "Enabling" Information Retrieval System: Modeling Information Flow. *Journal of the American Society for Information Science*, Vol. 50, No. 6, pp. 544–552.

Cole, Charles & Leide, John E. (2003): Using the User's Mental Model to Guide the Integration of Information Space into Information Need. *Journal of the American Society for Information Science and Technology*, Vol. 54, No. 1, pp. 39–46.

Collier, Andrew (1994): *Critical Realism - An Introduction to Roy Bhaskar's Philosophy.* London: Verso.

Conallen, Jim (1999): Modeling Web Application Architectures with UML. *Communications of the ACM*, Vol. 42, No. 10, pp. 63–70.

Conenberg, Adwolf G. (1999): *Kostenrechnung und Kostenanalyse.* Volume 4., Landsberg/Lech: moderne industrie.

Conklin, J. (1987): Hypertext: An Introduction and Survey. *IEEE Computer*, Vol. 20, No. 9, pp. 17–41.

Coughlan, Jane & Macredie, Robert D. (2002): Effective Communication in Requirements Elicitation: A Comparison of Methodologies. *Requirements Engineering*, Vol. 7, No. 1, pp. 60–74.

Culler, David E. & Hong, Wei (2005): Wireless Sensor Networks. *Communications of ACM*, Vol. 47, No. 6, pp. 30–33.

Curtis, Bill, Kellner, Marc I. & Over, Jim (1992): Process modeling. *Communications of the ACM*, Vol. 35, No. 9, pp. 75–90.

Cusumano, Michael A. & Yoffie, David B. (2000): *Competing on Internet time : lessons from Netscape and its battle with Microsoft*. New York, NY, USA: Simon & Schuster.

Cutter Consortium: *Poor Project Management Number-one Problem of Outsourced E-projects*. ⟨URL: http://www.cutter.com/research/2000/crb001107.html⟩ – visited on 2005-09-12.

Davis, Gordon B. & Olsen, Margrethe H. (1985): *Management Information Systems - Conceptual Foundations, Structure, and Development*. Volume 2., New York: McGraw-Hill.

Deetz, Stanley (1996): Describing Differences in Approaches to Organization Science: Rehtinking Burrell and Morgans and Their Legacy. *Organization Science*, Vol. 7, No. 2, pp. 191–207.

Deshpande, Yogesh & Ginige, Athula (2001): *Corporate Web Development: From Process Infancy to Maturity - A Case Study*. Volume 2016, Web engineering: managing diversity and complexity of web application development. Berlin u. a.: Springer, pp. 36–47.

Deshpande, Yogesh, Murugesan, San, Ginige, Athula, Hansen, Steve, Schwabe, Daniel, Gaedke, Martin & White, Bebo (2002): Web Engineering. *Journal of Web Engineering*, Vol. 1, pp. 3–17.

Dhyani, Devanshu, Ng, Wee Keong & Bhowmick, Sourav S. (2002): A Survey of Web Metrics. *ACM Computing Surveys (CSUR)*, Vol. 34, No. 4, pp. 469–503.

Doan, AnHai, Madhavan, Jayant, Dhamankar, Robin, Domingos, Pedro & Halevy, Alon (2003): Learning to match ontologies on the Semantic Web. *The VLDB Journal*, Vol. 12, No. 4, pp. 303–319.

Doan, AnHai, Madhavan, Jayant, Domingos, Pedro & Halevy, Alon (2002): Learning to map between ontologies on the semantic web. In WWW '02: Proceedings of the 11th international conference on World Wide Web. New York, NY, USA: ACM Press, pp. 662–673.

Dreyfus, Hubert L. (1979): *What computers still can't do: a critique of artificial reason*. Cambridge, Massachusetts: MIT Press.

Dreyfus, Hubert L. (1989): Misprenseting Human Intelligence. In Born, Rainer, editor: Artificial Intelligence - The Case Against. London: Routledge, pp. 41–54.

Driver, Michael J. (2000): Decision Style: Past, Present, and Future Research. In Riding, Richard J. & Rayner, Stephen G., editors: International Perspectives on Individual Differences: Volume 1 Cognitive Styles. Stamford: Ablex Publishing, pp. 41–64.

Dutta, Soumitra (1993): *Knowledge Processing & Applied Artificial Intelligence*. Oxford: Butterworth-Heinemann.

Dyke Parunak, H. van (1989): Hypermedia Topologies and User Navigation. In Proceedings of the 1st Conference on Hypertext and Hypermedia. Pittsburgh, Pennsylvania, United States: ACM Press, pp. 43–50.

Ehlers, Lars H. (2003): *Content Management Anwendungen: Spezifikation von Internet-Anwendungen auf Basis von Content-Management-Systemen*. Berlin: Logos Verlag, p. 264.

Eichinger, Christian (2004): Architektur von Web Anwendungen. In Kappel, Gerti, Pröll, Birgit, Reich, Siegfried & Retschitzegger, Werner, editors: Web Engineering: : Systematische Entwicklung von Web-Anwendungen. Heidelberg: dpunkt, pp. 77–100.

Engelbart, Douglas C. (1963): A Conceptual Framework for the Augmentation of Man's Intellect. In Howerton, Paul W. & Weeks, David C., editors: Vistas in Information Handling - The Augmentation of Man's Intellect by Machine. Volume 1, Washington: Spartan Books/Cleaver-Hume Press, pp. 1–29.

Estrin, Deborah, Culler, David E., Pister, Kris & Sukhatme, Gaurav (2002): Connecting the Physical World with Pervasive Networks. *IEEE Pervasive Computing*, Vol. 1, No. 1, pp. 59–69.

Falkenberg, Eckhard (1983a): Foundations of the Conceptual Schema Approach to Information Systems. In Holsapple, Clyde & Whinston, Andrew B., editors: Data Base Management: Theory and Applications. Dordrecht, NL: D. Reidel, pp. 3–17.

Falkenberg, Eckhard (1983b): Some Aspects of Conceptual Data Modelling. In Holsapple, Clyde & Whinston, Andrew B., editors: Data Base Management: Theory and Applications. Dordrecht, NL: D. Reidel, pp. 19–34.

Falkenberg, Eckhard, Hesse, Wolfgang, Lindgreen, Paul, Nilsson, Björn, Oei, Han, Rolland, Colette, Stamper, Ronald, Van, Assche, Frans, Verrijn-Stuart, Alexander & Voss, Klaus (1998): *FRISCO Report*. Leiden, Netherlands: International Federation of Information Processing (IFIP) – Technical report.

Fallside, David C. & Walmsley, Priscilla (2004): *XML Schema Part 0: Primer Second Edition*. ⟨URL: http://www.w3.org/TR/xmlschema-0/⟩ – visited on 2005-07-28.

Farhoomand, Ali F. & Drury, Don H. (2002): Managerial Information Overload. *Communications of ACM*, Vol. 45, No. 10, pp. 127–131.

Farkas, David K. & Farkas, Jean B. (2000): Guidelines for Designing Web Navigation. *Technical Communication*, Vol. 47, No. 3, pp. 341–358.

Fensel, Dieter (2001): *Ontologies: A Silver Bullet for Knowledge Management and Electronic Commerce*. Berlin u. a.: Springer, p. 147.

Ferstl, Otto K. & Sinz, Elmar J. (2001): *Grundlagen der Wirtschaftsinformatik*. 4th edition. München, Wien: Oldenbourg-Verlag.

Feyerabend, Paul (1975): *Against Method - Outline qf art anarchistic' theory of knowledge*. London: Western Printing Services.

Ford, Nigel (2000): Cognitive Styles and Virtual Environments. *Journal of the American Society for Information Science*, Vol. 51, No. 6, pp. 543–557.

Ford, Nigel (2004a): Creativity an Convergence in Information Science Research: The Roles of Objectivity and Suibjectivity, Constraint and Control. *Journal of the American Society for Information Science and Technology*, Vol. 55, No. 13, pp. 1169–1182.

Ford, Nigel (2004b): Modelling Cognitive Processes in Information Seeking: From Popper to Pask. *Journal of the American Society for Information Science*, Vol. 55, No. 9, pp. 769–782.

Fraternali, Piero (1999): Tools and approaches for developing data-intensive web applications: a survey. *ACM Computing Surveys (CSUR)*, Vol. 31, No. 3, pp. 227–263.

Fraternali, Piero & Paolini, Paolo (2000): Model-driven development of Web applications: the AutoWeb system. *ACM Transactions on Information Systems (TOIS)*, Vol. 18, No. 4, pp. 323–382.

Furnas, George W. & Zacks, Jeff (1994): Multitrees: Enriching and Reusing Hierarchical Structure. In Proceedings of the Conference on Human Factors in Computing Systems. Boston, Massachusetts, United States: ACM Press, pp. 330–336.

Gaedke, Martin, Nussbaumer, Martin, Jung, Oliver & Dieckmann, Markus (2004): Implementierungstechnologien für Web-Anwendungen. In Kappel, Gerti, Pröll, Birgit, Reich, Siegfried & Retschitzegger, Werner, editors: Web Engineering. Heidelberg: dpunkt, pp. 133–160.

Galliers, Robert D. (1992): Choosing Information Systems Research Approaches. In Galliers, Robert D., editor: Information Systems Research - Issues, Methods and Practical Guidelines. Oxford, England: Blackwell, pp. 144–162.

Galliers, Robert D. & Newell, Sue (2003): Back to the future: from knowledge management to the management of information and data. *Information Systems and e-Business Management*, Vol. 1, No. 1, pp. 5–13.

Galliers, Robert D. & Swan, Jacky A. (2000): There's More to Information Systems Development than Structured Approaches: Information Requirements Analysis as a Socially Mediated Process. *Requirements Engineering*, Vol. 5, No. 2, pp. 74–82.

Garzotto, Franca, Paolini, Paolo & Schwabe, Daniel (1991): HDM - a model for the design of hypertext applications. In Proceedings of the Third annual ACM conference on Hypertext. San Antonio: ACM Press, pp. 313–328.

Garzotto, Franca, Paolini, Paolo & Schwabe, Daniel (1993): HDM - a model-based approach to hypertext application design. *ACM Transactions on Information Systems*, Vol. 11, No. 1, pp. 1–26.

Ginige, Athula (2002): Web engineering: managing the complexity of web systems development. In Proceedings of the 4th international conference on Software engineering and knowledge engineering (SEKE'02). Ischia: ACM Press, pp. 721–729.

Ginige, Athula & Murugesan, San (2001): Web Engineering: An Introduction. *IEEE Multimedia*, Vol. 8, No. 1, pp. 14–18.

Gloor, Peter (1997): *Elements of Hypermedia Desing: techniques for navigation and visualization in cyberspace*. Bosten: Birkhäuser.

Gómez, Jaime & Cachero, Cristina (2002): OO-H Method: Extending UML to Model Web Interfaces. In Bommel, Patrick van, editor: Information Modeling for Internet applications. Hershey: Idea Group, pp. 144–173.

Gómez, Jaime, Cachero, Cristina & Pastor, Oscar (2000): Extending a Conceptual Modelling Approach to Web Application Design. In Wangler, Benkt & Bergman, Lars, editors: 12th International Conference on Advanved Information Systems Engineering (CAiSÄE). Volume 1789, Stockholm, Sweden: Springer, Lecture Notes in Computer Science, pp. 79–93.

Gómez, Jaime, Cachero, Cristina & Pastor, Oscar (2001): On Conceptual Modeling of Device-Independent Web Applications: Towards a Web Engineering Approach. *IEEE Multimedia*, Vol. 8, No. 2, pp. 26–39.

Goldfarb, Charles F. & Prescod, Paul (1998): *The XML Handbook*. Upper Saddle River, NJ: Prentice Hall.

Goldkuhl, G. & Lyytinen, Kalle (1982a): A Disposition for an Information Analysis Methodology based on Speech Act Theory. In Goldkuhl, G. & Lyytinen, Kalle, editors: Fifth Scandinavian Research Seminar on Systemeering Models. Dept. of Information Processing, University of Gothenburg, pp. 201–238.

Goldkuhl, G. & Lyytinen, Kalle (1982b): A Language Action View of Information Systems. In Ginzberg, M. & Ross, C., editors: Third International Conference on Information Systems. Ann Arbor, MI, pp. 13–30.

Green, F. & Rosemann, Michael (2002): Perceived Ontological Weakness of Process Modeling Techniques: Further Evidence. In The Xth European Conference on Information Systems (ECIS 2002). Gdânsk: Uniwersytetu Gdanskiego, pp. 312–321.

Green, Peter F. & Rosemann, Michael (2000): Integrated Process Modeling: An Ontological Evaluation. *Information Systems*, Vol. 25, No. 3, pp. 73–87.

Grünbacher, Paul (2004): Requirements Engineering für Web-Anwendungen. In Kappel, Gerti, Pröll, Birgit, Reich, Siegfried & Retschitzegger, Werner, editors: Web Engineering: Systematische Entwicklung von Web-Anwendungen. Heidelberg: dpunkt, Web Project Management. – chapter 2, pp. 29–47.

Gruber, Thomas R. (1993): A Translation Approach to Portable Ontology Specifications. *Knowledge Acquisition*, Vol. 5, No. 2, pp. 199–220.

Grundy, John C. & Venable, John R. (1996): Towards an integrated environment for method engineering. In Brinkkemper, Sjaak, Lyytinen, Kalle & Welke, Richard J.,

editors: Proceedings of the IFIP TC8, WG8.1/8.2 working conference on method
engineering on Method engineering : principles of method construction and tool
support. London, UK, UK: Chapman & Hall, Ltd., pp. 45–62.

Gu, Alice, Henderson-Sellers, Brian & Lowe, David (2002): Web Modelling Languages:
the gap between requirements and current exemplars. In Eighth Australian World
Wide Web Conference (AusWeb). Queensland, Australia, p. N/A.

Guarino, Nicola (1998): Formal Ontology and Information Systems. In International
Conference on Formal Ontologies in Information Systems (FOIS'98). Trento: IOS
Press, pp. 3–15.

Halasz, Frank & Schwartz, Mayer (1994): The Dexter hypertext reference model. *Communications of the ACM*, Vol. 37, No. 2, pp. 30–39.

Hansmann, Holger (2003): *Architekturen Workflow-gestützter PPS-Systeme - Referenzmodelle für die Koordination von Prozessen in der Auftragsabwicklung von Einzel- und Kleinserienfertigern.* Berlin: Logos.

Harbo, Ole, Ingwersen, Peter & Timmermann, P. (1977): Cognitive process in information storage and retrieval. In CC 77: International Workshop on the Cognitive Viewpoint. Ghent: Ghent University, pp. 214–218.

Harmsen, Anton Frank (1997): *Situational Method Engineering.* Utrecht: Moret Ernst & Young Management Consultants.

Harmsen, Frank & Saeki, M. (1996): Comparison of four method engineering languages.
In Brinkkemper, Sjaak, Lyytinen, Kalle & Welke, Richard J., editors: Proceedings
of the IFIP TC8, WG8.1/8.2 working conference on method engineering on Method
engineering : principles of method construction and tool support. London, UK,
UK: Chapman & Hall, Ltd., pp. 209–231.

Hassard, John (1999): Postmodernism, philosophy and management: concepts and controversies. *International Journal of Management Reviews*, Vol. 1, No. 2, pp. 171–195.

Hayes, John & Allinson, Christopher W. (1996): The Implications of Learning Style
for Training and Development: A Discussion of the Matching Hypotheses. *British Journal of Management*, Vol. 7, No. 1, pp. 63–73.

Herzberg, Frederick (1966): *Work and the nature of man.* Cleveland: World Publishing.

Herzberg, Frederick, Mausner, Bernard & Snyderman, Barbara Bloch (1967): *The motivation to work*. New York: Wiley.

Hesse, Wolfgang, Barkow, G., Braun, H. von, Kittlaus, H.-B. & Scheschonk, G. (1994): Terminologie der Softwaretechnik - Ein Begriffssystem für die Analyse und Modellierung von Anwendungssystemen - Teil 1: Begriffssystematik und Grundbegriffe. *Informatik Spektrum*, Vol. 17, pp. 39–47.

Hevner, Alan R., March, Salvatore T., Park, Jinsoo & Ram, Sudha (2004): Design Science in Information Systems Research. *MIS Quarterly*, Vol. 28, No. 1, pp. 75–105.

Hill, Jason, Horton, Mike, Kling, Ralph & Krishnamurthy, Lakshman (2004): The Platforms Enabling Wireless Sensor Networks. *Communications of ACM*, Vol. 47, No. 6, pp. 41–46.

Hill, Wilhelm, Fehlbaum, Raiymond & Ulrich, Peter (1989): *Organisationslehre 1*. Bern: UTB.

Hirschheim, Rudy (1985): Information Systems Epistemology: A Historical Perspective. In Mumford, Enid, Hirschheim, Rudy, Fitzgerald, Guy & Wood-Harper, Trevor, editors: Research Methods in Information Systems. Amsterdam: Elsevier, pp. 13–36.

Hirschheim, Rudy (1992): Information Systems Epistemology: An Historical Perspective. In Galliers, Robert D., editor: Information Systems Research: Issues, Methods and Practical Guidlines. Oxford: Blackwell, pp. 28–60.

Hirschheim, Rudy & Klein, Heinz K. (1989): Four paradigms of information systems development. *Communications of the ACM*, Vol. 32, No. 10, pp. 1199–1216.

Hirschheim, Rudy & Klein, Heinz K. (2003): Crisis in the IS Field? A Critical Reflection on the State of the Discipline. *Journal of the Association for Information Systems*, Vol. 4, No. 5, pp. 237–293.

Hirschheim, Rudy, Klein, Heinz K. & Lyytinen, Kalle (1995): *Information Systems Development and Data Modeling. Conceptual and Philosophical Foundations*. Cambridge: Cambridge University Press, p. 304.

Hirschheim, Rudy & Newman, Mike (1991): Symbolism and Information Systems Development: Myth, Metaphor and Magic. *Information Systems Research*, Vol. 2,

No. 1, pp. 29–62, 10477047 Not held at C.U. Libraries. See librarian for Interlibrary Loan.

Hitz, Martin & Leitner, Gerhard (2004): Usability von Web-Anwendungen. In Kappel, Gerti, Pröll, Birgit, Reich, Siegfried & Retschitzegger, Werner, editors: Web Engineering: Systematische Entwicklung von Web-Anwendungen. Heidelberg: dpunkt, pp. 265–295.

Hofstede, A. H. M. ter, Proper, H. A. & Weide, Th. P. van der (1996): Query Formulation as an Information Retrieval Problem. *The Computer Journal*, Vol. 39, pp. 255–274.

Holten, Roland (1999): *Entwicklung von Führungsinformationssystemen. Ein methodenorientierter Ansatz*. Wiesbaden, Germany: Gabler, p. 306.

Holten, Roland (2001): *The MetaMIS Approach for the Specification of Management Views on Business Processes*. Westfälische Wilhelms-Universität Münster, Institut für Wirtschaftsinformatik, Working Paper 84, Universität Münster Institut für Wirtschaftsinformatik – Technical report.

Holten, Roland (2003a): *Integration von Informationssystemen. Theorie und Anwendung im Supply Chain Management*. Münster: Westfälische Wilhelms-Universität – Technical report.

Holten, Roland (2003b): Specification of Management Views in Information Warehouse Projects. *Information Systems*, Vol. 28, No. 7, pp. 709–751.

Holten, Roland (2004): *Integration von Informationssystemen - Theorie und Anwendung im Supply Chain Management*. Habilitation Treatise University of Münster.

Holten, Roland & Dreiling, Alexander (2002): *Specification of Fact Calculations within the MetaMIS Approach*. Westfälische Wilhelms-Universität Münster, Institut für Wirtschaftsinformatik, Working Paper 88, Universität Münster Institut für Wirtschaftsinformatik – Technical report.

Holten, Roland, Dreiling, Alexander & Becker, Jörg (2004): *Ontology-Driven Method Engineering for Information Systems Development*. Hershey: IDEA Group Publishing, Ontological Analysis, Evaluation, and Engineering of Business Systems Analysis Methods.

Holten, Roland, Dreiling, Alexander & Schmid, Benedikt (2002): Management Report Engineering - A Swiss Re Business Case. In Proceedings of the Data Warehouse 2002. Heidelberg: Physica-Verlag, pp. 421–437.

Hopper, Trevor & Powell, Andrew (1985): Making Sense of Research into the Organizational and Social Aspects of Management Accounting: A Review of its Underlying Assumptions. *Journal of Management Studies*, Vol. 22, No. 5, pp. 429–465.

Hors, Arnaud Le, Hégaret, Philippe Le, Wood, Lauren, Nicol, Gavin, Robie, Jonathan, Champion, Mike & Byrne, Steve (2004): *Document Object Model (DOM) Level 3 Core Specification.* ⟨URL: http://www.w3.org/TR/2004/REC-DOM-Level-3-Core-20040407/⟩ – visited on 2005-07-26.

Huizingh, Eelko K.R.E. (2000): The content and design of web sites: an empirical study. *Information & Management*, Vol. 37, No. 3, pp. 123–134.

Ingwersen, Peter (1992): *Information Retrieval Interaction.* London: Taylor Graham.

Ingwersen, Peter (1996): Cognitive Perspectives of Information Retrieval Interaction: Elements of a Cognitive IR Theory. *Journal of Documentation*, Vol. 52, No. 1, pp. 3–50.

Inmon, William H. (1996): *Building the Data Warehouse.* 2nd edition. New York u. a.: John Wiley & Sons, p. 401.

Inmon, William H. (2002): *Building the Data Warehouse.* 3rd edition. New York u. a.: John Wiley & Sons.

Inmon, William H. & Hackathorn, Richard D. (1994): *Using the Data Warehouse.* New York u. a.: John Wiley & Sons, p. 304.

Internet Engineering Task Force: *Internet Protocol (Request for Comments No. 791).* ⟨URL: http://www.ietf.org/rfc/rfc791.txt⟩ – visited on 2005-07-14.

Isakowitz, Tomas, Bieber, Michael & Vitali, Fabio (1998): Web Information Systems. *Communications of the ACM*, Vol. 41, No. 7, pp. 78–80.

Isakowitz, Tomas, Stohr, Edward A. & Balasubramanian, P. (1995): RMM: a methodology for structured hypermedia design. *Communications of the ACM*, Vol. 38, No. 8, pp. 34–44.

Janiesch, Christian, Brelage, Christian & Holten, Roland (2005): Exploration of Conceptual Models: Application of the GoM Framework. In 16th Information Resources Management Association Conference (IRMA 2005). San Diego, CA, USA, pp. 524–527.

Jansen, Bernard J. & Spink, Amanda (2006): How are we searching the World Wide Web? A comparison of nine search engine transaction logs. *Information Processing & Management*, Vol. 42, No. 1, pp. 248–263.

Kamlah, Wilhelm & Lorenzen, Paul (1984): *Logical Propaedeutic. Pre-School of Reasonable Discourse*. Lanham: University Press of America.

Kappel, Gerti, Pröll, Birgit, Reich, Siegfried & Retschitzegger, Werner (2004): Web Engineering - Die Disziplin zur systematischen Entwicklung von Web-Anwendungen. In Kappel, Gerti, Pröll, Birgit, Reich, Siegfried & Retschitzegger, Werner, editors: Web Engineering: Systematische Entwicklung von Web-Anwendungen. Heidelberg: dpunkt, pp. 1–28.

Kappel, Gerti, Retschitzegger, Werner, Pröll, Birgit, Unland, Rainer & Vojdani, Bahram (2003): Architektur von Web-Informationssystemen. In Rahm, Erhard & Vossen, Gottfried, editors: Web & Datenbanken. Heidelberg: dpunkt, pp. 101–134.

Kautz, Karlheinz & Nørbjerg, Jacob (2003): Persistent Problems in Information Systems Development. The Case of the World Wide Web. In Proceedings of the 11th European Conference on Information Systems (ECIS 2003). Naples.

Khan, Kushal & Locatis, Craig (1998): Searching through Cyberspace: The Effects of Link Display and Link Density on Information Retreival from Hypertext on the World Wide Web. *Journal of the American Society for Information Science*, Vol. 49, No. 2, pp. 176–182.

Klein, Heinz K. & Myers, Michael D. (1999): A Set of Principles for Conducting and Evaluating Interpretive Field Studies in Information Systems. *MIS Quarterly*, Vol. 23, No. 1, pp. 67–93.

Klyne, Graham & Carroll, Jeremy J.: *Resource Description Framework (RDF): Concepts and Abstract Syntax*. ⟨URL: http://www.w3.org/TR/rdf-concepts/⟩ – visited on 2005-07-25.

Knackstedt, Ralf (2004): *Fachkonzeptionelle Referenzmodellierung einer Managementunterstützung mit quantitativen und qualitativen Daten -Methodische Konzepte zur Konstruktion und Anwendung*. Ph. D thesis, University of Münster.

Koertge, Noretta (1997): Popper's Contributions to Our Understanding of Social Science. *Foundations of Science*, Vol. 2, No. 2, pp. 365–370.

Krcmar, Helmut (2003): *Informationsmanagement.* 3rd edition. Berlin: Springer.

Krogstie, John & Solvberg, Arne (1996): A Classification of Methodological Frameworks for Computerized Information Systems Support in Organizations. In Brinkkemper, Sjaak, Lyytinen, Kalle & Welke, Richard J., editors: Proceedings of the IFIP TC8, WG8.1/8.2 working conference on method engineering: principles of method construction and tool support. London, UK, UK: Chapman & Hall, Ltd., pp. 278–295.

Kuhn, Thomas S. (1996): *The Structure of Scientific Revolutions.* Chicago: The University of Chicago Press.

Kuropka, Dominik (2003): *Modelle zur Repräsentation von natürlichsprachlichen Dokumenten.* Ph. D thesis, University of Münster.

Lancaster, Frederick Wilfried (1991): *Indexing and abstracting in theory and practice.* London: Library Association Publishing.

Land, Frank (1992): The Information System Domain. In Galliers, Robert D., editor: Information Systems Research: Issues, Methods and Practical Guidlines. Oxford: Blackwell, pp. 6–13.

Landow, George P. (1997): *Hypertext 2.0.* Balitmore: Johns Hopkins University Press.

Lang, Michael (2003): Hypermedia Systems Development: A Comparative Study of Software Engineers and Graphic Designers. *Communications of the Association for Information Systems,* Vol. 12, No. Article 16, p. N/A.

Langefors, Börje (1973): *Theoretical Analysis of Information Systems.* Philadelphia, PA: Auerbach.

Langefors, Börje (1977): Information Systems Theory. *Information Systems,* Vol. 2, pp. 207–219.

Langefors, Börje (1980): Infological Models and Information User Views. *Information Systems,* Vol. 5, No. 1, pp. 17–32.

Larson, Kevin & Czerwinski, Mary (1998): Web page design: implications of memory, structure and scent for information retrieval. In Proceedings of the SIGCHI conference on Human factors in computing systems. Los Angeles, California, United States: ACM Press/Addison-Wesley Publishing Co., pp. 25–32.

Laudon, Kenneth C. & Lauden, Jane Price (1993): *Business information systems: a problem solving approach*. Fort Worth: Dryden Press.

Lee, Allen S. (1989): A Scientific Methodology for MIS Case Studies. *MIS Quarterly*, Vol. 13, No. 1, pp. 32–50.

Lee, Allen S. (1999): Researching MIS. In Currie, Wendy L. & Galliers, Robert D., editors: Rethinking Management Information Systems: An Interdisciplinary Perspective. Oxford: Oxford University Press, pp. 7–27.

Lehner, Franz (1995): Grundfragen und Positionierung der Wirtschaftsinformatik. In Franz Lehner, Knut Hildebrand & Maier, Ronald, editors: Wirtschaftsinformatik: theoretische Grundlagen. München: Hanser, pp. 1–71.

Lennon, Jennifer A. (1997): *Hypermedia systems and applications: World Wide Web and beyond*. Berlin: Springer.

Levy, David M. (2005): To grow in wisdom: vannevar bush, information overload, and the life of leisure. In JCDL '05: Proceedings of the 5th ACM/IEEE-CS joint conference on Digital libraries. New York, NY, USA: ACM Press, pp. 281–286.

Liestol, Gunnar (1994): Wittgenstein, Genette, and the Reader's Narrative in Hypertext. In Landow, George P., editor: Hyper Text Theory. Baltimore: Johns Hopkins University Press, pp. 87–120.

Liu, Chang & Arnett, Kirk P. (2000): Exploring the factors associated with Web site success in the context of electronic commerce. *Information & Management*, Vol. 38, No. 1, pp. 23–33.

Lorenz, Kuno (1995a): Metasprache. In Mittelstraß, Jürgen, editor: Enzyklopädie Philosophie und Wissenschaftstheorie. Part 2: H-O. Stuttgart: J. B. Metzler, p. 875.

Lorenz, Kuno (1995b): Objektsprache. In Mittelstraß, Jürgen, editor: Enzyklopädie Philosophie und Wissenschaftstheorie. Part 2: H-O. Stuttgart: J. B. Metzler, pp. 1054–1055.

Lorenz, Kuno (1996): Komplex. In Mittelstraß, Jürgen, editor: Enzyklopädie Philosophie und Wissenschaftstheorie 4. Stuttgart: J. B. Metzler, pp. 427–428.

Lu, Hongjun & Feng, Ling (1998): Integrating database and World Wide Web technologies. *World Wide Web*, Vol. 1, No. 1, pp. 73–86.

Luger, George F. & Stubblefield, William A. (1993): *Artificial Intelligence - Structures and Strategies for Complex Problem Solving.* 2nd edition. Redwood City, CA, USA: Benjamin/Cummings.

Lyytinen, Kalle (1985): Research Methods in Information Systems: Using Action Research. In Mumford, Enid, Hirschheim, Rudy, Fitzgerald, Guy & Wood-Harper, Trevor, editors: Research Methods in Information Systems. Amsterdam: Elsevier, pp. 219–236.

Lyytinen, Kalle (1987a): Different perspectives on information systems: problems and solutions. *ACM Computing Surveys*, Vol. 19, No. 1, pp. 5–46.

Lyytinen, Kalle (1987b): A taxonomic Perspective of Information Systems Development: Theoretical Constructs and Recommendations. In Boland, Richard J. & Hirschheim, Rudy, editors: Critical Issues in Information Systems Research. Chichester: John Wiley, pp. 3–41.

Lyytinen, Kalle, Rose, Gregory & Welke, Richard J. (1998): The Brave New World of Development in the Internetwork Computing Architecture (InterNCA): Or How Distributed Computing Platforms Will Change Systems Development. *Information Systems Journal*, Vol. 8, No. 3, pp. 241–253.

MacDonald, Margaret S. & Oettinger, Anthony G. (2002): Information Overload: Managing Intelligence Technologies. *Harvard International Review*, Vol. 24, No. 3, pp. 44–48.

Mack, Robert, Ravin, Yael & Byrd, Roy. J. (2001): Knowledge Portals and the Emerging Digitial Knowledge Workplace. *IBM Systems Journal*, Vol. 40, No. 4, pp. 925–955.

Manola, Frank & Miller, Eric: *RDF Primer.* ⟨URL: http://www.w3.org/TR/rdf-primer/⟩ – visited on 2005-07-27.

Marttiin, P., Harmsen, Frank & Rossi, M. (1996): A functional framework for evaluating method engineering environments: the case of Maestro II/ Decamerone and MetaEdit+. In Brinkkemper, Sjaak, Lyytinen, Kalle & Welke, Richard J., editors: Proceedings of the IFIP TC8, WG8.1/8.2 working conference on method engineering on Method engineering : principles of method construction and tool support. London, UK, UK: Chapman & Hall, Ltd., pp. 63–86.

Mathiassen, Lars & Munk-Madsen, Andreas (1986): Formalizations in Systems Development. *Behaviour and Information Technology*, Vol. 5, No. 2, pp. 145–155.

Mattern, Friedemann & Römer, Kay (2003): Drahtlose Sensornetze. *Informatik Spektrum*, Vol. 26, No. 3, pp. 191–194.

Mayrhauser, Anneliese von (1990): *Software engineering: methods and management*. San Diego, CA: Academic Press.

McGrath, Joseph Edward (1991): Time, Interaction and performance (TIP): A theory of groups. *Small Group Research*, Vol. 22, No. 2, pp. 147–174.

McGuinness, Deborah L. & Harmelen, Frank van: *OWL Web Ontology Language Overview*. ⟨URL: http://www.w3.org/TR/owl-features/⟩ – visited on 2007-07-31.

Mecca, Giansalvatore, Atzeni, Paolo, Masci, A., Sindoni, G. & Merialdo, Paolo (1998): The Araneus Web-based management system. In Proceedings of the ACM SIGMOD international conference on Management of data. Seattle: ACM Press, Seattle, Washington, United States, pp. 544–546.

Merialdo, Paolo, Atzeni, Paolo & Mecca, Giansalvatore (2003): Design and development of data-intensive web sites: The Araneus approach. *ACM Transactions on Internet Technology*, Vol. 3, No. 1, pp. 49–92.

Mey, Marc de (1980): The relevance of the cognitive paradigm for information science. In Harbo, Ole & Kajberg, Leif, editors: Theory and application of Information Research. London: Mansell, pp. 48–61.

Mey, Marc de (1982): *The cognitive paradigm*. Dordrecht, Holland: D. Reidel Publishing.

Mühlen, Michael zur (2002): *Workflow-based Process Controlling - Foundations, Design and Applikation of Workflow-driven Process Information Systems*. Ph. D thesis, University of Münster.

Mittelstraß, Jürgen (1995): Erkenntnistheorie. In Mittelstraß, Jürgen, editor: Enzyklopädie Philosophie und Wissenschaftstheorie. Part 1: A-G. Stuttgart: J. B. Metzler, pp. 576–577.

Montoya-Weiss, Mitzi M., Massey, Anne P. & Song, Michael (2001): Getting it Together: Temporal Coordination and Conflict Management in Global Virtual Teams. *Academy of Management Journal*, Vol. 44, No. 6, pp. 1251–1262.

Moody, Daniel L., Sindre, Guttorm, Brasethvik, Terje & Sløvberg, Arne (2002): Evaluating the Quality of Process Models: Empirical Testing of a Quality Framework. In 21st International Conference on Conceptual Modeling (ER 2002). Tampere: Springer, pp. 380–396.

Mullock, Kelvin, Birch, Tom & Breems, Suzanne den (2004): Electronic Invoicing: European developments. *International Tax Review*, Vol. 18, pp. 37–41.

Muylle, Steve, Moenaert, Rudy & Despontin, Marc (2004): The conceptualization and empirical validation of web site user satisfaction. *Information & Management*, Vol. 41, No. 1, pp. 543–560.

Nelson, Theodor Holm (1965): Complex information processing: a file structure for the complex, the changing and the indeterminate. In Proceedings of the 1965 20th ACM national conference. Cleveland, Ohio, United States: ACM Press, pp. 84–100.

Nelson, Theodor Holm (1993): *Literary Machines*. Sausalito, CA: Mindful Press.

Nelson, Theodor Holm (1999a): The unfinished revolution and Xanadu. *ACM Computing Surveys*, Vol. 31, No. 4, pp. 37–43.

Nelson, Theodor Holm (1999b): Xanalogical structure, needed now more than ever: parallel documents, deep links to content, deep versioning, and deep re-use. *ACM Computing Surveys*, Vol. 31, No. 4, pp. 33–64.

Neumaier, Otto (1989): A Wittgensteinnian View of Artificial Intelligence. In Born, Rainer, editor: Artificial Intelligence - The Case Against. London: Routledge, pp. 132–173.

Newell, Allen & Simon, Herbert A. (1972): *Human Problem Solving*. Englewood Cliffs: Prentice-Hall.

Niehaves, Björn (2004): A Framework for Analysing the Epistemological Assumptions of Research Methods. In Khosrow-Pour, M., editor: Innovation Through Information Technology. 2004 IRMA International Conference. New Orleans/LA, U.S.A., pp. 57–60.

Niehaves, Björn (2005): Epistemological Perspectives on Pluralist IS Research. In ECIS 2005. Regensburg, Germany.

Niehaves, Björn, Dreiling, Alexander, Ribbert, Michael & Holten, Roland (2004): Conceptual Modeling - An Epistemological Foundation. In Bullen, C.V. & Stohr, Edward A., editors: American Conference on Information Systems AMCIS 2004. New York, U.S.A..

Nielsen, Jakob (1990): The Art of Navigating Through Hypertext. *Communications of ACM*, Vol. 33, No. 3, pp. 296–310.

Nielsen, Jakob (1999): User Interface Directions for the Web. *Communications of ACM*, Vol. 42, No. 1, pp. 65–72.

Nielsen, Jakob (2000): *Designing Web Usability: The Practice of Simplicity*. Indianapolis, Ind: New Riders.

Noy, Natalya F. & Musen, Mark A. (2002): Evaluating Ontology-Mapping Tools: Requirements and Experience. In OntoWeb-SIG3 Workshop at the 13th International Conference on Knowledge Engineering and Knowledge Management EKAW 2002. Siguenza: Springer, pp. 1–14.

Ocker, Rosalie & Hiltz, Starr Roxanne (1995): The effects of distributed group support and process structuring on software requirements. *Journal of Management Information Systems*, Vol. 12, No. 3, pp. 127–153.

Odell, James J. (1996): A primer to method engineering. In Proceedings of the IFIP TC8, WG8.1/8.2 working conference on method engineering on Method engineering : principles of method construction and tool support. London, UK, UK: Chapman & Hall, Ltd., pp. 1–7.

Oei, J. L. H., Hemmen, J. G. T. van, Falkenberg, Eckhard & Brinkkemper, Sjaak (1992): *The Meta Model Hierarchy: A Framework for Information Systems Concepts and Techniques*. Nijmegen, Netherlands: Department of Information Systems, University of Nijmegen – Technical report.

Olle, T. William (1983): A Tutorial On Data Modelling Using Entity Types, Attributes And Relationships. In Holsapple, Clyde & Whinston, Andrew B., editors: Data Base Management: Theory and Applications. Dordrecht, NL: D. Reidel, pp. 35–58.

Orlikowski, Wanda J. & Iacono, C. Suzanne (2001): Research Commentary: Desperately Seeking the 'IT' in IT Research-A Call to Theorizing the IT Artifact. *Information*

Systems Research, Vol. 12, No. 2, pp. 121–134, 10477047 Not held at C.U. Libraries. See librarian for Interlibrary Loan.

Ortner, Erich (2002): Sprachingenieurwesen - Empfehlungen zur inhaltlichen Weiterentwicklung der (Wirtschafts)informatik. *Informatik Spektrum*, Vol. 25, No. 1, pp. 39–51.

Palmer, Jonathan W. (2002): Web Site Usability, Design, and Performance Metrics. *Information Systems Research*, Vol. 13, No. 2, pp. 151–167, 10477047 Not held at C.U. Libraries. See librarian for Interlibrary Loan.

Papazoglou, M. P., Proper, H. A. & Yang, J. (2001): Landscaping the Information Space of Large Multi-Database Networks. *Data & Knowledge Engineering*, Vol. 36, No. 3, pp. 251–281.

Pask, Gordon (1975): *Conversation, Cognition and Learning - A Cybernetic Theory and Methodology*. Amsterdam, NL: Elsevier.

Pfeffer, Jeffrey (1993): Barriers to the advance of organizational science: Paradigm development as a dependable variable. *Academy of Management Review*, Vol. 18, No. 4, pp. 599–620.

Popper, Karl Raimund (1969): *Conjectures and Refutations*. Volume 3. ed., London: Routledge & Kegan Paul Limited.

Popper, Karl Raimund (1979): *Objective Knowledge - An Evolutionary Approach*. Revised Edition edition. Oxford: Oxford University Press.

Postel, J. & Reynolds, J. (1985): *File Transfer Protocol (FTP) (Request for Comments No. 959)*. ⟨URL: http://www.ietf.org/rfc/rfc0959.txt?number=959⟩ – visited on 2005-07-16.

Rasmussen, Jens, Pejtersen, Anneliese Mark & Goodstein, L. P. (1994): *Cognitive Systems Engineering*. New York: Wiley.

Ratcliff, B. (1987): *Software engineering: principles and methods*. Oxford: Blackwell Scientific Publications.

Retschitzegger, Werner & Schwinger, Wieland (2000): Towards Modeling of DataWeb Applications - A Requirements' Perspective. In Americas Conference on Information Systems (AMCIS). Long Beach, CA, USA, pp. 149–155.

Ribbert, Michael, Niehaves, Björn, Dreiling, Alexander & Holten, Roland (2004): An Epistemological Foundation of Conceptual Modeling. In Leino, T., Saarinen, T. & Klein, S., editors: 12th European Conference on Information Systems (ECIS). Turku, Finland.

Rich, Elaine & Knight, Kevin (1991): *Artificial Intelligence*. 2nd edition. New York: McGraw-Hill.

Riding, Richard J. (2000): Cognitive Style: A Review. In Riding, Richard J. & Rayner, Stephen G., editors: International Perspectives on Individual Differences: Volume 1 Cognitive Styles. Stamford: Ablex Publishing, pp. 315–344.

Riebel, Paul (1979a): Gestaltungsprobleme einer zweckneutralen Grundrechnung. *Zeitschrift für betriebswirtschaftliche Forschung*, Vol. 31, pp. 863–893.

Riebel, Paul (1979b): Zum Konzept einer zweckneutralen Grundrechnung. *Zeitschrift für betriebswirtschaftliche Forschung (ZfbF)*, Vol. 31, No. 1, pp. 785–798.

Riebel, Paul (1992): *Einzelerlös-, Einzelkosten- und Deckungsbeitragsrechung als Kern einer ganzheitlichen Führungsrechung*. Wiesbaden: Gabler Verlag, Handbuch Kostenrechnung, pp. 247–299.

Riebel, Paul & Sinzig, Werner (1981): Zur Realisierung der Einzelkosten und Deckungsbeitragsrechnung mit einer relationalen Datenbank. *Zeitschrift für betriebswirtschaftliche Forschung*, Vol. 33, pp. 457–489.

Rivlin, Ehud, Botafogo, Rodrigo A. & Shneiderman, Ben (1994): Navigating in Hyperspace. Designing a Structure-Based Toolbox. *Communications of ACM*, Vol. 37, No. 2, pp. 87–96.

Robey, Daniel & Markus, M. Lynne (1984): Rituals In Information System Design. *MIS Quarterly*, Vol. 10, No. 1, pp. 5–15.

Rolland, Colette & Prakash, Naveen (1996): A proposal for context-specific method engineering. In Proceedings of the IFIP TC8, WG8.1/8.2 working conference on method engineering on Method engineering : principles of method construction and tool support. London, UK, UK: Chapman & Hall, Ltd., pp. 191–208.

Rosemann, Michael (1996): *Komplexitätsmanagement in Prozeßmodellen*. Wiesbaden: Gabler Verlag, p. 297.

Rosemann, Michael & Green, Peter F. (2002): Developing a meta model for the Bunge-Wand-Weber ontological constructs. *Information Systems*, Vol. 27, No. 2, pp. 75–91.

Roth, Gerhard (1992): Das konstruktive Gehirn: Neurobilologische Grundlagen von Warhnehmung und Erkenntnis. In Schmidt, Siegfried J., editor: Kognition und Gesellschaft - Der Diskurs des Radikalen Konstruktivismus 2. Volume 1, Frankfurt: suhrkamp, pp. 277–336.

Roth, Gerhard (1997): *Das Gehirn und seine Wirklichkeit - Kognitive Neurobiologie und ihre philosophischen Konsequenzen.* Frankfurt: suhrkamp.

Rowan, John & Reason, Peter (1981): On making sense. In Reason, Peter & Rowan, John, editors: Human Inquiry: A Sourcebook of New Paradigm Research. Chichester: John Wiley & Sons, pp. 113–137.

Rumbaugh, James, Blaha, M., Premerlani, W., Eddy, F. & Lorenson, W. (1991): *Object-oriented modeling and design.* Englewood Cliffs: Prentice-Hall.

Rumbaugh, James, Jacobson, Ivar & Booch, Grady (1998): *Unified modeling language reference manual.* Reading, Mass: Addison-Wesley.

Sadler-Smith, Eugene (2000): Cognitive Style and Learning in Organizations. In Riding, Richard J. & Rayner, Stephen G., editors: International Perspectives on Individual Differences: Volume 1 Cognitive Styles. Stamford: Ablex Publishing, pp. 181–213.

Scacchi, Walt (1985): Applying Social Analysis of Computing to System Design. In Proceedings of the Development and Use of Computer-Based Systems Tools. Aarhus, Denmark, pp. 477–499.

Scharl, Arno (1998): Reference Modelling of Commercial Web Information Systems Using the Extended World Wide Web Design Technique (eW3DT). In Proceedings of the Hawaii International Conference on System Science. Hawaii, USA, pp. 476–484.

Scharl, Arno (2000): *Evolutionary Web Development.* London: Springer.

Scheer, August-Wilhelm (1992): *Architecture of Integrated Information Systems - Foundations of Enterprise Modelling.* Berlin u. a.: Springer, p. 219.

Scheer, August-Wilhelm (1994): *Business Process Engineering. Reference Models for Industrial Enterprises.* 2nd edition. Berlin u. a.: Springer, p. 770.

Scheer, August-Wilhelm (1998): *Wirtschaftsinformatik: Referenzmodelle für industrielle Geschäftsprozesse.* 2nd edition. Berlin: Springer.

Scheer, August-Wilhelm (1999): *ARIS - Business Process Modeling.* 2nd edition. Berlin u. a.: Springer, p. 218.

Scheer, August-Wilhelm (2001): *ARIS - Modellierungsmethoden, Metamodelle, Anwendungen.* 4th edition. Berlin u. a.: Springer.

Schellhase, Jörg (2001): *Entwicklungsmethoden und Architekturkonzepte für Web-Applikationen - Erstellung und Administration Web-basierter Lernumgebungen.* Wiesbaden: Gabler.

Schöning, Harald & Waterfeld, Walter (2003): XML Schema. In Rahm, Erhard & Vossen, Gottfried, editors: Web & Datenbanken - Konzepte, Architekturen, Anwendungen. Heidelberg: dpunkt, pp. 33–64.

Schütte, Reinhard (1998): *Grundsätze ordnungsmäßiger Referenzmodellierung. Konstruktion konfigurations- und anpassungsorientierter Modelle.* Wiesbaden: Gabler Verlag.

Schütte, Reinhard & Zelewski, Stephan (2001): *Epistemological Problems in Working with Ontologies.* Institut für Produktion und industrielles Informationssmanagement (13). – Technical report.

Schultze, Ulrike & Stabell, Charles (2004): Knowing What You Don't Know? Discourses and Contradictions in Knowledge Management Research. *Journal of Management Studies*, Vol. 41, No. 4, pp. 549–573.

Schwabe, Daniel, Rossi, Gustavo & Barbosa, Simone D. J. (1996): Systematic hypermedia application design with OOHDM. In Seventh ACM conference on Hypertext and Hypermedia. Bethesda: ACM Press, pp. 116–128.

Schwaber, Ken (2004): *Agile Project Management with Scrum.* Redmond: Microsoft Press.

Schwemmer, Owald (1995): Ontologie. In Mittelstraß, Jürgen, editor: Enzyklopädie Philosophie und Wissenschaftstheorie. Part 2: H-O. Stuttgart: J. B. Metzler, pp. 1077–1079.

Schwinger, Werner & Koch, Nora (2004): Modellierung von Web-Anwendungen. In Gerti Kappel, Birgit Pröll, Siegfried Reich & Retschitzegger, Werner, editors: Web Engineering: Systematische Entwicklung von Web-Anwendungen. Heidelberg: dpunkt.– chapter 3, pp. 49–75.

Scott, Bernard (2001a): Conversation Theory: A Constructivist, Dialogical Approach to Educational Technology. *Cybernetics & Human Knowing*, Vol. 8, No. 5, pp. 25–46.

Scott, Bernard (2001b): Gordon Pask's Conversation Theory: A Domain Independent Constructivist Model of Human Knowing. *Foundations of Science*, Vol. 6, No. 4, pp. 343–360.

Seiffert, Helmut (1996): *Einführung in die Wissenschaftstheorie 2*. 10th edition. München: Beck.

Serries, Thomas (2004): *Situationsbezogene Informationsversorgung in der Industriellen Auftragsabwicklung - Erweiterte OLAP-Techniken für Workflow-einbeziehende PPS*. Berlin: Logos.

Shah, Abad (2003): OODM: An Object-Oriented Design Methodology for Development of Web Applications. In Bommel, Patrick van, editor: Information Modeling for Internet applications. Hershey: Idea Group, pp. 189–229.

Shannon, Claude E. (1948): A Mathematical Theory of Communication. *The Bell System Technical Journal*, Vol. 27, pp. 379–423 and 623–656.

Shannon, Claude E. (1949): The Mathematical Theory of Communication. In Shannon, Claude E. & Weaver, Warren, editors: The Mathematical Theory of Communication. Urbana, Illinois: University of Illinois Press, pp. 29–125.

Siegwart, Geo (1996a): System. In Mittelstraß, Jürgen, editor: Enzyklopädie Philosophie und Wissenschaftstheorie 4. Stuttgart: J. B. Metzler, pp. 183–185.

Siegwart, Geo (1996b): Systemtheorie. In Mittelstraß, Jürgen, editor: Enzyklopädie Philosophie und Wissenschaftstheorie 4. Stuttgart: J. B. Metzler, pp. 190–194.

Simpson, Rosemary, Renear, Allen, Mylonas, Elli & Dam, Andries van (1996): 50 years after As we may think: the Brown MIT Vannevar Bush symposium. *ACM Interactions*, Vol. 3, No. 2, pp. 47–67.

Sinz, Elmar J. (1988): Das strukturierte Entity-Relationship-Modell (SER-Modell). *Angewandte Informatik*, Vol. 30, No. 5, pp. 191–202.

Sinzig, Werner (1990): *Datenbankorientiertes Rechnungswesen. Grundzüge einer EDV-gestützten Realisierung der Einzelkosten- und Deckungsbeitragsrechnung.* Volume 3. Ed., Berlin: Springer.

Smith, Michael K., Welty, Chris & McGuinness, Deborah L.: *OWL Web Ontology Language Guide.* ⟨URL: `http://www.w3.org/TR/2004/REC-owl-guide-20040210/`⟩ – visited on 2005-07-29.

Sodhi, Jag (1991): *Software engineering: methods, management and CASE tools.* Blue Ridge Summit, PA: TAB Books.

Solvberg, Arne & Kung, David Chenho (1993): *Information System Engineering - An Introduction.* Berlin: Springer.

Sommerville, Ian (2001): *Software Engineering.* 6th edition. Edinburgh: Addison-Wesley.

Sowa, John F. (1999): *Knowledge representation: logical, philosophical and computational foundations.* Pacific Grove: Brooks Cole.

Sowa, John F. (2000): Ontology, Metadata, and Semiotics. In ICCS '00: Proceedings of the Linguistic on Conceptual Structures. London, UK: Springer-Verlag, pp. 55–81.

Sowa, John F. & Zachman, John A. (1992): Extending and formalizing the framework for information systems architecture. *IBM Systems Journal*, Vol. 31, No. 3, pp. 590–616.

Spangler, Scott, Kreulen, Jeffrey T. & Lessler, Justin (2003): Generating and Browsing Multiple Taxonomies Over a Document Collection. *Journal of Management Information Systems*, Vol. 19, No. 4, pp. 191–212, 22p 1 chart, 8bw.

Speck, Mario C. (2001): *Geschäftsprozessorientierte Datenmodellierung - Ein Referenz-Vorgehensmodell zur fachkonzeptionellen Modellierung von Informationsstrukturen.* Berlin: Logos.

Standish Group: *The CHAOS Report.* ⟨URL: `http://www.standishgroup.com/sample_research/chaos_1994_1.php`⟩ – visited on 2005-09-12.

Stapleton, Jennifer (2003): *DSDM Business Focused Development.* Volume 2., The Agile Software Development Series. London: Addison-Wesley.

Stonier, Tom (1992): *Beyond Information: the natural history of intelligence*. Berlin: Springer.

Stonier, Tom (1997): *Information and Meaning - An Evolutionary Perspective*. Berlin: Springer.

Strahringer, Susanne (1996): *Metamodellierung als Instrument des Methodenvergleichs - Eine Evaluierung am Beispiel objektorientierter Analysemethoden*. Aachen: Shaker Verlag, p. 400.

Strobel, Claus (2004): *Web-Technologien: in E-Commerce-Systemen*. München, Wien: Oldenbourg.

Styhre, Alexander (2003): *Understanding Knowledge Management - Critical and Postmodern Perspectives*. Trelleborg: Berlings Skogs.

Sutton, David C. (2000): Linguistic Problems with Requirements and Knowledge Elicitation. *Requirements Engineering*, Vol. 5, No. 2, pp. 114–124, TY - JOUR.

Tanenbaum, Andrew S. (1981): Network Protocols. *ACM Computig Surveys*, Vol. 13, No. 4, pp. 453–489.

Teichert, Dieter (1996): Zirkel, hermeneutischer. In Mittelstraß, Jürgen, editor: Enzyklopädie Philosophie und Wissenschaftstheorie. Part 4: SP-Z. Stuttgart: J. B. Metzler, pp. 850–851.

Teorey, Toby J., Yang, Dongqing & Fry, James P. (1986): A logical design methodology for relational databases using the extended entity-relationship model. *ACM Computing Surveys*, Vol. 18, No. 2, pp. 197–222.

Teubner, Rolf Alexander (1999): *Organisations- und Informationssystemgestaltung: theoretische Grundlagen und integrierte Methoden*. Wiesbaden: Gabler Verlag.

Thalheim, Bernhard & Düsterhöft, Antje (2001): SiteLang: Conceptual Modeling of Internet Sites. In Kunii, Hideko S., Jajodia, Sushil & Solvberg, Arne, editors: Conceptual Modeling - ER 2001, 20th International Conference on Conceptual Modeling. Yokohama: Springer, pp. 179–192.

Thalheim, Bernhard & Düsterhöft, Antje (2003): Systematic Development of Internet Sites: Extending Approaches of Conceptual Modeling. In Bommel, Patrick van, editor: Information Modeling for Internet applications. Hershey: Idea Group, pp. 80–102.

Theng, Yin Leng (2003): Designing Hypertext and the Web with the Heart and the Mind. In Bommel, Patrick van, editor: Information Modeling for Internet applications. Hershey: Idea Group, pp. 299–319.

Thüring, Manfred, Hannemann, Jörg & Haake, Jörg M. (1995): Hypermedia and cognition: designing for comprehension. *Communications of the ACM*, Vol. 38, No. 8, pp. 57–66.

Tolvanen, Juha-Pekka (1998): *Incremental Method Engineering with Modeling Tools - Theoretical Principles and Empirical Evidence*. Ph. D thesis, University of Jyväskylä.

Troyer, Olga De & Decruyenaere, Tom (2000): Conceptual modelling of web sites for end-users. *World Wide Web*, Vol. 3, No. 1, pp. 27–42.

Veraart, Albert & Wimmer, Rainer (1996): Hermeneutik. In Mittelstraß, Jürgen, editor: Enzyklopädie Philosophie und Wissenschaftstheorie 4. Stuttgart: J. B. Metzler, pp. 85–90.

Vessey, Iris, Jarvenpaa, Sirkka L. & Tractinsky, Noam (1992): Evaluation of vendor products: CASE tools as methodology companions. *Communications of the ACM*, Vol. 35, No. 4, pp. 90–105.

Vidgen, Richard (2002): Constructing a web information system development methodology. *Information Systems Journal*, Vol. 12, No. 3, pp. 247–261.

Vossen, Gottfried (1999): *Datenmodelle, Datenbanksprachen und Datenbank-Management-Systeme*. 3rd edition. München u. a.: Oldenbourg.

Walsham, Geoff (1993): *Interpreting information systems in organizations*. Chichester, GB: John Wiley & Sons.

Walsham, Geoff (1995): The Emergence of Interpretivism in IS Research. *Information Systems Research*, Vol. 6, No. 4, pp. 376–394.

Wand, Yair, Monarchi, David E., Parsons, Jeffrey & Woo, Carson C. (1995): Theoretical foundations for conceptual modelling in information systems development. *Decision Support Systems*, Vol. 15, No. 4, pp. 285–304.

Wand, Yair, Storey, Veda C. & Weber, Ron (1999): An ontological analysis of the relationship construct in conceptual modeling. *ACM Transactions on Database Systems (TODS)*, Vol. 24, No. 4, pp. 494–528.

Wand, Yair & Weber, Ron (1989): *An ontological evaluation of systems analysis and design methods.* Amsterdam: North-Holland publishing Company, Information Systems Concepts: An In-depth Analysis, pp. 79–107.

Wand, Yair & Weber, Ron (1990a): *Mario Bunge's Ontology as a formal foundation for information systems concepts.* Atlanta: Rodopi, Studies on Mario Bunge's Treatise, pp. 123–149.

Wand, Yair & Weber, Ron (1990b): An Ontological Model of an Information System. *IEEE Transactions on Software Engineering*, Vol. 16, No. 11, pp. 1282–1292.

Wand, Yair & Weber, Ron (1993): On the ontological expressiveness of information systems analysis and design grammars. *Journal of Information Systems*, Vol. 3, No. 4, pp. 217–237.

Wand, Yair & Weber, Ron (2002): Research Commentary: Information Systems and Conceptual Modeling - A Research Agenda. *Information Systems Research*, Vol. 13, No. 4, pp. 363–376.

Weaver, Warren (1949): Recent Contributions to the Mathematical Theory of Communication. In Shannon, Claude E. & Weaver, Warren, editors: The Mathematical Theory of Communication. Urbana, Illinois: University of Illinois Press, pp. 29–125.

Weber, Ron (2004): The Rhetoric of Positivism Versus Interpretivism: A Personal View. *MIS Quarterly*, Vol. 28, No. 1, pp. iii–xii.

Wedekind, Hartmut (1981): *Datenbanksysteme I. Eine konstruktive Einführung in die Datenverarbeitung in Wirtschaft und Verwaltung.* 3rd edition. Mannheim u. a.: Spektrum Akademischer Verlag, p. 325.

Weick, Karl E. (1995): *Sensemaking in Organizations.* Thousand Oaks, CA, USA: SAGE.

Welke, Richard J. (1983): IS/DSS: DBMS Support for Information Systems Development. In Holsapple, Clyde & Whinston, Andrew B., editors: Data Base Management Theory and Applications. Dordrecht: D. Reidel, pp. 195–250.

Whorf, Benjamin L. (1956): *Language, Thought, and Reality - Selected Writings of Benjamin Lee Whorf.* Boston: Technology Press.

Wiener, Norbert (1948): *Cybernetics; or, Control and Communication in the Animal and the Machine.* New York: Technology Press.

Wilde, Erik (1999): *Wilde's WWW - Technical Foundations of the World Wide Web.* Berlin: Springer.

Willmott, Hugh (1990): Beyond Paradigmatic Closure In Organisational Inquiry. In Hassard, John & Pym, D., editors: The Theory and Philosophy of Organisations. New York: Routledge, p. N/A.

Willmott, Hugh (1993): Breaking the Paradigm Mentality. *Organization Studies*, Vol. 14, No. 5, pp. 681–719.

Wittgenstein, Ludwig (1922): *Tractatus Logico-Philosophicus.* New York, NY, USA: Routledge & Kegan Paul.

Wittgenstein, Ludwig (1963): *Philosophical Investigations.* Oxford: Basil Blackwell, Combined Edition English and German.

(WKWI), Wissenschaftliche Kommission der Wirtschaftsinformatik (1994): Profil der Wirtschaftsinformatik. Ausführungen der Wissenschaftlichen Kommission der Wirtschaftsinformatikord. *Wirtschaftsinformatik*, Vol. 36, pp. 80–81.

Wolf, Gary (1995): The Curse of Xanadu. *Wired,*, No. Issue 3.06, p. N/A ⟨URL: http://www.wired.com/wired/archive/3.06/xanadu_pr.html⟩.

Wood-Harper, Trevor (1985): Research Methods in Information Systems: Using Action Research. In Mumford, Enid, Hirschheim, Rudy, Fitzgerald, Guy & Wood-Harper, Trevor, editors: Research Methods in Information Systems. Amsterdam: Elsevier, pp. 169–191.

World Wide Web Consortium: *XHTML 1.0 The Extensible HyperText Markup Language (Second Edition).* ⟨URL: http://www.w3.org/TR/xhtml1/⟩ – visited on 2005-07-28.

Wyssusek, Boris (2004): Ontology and Ontologies in Information Systems Analysis and Design: A Critique. In Proceedings of the Tenth Americas Conference on Information Systems (AMCIS). New York, NY, pp. 4303–4308.

Wyssusek, Boris & Klaus, Helmut (2005): Ontological foundations of information systems analysis and design: extending the scope of the discussion. In Green, Peter F.

& Rosemann, Michael, editors: Business systems analysis with ontologies. Hershey: Idea Group Publishing, pp. 322–344.

Zachman, John A. (1987): A Framework for Information Systems Architecture. *IBM Systems Journal*, Vol. 26, No. 3, pp. 276–292.

Zachmann, John A. & Sowa, John F. (1992): Extending and formalizing the Framework for Information Systems Architecture. *IBM Systems Journal*, Vol. 31, No. 3, pp. 590–616.

Zhang, Ping & Dran, Gisela M. von (2000): Satisfiers and Dissatisfiers: A Two-Factor Model for Website Design and Evaluation. *Journal of the American Society for Information Science*, Vol. 51, No. 14, pp. 1253–1268.

Appendix

A Language-based Metamodels for Method Comparison

section Language-based metamodels are constructed in order to normalize the linguistic means provided by the modelling approaches in a unified way. Refer to Section 2.2.6 for a description of metamodels and their construction principle. The metamodels depict the main concepts of the modelling techniques, which could be derived by publications. Obviously, a comparison has to consider unavoidable inaccuracies, since abstraction levels and naming of concepts can not be aligned among the modelling approaches. However, the metamodels are very useful for capturing the main modelling principles and concepts in a uniform and semi-formal way. Refer to the Section 2.2.7 for brief descriptions of the modelling approaches in natural language.

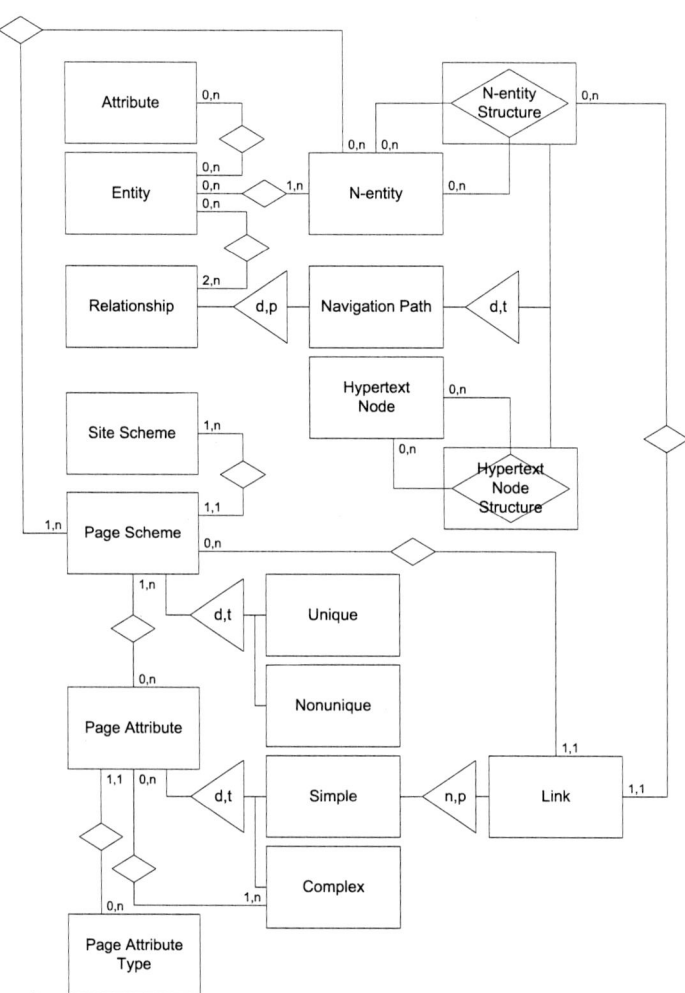

Figure A-1: Language-based Metamodel Araneus

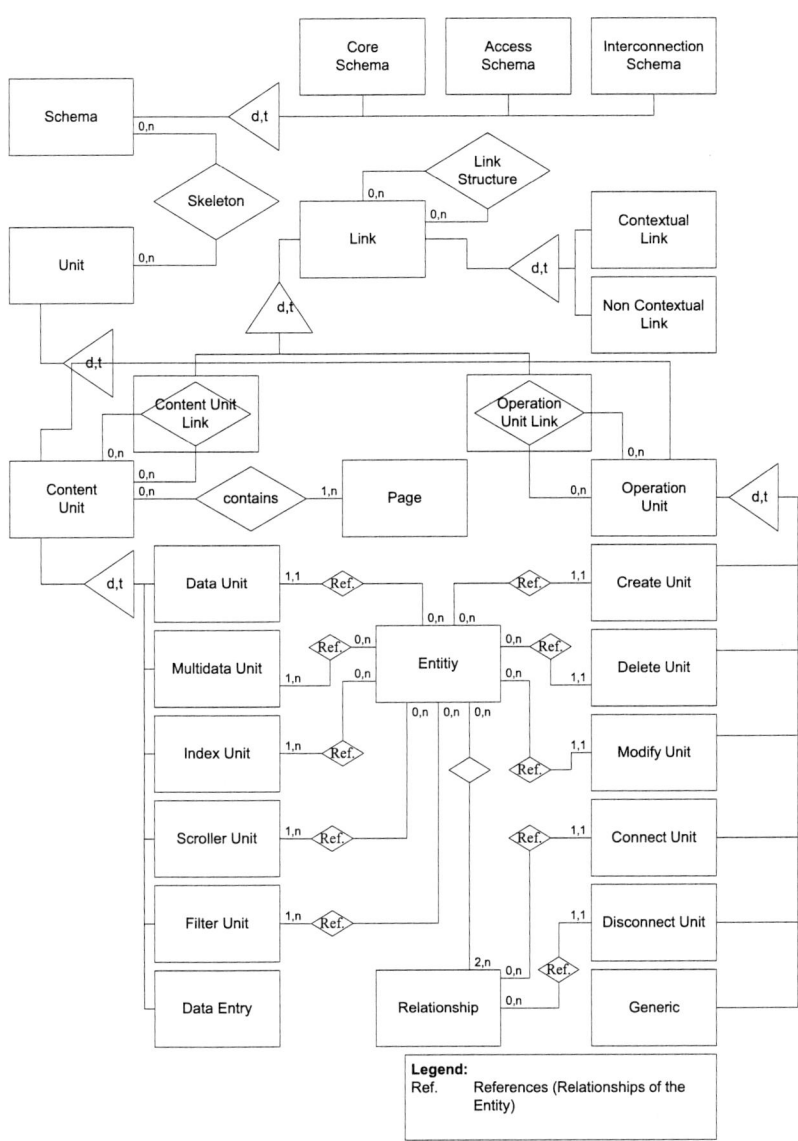

Figure A-2: Language-based Metamodel WebML

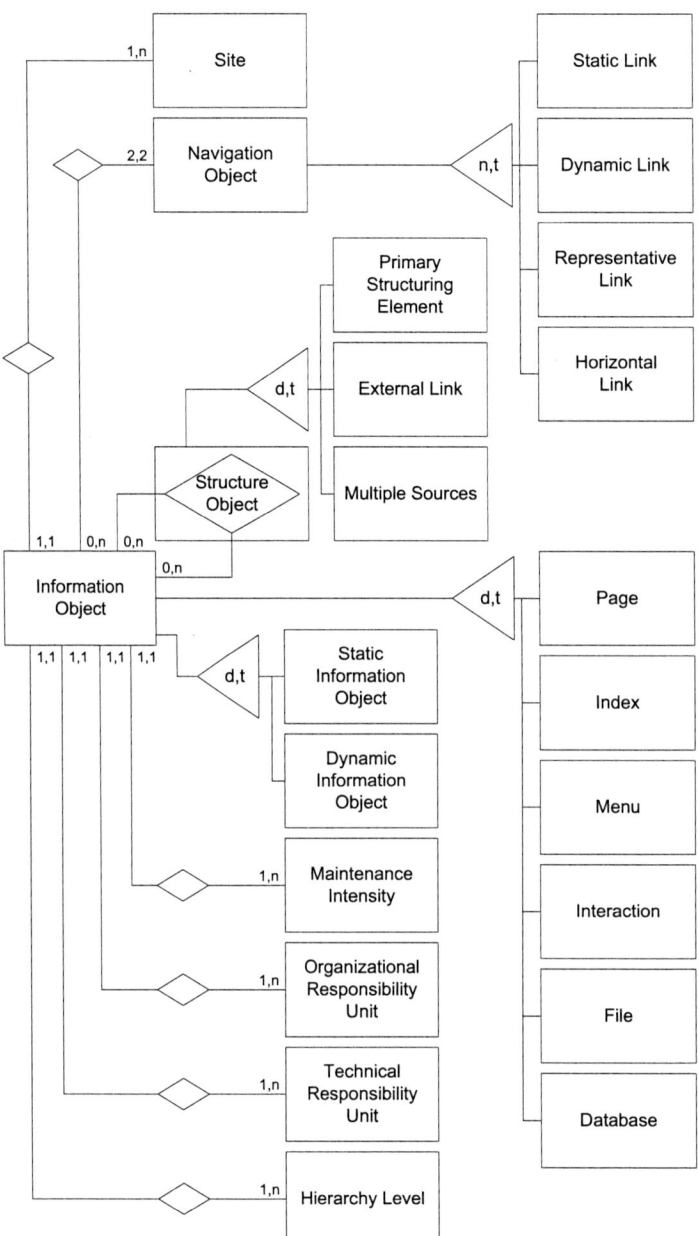

Figure A-3: Language-based Metamodel eW3DT

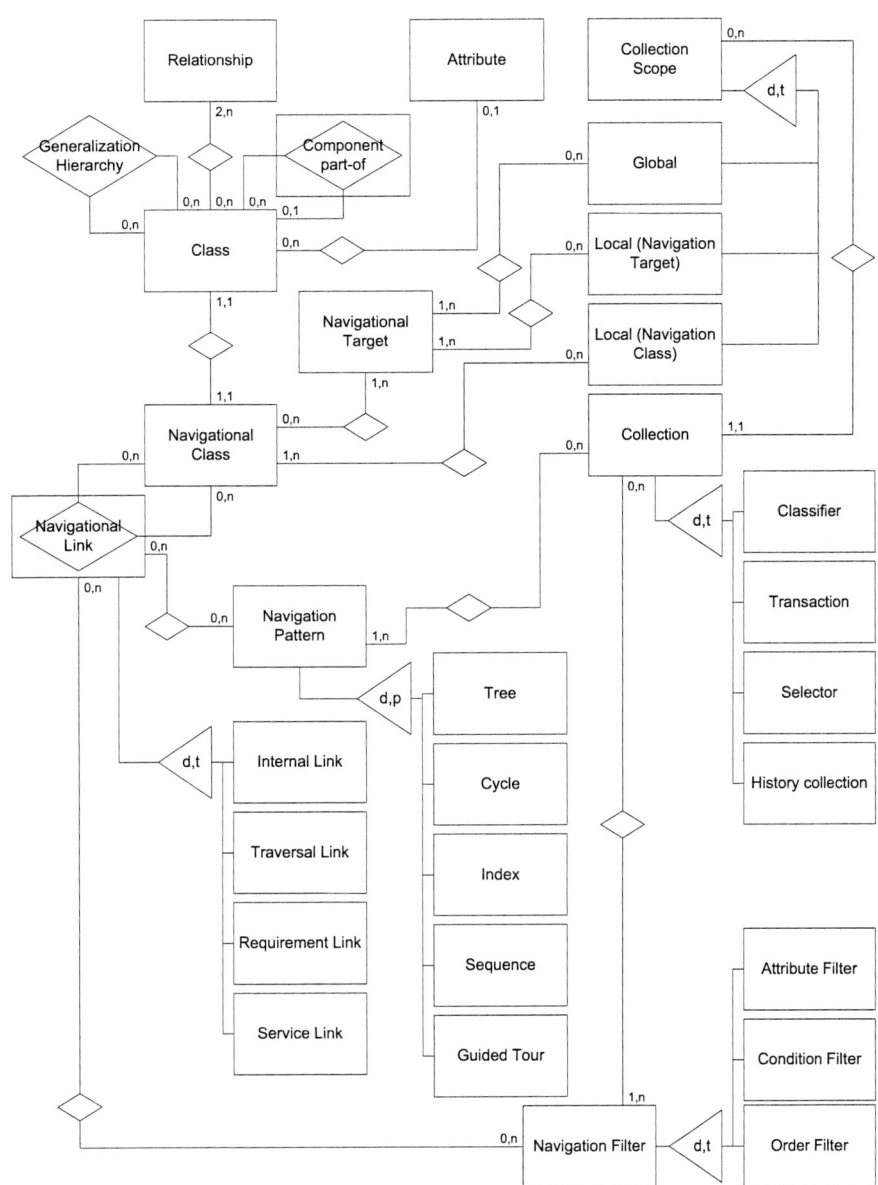

Figure A-4: Language-based Metamodel OO-H

Author Index

Bisher erschienene und geplante Bände der Reihe
Advances in Information Systems and Management Science

ISSN 1611-3101

Bd. 1: Lars H. Ehlers

Content Management Anwendungen.

Spezifikation von Internet-Anwendungen
auf Basis von Content Management Systemen

ISBN 3-8325-0145-2   40.50 €
285 Seiten, 2003

Content Management Anwendungen stellen für Unternehmen die Chance einer attraktiven und einfach zu pflegenden Präsenz im Internet dar. Umfangreiche Inhalte auf den Web-Seiten und regelmäßige Aktualisierungen lassen sich so realisieren. Dabei stellen Content Management Systeme (CMS) die technologische Basis zum Aufbau dieser Anwendungen dar.
Dieses Buch verdeutlicht dem Leser wichtige Internet-Grundlagen und die Eigenschaften von Content Management Systemen. Darauf aufbauend liefert Lars H. Ehlers umfangreiche Gestaltungsempfehlungen für die fachkonzeptionelle Modellierung von Content Management Anwendungen.
Aus dem Inhalt:

- Internet: Grundlagen des Hypertextes, Möglichkeiten von HTML sowie client- und serverseitigen Skriptsprachen, Übersicht von Planungsansätzen für Internet-Anwendungen

- Content Management Systeme: Komponenten, Erweiterungsmöglichkeiten, Metamodell; Fragebogen zur Systemauswahl

- Content Management Anwendungen: Erstellung, enthaltene Dimensionen, Modellierung von Präsentation, Navigation und Content

Bd. 2: Stefan Neumann

Workflow-Anwendungen
in technischen Dienstleistungen.

Eine Referenz-Architektur für die Koordination
von Prozessen im Gebäude- und Anlagenmanagement

ISBN 3-8325-0156-8   40.50 €
310 Seiten, 2003

Technische Dienstleistungen werden von Unternehmen, die sich auf ihre Kernkompetenzen konzentrieren, in zunehmendem Maße an externe Anbieter vergeben. Aufgrund der Komplexität, Variantenvielfalt und zwischenbetrieblichen Ausrichtung dieser Leistungen stoßen heutige Anwendungssysteme zur Unterstützung der Auftragsabwicklung an ihre Grenzen. Vor diesem Hintergrund stellen Workflowmanagementsysteme viel versprechende Lösungsmöglichkeiten bereit.
Stefan Neumann analysiert am Beispiel der Bewirtschaftung von Gebäuden und technischen Einrichtungen (Facility Management) umfassend die besonderen Anforderungen

technischer Dienstleistungen an die Gestaltung von Informationssystemen. Darauf aufbauend entwirft er eine neuartige Systemarchitektur, die basierend auf dem Workflow-Ansatz eine verbesserte, durchgängig integrierte Definition, Planung, Steuerung und Kontrolle technischer Dienstleistungen ermöglicht.

Das Buch richtet sich an Dozenten und Studenten der Wirtschaftsinformatik und der Betriebswirtschaftslehre sowie an Organisations- und Anwendungssystemgestalter im Servicemanagement.

Aus dem Inhalt:

- Informationssysteme in technischen Dienstleistungen: Charakterisierung technischer Dienstleistungen und des technischen Facility Management, Referenz-Ordnungsrahmen für Dienstleistungs-Informationssysteme, verfügbare Systeme und Referenzmodelle

- Workflowmanagement: Grundlagen, Architekturen, Nutzen, Integration von Workflow- und Fachkomponenten

- Architektur Workflow-basierter Anwendungen im technischen Facility Management: Fachkonzepte für Workflow-Komponenten, Leistungs- und Prozessgestaltung, Anlagenmanagement, Projektplanung und -steuerung, Serviceauftragsabwicklung.

Bd. 3: Christian Probst

Referenzmodell für IT-Service-Informationssysteme.

ISBN 3-8325-0161-4   40.50 €

315 Seiten, 2003

IT-Service-Informationssysteme werden in Unternehmen zur Unterstützung des IT-Service-Managements eingesetzt. Sie sind unabdingbare Voraussetzung, um Beratung, Entwicklung, Einführung, Betrieb, Unterstützung und Stilllegung zu bzw. von IT-Services effektiv und effizient zu realisieren. Hierfür müssen neben der Komplexität und Kompliziertheit der Komponenten eines IT-Services (Hardware, Software und Carrier-Services) sowohl die hohe Innovationsgeschwindigkeit in der IT als auch eine variable Leistungstiefe flexibel und ökonomisch beherrscht und durch geeignete Systeme unterstützt werden. Obschon heute de facto jede größere Organisation essenziell von IT-Dienstleistungen abhängig ist, kann ein beachtliches Theoriedefizit hinsichtlich der Gestaltung von IT-Service-Informationssystemen festgestellt werden.

Hier setzt Christian Probst in seiner Dissertation an, in der er Literatur und bestehende Ansätze der Referenzmodellierung im Umfeld des IT-Service-Managements (u. A. ITIL, eTOM und DMTF DMI/ CIM) analysiert und daraus praktische Gestaltungsempfehlungen in Form eines ganzheitlichen Ordnungsrahmens ableitet, der durch über 200 Prozess-, Funktions- und Datenmodelle umfassend detailliert wird.

Das Buch richtet sich an Dozenten und Studenten der Wirtschaftsinformatik und der Betriebswirtschaftslehre sowie an IT-Service-Manager, Organisations- und Anwendungssystemgestalter im IT-Service-Management.

Bd. 4: Jan vom Brocke

Referenzmodellierung.

Gestaltung und Verteilung von Konstruktionsprozessen

ISBN 3-8325-0179-7   40.50 €

424 Seiten, 2003

Referenzmodelle sind der Schlüssel zur wirtschaftlichen Konstruktion leistungsfähiger Informationssysteme. Wie Informationsmodelle so zu konstruieren sind, dass sie der angestrebten Referenzfunktion in Theorie und Praxis gerecht werden, zeigt die vorliegende Arbeit.

Jan vom Brocke entwickelt hierzu das Konzept der Verteilten Referenzmodellierung (VRM), in dem er innovative Ansätze des Software Engineering (z. B. Open Source und Component Based Software Engineering) für die Referenzmodellierung erschließt. Die Arbeit gibt umfangreiche Gestaltungsempfehlungen, nach denen Referenzmodelle im Netzwerkverbund verteilt agierender Akteure komponentenorientiert entwickelt und in Austausch- und Diskursprozessen flexibel an neue Anforderungen angepasst werden können. Als Basis schafft Jan vom Brocke konzeptionelle Grundlagen zur Gestaltung von Konstruktionsprozessen und liefert eine differenzierte Analyse des State-of-the-Art der Referenzmodellierung.

Die Arbeit von Jan vom Brocke ist mit einem Dissertationspreis der Universität Münster ausgezeichnet worden. Die innovativen Forschungsergebnisse werden als richtungsweisend für die wissenschaftliche Entwicklung der Referenzmodellierung eingestuft. Durch die Konstruktion von Metamodellen und die Implementierung der Internetplattform referenzmodelle.de sind die Ergebnisse unmittelbar in der Praxis einsetzbar. Die umfassende Aufbereitung des Themengebiets und dessen strukturierte Darstellung machen das Buch zu einem Standardwerk für Dozenten und Studenten der Wirtschaftsinformatik.

Bd. 5: Holger Hansmann

Architekturen Workflow-gestützter PPS-Systeme.

Referenzmodelle für die Koordination von Prozessen
der Auftragsabwicklung von Einzel- und Kleinserienfertigern

ISBN 3-8325-0282-3   40.50 €

299 Seiten, 2003

Die Komplexität der Produktionsplanung und -steuerung (PPS) stellt hohe Anforderungen an Anwendungssysteme. Heutige PPS-Systeme bieten zwar eine umfassende Unterstützung einzelner PPS-Funktionen, weisen jedoch eine Reihe von Defiziten auf. Insbesondere erlauben sie keine ganzheitliche und unternehmensindividuell spezifizierbare Prozessgestaltung, -steuerung und -kontrolle und unterstützen nur in eingeschränktem Maße eine flexible Integration zusätzlich benötigterAnwendungssysteme. Einen Ansatz, diesen Defiziten zu begegnen, stellt die Integration von PPS-Systemen mit dar, die eine automatisierte und individuell anhandvon Prozessmodellen spezifizierbare Prozesskoordination ermöglichen.

In diesem Buch vermittelt Holger Hansmann dem Leser essentielle Grundlagen der PPS und des Workflow-Managements und analysiert umfassend die spezifischen Anforderungen der industriellen Auftragsabwicklung an die Gestaltung von Workflow-Anwendungen. Darauf aufbauend entwirft er eine neuartige Systemarchitektur für Workflow-gestützte PPS-Systeme, die eine effizientere und durchgängig integrierte Definition, Planung, Steuerung und Kontrolle industrieller Geschäftsprozesse ermöglicht.

Bd. 6: Michael zur Muehlen

Workflow-based Process Controlling.

Foundation, Design, and Application of workflow-driven Process Information Systems

ISBN 3-8325-0388-9   40.50 €

315 Seiten, 2004

Workflow-based Process Controlling Systems provide companies with the ability to measure the operational performance of their business processes in a timely and accurate fashion. The combination of workflow audit trails with data warehouse technology and operational business data allows for complex analyses that can support managers in their assessment of an organization?s performance. The increasing maturity of business process management and data warehouse systems enables the design and development of advanced process-oriented management information systems.

Michael zur Muehlen discusses the integration of workflow audit trail data with existing data warehouse structures and develops a reference architecture for process-oriented management information systems. Starting with an organizational and technical analysis of process organizations, this book provides a comprehensive documentation of business process management, workflow technology, and existing standardization efforts The proposed reference architecture is validated in an industry context. A prototypical implementation of the reference architecture and its integration with a commercial business process management system are demonstrated as well.

This book is directed at both practitioners and academics in the fields of business process management, management accounting, and information systems research.

Bd. 7: Martin B. Schultz

Anreizorientiertes Investitionscontrolling mit vollständigen Finanzplänen.

Ein Referenzprozessmodell für Inverstment Center

ISBN 3-8325-0420-6   40.50 €

380 Seiten, 2005

Am Investitionsprozess in dezentralisierten Unternehmen sind zahlreiche Akteure mit individuellen und häufig divergierenden Interessen beteiligt. Um die Effektivität und Effizienz des Prozesses sicherzustellen, ist das Investitionscontrolling phasenübergreifend anreizorientiert auszugestalten. Hierzu wird in dem Buch von Martin B. Schultz folgenden Fragen nachgegangen:

Wie ist die Führung als Empfänger von Anreizen begrifflich abzugrenzen und welche Faktoren beeinflussen die Rationalität der Führung?

Wie ist eine zweckmäßige Controllingkonzeption auszugestalten, die die Anreizorientierung integrativ umfasst?

Welche konstituierenden Eigenschaften weist das Investitionscontrolling in Investment Centern auf?

Wie hat ein Ordnungsrahmen für das anreizorientierte Investitionscontrolling in Investment Centern auszusehen, der sowohl die Gestaltung der Instrumente und Informationssysteme als auch deren Nutzung zu strukturieren vermag?

Welche Instrumente sind im Rahmen des anreizorientierten Investitionscontrollings in Investment Centern auf welche Weise einzusetzen?

Wie sollte der Ablauf eines Investitionsprozesses gestaltet sein, der die Aktivitäten des anreizorientierten Investitionscontrollings umfasst und der als Referenzprozessmodell für die Implementierung in Unternehmen dienen kann?

Wie ist ein computergestütztes Controllinginstrument auszugestalten, mit dem der Investitionsprozess in Investment Centern phasenübergreifend begleitet werden kann?

Für die vorliegende Arbeit wurde Martin B. Schultz mit dem Österreichischen Controllerpreis 2004 ausgezeichnet.

Bd. 8: Norman Lahme

Information Retrieval im Wissensmanagement.

Ein am Vorwissen orientierter Ansatz zur Komposition von Informationsressourcen

ISBN 3-8325-0526-1   40.50 €
274 Seiten, 2004

Die Suche nach relevanten Informationsressourcen ist eine regelmäßige Aufgabe für die Mitglieder einer Organisation. Zu ihrer Unterstützung bei dieser Aufgabe können Information Retrieval-Systeme als Werkzeuge des Wissensmanagements zum Einsatz gelangen. Derzeitige Ansätze hierzu lassen jedoch Unterschiede zwischen den Informationsressourcen hinsichtlich ihrer Verstehbarkeit unberücksichtigt.

Norman Lahme entwickelt zur Berücksichtigung dieser Unterschiede eine verstehbarkeitsorientierte Information Retrieval-Methode. Nach dieser wird zu einer Anfrage eines Nachfragers von Informationen eine an dessen Vorwissen orientierte und somit grundsätzlich verstehbare Komposition von Informationsressourcen ermittelt, die im Hinblick auf die zu ihrer Internalisierung durchschnittlich benötigte Zeit optimal ist. Zu seiner Methode erstellt er zudem einen effizienten Algorithmus, der auf Erkenntnissen aus der künstlichen Intelligenz aufbaut, sowie ein Softwareprodukt, das den Algorithmus implementiert und die Anwendung und Erprobung der Methode erlaubt.

Das Buch wendet sich an Dozenten und Studenten der Informatik, der Betriebswirtschaftslehre und der Wirtschaftsinformatik sowie an Praktiker, die sich mit der informationstechnischen Unterstützung des Wissensmanagements befassen.

Bd. 9: Jörg Bergerfurth

Referenz-Informationsmodelle für das Produktionscontrolling.

Nutzerspezifische Analyse- und Auswertungssichten für produktionsbezogene Aufgaben

ISBN 3-8325-0492-3   40.50 €
275 Seiten, 2004

Einer aufgabenspezifischen Versorgung mit betriebswirtschaftlich relevanten Informationen kommt im Rahmen des Produktionscontrollings große Bedeutung zu. Bei der Umsetzung von Konzepten zum Produktionscontrolling in Informationssystemen werden jedoch häufig Mängel bzgl. der nutzerindividuellen Informationsversorgung festgestellt. Die vorhandenen Daten der operativen bzw. datenerzeugenden Systeme werden nicht für eine ganzheitliche Betrachtung controllinggerecht zusammengeführt. Instrumente zur Informationsaufbereitung insbesondere Kennzahlensysteme werden zumeist unzureichend eingesetzt. Zudem sind die Auswertungen nicht aktuell genug und unflexibel, so dass die Transparenz der Produktion gering ist. Die von Jörg Bergerfurth entwickelten

Referenz-Informationsmodelle bieten auf fachkonzeptioneller Ebene eine Grundlage für ein umfassendes **Produktionscontrolling**. Die Modelle ermöglichen neben der breiten Abdeckung der Produktionsbereiche auch sehr flexible und individuelle **Analyse- und Auswertungssichten**. Die dokumentierten Modelle dienen auf fachkonzeptioneller Ebene als Vorlage für die Informationssystemgestaltung, wie bspw. den Aufbau eines Data-Warehouses. Das Buch richtet sich an Dozenten und Studenten der Wirtschaftsinformatik und der Betriebswirtschaftslehre sowie an Anwendungssystemgestalter in den Produktionsbereichen.

Bd. 10: Dominik Kuropka

Modelle zur Repräsentation natürlichsprachlicher Dokumente.

Ontologie-basiertes Information-Filtering und -Retrieval mit relationalen Datenbanken

ISBN 3-8325-0514-8   40.50 €
264 Seiten, 2004

Kostengünstige Massenspeicher und die zunehmende Vernetzung von Rechnern haben die Anzahl der Dokumente, auf die ein einzelnes Individuum zugreifen kann (bspw. Webseiten) oder die auf das Individuum einströmen (bspw. E-Mails), in den letzten Jahren rapide ansteigen lassen. In immer mehr Bereichen der Wirtschaft, Wissenschaft und Verwaltung nimmt der Bedarf an hochwertigen Information-Filtering und -Retrieval Werkzeugen zur Beherrschung der Informationsflut zu. Zur computergestützten Lösung dieser Problemstellung sind Modelle zur Repräsentation natürlichsprachlicher Dokumente erforderlich, um formale Kriterien für die automatisierte Auswahl relevanter Dokumente definieren zu können.

Dominik Kuropka gibt in seiner Arbeit eine umfassende Übersicht über den Themenbereich der Suche und Filterung von natürlichsprachlichen Dokumenten. Es wird eine Vielzahl von Modellen aus Forschung und Praxis vorgestellt und evaluiert. Auf den Ergebnissen aufbauend wird das Potenzial von Ontologien in diesem Zusammenhang eruiert und es wird ein neues, ontologie-basiertes Modell für das Information-Filtering und -Retrieval erarbeitet, welches anhand von Text- und Code-Beispielen ausführlich erläutert wird.

Das Buch richtet sich an Dozenten und Studenten der Informatik, Wirtschaftsinformatik und (Computer-)Linguistik sowie an Systemdesigner und Entwickler von dokumentenorientierten Anwendungssystemen und Werkzeugen.

Bd. 11: Christoph Köster

Kosten- und Prozesscontrolling in der Versicherungswirtschaft.

Ontologie-basiertes Information-Filtering und -Retrieval mit relationalen Datenbanken

ISBN 3-8325-0519-9   40.50 €
272 Seiten, 2004

Kostencontrolling und -management als Instrumente der Unternehmenssteuerung sehen sich in jüngerer Vergangenheit heftiger Kritik ausgesetzt. Insbesondere den traditionellen Methoden der Kostenrechnung wird die Relevanz für rationale Entscheidungsfindungen abgesprochen, weil sie sich nicht den Gegebenheiten aktueller Umwelt- und Rahmenbedingungen angepasst haben. Mit der Ausrichtung der Organisation des Versicherungs-Unternehmens auf die elementaren Geschäftsprozesse und der Gewinnung von kostenrelevanten Daten aus Dokumenten- und Workflow-Management-Systemen (DMS / WfMS) mittels Audit-Trails wird ein überzeugender Lösungsansatz vorgestellt. Besonders in der personalkostenintensiven Versicherungswirtschaft, deren Gemeinkosten im Wesentlichen durch die Sachbearbeitung in Sparten entstehen, ist eine präzise verursachungsgerechte Verrechnung der Kosten für ein erfolgreiches Kostencontrolling von größter Bedeutung. Da im Wesentlichen einzelne Aktivitäten als Bestandteil von Versicherungsvorgängen mit den dazugehörenden Dokumenten Personalkosten auslösen, wird ein Weg aufgezeigt, wie aus DMS / WfMS ermittelte Audit-Trail-Daten zur Etablierung eines effizienten Kosten- und Prozesscontrollings und -monitorings genutzt werden können. Mit Hilfe des kombiniert-integrierten Einsatzes von adäquaten Kostencontrolling- und -managementinstrumenten und Informationstechnologie werden Möglichkeiten geschaffen, der Führungsebene von Versicherungsunternehmen umfassende und zeitnahe Instrumente zur Planung, Überwachung und Kontrolle von Geschäftsprozessen und Kosten an die Hand zu geben.

Bd. 12: Andreas Rottwinkel

Management von Partnerkontakten in Versicherungsunternehmen.

Referenzmodelle für die
Koordination von Partnerkontakten

ISBN 3-8325-0523-7   40.50 €
230 Seiten, 2004

Ein Partnerkontakt dokumentiert den Informationsaustausch zwischen einem Unternehmen und dessen Partner sowie den aktuellen Stand der Bearbeitung dieses Ereignisses. Ausgehend von den Problemstellungen bei der Kontaktbearbeitung in Versicherungsunternehmen stellt Andreas Rottwinkel in seiner Dissertation mit Computer-Supported Cooperative Work, Dokumenten-Management, Workflow-Management und Customer-Relationship-Management bestehende Ansätze vor, die sich bei Versicherern bisher nicht behaupten konnten. Mit dem Management von Partnerkontakten wird ein neuer Ansatz konzipiert, in dem spartenübergreifend nicht nur Kunden, sondern auch Partner wie Makler, Werkstätten oder Rechtsanwälte fokussiert werden.
Mit Referenzmodellen für die Koordination von Partnerkontakten unterstützt Andreas Rottwinkel fachkonzeptuell die Einführung von Partnerkontaktsystemen in Versicherungsunternehmen. Eine Einbettung finden diese Modelle zur Beschreibung von Informationssystemen im Versicherungs-V-Modell einem Ordnungsrahmen für Versicherungsinformationssysteme.
Das Buch richtet sich an Dozenten und Studenten der Wirtschaftsinformatik und der Betriebswirtschaftslehre sowie an IT-Manager, Organisations- und Anwendungssystemgestalter.

Data Mining mit Genetischen Algorithmen.

ISBN 3-8325-0522-9   40.50 €
280 Seiten, 2004

Die Weiterentwicklung von Hardware und Datenbanken hat in den letzten Jahren zu einer rasanten Steigerung des Interesses an der automatisierten Auswertung von Massendaten geführt. Das Data Mining, dessen Potenzial bisher nur in Ansätzen genutzt wird, soll wissenschaftlich gestützte und praktisch anwendbare Verfahrensweisen dafür liefern. Auch wenn statistische Methoden viele Fragen beantworten können, bleibt doch der Bedarf an innovativen Herangehensweisen, um noch mehr Informationen aus den Daten herauszuholen.

Mit Genetischen Algorithmen, einer Gruppe von Verfahren, die Mechanismen der natürlichen Evolution nachahmen, werden komplexe Optimierungsprobleme oft überzeugend gelöst. Der Anwender eines solchen Algorithmus muss allerdings dafür sorgen, dass Codierung und Auswahl von Parametern zur Problemstellung passen.

Ulrich Kathöfer entwickelt in diesem Buch eine Reihe von Erweiterungen der Standard-Algorithmen, die für spezifische Problemstellungen des Data Mining zu besseren, robusteren oder schneller erreichbaren Ergebnissen führen. Anwendbar sind die Ergebnisse auch für andere Fragestellungen, in denen Optimierung eine Rolle spielt.

Das Buch richtet sich sowohl an Dozenten und Studierende der Mathematik, Informatik und Wirtschaftsinformatik als auch an Praktiker, die Genetische Algorithmen insbesondere im Bereich der Datenanalyse einsetzen wollen.

Controlling im Onlinehandel.
Ein kennzahlenorientierter Ansatz für Onlineshops

ISBN 3-8325-0540-7   40.50 €
300 Seiten, 2004

Die Erscheinungsformen und Auswirkungen der Internetökonomie werden derzeit vielfältig diskutiert, insbesondere da der prognostizierte Geschäftserfolg vieler Internetunternehmen bis heute ausbleibt. Die euphorischen Vorhersagen aus den Zeiten des New Economy Booms konnten keineswegs erfüllt werden. Studien belegen, dass diejenigen Unternehmen der Internetökonomie, die trotz der wirtschaftlichen Krise inzwischen langfristige wirtschaftliche Erfolge aufweisen, eine systematische Unternehmenssteuerung auf strategischer und operativer Ebene betreiben. Die Bedeutung von Controlling ist den Unternehmen bewusst und die Einrichtung von Controllingsystemen wird von der Unternehmensführung vor allem für den Onlinehandel mit Nachdruck gefordert.

Anita Hukemann präsentiert einen Lösungsansatz für die Etablierung von Controllingsystemen im Onlinehandel. Kennzeichnend für die Arbeit ist die umfassende Katalogisierung und Systematisierung der vielfältigen Controllinginstrumente. Als Basis dient die Datengrundlage des Onlinehandels, die für Controllingzwecke nutzbar gemacht werden muss, um darauf aufbauend originäre Instrumente zu entwickeln. Bei der Gestaltung der Controllinginstrumente wurden sowohl etablierte Methoden des Handelscontrollings berücksichtigt als auch eine Adaption der klassischen Instrumente vorgenommen. Von großem praktischem Nutzen für den Aufbau eines Kennzahlensystems für den Onlinehandel wird die Herleitung und Entwicklung von über 80 spezifischen Controllingkennzahlen angesehen.

Bd. 15: Thomas Serries

Situationsbezogene Informationsversorgung in der industriellen Auftragsabwicklung.

Erweiterte OLAP-Techniken für Workflow-einbeziehende PPS

ISBN 3-8325-0632-2   40.50 €
308 Seiten, 2004

Die Effizienz der industriellen Auftragsabwicklung ist ein entscheidendes Merkmal für den betriebswirtschaftlichen Erfolg auftragsorientierter Einzel- und Kleinserienfertiger. Obwohl mit PPS- bzw. Workflowmanagementsystemen ausgereifte Koordinationsinstrumente vorhanden sind, zeigt die Praxis, dass ihr alleiniger Einsatz keinen reibungslosen Produktionsablauf garantieren kann. Manuelle Eingriffe in die Planungen und Prozessabläufe sind vielfach unumgänglich. PPS- und Workflowmanagementsysteme halten umfangreiche Daten bereit, die zum Treffen einer zielgerichteten Entscheidung notwendig sind. Ihre Auswertungsmöglichkeiten werden den Anforderungen an die benötigten Informationen jedoch nur eingeschränkt gerecht.

Thomas Serries untersucht, inwieweit OLAP-Techniken diese Anforderungen im Sinne einer situationsbezogenen Informationsversorgung in der industriellen Auftragsabwicklung unterstützen können. Für die sich aus den Datenstrukturen zur Abbildung mehrdimensionaler Informationsräume ergebenden Restriktionen werden Erweiterungen an OLAP-Techniken entwickelt, die die domänenspezifischen Datenstrukturen der Workflow-einbeziehenden PPS für mehrdimensionale Auswertungen zugänglich machen und dennoch von der industriellen Auftragsabwicklung unabhängig sind.

Das Buch richtet sich an Dozenten und Studenten der Wirtschaftsinformatik sowie an Anwendungssystemgestalter, insbesondere in produktionsnahen Bereichen, und die Hersteller von OLAP- und Data-Warehouse-Systemen.

Bd. 16: Thomas Zabel

Klassifikation mit Neuronalen Netzen.

CARTE Cooperative Adaptive Resonance Theory Ensembles

ISBN 3-8325-0803-1   40.50 €
220 Seiten, 2005

Für die betriebswirtschaftliche Entscheidungsfindung besteht die Notwendigkeit, bislang unbekannte Zusammenhänge und wertvolle Information aus einer immer größer werdenden Datenbasis zu ermitteln. Dies erfordert eine neue Generation von intelligenten und möglichst automatischen Modellen und Techniken, die den Anwender bei der Analyse der Daten unterstützen. Derzeitige Ansätze zur Klassifikation auf Basis neuronaler Netze weisen Schwächen auf. Die in dieser Arbeit entwickelten Klassifikatoren basieren auf der Adaptiven Resonanz Theorie und der Bildung von Ensembles.

Thomas Zabel entwickelt in diesem Buch eine Methode zur Erstellung von Klassifikatoren auf Basis der Adaptiven Resonanz Theorie. Zu seiner Methode erstellt er zudem einen effizienten Algorithmus, der auf Erkenntnissen der Ensemblebildung aufbaut, sowie ein Softwareprodukt, das den Algorithmus implementiert und die Anwendung und die Erprobung der Methode ermöglicht. Mithilfe des Softwareprodukts wird eine empirische Untersuchung von Versicherungsdaten unter der Fragestellung Erkennung von aktiven bzw. inaktiven Versicherungsagenturen durchgeführt. Die Klassifikationsqualität der verwendeten Methoden erweist sich als zufrieden stellend.

Das Buch wendet sich an Dozenten und Studierende der Mathematik, Informatik, Wirtschaftsinformatik und Betriebswirtschaftslehre sowie an Praktiker, die Neuronale Netze insbesondere im Bereich der Datenanalyse einsetzen wollen.

Bd. 18: Rainer Babiel

Content Management in der öffentlichen Verwaltung.

Ein systemgestaltender Ansatz für die Justizverwaltung NRW

ISBN 3-8325-0927-5   40.50 €
226 Seiten, 2005

Informationsfreiheitsgesetze bilden die rechtliche Grundlage für den Wandel von Amts-geheimnis verpflichteten Behörden zur modernen, transparenten öffentlichen Verwaltung. Die Öffentlichkeit erhält beinahe unbeschränkten Zugang zu allen Unterlagen und Do-kumenten staatlicher Stellen. Mit dieser Transparenz kommen neue Aufgaben auf die Behörden zu, deren Erfüllung durch Content Management als Domäne der Wirtschafts-informatik ohne zusätzlichen Personalaufbau effizient zu gestalten scheint.

Im Rahmen der vorliegenden Arbeit werden die theoretischen und rechtlichen Rahmen-bedingungen für ein effizientes Informationsmanagement öffentlicher Einrichtungen be-leuchtet und anhand der konkreten Systemimplementierung für die Justizverwaltung NRW konkretisiert. Die sich anschließende Wirtschaft-lichkeitsbetrachtung sowie die Er-gebnisse der durchgeführten Nutzerbefragung zeigen den Erfolg des gestalteten System eindrucksvoll auf.

Bd. 19: Michael Ribbert

Gestaltung eines IT-gestützten Kennzahlensystems für das Produktivitätscontrolling operativer Handelsprozesse.

Ein fachkonzeptioneller Ansatz am Beispiel des klassischen Lager-geschäfts des Lebensmittelgroßhandels

ISBN 3-8325-0944-5   40.50 €
292 Seiten, 2005

Der Lebensmittelhandel in Deutschland sieht sich einem intensiven Wettbewerb ausge-setzt. Um dauerhaft am Markt bestehen zu können, ist der effiziente Ressourceneinsatz eine unabdingbare Voraussetzung. Die fehlende rechtliche Beschränkung bzgl. der Adap-tion von Betreiberkonzepten gepaart mit einer hohen Umstellungsflexibilität begründen die hohe Bedeutung der internen Unternehmensprozesse, um dauerhaft Wettbewerbsvor-teile erzielen zu können. Die Effizienz von Prozessen lässt sich durch die Betrachtung der erbrachten Leistungen und der dafür eingesetzten Ressourcen beurteilen, was mit einer Bewertung der Produktivität der Prozesse gleichzusetzen ist. Michael Ribbert entwickelt hierzu eine Methode, welche mittels eines Vorgehensmodells und durch die integrierte An-wendung ausgesuchter Controllinginstrumente zur Definition eines Kennzahlensystems für das prozessorientierte und multidimensionale Produktivitätscontrolling im Handel genutzt werden kann. Die Anwendung der Methode am Beispiel von Referenzprozessen des klassischen Lagergeschäfts des Lebensmittelgroßhandels und die Überführung der Ergebnisse in fachkonzeptionelle Modelle ergeben Referenzmodelle, die für die Ableitung und Spezifikation unternehmensindividueller Controllingkonzepte und unterstützender IT-Systeme genutzt werden können. Das Buch richtet sich an Dozenten und Studenten der Wirtschaftsinformatik und der Betriebswirtschaftslehre sowie an Anwendungssystem-gestalter der Handelsdomäne.

Bd. 20: Peter Westerkamp

Flexible Elearning Platforms:
A Service-Oriented Approach

ISBN 3-8325-1117-2   40.50 €

320 Seiten, 2005

Although the benefits of Service-Oriented Architectures (SOA) are well-understood in the area of software engineering, elearning platforms are commonly still implemented in the form of monolithic applications. The latter resemble one another to a large extend, but a reuse of functionalities between platforms in the form of services is uncommon or impossible. The reuse of elearning content is addressed by many competing standards and specifications making the physical exchange of these learning objects difficult.

The book of Peter Westerkamp transfers the concepts of SOAs to the field of elearning. It starts with a short overview of the elearning field and discusses different approaches to implement a SOA for elearning. In addition, it defines reasonable elearning services based on existing elearning architecture standards. It turns out that the consequent design and implementation of elearning functionalities in the form of Web services provides mechanisms to reuse elearning functionalities and to create flexible platforms that can easily be adapted to the individual needs of learners. By using already existing standards from the field of Web services, functionalities can easily be integrated. Content, too, is delivered in the form of Web services, which makes a physical distribution of learning objects obsolete. This means that several elearning standards and specifications are also obsolete because content is stored only once on the server of the content provider and accessed via Web services.

The book covers models of the internal and external architecture of a Web-services-based elearning environment. The service concept for elearning is implemented in the Learn-Serve environment and can be interpreted as a more general model for elearning Web services. The book also covers economical and organizational perspectives of elearning Web services and discusses differences to monolithic platforms.